Just War Theory

Principle and Practice

Iacovos Kareklas

LEXINGTON BOOKS
Lanham • Boulder • New York • London

Published by Lexington Books
An imprint of The Rowman & Littlefield Publishing Group, Inc.
4501 Forbes Boulevard, Suite 200, Lanham, Maryland 20706
www.rowman.com

86-90 Paul Street, London EC2A 4NE

British Library Cataloguing in Publication Information Available

Library of Congress Cataloging-in-Publication Data

Names: Kareklas, Iakōvos, 1976- author.
Title: Just war theory : principle and practice / Iacovos Kareklas.
Description: Lanham : Lexington Books, 2024. | Includes bibliographical references and index.
Identifiers: LCCN 2024008780 (print) | LCCN 2024008781 (ebook) | ISBN 9781666947335 (cloth) | ISBN 9781666947342 (epub)
Subjects: LCSH: Just war doctrine. | War (International law) | Self-defense (International law) | Intervention (International law) | Humanitarian intervention.
Classification: LCC KZ6396 .K35 2024 (print) | LCC KZ6396 (ebook) | DDC 172/.42--dc23/eng/20240310
LC record available at https://lccn.loc.gov/2024008780
LC ebook record available at https://lccn.loc.gov/2024008781

Contents

List of Abbreviations

A.J.I.L/American J.I.L: *American Journal of International Law*
B.YB.I.L/British YB.I.L: *British Yearbook of International Law*
C.O.: Colonial Office
F.O.: Foreign Office
G.A.: General Assembly
G.A.O.R: General Assembly Official Records
H.M.S.O: Her Majesty's Stationery Office
I.C.J. Reports: International Court of Justice Reports
IG: Inscriptiones Graecae
I.L.M: International Legal Materials
I.L.C. Yearbook: *International Law Commission Yearbook*
I.L.R: International Law Reports
M.L.R: *Modern Law Review*
NATO: North Atlantic Treaty Organization
P.C.I.J: Permanent Court of International Justice
S.C.: Security Council
S.C.O.R: Security Council Official Records
SEG: Sylloge Inscriptionum Graecarum
U.N.: United Nations
U.N. Charter: United Nations Charter

Introduction

The present monograph constitutes a full analysis of Just War Theory in every one of its aspects; therefore, the book constitutes a complete exposition of the corpus of International Law called *Jus ad Bellum*. Simultaneously, there is a chapter that explores Humanitarian Law of Armed Conflict, called *Jus in Bello*. This comprises the rules that should govern an armed conflict and is called humanitarian precisely because it aims at safeguarding humanitarian values and human rights in time of war. Consequently this book covers the Law of War in its entirety, both the *Jus ad Bellum* category—justifications of war—as well as the *Jus in Bello* category, albeit only to some limited extent.

Just War Theory, as this is analyzed in the monograph, presents a peculiarity. Not only the basic aspects of *Jus ad Bellum* are analyzed, but the theory of just war is developed in further depth. It is noteworthy that in a special first chapter, reference is made to the way through which Thucydides has influenced the contemporary theory of just war, particularly the legal basis of humanitarian intervention.

Let me briefly refer to some of the basic chapters of the monograph, so that I may provide a general picture of the book contents.

Two extensive chapters on self-defense are presented. Both individual as well as collective self-defense are analyzed in the light of state practice and the United Nations Charter. Special reference is made to the concept of pre-emptive self-defense, which the author wholeheartedly endorses.

In the chapter entitled "National Liberation Wars," my aim is to prove, in the first part, that International Law allows or recognizes the Use of Force that is, war—in the aid of self-determination. In the second part, I aim at presenting the rather-neglected diplomatic background leading to the Navy Battle of Navarino, the most decisive battle of the Greek Revolution (and the first intervention in aid of self-determination in the history of modern International Law), and at critically approaching this war incident. There is a separate chapter on the diplomatic background of the Navy Battle of Navarino, which proves that this war incident is also the first paradigm example of humanitarian intervention in the history of modern International Law and that this very intervention was launched not merely upon the basis of the strategic interests of the Great Powers, but was largely moved by humanitarian sentiments. The political analysis is fundamentally based on Colonial and Foreign Office Files.

Furthermore, the chapter on humanitarian intervention is quite unique in Greek bibliography. The existence of a right of humanitarian intervention in International Law is well documented through international treaties, decisions of the International Court of Justice, and textbooks of eminent professors of international law and politics since the Renaissance. The author, however, does not hesitate to criticize interventions that were launched in the first instance for humanitarian purposes but also promoted political interests, such as the intervention of NATO in Kosovo in 1999. The intervention in Kosovo, however, was certainly imperative in view of aggravated war crimes committed by the Serbs against Albanian minorities. Nevertheless, the author still boldly believes that the protection of human rights and humanitarian values is superior to State sovereignty, and this implies that humanitarian interventions are lawful and imperative when the motives of the intervening States genuinely conform to the requirements of humanity.

The chapter "Military Intervention by Treaty Right: The Turkish Military Intervention of Cyprus" examines the legal and diplomatic background of the Turkish intervention 1974. On the one hand, the main legal argument put forward by Turkey in order to justify the intervention, which was based on the Republic of Cyprus Treaty of Guarantee, is put under scrutiny; international legal theories on the legality of intervention envisaged by the Treaty are judiciously presented (this is, in fact, the pivotal International Law question analyzed in the present chapter, which goes far beyond the issue of the Turkish invasion, hence it is of utmost importance). On the other hand, the diplomatic background to the Treaty in question is explored in the light of available Foreign Office Files, UN documents, and UK Parliamentary debates in an effort to verify whether a right to military intervention was expressly provided for. Then the conduct of Turkey is tackled on the hypothesis that it did have a right to intervene. Finally, it is stressed how the preceding discussion can be useful for security arrangements in the context of the current negotiations for a settlement to the pending Cyprus question.

It is proved by the use of most powerful arguments that the Treaty of Guarantee of the Cyprus Republic does not provide for a right of intervention, but Turkey interpreted that the Treaty provides such a right in an effort to promote political expediencies. It is also evident that even if one supports the view that the Treaty provides for a right of military intervention, this view is contrary to International Law as it currently stands; it goes against the principles of the UN Charter and International Law theory.

The chapter on International Humanitarian Law firstly tackles the rules governing the conduct of hostilities. Secondly, it examines the Legal Opinion of the International Court of Justice 1996 on the Threat or Use of Nuclear Weapons on the basis of the Law of Armed Conflict. In relation to that, International Criminal Law is concisely analyzed, since violations of the Law of Armed Conflict amount to the commission of war crimes and international crimes in general.

Another significant chapter examines the right of pro-democratic intervention, which might be seen as a kind of humanitarian intervention or a type of intervention in its own right. State practice and academic opinions are extensively cited, and although it is concluded that such a right is not yet fully recognized in International Law, it is submitted (and hereby also lies the originality of this monograph) that this right ought soon to be given effect in international politics and law. Despite the fact that a State cannot impose a constitution or governmental regime upon another State, since this would be in contravention to the notion of internal self-determination, it is equally—if not more—important to concede to the reality that gross violations of human rights, including that of democracy, should no longer be tolerated by the international community.

The monograph comprises an extensive chapter, which explores United Nations peacekeeping and enforcement action. There is a comprehensive analysis of the Observer Group in Lebanon and the UN operation in the Congo. Particular emphasis is placed upon the great diplomatic efforts that consequently led to the establishment of the State of Israel. The affairs explored are documented through Resolutions of the United Nations Security Council and General Assembly.

A final chapter analyses a special issue in International Law, namely whether collective security through enforcement action may be achieved through a Resolution of the United Nations General Assembly instead of the Security Council. This topic is virtually based on a legal opinion that I have been kindly asked and exhorted to prepare for the Changing Character of War Centre of Pembroke College in the University of Oxford. It is particularly topical in view of the Russian invasion in Ukraine and offers to academia as well as to the real world of politics a doctrinal and policy tool on the basis of which they can justify a future diplomatic and military action for humanitarian and peacekeeping purposes.

Consequently, the monograph may be seen as a useful tool for policy makers in the UK Foreign and Commonwealth Office, the UK Ministry of Defence, the US State Department, the US Pentagon; for academics; and for both undergraduate as well as postgraduate-doctoral students of International Law, International Relations, and History (particularly History of Political

Thought), who would like to study in depth certain aspects of international justice, international relations theory, and diplomacy.

The monograph is largely the product of a project conducted in the course of a Fellowship at the Changing Character of War Centre of Pembroke College in the University of Oxford. It is, in fact, the product of two decades of serious research and study of the International Law of War. While writing this book, I have used the excellent resources of the Old Bodleian Library and of the Bodleian Law Library at Oxford University. I would like to give my warmest thanks to the staff of these Libraries for their kind assistance.

Last, but certainly not least, I would like to express my deepest thanks to the publisher, Rowman and Littlefield: Lexington Books, a foremost law publisher of the United States of America. I admire the professionalism of its staff, and I am very glad, indeed, that this work sees the light through this publisher.

Chapter 1

Philosophy of Just War in Classical Greek International Law and Grounds of Lawful War in Thucydides

The aim of the present chapter is, firstly, to unearth the philosophical grounds of just war in classical Greece. Secondly, it aims to indicate specifically that neither the causes nor the theoretical grounds of the Peloponnesian War in the *History of Thucydides* are in conformity with previously established grounds of warfare. Thirdly, it shall be proved that the philosophical underpinnings of war in Thucydides have formed the theoretical and legal basis of contemporary kinds of military intervention in International Law. In this context, the contribution of Thucydides to the Theory of the International Law of War will be duly emphasized.

An in-depth study of Greek law and civilization in general makes manifest the existence of a concept of International Law in the ancient Greek world. It is necessary to clarify at the outset that Greek authors distinguished between unwritten (ἄγραφος) and written law. Unwritten law is defined by Aristotle as the universal law, that is universally recognized principles of morality, whereas written law is the statutes of any given State.[1] Unwritten law is otherwise called natural law or divine law. This distinction is drawn in the *Nicomachaean Ethics*, where Aristotle suggests that: civil justice is partly natural, and partly conventional; that is natural, which possesses the same validity everywhere, and does not depend on being deliberately adopted or not; while that is conventional, which in the first instance does not matter whether it assumes one form or another, it matters only when it has been laid down.[2] A certain application of these conceptions and distinctions is seen in the sphere of the Greek Law of Nations. Writers frequently refer to "the laws of the Hellenes," "the common laws of Hellas," "the laws of mankind," "the laws common to men." Therefore, expressions such as the following are constantly used: τά τῶν Ἑλλήνων νόμιμα,[3] τά πάντων ἀνθρώπων νόμιμα, τά κοινά τῶν Ἑλλήνων νόμιμα.[4] A large number of important rules and practices of International Law are implied in these expressions. The underlying principles belong predominantly to the category of unwritten laws, deriving their juridical force from tradition and custom, and having for their sanction the will of the gods.

The most common grounds considered sufficient for the commencement of operations of war in classical Greece were: violation of a treaty, desertion from an alliance or confederation, offenses committed against allies, refusal to receive ambassadors on invalid grounds, breach of neutrality, violation of territorial integrity, and, highly importantly, desecration of sacred places.[5] History offers examples.

A serious injury intentionally committed against an ally was usually considered as an offense against that ally's confederates, and so a ground for just war on the part of the latter. Penelope, rebuking Antinous for compassing the death of Telemachus, says: "Do you not remember how your father fled to this house in fear of the people, who were incensed against him for having joined some Taphian pirates, and plundered the Thesprotians, who were at peace with us?"

Ἡ οὐκ οἶσθ,' ὅτε δεῦρο πατήρ τεός ἵκετο φεύγων
δῆμον ὑποδδείσας; δή γάρ κεχολώατο λίην,
οὕνεκα ληΐστηρσιν ἐπισπόμενος Ταφίοισιν
ἤκαχε Θεσπρωτούς. Οἱ δ'ἡμιν ἄρθμιοι ῆσαν.[6]

When the province of Macedonia fell by lot to Publius Sulpicius (202 BC), he proposed to the people that on account of the injuries and hostilities committed against the Athenians, who were allies of Rome, they should proclaim war against Philip. In the following year, the Athenians having put to death two Acarnanians for straying into their mysteries, the countrymen of the victims appealed for help to who, as they were his lawful allies, permitted them to levy troops in Macedonia. With these reinforcements, they invaded Attica without a formal declaration of war. Accordingly, envoys were sent to Rome to report the attack made by an old ally of the Romans. Therefore, the Senate of Rome, in the following year, proposed to the *comitia* a declaration of war in consequence of this attack on a State in alliance with Rome.[7]

Supplying assistance to the enemy belligerent, or any other flagrant act of violation of neutrality was certainly a cause of war. So, Demetrius, during his war against the Athenians, captured a ship which was loaded with wheat bound for Athens, and hanged the captain and pilot, a measure, says Plutarch, which terrified other merchants so much that they avoided Athens, and a terrible famine pursued there.[8]

The desecration of sacred places was especially, amongst the Hellenes, considered a cause for embarking upon just war against the offenders. Thus the reason of the Greek offensive war against the Persians was to exact just retribution for their profanation of sacred places. The Athenians declined to come to terms with Xerxes, and expressed their determination to avenge the destruction by him of their temples and images of gods and heroes. *Πρῶτα μέν καί μέγιστα, τῶν θεῶν τά ἀγάλματα καί τά οἰκήματα ἐμπεπρησμένα τέ καί συγκεχωσμένα, τοῖς ἡμέας ἀναγκαίως ἔχει τιμωρέειν ἔς τά μέγιστα μᾶλλον, ἤπερ ὁμολογέειν τῷ ταῦτα ἐργασαμένῳ.*[9]

The devastation of Persia by Alexander the Great provides a further proof of the vengeance exacted by the Greeks upon their enemies, primarily, if not solely, because the latter did not treat with respect the sacred locations of Hellas.[10]

Even more emphatic was the defensive war of the Greeks when they took up arms to defend their homeland in the course of the Persian wars. Particularly their valor, as shown in the navy battle of Salamis in 480 BC, marvelously reported by Aeschylus, needs be cited:

> O ye sons of Hellas, go forth, free your homeland, free your women and children, the temples of your ancestral gods, the tombs of your forefathers. Now, you are fighting for them all.
>
> (*Ὦ παῖδες Ἑλλήνων,* ἴτε, Ἐλευθεροῦτε πατρίδα, ἐλευθερουτε δέ παιδας, γυναίκας, θεῶν τέ πατρώων ἔδη, θήκας τέ προγόνων, νῦν ὑπέρ πάντων ἀγών)[11]

In this context, it is of crucial significance to mention the role of Amphictionies in classical Greece. Amphictionies were alliances or confederations in ancient Greece. Amphictionies denoted the establishment of very strong political and religious ties among city-states, which shared religious ceremonies and temples.[12] Many amphictionies existed in ancient Greece, notably that of Thermopylae, Delos, and Delphi. The Delphic amphictiony was by far the most eminent and powerful. It was an international association, as it was composed of twelve tribes or nations, linked with close ties of kinship. It is often referred to as the Congregation of the Greeks or, in fact, the Council of the Hellenes—*τό κοινόν τῶν Ἑλλήνων Συνέδριον*. There existed two categories of representatives, namely the *ἱερομνήμονες*, otherwise called *Ἀμφικτιόνων οἱ Σύνεδροι*, councilors, and the *πυλαγόραι*. The former, who comprised the formal Congregation, had the privilege to demarcate the territorial boundaries of the sacred places and sacred lands.[13] As a rule, the fundamental principles that the Congregation was called to implement were decided upon and ratified through formal oath. In the case of the Delphic Amphictiony, the practice of the Councilors and in essence of allies who pursued identical policies has been preserved up to nowadays and is no doubt one of the most ancient texts of treaties, providing for the formation of an alliance, in the Western world. The members, or Councilors, took an oath that they would in no event destroy any member city-state of the Amphictiony, nor would they cut it off from the supply of drinking water in the course of either war or peace; that they would declare war against anyone who would violate this law and should destroy their cities; and that they would punish in every manner anyone who would plunder the property of the god and his accomplices in such an act.[14]

Generally speaking, the real objective of war was to effect a reparation, previously denied, of some serious act that had without reason been inflicted, or, more importantly, to exact due revenge of a wrong in conformity and compliance with divine injunctions. Thus, Xenophon exhorted his men to have regard to moderation and honor, and not to plunder any city that was not in any way guilty of offenses against them.[15] The purpose, declares Polybius, for which good men make war is not to destroy and annihilate the wrongdoers, but to alter the wrongful acts. Nor is it their object to involve the innocent in the destruction of the guilty—*ού γάρ έπ'άπωλεία δεῖ καί ἀφανισμῷ τοῖς ἀγνοήσασι* πολεμεῖν *τούς ἀγαθούς ἄνδρας, ἀλλ'ἐπί μεταθέσει τῶν ἡμαρτημένων, οὐδέ συναιρεῖν τά μηδέν ἀδικοῦντα τοῖς ἠδικηκόσιν*. This, however, has not always been the sole, let alone the most significant and justifiable, aim of war among the Greeks. The same aforementioned doctrine had long before been affirmed by Plato. In the Republic, where Socrates and Glaucon discuss what acts ought to be forbidden in warfare, but distinguish between war against Greeks and that against barbarians, Socrates suggests that the armed conflict, with the Greeks, must be conducted entirely with a view to conciliation. The rule ought to be not enslavement or destruction of the enemy. "And as they are Hellenes themselves they will not devastate Hellas, nor they burn houses, nor even suppose that the whole population of a city—men, women, and children—are equally their enemies, for they know that the guilt of war is always confined to a few persons and that the many are their friends. And for all these reasons they will be unwilling to devastate their lands and raze their houses; their enmity to them will only last until the many innocent sufferers have compelled the guilty few to give satisfaction."[16] Contrast, though, the firm view of Aristotle, as expressed in the *Rhetoric*, that punishment and just retribution ought to be in every case the predominant object—*διά θυμόν καί* ὀργήν *τά τιμωρητικά*.

If we now turn to the causes of the Peloponnesian War, we cannot help but see that these very causes have little resemblance to the grounds of war as above elaborated. As a preliminary it should be stressed that this was a civil war among the Greeks, not an international armed conflict as the notion is nowadays comprehended. However, the war erupted between city-states of the classical Greek world, so from this perspective, it may, too, be termed as an inter-state war. What is more, Thucydides invented the distinction between the remote and deeper causes of the war and the immediate causes of it. The immediate causes of the Peloponnesian War are well-known, and there is no need to refer to them extensively: the events at Epidamnus, the political situation in Corcyra, the Megarian decree, and the incidents at Potidaea. In *The History of the Peloponnesian War*, Thucydides considered the immediate causes, which, in fact, went back almost five years before the commencement of hostilities, to be less important than the remote causes, which arose from the growth of the Athenian Empire during the fifty years before the outbreak of the war. The standpoint of Thucydides that the war was the eventual and inevitable sequence of that empire's growth has been widely accepted among scholars and is hereby, too, endorsed. Thucydides's main statement of the causes of the war runs as follows:

> *Διότι δ'ἔλυσαν τάς αἰτίας προύγραψα πρώτον καί τάς διαφορᾶς του μή τινά ζητησαι ποτέ ἐξ ὅτου τοσουτος πόλεμος τοῖς Ἑλλησι κατέστη.* Τήν μέν γάρ ἀληθεστάτην πρόφασιν, ἀφανεστάτην δέ λόγω, τούς Ἀθηναίους ἡγοῦμαι μεγάλους γιγνομένους, καί φόβον παρέχοντας τοῖς Λακεδαιμονίοις ἀναγκᾶσαι ἕς τό πολεμοιν. Αἵ δ'ἕς τό φανερόν λεγόμεναι αἰτίαι αἰδ'ἦσαν ἑκατέρων, ἀφ'ὧν λύσαντες τάς σπονδᾶς ἕς τοόν πόλεμον κατέστησαν.
>
> The reasons why they broke it [the peace] and the grounds of their quarrel I have first set forth, that no one may ever have to inquire for what cause the Hellenes became involved in so a great war. The truest explanation, although it has been the least often advanced, I believe to have been the growth of Athens to greatness, which brought fear to the Lacedaemonians and forced them to war. But the reasons publicly alleged on either side which led them to break the truce and involved them in the war were as follows.[17]

The imperial policy of Athens and ambitions of its ruling elite, which became manifest particularly on the eve of the Sicilian expedition, readily justified or at least explained a policy of counterimperialism on the part of Sparta that eventually led to war. These causes are far more similar to causes of contemporary wars that are characterized by an imperial spirit, that is, wars that are usually the consequence of imperialistic ambitions.

I cannot agree with Kagan, who attempts to disprove the statement of Thucydides, and allege that the immediate causes of the war were far more important than the remote ones.[18] Also, economic causes of various forms have been suggested as the real cause of the armed conflict. The proposition of Cornford that there was a party of merchants from Peiraeus who hoped to make gains by seizing control of the routes to the west through Megara, Acarnania, and Corcyra and forced Pericles to lead Athens to war is mostly an imaginary proposition.[19] Clearly, the interest of Athens in Corcyra was strategic and not economic. Although there were aggressively imperialistic Athenians who hoped to gain economically from the extension of their empire, the mere fact is that they did not formulate Athenian policy.[20] That policy was made by Pericles, who had previously fought them successfully and was not influenced by them at the stage of the final crisis. The interests of the merchants may only have had some part in the decision made by the Athenian people to embark upon an expedition in Sicily.

Noteworthy is a version of the Thucydidean thesis that the war was the inevitable outcome of the division of the Greek world into two power blocs.[21] This Thucydidean view is reinforced by the weapons of contemporary political science, notably international relations theory. The condition that troubled the Greek world and brought about the war is to be found in the term *bipolarity*. *Bipolarity* is used to describe a condition in which exclusive control of international politics is concentrated in two great powers solely responsible for the preservation of peace or the making of war expeditions. Such a thesis seems to be convincing, but not distinct from the remote and real causes of the war, as the influence and policies exerted by the two great states of the Greek world was actually the product of their respective inclinations, ambitions, ideologies, and imminent idiosyncrasies.

The more important contribution of Thucydides, however, in my view, is to be traced in the grounds of war as described in his *History*. In this third part of the article, an analysis will ensue, indicating that the grounds, more properly the justifications, of war as elaborated by this great author, have provided the legal basis of some fundamental forms of armed intervention in the modern world, in the sphere of International Law science in particular.

The Thucydidean historical work sets an authoritative example of the Use of Force in the sense of armed intervention in international relations. The affairs that follow should be seen in light of the fact that the Greek cities in ancient times were states themselves.[22] First, Book IV of the *History of the Peloponnesian War* may at first sight be said to pose an example of self-defense in International Law, particularly of protection of nationals abroad, this being a facet or category of self-defense of states. On its way to Sicily, the Athenian fleet was met with a sea storm, which forced the ships to seek refuge in the Peloponnese (Pylos). Since the war between Athens and Sparta was at its height, the Athenian Navy members were arrested by the Lacedaemonians. Cleon, the Athenian demagogue, forcefully urged the Athenian Assembly for a military campaign to prevent their fellow citizens from being massacred. The incident may be described as an operation to save nationals abroad (since the Athenian prisoners of war were not subjects of the Spartans).

In modern International Law, serious efforts have been made to limit the use of force by states. One of the cornerstones of International Law is the general prohibition of the Use of Force as enshrined in the Charter of the United Nations.[23] UN Charter Article 2(4) provides: all members shall refrain in their international relations from the threat or use of force against the territorial integrity or political independence of any State, or in any manner inconsistent with the purposes of the United Nations. However, Self-Defense of States is a commonly accepted exception to the general prohibition of the Use of Force as embodied in the UN Charter. Article 51 of the Charter stipulates that: "nothing in the present Charter shall impair the inherent right of individual or collective self-defense if an armed attack occurs against a member of the United Nations, until the Security Council has taken the measures necessary to maintain international peace and security. Measures taken by Members in the exercise of this right of self-defense shall be immediately reported to the Security Council and shall not in any way affect the authority and responsibility of the Security Council under the present Charter to take at any time such action as it deems necessary in order to maintain international peace and security."[24] The protection of nationals abroad forms one of the four facets of the right to self-defense. An attack against nationals of a state who happen to be abroad or failure for them to be succored in accordance with International Law stipulations, gives the right to this state to use armed force in order to protect its nationals without securing the consent of the foreign government. The right of a state to take military action to protect its nationals in mortal danger is recognized by all legal authorities in International Law. In *Self Defense in International Law*, Professor Bowett states that the right of the state to intervene by the use or threat of force for the protection of its nationals suffering injuries within the territory of another state is generally admitted, both in the writings of jurists and in the practice of states.[25]

On June 27, 1976, an Air France airliner bound for Paris from Tel Aviv was hijacked over Greece after leaving the Athens airport. Two of the hijackers appear to have been West German nationals; the other two held Arab passports. The airliner was diverted to Entebbe airport in Uganda, where the Jewish passengers (about one hundred) were separated from the others, and the latter were released. The hijackers demanded the release of about fifty Palestinian terrorists imprisoned in various countries. The evidence seems to suggest that Uganda did not take such steps as it might have done against the hijackers and, indeed, helped them, although Uganda denied this. On July 3, 1976, Israel flew transport aircraft and soldiers to Entebbe and rescued the hostages by force. The hijackers were killed during the operation, as were some Ugandan and Israeli soldiers. There was also extensive damage to the Ugandan aircraft and the airport.[26]

The military operation at Pylos has, in a magnificent manner, also generated the criteria for a legitimate use of force applicable in all cases of military intervention, including self-defense. These were formulated in the speech of the Athenian general Demosthenes only a while before the commencement of the military rescue operation: "Men who have gathered in this venture, let no one of you wish to be esteemed a man of rationality; but, instead, with plain courage, which *leaves no moment for deliberation*, let him attack the opponents and even be optimistic that he will eventually be victorious. When matters reach a point of *overwhelming necessity*, as the present case is, crude reflection is least needed in view of the *instant* danger."[27] Note the striking similarity between the terminology used in this text, and the one employed in the *Caroline Case* (1840),[28] which traditionally and in a universally acceptable proposition sets limits to the use of armed force in contemporary International Law: 'It will be for Her Majesty's Government to show a necessity of self-defense, instant, overwhelming, leaving no moment for deliberation.' These were the words of Mr. Webster, US secretary of state, to British minister Mr. Fox (April 24, 1841). It makes one wonder whether Mr. Webster was a fervent reader of Thucydides. In fact, research I have done into his biography have revealed that, indeed, he studied Thucydides to a significant extent. This may only be coincidental. But it remains a true fact that the terminology used both at the Pylos incident and in the Caroline affair is identical. And it remains an undisputable fact that the International Law principles laid down in the Caroline Case, known as the Caroline test, were put forward some 2,400 years ago in Pylos, as reported by Thucydides in *The History of the Peloponnesian War*. State practice in the field of the Law of War in the twentieth century that has developed in the same pattern as the rescue operation of Pylos (and Sphacteria) affirms the principles born out of the Peloponnesian War. A criterion is that the use of force must correspond to the dictates of the proportionality principle. The Caroline case principle may be seen as one that sets limits to the use of force in general and calls for adherence to proportionality. The classic formulation of Mr. Webster in this context may also be quoted: "did nothing unreasonable or excessive; since the act is justified by the necessity of self-defense, must be limited by that necessity, and kept clearly within it."

Turning back to Thucydides, and examining for a moment the war incident of Pylos from a purely philological (and political) perspective, one cannot fail to see the rather unfair treatment of Cleon on the part of Thucydides. In paragraph 28.5 of Book IV, where Cleon is described as struggling to persuade the Athenian assembly to undertake a military operation in Pylos to rescue the Athenian hostages, Thucydides, verbatim, says: *ἐνέπεσε μέν τί καί γέλωτος τή κουφολογία αὐτοῦ. Ἀσμένοις δ'ὅμως ἐγίγνετο τοῖς σώφροσι τῶν ἀνθρώπων, λογιζομένοις δυοιν ἀγαθοίν τοῦ ἑτέρου τεύξεσθαι. Ἤ Κλέωνος ἀπαλλαγήσεσθαι, ὅ μᾶλλον ἤλπιζον, ἤ σφαλείσι γνώμης Λακεδαιμονίους σφίσι χειρώσασθαι.*[29] The prejudice against Cleon is evident, though Thucydides to his credit seems to take a measured stance when he subsequently (much at the end of the Athenian military campaign) does not hesitate to emphasize the success of Cleon. *Καί τοῦ Κλέωνος, καῖπερ μανιώδης οὖσα, ή ὑπόσχεσις* ἀπέβη (and the promise of Cleon, mad though it was, proved to be successful, paragraph 40). The proverbial objectivity of Thucydides is further confirmed at paragraph 21.3, where it is stated that Cleon was a prominent and most influential demagogue. That statement, of course, carries some irony, but it still accurately depicts Cleon himself, who, indeed, exerted influence among the populace.[30]

Cornford's view that Thucydides emphasized and exaggerated the element of chance in the Athenian victory, in order, according to him, to minimize Cleon's success, in reality it would serve rather to minimize that of Demosthenes, with whom Thucydides is generally supposed to have been on friendly terms.[31] The war incident at Pylos and Sphacteria was certainly affected by the fortune of war, not chance in the strict sense of the word. The navy battle that took place in the harbor of Pylos remains one of the most impressive ones in the history of naval warfare, and it is worth quoting the historian at this point.[32]

The military operation at Pylos can also be viewed as a paradigm example of unilateral humanitarian intervention, if by extension of the doctrine of self-defense one accepts the existence of a similar right of intervention for humanitarian purposes. The speech of General Demosthenes again lays down the premises of humanitarian intervention. A state can lawfully use armed force to prevent a humanitarian catastrophe of its nationals, especially if such a danger is imminent. Such was the action of the Athenian State in Pylos. And, certainly, in modern International Law, this form of the use of force should conform to the requirements of the principle of proportionality as this was developed in the Caroline case, cited above. A UK Foreign Office Policy Document gives an accurate definition of *humanitarian intervention*: "a substantial body of opinion and of practice has supported the view that when a State commits cruelties against and persecution of its nationals in such a way as to deny their fundamental human rights and to shock the conscience of mankind, intervention in the interests of humanity is legally permissible."[33]

To put this issue into a contemporary context and to address the fundamental issue of the moral justification of humanitarian intervention would require a whole inquiry into the ethical foundations of the international legal system. The tension focuses between sovereignty and human rights.

At first sight, there is a legal duty to refrain from interfering in the internal affairs of other states. Each state is bound to respect the sovereignty of its neighbor states. This view has its roots in legal positivism. The German philosopher Wolff was the first to separate the international law principles from the ethics of the individual. Great academic debate has erupted over the general prohibition of the use of force as stipulated in Article 2(4) of the UN

Charter,[34] especially the wording "against the territorial integrity or political independence of any State."[35]

It is necessary to show that a right of unilateral humanitarian intervention is compatible with Article 2(4) of the UN Charter.[36] The only exceptions to the general prohibition of the threat or use of force are the "inherent right of individual or collective self-defense in the face of an armed attack against a State" in Article 51 of the UN Charter, and enforcement actions by the Security Council or by a regional organization or group of states authorized to use force by the Security Council under Chapter VII of the Charter. Neither of these provisions is applicable to unilateral humanitarian intervention. Two arguments may be employed: that a genuine humanitarian intervention would not be a use of force against the "territorial integrity or political independence" of another state, or that it would not be "inconsistent with the Purposes of the United Nations." It is noteworthy that in their commentary on the Charter, Goodrich and Hambro observed that it is possible to construe the language as allowing certain limited uses of force, such as a temporary intervention for protective purposes.[37] Teson, noting that the promotion of human rights is as important a purpose in the Charter as the control of international conflict, concludes that to argue that humanitarian intervention is prohibited by Article 2(4) is a distortion.[38]

Article 2(4) must be read and interpreted in conjunction with the purposes of the United Nations, one of which is the promotion of human rights. The Preamble to the Charter reads as follows: "We the peoples of the United Nations determined . . . to reaffirm faith in fundamental human rights, in the dignity and worth of the human person, in the equal rights . . . of nations large and small. . . . " Article 1(3) states: "To achieve international co-operation in solving international problems of an economic, social, cultural, or humanitarian character, and in promoting and encouraging respect for human rights and for fundamental freedoms for all."[39] Further, Article 55(c) of the Charter declares that the United Nations shall promote "universal respect for, and observance of human rights and fundamental freedoms for all without distinction as to race, sex, language, or religion." More importantly, by Article 56 "all members pledge themselves to take joint and separate action in co-operation with the Organization for the achievement of the purposes set forth in Article 55."[40]

The deduction from the above should be that the right of unilateral humanitarian intervention is clearly not incompatible with Article 2(4) of the UN Charter.

Apart from the legal debate, however, I would suggest, from the moral standpoint, that the rights of states under international law derive from individual rights. The proper role of the state is to ensure the protection of the rights of the individuals. As Hersch Lauterpacht very well put it, "states are like individuals; it is due to the fact that states are composed of individual human beings. . . . The dignity of the individual human being is a matter of direct concern to international law." Lauterpacht's rationale for humanitarian intervention is that "ultimately, peace is much more endangered by tyrannical contempt for human rights than by attempts to assert, through intervention, the sanctity of human personality."[41] Therefore, in my opinion, state sovereignty must give way to the protection of human rights whenever these are flagrantly violated.[42] In view of the preceding theoretical discussion in this section, I strongly submit that states have a moral right, to say the least, to unilaterally intervene in cases of overwhelming humanitarian necessity. The writings of learned jurists should, in my submission, be taken much more seriously into account, and perhaps cease to be seen merely as subsidiary sources of public international law (despite Article 38(1)(d) of the ICJ Statute).

A further instance, which could have crystalized into a clear example of humanitarian intervention in *The History of Thucydides*, and eventually did not materialize as such, is provided in Book III. The island of Lesbos (member of the Athenian Empire-Commonwealth or Confederation of city-states) revolted from Athens. The Athenians set sail against the Mytilenians (the inhabitants of Lesbos), warning them that if they were to refuse an order to surrender, they would demolish their fortifications. An embassy of Mytilenians sought the help of Sparta thus: "Come to the help of Mytilene. It is our lives that we are risking; an even more general calamity will follow if you will not listen to us."[43] The very basic criteria for humanitarian intervention were, in this case, fulfilled: (i) the Mytilenians were subjects of a State (Athens), (ii) they consented to the military intervention undertaken for their own sake, and (iii) they faced imminent danger of humanitarian catastrophe.[44] The Spartans, indeed, dispatched a fleet that reached the coast of Lesbos but never engaged in fighting. The conservative foreign policy of Sparta dictated that the military forces of the state were to keep an eye on a possible revolt of the Helot population in the Peloponnese.[45] This affair serves, if nothing else, as an instance clearly showing that humanitarian disaster may, indeed, be the outcome of non-intervention, as it eventually was with the Mytilenians. Therefore, it may be inferred that humanitarian intervention in cases of instant necessity is a must.

The History of Thucydides has undoubtedly laid down the foundations of modern International Law of War. State practice of ancient times—indeed, the custom of the states of ancient Greece—cannot be neglected.[46] The adoption of the UN Charter is not meant to suggest that pre-charter international customary law has automatically been abrogated. Instead, customary law can, indeed, be considered as part and parcel of a unified International Law tradition, as living international custom, living law, may still find appeal in the modern world.

NOTES

1. Aristotle, *Rhetoric*, *Ars Rhetorica*, *Oxford Classical Texts* (Oxford: Oxford University Press, 1959), i. 10: *νόμος δ'ἐστίν ὁ μέν ἴδιος, ὁ δέ κοινός. Λέγω δέ ἴδιον μέν καθ'ὅν γεγραμμένον πολιτεύονται. Κοινόν δέ ὅσα ἄγραφα παρά πᾶσιν ὁμολογεῖσθαι δοκεῖ.*

2. *Τοῦ δέ πολιτικοῦ δικαίου τό μέν φυσικόν ἐστι τό δέ νομικόν, φυσικόν μέν τό πανταχοῦ τήν αὐτήν ἔχον δύναμιν, καί οὐ τω δοκεῖν ἤ μή, νομικόν δέ ὁ ἐξ ἀρχῆς μέν οὐθεν διαφέρει οὕτως ἤ ἄλλως, ὅταν δέ θῶνται.* (*Nicomachaean Ethics*, *Loeb Classical Library* 73, Cambridge, Massachusetts: Harvard University Press, 1926), v. 10.

3. Thucydides, *History of the Peloponnesian War*, *Loeb Classical Library*, (Cambridge, Massachusetts: Harvard University Press, 1920), iv. 97.

4. *Ibid.* i. 3, i. 118; Plutarch, *Pericles*, *Lives* Volume III, *Loeb Classical Library* 65, (Cambridge, Massachusetts: Harvard University Press, 1916), 17.

5. A formal declaration of war was not a necessary prerequisite for commencing military operations, though in the Peloponnesian War, the instance of envoy Melisippus sent to the camp of the Lacedaemonians by General Pericles on part of the Athenians, only before the commencement of armed conflict, goes to the contrary. On his way back, he notoriously exclaimed μεγάλα κακά ἄρξονται τοῖς Ἕλλησι. Interestingly, in the Roman Law of Nations (*Ius Gentium*), a demand for satisfaction was laid down before declaring war. The Romans, before declaring war, dispatched ambassadors to foreign countries, against which they had a grievance, with a formal demand in the name of the Roman government and people to make reparations for any injury suffered. In case of refusal, a declaration of war was pronounced. This criterion of legitimacy of war is echoed in the words of Cicero, who says that "the laws and customs of war are religiously recorded in the code of the Roman people, in pursuance of which no war is deemed to be just or legitimate, unless it is duly declared after a formal demand for satisfaction has been made" (Cicero, *On Duties* [*De Officiis*], *Loeb Classical Library* 30, Cambridge, Massachusetts: Harvard University Press, 1931, i. II. 36: Ac belli quidem aequitas sanctissime fetiali populi Romani iure perscripta est. Ex quo intelligi potest nullum bellum esse iustum nisi quod aut rebus repetitis geratur aut denunciatum ante sit et indictum).

6. *The Odyssey of Homer* (Harper Collins Publishers, 2007), xvi. 425–28.

7. Livy, *History of Rome* volume VIII, *Loeb Classical Library* (Cambridge, Massachusetts: Harvard University Press, 1936), XXX. 42.

8. Plutarch, *Demetrius, Lives Volume IX*, *Demetrius and Anthony*, *Loeb Classical Library* 101, (Cambridge, Massachusetts: Harvard University Press, 1920), 33.

9. Herodotus, *The Persian Wars*, *Loeb Classical Library* 118 (Cambridge, Massachusetts: Harvard University Press, 1921), viii, I44.

10. Arrian in his *Anabasis of Alexander*, ably presents the patriotic, warlike, and justly vengeful temper of Alexander the Great as expressed in his: *ἄπιτε πάντες καί ἀπελθόντες οἴκοι ἀπαγγείλατε ὅτι τόν βασιλέα ὑμῶν Ἀλέξανδρον, τόν νικήσαντα Μήδους τέ καί Πέρσας . . . καί τόν Ἰνδόν ποταμόν διαβάντα, καί τόν Ὕφασιν διαπεράσαντα ἄν εἰ μή ὑμεις ἀποκνήσατε, οἴχεσθε καταλοιπόμενοι, παραδιδόμενοι φυλάττειν τοῖς νενικημένοις βαρβάροις. Ταῦτα ἴσως εὐκλεά ἔστε ἀπαγγελθέντα. Ἄπιτε.*

(Arrian, *Anabasis of Alexander, Books I-IV, Loeb Classical Library* 236, Cambridge, Massachusetts: Harvard University Press, 1976), 234, VII, 6.

11. Aeschylus, *Persians, Loeb Classical Library* (Cambridge, Massachusetts: Harvard University Press, 1926), 402.

12. The term *αμφικτιονία* originates in the term *αμφικτίονες*, practically a synonym of *περικτίονες,* commonly called *περίοικοι,* which means neighbors.

13. *Ιερά χώρα* (A. Bockh, *Corpus Inscriptionum Graecarum*, Officina Academica, 1171).

14. See I. Kareklas, ΔΙΕΘΝΕΣ ΔΙΚΑΙΟΝ ΚΑΙ ΕΛΛΗΝΙΚΟΣ ΠΟΛΙΤΙΣΜΟΣ (Athens, 2010), 19 for the text: *Μηδεμίαν πόλιν τῶν Ἀμφικτυονίδων ἀνάστατον ποιήσειν μηδ'ὑδάτων ναματιαίων εἴρξειν μητ'ἐν πολέμω μήτ'ἐν εἰρήνη, ἐάν δέ τίς ταῦτα παραβῆ, στρατεύσειν ἐπί τοῦτον καί τάς πόλεις ἀναστήσειν, καί ἐάν τίς εἰ συλα τά τοῦ θεοῦ εἰ συνείδη τί ἤ βουλεύση τί κατά τῶν ἱερῶν τιμωρήσειν καί χειρί καί ποδί καί φωνή καί πάσει δυνάμει*. See also extensively on the issue of Amphictionies *Idem*), 15–22.

15. Xenophon, *Anabasis, Loeb Classical Library* 90 (Cambridge, Massachusetts: Harvard University Press, 1998), vii. I. 29.

16. Plato, *Republic*, *Loeb Classical Library* 276 (Cambridge, Massachusetts: Harvard University Press, 2013), v. 471A: *Οὐδ'ἄρα τήν Ἑλλάδα Ἕλληνες ὄντες κερουσιν, οὐδέ οἰκήσεις ἐμπρήσουσιν, οὐδέ ὁμολογήσουσιν ἐν ἑκάστη πόλει πάντας ἐχθρούς αὐτοις εἶναι, καί ἄνδρας καί γυναίκας καί παιδας, ἀλλ'ὀλίγους ἀεί ἐχθρούς τους αἰτίους τῆς διαφορᾶς. Καί διά ταῦτα πάντα οὔτε τήν γῆν ἐθελήσουσι κείρειν αὐτῶν, ὡς φίλων των πολλῶν, οὔτε οἰκίας ἀνατρέπειν. Ἀλλά μέχρι τούτου ποιήσονται τήν διαφοράν, μέχρι οὐ ἄν οἱ αἴτιοι ἀναγκασθῶσιν ὑπό τῶν ἀναιτίων ἀλγούντων δοῦναι δίκην.*

17. Thucydides, *History of the Peloponnesian War,* translated by C.F. Smith, *Loeb Classical Library* (Cambridge, Massachusetts: Harvard University Press, 1921), I, 23.

18. See D. Kagan, *The Outbreak of the Peloponnesian War* (Cornell University Press, 1989), 345–46: "Our investigation has led to conclude that his judgment is mistaken. We have argued that Athenian power did not grow between 445 and 435, that the imperial appetite of Athens was not insatiable and gave good evidence of being satisfied, that the Spartans as a state seem not to have been unduly afraid of the Athenians, at least until the crisis had developed very far, that there was good reason to think that the two great powers and their allies could live side by side in peace indefinitely, and thus that it was not the underlying causes but the immediate crisis that produced the war."

19. C.F. Cornford, *Thucydides Mythistoricus* (London, Edward Arnold, 1907), 1–51.

20. On this I agree with Kagan. See *The Outbreak of the Peloponnesian War, ibid.*, 345–56.

21. P.J. Fliess, *Thucydides and the Politics of Bipolarity* (Baton Rouge, 1966). See also the fundamental work of Polly Low, *Interstate Relations in Classical Greece. Morality and Power, Cambridge Classical Studies* (Cambridge: Cambridge University Press, 2007) for an international or interstate relations perspective in Thucydides.

22. It is precisely because of the fact that the Greek cities were themselves recognized as States—albeit with common origins of blood, language, and religion- that

the Peloponnesian War, though often described as the greatest 'Civil War' in antiquity, was in fact an international conflict.

23. Previous efforts had been made to the same effect including primarily the Covenant of the League of Nations 1919, of which Article 12(1) provided: the members of the League agree that, if there should arise between them any dispute likely to lead to a rupture, they will submit the matter either to arbitration or judicial settlement or to inquiry by the Council, and they agree in no case to resort to war until three months have passed after the award by the arbitrators or the judicial decision or the report by the Council. Secondly, and more persistently, the Kellogg-Briand Pact 1928 declared: The High Contracting Parties solemnly declare that they condemn recourse to war for the solution of international controversies, and renounce it as an instrument of national policy in their relations with one another. The High Contracting Parties agree that the settlement or solution of all disputes or conflicts of whatever nature or whatever origin they may be, which may arise among them, shall never be sought except by pacific means.

24. The International Law of War and its first and foremost category, jus ad bellum, which provides for the legal justifications of war, recognizes four instances of lawful war: (1) individual and collective self-defense, (2) humanitarian intervention, though there exist views as to the opposite, (3) collective military action under Chapter VII of the UN Charter after a decision of the Security Council has been made, when regional or international security is at stake, and (4) war in aid of self-determination.

25. In the *Law of Nations* (6th edition, Oxford: Oxford University Press, 2012), 427, Brierly states as follows: every effort must be made to get the United Nations to act. But, if the United Nations is not in a position to move in time and the need for instant action is manifest, it would be difficult to deny the legitimacy of action in defense of nationals which every responsible Government would feel bound to take if it had the means to do so; this is, of course, on the basis that the action was strictly limited on securing the safe removal of the threatened nationals.

26. 15 *International Legal Materials* 1224 (1976). A similar Case is the *US Diplomatic and Consular Staff in Tehran Case*. On November 4, 1979, several hundred Iranian students and other demonstrators took possession of the United States Embassy in Tehran by force. They did so in protest at the admission of the deposed Shah of Iran into the United States for medical treatment. The demonstrators were not opposed by the Iranian security forces who "simply disappeared from the scene." United States consulates elsewhere in Iran were similarly occupied. The demonstrators were still in occupation when the International Court of Justice was called to give a judgment. They had seized archives and documents and continued to hold fifty-two United States nationals (women had been released). Fifty were diplomatic or consular staff; two were private citizens. In an earlier judgment, the Court had indicated interim measures at the request of the United States. In the present judgment, the Court ruled on the United States request for a declaration that Iran had infringed a number of treaties, including the 1961 and 1963 Vienna Conventions on Diplomatic and Consular Relations respectively. It also asked for a declaration calling for the release of the hostages, the evacuation of the Embassy and consulates, the punishment of the persons responsible and the payment of reparation. In April 1980, while the case was

pending, United States military forces entered Iran by air and landed in a remote desert area in the course of an attempt to rescue the hostages. The United States justified its action, in a report to the Security Council pursuant to Article 51 of the UN Charter, as being in "exercise of its inherent right of self-defence with the aim of extricating American nationals who are and remain the victims of the Iranian armed attack on our Embassy." The attempt was abandoned because of equipment failure. United States military personnel were killed in an air collision as the units withdrew. No injury was done to Iranian nationals or property (*International Court of Justice Reports* 1980, 3). The Court by thirteen votes to two, decided that the Islamic Republic of Iran had violated obligations owed by it to the United States of America under international conventions in force between the two countries, as well as under long-established rules of general International Law. The Court also decided that Iran must immediately take all steps to redress the situation resulting from the events of November 4, 1979, including the release of the hostages and the return of the premises and documents to the United States, and that Iran was under an obligation to make reparation to the United States. Iran, which declined to participate in the proceedings, did not comply with the judgment of the Court in any respect. The hostages were ultimately released in January 1981 as a result of a negotiated settlement with the United States.

27. Thucydides, *History of the Peloponnesian War, Loeb Classical Library* (Cambridge, Massachusetts: Harvard University Press, 1972), Book IV, para. XXXVIII. (emphasis added).

28. The case arose out of the Canadian Rebellion of 1837. The rebel leaders, despite steps taken by United States authorities to prevent assistance being given to them, managed on December 13, 1837, to enlist Buffalo in the United States the support of a large number of American nationals. The resulting force established itself in Navy Island in Canadian waters from which it raided the Canadian shore and attacked passing British ships. The force was supplied from the United States shore by an American ship, the *Caroline*. On the night of December 29–30, the British seized the Caroline, which was then in the American port of Schlosser, fired her and sent her over Niagara Falls. Two United States nationals were killed. The legality of the British act was discussed in detail in correspondence in 1841–1842 when Great Britain sought the release of a British subject, McLeod, who had been arrested in the United States on charges of murder and arson out of the incident. (Harris, *Cases and Materials on International Law*, London: Sweet and Maxwell, 1991), 848. See Jennings, *American Journal of International Law*, 32, 1938, 82.

29. This prompted the Athenians to burst out laughing at his empty talk, while the wise heads among them reflected with satisfaction that they would get one or other of two benefits: either they would be rid of Cleon—the result they expected; or if they were wrong about this, they would have the Spartans as their prisoners (Thucydides, *The War of the Peloponnesians and the Athenians*, *Cambridge Texts in the History of Political Thought*, edited by Jeremy Mynott, Cambridge: Cambridge University Press, 2013)

30. Gomme, in my view, rightly observes that this is 'certainly an unexpected description of Kleon after the very similar one in iii. 36. 6, and the prominent and characteristic part there played by him, and not to be justified by Stahl's argument that

Kleon's influence was not constant and probably weakened after the second debate over Mytilene' (*A Historical Commentary on Thucydides*, volume III, Oxford: Oxford University Press, 1956).

31. I agree with Gomme: Certainly the word *τυγχάνειν* occurs frequently: 5.1 (the Spartan festival), 9.1 (the arrival of the Messenian vessels), 13.4 (the omission to block the entrances), and 18.3 (*τύχη*); also 30.2 (the fire on Sphakteria). But as pointed out in the nn. on i. 57. 6, and iv. 9. 1, *τυγχάνειν* does not necessarily mean that an event was accidental, but that it was contemporaneous. 'The Spartans were at that time holding a festival': the most that is meant is that Demosthenes had not timed the arrival at Pylos in order to coincide with it. 'The Messenian vessels had just arrived': that the Messenians had arrived by arrangement with Demosthenes is obvious and is implied by 3.3; but to arrive at exactly the expected time was to some extent fortuitous and fortunate. It was similarly fortunate for the Athenians, and again not planned by them, that the Spartans had not blocked the entrances; but it was not chance. The only events that were really accidental were the storm (3.1, *κατά τύχην*) and the fire on the island; and in the latter case Thucydides makes this clear by *ἄκοντος* and *ἔλαθε*—he does not use. means 'the fortune of war,' which may be no more due to accident than *τό ευτυχησαι*, 17.4 or *τη παρούση τύχη*, 14.3 (*A Historical Commentary on Thucydides, ibid.*, 488–89).

32. *Ἔς τουτό τέ περιέστη ή τύχη, ὥστε Ἀθηναίους μέν ἐκ γῆς τέ καί ταύτης Λακωνικῆς ἀμύνεσθαι ἐκείνους ἐπιπλέοντας, Λακεδαιμονίους δέ ἔς τήν ἑαυτῶν τέ καί πολεμίαν οὖσαν ἐπ'Ἀθηναίους ἀποβαίνειν. Ἐπεῖ πολύ γάρ ἐποίει τῆς δόξης ἐν τῷ τότε τοῖς μέν ἠπειρώταις μάλιστα εἶναι καί τά πεζά κρατίστοις, τοῖς δέ θαλασσίοις τέ καί ταῖς ναυσίν πλεῖστον προέχειν.* (Thucydides, *History of the Peloponnesian War*, Loeb Classical Library, Boston, Harvard University Press, 1923, 4.1.2.).

33. UK Foreign Office Policy Document NO. 148 reprinted in United Kingdom Materials in International Law 1986, 57 *British Yearbook of International Law* 614 (1986).

34. See generally, I. Brownlie, *International Law and the Use of Force by States* (Oxford University Press, 1963).

35. Walzer proposed that 'any use of force by one state against the political independence of another constitutes aggression and is a criminal act'(*Just and Unjust Wars*, Basic Books, 2006*),* 61.

36. UN Charter Article 2 (4): 'All Members shall refrain in their international relations from the threat or use of force against the territorial integrity or political independence of any state, or in any other manner inconsistent with the Purposes of the United Nations.'

37. Goodrich and Hambro, *Charter of the United Nations: Commentary and Documents* (Boston: World Peace Foundation, 1946), 68–69.

38. Teson, *Humanitarian Intervention* (Transnational Publishers, 1988), 151.

39. UN Charter, Article 1(3) (emphasis added).

40. UN Charter, Article 56 (emphasis added).

41. H. Lauterpacht, *International Law and Human Rights* (London, 1950), 32 (emphasis original). H. Lauterpacht is late Whewell Professor of International Law in the University of Cambridge.

42. Most legal scholars who are opposed to humanitarian intervention emphasizing the danger of abuse, are putting forward a policy objection rather than a principled argument. However, all rights are capable of being abused. The right of self-defence has undoubtedly been the subject of abuse, but it is never seriously suggested that International Law should not include the right of a State to defend itself.

43. Thucydides, *History of the Peloponnesian War, ante*, Book II, 14.

44. The basic criteria for humanitarian intervention were fulfilled, but the Mytilenaians's constitution was an oligarchy; the majority of the citizens of Mytilene may well have seen things very differently (on this point see G. de Ste. Croix, *The Origins of the Peloponnesian War* (Cornell University Press, 1972).

45. See, however, Hornblower, *A Commentary on Thucydides Volume I* (Oxford University Press, 1997), where he argues that the standards of the ancient Greeks were not ours, and by our standards the Spartans were probably among the least 'humane' of all ancient Greeks.

46. Thucydides, having detected the unchangeable character of human nature, ably predicted: 'My work is not a piece of writing designed to meet the taste of an immediate public, but was done to last for ever' (*History of the Peloponnesian War, ante,* Book I, 22).

Chapter 2

Grotius and the Tradition of Just War Theory

On the Law of War and Peace

WHETHER IT IS EVER LAWFUL TO WAGE WAR

This chapter is exclusively based on Grotius's *De Jure Belli ac Pacis*. Most of the citations are laid down in the way they appear in the edition of the Carnegie Foundation for Peace (1916).

That war is not in conflict with the law of nature is proved by several considerations:

> 1. Having seen what the sources of law are, let us come to the first and most general question, which is this: whether any war is lawful, or whether it is ever permissible to war. This question, as also the others which follow, must be first taken up from the point of view of the law of nature.

Marcus Tullius Cicero, both in the third book of his treatise *On End* and in other places, following Stoic writings learnedly argues that there are certain first principles on nature—"first according to nature," as the Greeks phrased it—and certain other principles that are later manifest but that are to have the preference over those first principles. He calls first principles of nature those in accordance with which every animal from the moment of its birth has regard for itself and is impelled to preserve itself, to have zealous consideration for its own condition and for those things that tend to preserve it, and also shrinks from destruction and things that appear likely to cause destruction. Hence also it happens, he says, that there is no one, if the choice were presented to him, who would not prefer to have all the parts of his body in proper order and whole rather than dwarfed or deformed; and that it is one's first duty to keep oneself in the condition that nature gave to him, then to hold to those things that are in conformity with nature and reject those things that are contrary thereto.

> 2. But after these things have received due consideration [Cicero continues], there follows a notion of the conformity of things with reason,[1] which is superior to the body. Now this conformity, in which moral goodness becomes the paramount object, ought to be accounted of higher import than the things to which alone instinct first directed itself, and right reason ought to be more dear to us than those things through whose instrumentality we have been brought to it.

Since this is true and without other demonstration would easily receive the assent of all who are endowed with sound judgment, it follows that in investigating the law of nature, it is necessary first to see what is consistent with those fundamental principles of nature, and then to come to that which, though of later origin, is nevertheless more worthy—that which ought not only to be grasped, if it appear, but to be sought out by every effort.

> 3. According to the diversity of the matter, that which we call moral goodness at times consists of a point, so to speak, so that if you depart from it even the least possible distance you turn aside in the direction of wrong-doing; at times it has a wider range, so that an act may be praiseworthy if performed, yet if it be omitted altogether or performed in some other way no blame would attach, the distinction being generally without an intermediate stage, like the transition from being to not-being. Between things opposed in a different way, however, as white and black, a mean may be found either by effecting a combination of the two or by finding an intermediate between them.

It is with this latter class of actions that both divine and human laws are wont to concern themselves, in order that those acts which were in themselves merely praiseworthy might become also obligatory. But we said above, in discussing the law of nature, that the question is this, whether an act can be performed without injustice; and injustice is understood to be that which is utterly repugnant to a rational and social nature.

> 4. In the first principles of nature there is nothing which is opposed to war; rather, all points are in its favor. The end and aim of war being the preservation of life and limb, and the keeping or acquiring of things useful to life, war is in perfect accord with those first principles of nature. If in order to achieve these ends it is necessary to use force, no inconsistency with the first principles of nature is involved, since nature has given to each animal strength sufficient for self-defense and self-assistance. 'All

kinds of animals,' says Xenophon, 'understand some mode of fighting, and they have learned this from no other source than nature.'[2]

Horace has said:

With tooth the wolf, with horn the bull attacks;
And why, unless by inner feeling guided?

Lucretius presents the thought more fully:

Each creature feels the strength which it can use.
Felt by the calf his horns are, ere they stand
Upon his forehead; and with them he butts
Angrily, and threatening, forward thrusts.[3]

The same idea is thus expressed by Galen: "We see that each animal uses for its protection that in which it is strongest. For the calf whose horns have not yet sprouted threatens with that part, and the colt kicks before its hoofs are hard, and the puppy tries to bite when its teeth are not yet strong." Galen also remarks (*On the Use of Parts*, I) that man is an animal born for peace and war. Weapons, to be sure, are not born with him, but he has hands suited for fashioning and handling weapons; and we see that babies of their own accord, and without being taught by any one, use their hands in place of weapons.[4] So Aristotle,[5] too, says that in the case of man, the hand has the place of spear, sword, and all other weapons, because he is able to take and hold everything with the hand.

5. Right reason, moreover, and the nature of society, which must be studied in the second place and are of even greater importance, do not prohibit all use of force, but only that use of force which is in conflict with society, that which attempts to take away the rights of another. For society has in view this object, that through community of resource and effort each individual be safeguarded in the possession of what belongs to him.

It is easy to understand that this consideration would hold even in private ownership (as we now call it) had it not been introduced; for life, limbs, and liberty would in that case be the possessions belonging to each, and no attack could be made upon these by another without injustice. Under such conditions the first one taking possession would have the right to use things not claimed and to consume them up to the limit of his needs, and anyone depriving him of that right would commit an unjust act. But now that private ownership has by law or usage assumed a definite form, the matter is much easier to understand. I shall express the thought in the words of Cicero:

> Just as in case each member of the body should have a feeling of its own, so that it might think that it could gain in vigor by drawing to itself the vigor of the nearest member, the whole body would of necessity be weakened and utterly perish, so, if every one of us should seize upon the possessions of others for himself and carry off from each whatever he could, for his own gain, human society and the community of life would of necessity be absolutely destroyed. For, since, nature does not oppose, it has been granted that each prefer that whatever attributes to the advantage of life be acquired for himself rather than for another; but nature does not allow us to increase our means of subsistence, our resources and our riches, from the spoil of others.[6]

It is not, then, contrary to the nature of society to look out for oneself and advance one's own interests, provided the rights of others are not infringed; and consequently the use of force that does not violate the rights of others is not unjust. This thought also Cicero has presented: "Since there are two ways of settling a difference, the one by argument, the other by force, and since the former is characteristic of man, the latter of brutes, we should have recourse to the second only when it is not permitted to use the first."[7] "What can be done," says the same writer in another passage, "against force without force?"[8]

In Ulpian, we read: "Cassius writes that it is permissible to repel force by force, and this right is bestowed by nature. From this moreover it appears, he says that it is permissible to repel arms by means of arms."[9] Ovid had said: "The laws permit arms against armed men to bear."[10]

That war is not in conflict with the law of nature is proved from history:

> 1. Our statement that not all war is in conflict with the law of nature is more fully proved from sacred history. For Abraham with his servants and allies had taken up arms and had won the victory over the four kings who had sacked Sodom; and God approved the deed through his priest Melchizedek. This in the first Melchizedek addressed him: 'Praise be to God Most High, who has delivered thine enemies into thine hand.'[11] But Abraham had taken up arms, as is evident form the narrative, without a special command of God; in accordance with the law of nature, therefore, did he act, a man not only most holy but also most wise—so recognized even by the testimony of foreigners, Berosus and Orpheus.
>
> I shall not appeal not the history of the seven peoples whom God delivered to the Israelites to be destroyed; for in that case there was a special command to execute a judgement of God upon peoples guilty of the greatest crimes. These wars therefore in holy writ are properly called the wars of God, since they were undertaken by the command of God, not the discretion of men. Having a more direct bearing on our subject is the war which the Jews, under the leadership of Moses, by arms repelled

the Amalekites who were attacking them.[12] This act, which God had not commanded in advance, He approved afterward.

2. But further, God laid down for His own people general and perpetual laws in regard to the mode of carrying on war (Deuteronomy, xx. 10. 15) showing by this very act that a war can be just even without having been specifically commanded by Him. For in these passages He plainly distinguishes the case of the seven peoples from that of other peoples; and since in the same passages He presents no ordinance dealing with the just causes for undertaking war, by this very fact He shows that these are clearly enough known from nature. A just cause of war, for example, is the defence of territory; another is the maltreatment of envoys, in the war of David against the Ammonites.

That war is not in conflict with the law of nature is proved from general agreement:

1. Our thesis is proved also by the general agreement of all nations and especially among the wise. Well known is the passage of Cicero in regard to force used in the defence of life, in which he bears witness to the nature herself:

> 'There is this law which is not written, but born with us; which we have not learned, have not received, have not read, but which we have caught up, have sucked in, yes have wrung out from nature herself; a law regarding which we have not been instructed, but in accord with which we have been made; to which we have not been trained, but with which we are imbued—the law that if our life has been placed in jeopardy by any snare, or violence, or weapons either of brigands or of enemies, every possible means of securing safety is morally right.'[13]

The same writer in another passage adds:

> 'This law reason has enjoined upon the learned, necessity upon barbarians, custom upon nations, and nature herself upon wild beasts, that always, with whatever means of defence they possess, they ward off all violence from body, from head, from life itself.'[14]
>
> The jurist Gaius says: 'Natural reason permits defence of oneself against danger';[15] the jurist Florentinus, 'In accordance with this law it comes about that whatever each may have done in defence of his person he is thought to have done lawfully.'[16] 'For there is,' says Josephus, 'that law of nature which applies in the case of all creatures, that they wish to live; and therein lies the reason why we consider those as enemies who clearly wish to rob us of life.'[17]

2. So obvious is the fairness if this principle that even among brutes which, as we have said, have not the substance of legal rights but only a shadowy appearance of them, we may distinguish between the use of force which attempts an injury and that which wards it off. For Ulpian, having said that an animal devoid of sense, that is, of the use of reason, is incapable of doing what is legally wrong, nevertheless immediately adds that when rams or bulls have fought, and one has killed the other, on the authority of Quintus Mucius a distinction ought to be made. If the animal which started the fight should be killed, an action would not lie. A passage of Pliny will serve to throw light on what has been said:

> 'The fierceness of lions does not manifest itself in attacks upon lions, the bites of serpents are not directed to serpents; but if violence is attempted there is no creature which does not manifest anger, which does not possess a spirit impatient of injury and will not show a ready liveliness in defending itself if you do it harm.'[18]

Proof is adduced that war is not in conflict with the law of nations:

1. It is sufficiently well-established, therefore, that not all wars are at variance with the law of nature; and this may also be said to be true of the law of nations.
2. That wars, moreover, are not condemned by the volitional law of nations, histories, and the laws and customs of all peoples fully teach us. Rather, Hermogenianus said that wars were introduced by the law of nations;[19] but I think that this statement ought to be understood as having a meaning slightly different from that ordinarily given to it, namely, that a definite formality in the conduct of war was introduced by the law of nations, and that particular effects follow wars waged in accordance with such formality under the law of nations. Hence arises the distinction, which we shall have to make use of later, between a war which, according to the law of nations, is formally declared and is called legal, that is a complete war; and a war not formally declared, which nevertheless does not on that account cease to be a legal war, that is according to law. For as regards other wars, provided the cause be just, the law of nations does not indeed lend them support, but it does oppose them. It has been established by the law of nations, says Livy that arms are to be warded off by arms. And Florentinus declares that the law of nations authorizes us to ward off violence and injury in order to protect our body.[20]

Proof is adduced that war was not in conflict with the divine volitional law before the time of the Gospel, and objections are answered:

1. A greater difficulty presents itself in connection with the divine volitional law. Let no one at this point raise the objection that the law of nature is

unchangeable; and that in consequence nothing can be established by God which is contrary to it. For this holds true inn respect to those things which the law of nature forbids or enjoins, but not in respect to the things which by the law of nature are permissible only. Things of the latter class, since they do not properly belong to the sphere of the law of nature but are outside that sphere, can be both forbidden and enjoined.

2. First, therefore, as against war some are accustomed to bring forward the law given to Noah and his posterity, in which God thus speaks:[21]

> 'And surely your blood, the blood of your lives, will I require; from every beast will I require it; and at the hand of man, even at the hand of every man's brother, will I require the life of man. Whoso sheddeth man's blood, by man shall his blood be shed: for in the image of God made He man.'

The first part of this passage, then, in which the requiring of blood is mentioned, they understand as altogether general; and they suppose that the second part, about the shedding of blood in turn, is in the nature of a menace, not an expression of approval. Neither interpretation is to me convincing. For the prohibition in regard to the shedding of blood has no wider application than the commandment, 'Thou shalt not kill'; but this commandment, it is clear, has not proved to be an obstacle either to capital punishments or to wars. The rule of law then as well as the former, had in view not so much the ordaining of something new as the declaration and repetition of a rule of law of nature which had been effaced by degenerate usage. Hence these words are to be taken in a sense which conveys the idea of moral fault, just as by the word of homicide we understand not the slaying of man in general, but a premeditated murder of an innocent man. What follows in regard to the shedding of blood in turn seems to me to contain not a statement of bare fact, but a provision of law.

3. I explain the matter thus. According to nature it is not unfair that each suffer to the full extent of the evil he has committed, in accordance with the principle which is called the law of Radamanthus: if each shall suffer all that he has done, it will be fair and right.[22]

Seneca the father phrased the idea thus: 'By a most just recompense of suffering each through his own punishment undergoes what he devised for another.'[23] In accordance with the viewpoint of this natural equity Cain, conscious of parricide, had said: 'Whosoever findeth me shall slay me.'[24]

In those first times, however, either on account of the scarcity of men or because criminals were few in number and so there was less need of an example, that which seemed to be permitted by nature God repressed by a command; He desired that contact and intercourse with a murderer be avoided, but that life be not taken from him. A similar regulation Plato established among his laws;[25] that such was the practice formerly in vogue Euripides informs us in these verses:

How well the prescient age of our forebears
Decreed, that whoso murder had committed
Should far from way and sight of men depart,
By flight, not death, his dreadful crime atone!

To the same point the following passage of Thucydides relates: 'It is believable that in antiquity penalties were light[26] even for great crimes; but as these in the course of time came to be viewed with contempt, recourse was had to the death penalty.'[27]

4. Upon the one striking example was based a conclusion in regard to the divine will, and this passed over into law. Thus Lamech, having committed a similar crime, in the light of that example promised himself exemption from punishment.[28]
5. But since already before the Flood, in the period of the giants, a general orgy of murders had prevailed, in the renewal of the human race after the Flood God judged that several measures must be taken, in order that the same custom might not become fixed; and having done away with the mildness of the former age, He Himself permitted that the man who had killed a murderer[29] should be innocent—a measure which nature declared was not unfair.[30] Afterward, when courts were established, for very weighty reasons this permission was restricted to judges alone. Nevertheless, a trace of the older custom remained in the light of the next of kin of a murdered man; this right was recognized even after the law of Moses.
6. In favour of our interpretation we have the great authority of Abraham who, being not ignorant of the law given to Noah, took up arms against the four kings, obviously in the belief that his action was not in conflict with that law. In like manner also Moses ordered that the Amalekites, who were attacking the people, be resisted by force of arms; he made use, as we see, of the law of nature, for it does not appear that God had been specifically consulted in regard to this act.[31] Furthermore, it is clear that capital punishment was already applied not only to murderers but also to other criminals, and not merely among foreign peoples but among the favoured recipients of the holy teaching.[32]
7. Beyond doubt interpretation of the divine will, with the help of natural reason, had proceeded from like to like, so that it seemed not unfair to apply to others who were guilty of exceptional crimes the penalty which had been appointed for the murderer. For there are certinl things which are rated of equal value with life, as reputation, maidenly chastity, and conjugal fidelity; and things without which life cannot be safe, such as respect for the governing power which maintains the social order. Those who attack these things seem no better than murderers.
8. In this connection belongs the ancient tradition which is found among the Jews, that several laws were given by God to the sons of Noah, of which not all were recorded by Moses, because it was sufficient for his

purpose that these were afterwards included in the particular law of the Jews. Thus it is evident that there was an old law against incestuous marriages,[33] although this was not mentioned by Moses in the proper place. Among the ordinacnes which God gave to the sons of Noah they say that the following also had a place, that not only murder but also adultery, incest and robbery with violence should be punished with death.

9. Now the law which was given through the agency of Moses justifies the inflicting of capital punishment by reasons which carry not less weight among other peoples than with the Jewish people; examples are to be found in *Leviticus*, xviii. 24, 25, 27, 28; *Psalms*, ci. 5; and *Proverbs*, xx. 8. Of murder it is specifically said that no expiation can be made for the land except for shedding the blood of the murderer.[34] Besides, it is absurd to think that on the one hand the Jewish people were allowed to protect their moral code and the safety of both the state and of individuals by means of capital punishment and to defend themselves by war, and that, on the other hand, the same course of action was not at the time permissible to other kings and nations, while, nevertheless, those kings or nations were never warned by the prophets, as they were frequently warned in regard to other sins, that the use of capital punishment and wars of every kind were viewed with disapproval by God.
10. Who, on the contrary, would not believe that, since the law of Moses with reference to judgments embodied a faithful expression of the divine will, the nations would have acted rightly and fittingly in taking this as a model for themselves? It is believable that at any rate the Greeks, the Attic Greeks in particular, did this; hence it came about that there is so great similarity between the ancient Attic law, together with that part of the Roman law of the Twelve Tables derived from it, and the Hebraic laws.[35] These considerations seem sufficient to make it plain that the law given to Noah did not have the meaning attributed to it by those who on the strength of it oppose all wars.

Preliminary considerations bearing upon the question whether war is in conflict with the law of the Gospel:

1. The arguments against war which are drawn from the Gospel have greater plausibility. In examining them I shall not assume, as many do, that in the Gospel outside of the ordinances relating to belief and to the sacraments there is nothing which does not belong to the law of nature; for I do not think that is true, at least in the sense in which most people take it.
2. I willingly recognize the fact that in the Gospel nothing is enjoined upon us which does not have the quality of natural moral goodness; but I do not see why I should grant that we are not bound by the laws of Christ beyond the limit of obligation imposed by the law of nature of and by itself. It is amazing to see how those who think differently labour in the effort to prove that things which are forbidden by the Gospel are not permissible

by the law of nature, as concubinage, divorce and polygamy. These things in fact are of such a nature that reason itself declares that it is morally better to abstain from them, but they are not such that wickedness would be manifest in them without divine law. Again, who would say that we are bound by the law of nature to do that which the law of Christ enjoins, that we expose ourselves to the danger of death for others?[36]

3. I shall not even follow those who make another by no means slight assumption, that Christ in delivering the precepts which are found in the first chapter of *Matthew* and immediately thereafter, was speaking only as an expounder of the law given through the agency of Moses. Of an altogether different import are the words so often repeated: 'Ye have heard that it was said to them of old time—but I say unto you.' The contrast here, as in the Syriac and other versions, shows that the meaning is, 'to them of old time,' not 'by them of old time'; so 'to you,' not 'by you.' Now 'they of old time' were none other than those who were living in the time of Moses. For the things which are declared to have been said to them 'of old time' are not utterances of men learned in the law but of Moses, either word for word, or in substance. These utterances are:

> Thou shalt not kill;[37]
> Whoso hath killed a man shall be held in judgement;[38]
> Thou shalt not commit adultery;[39]
> Whoso putteth away his wife, let him give to her a bill of divorcement;[40]
> Thou shalt not swear faulsely, but thou shalt render unto the Lord that which thou hast sworn;[41]
> An eye for an eye, a tooth for a tooth—supply 'it may be permitted to demand in judgement';[42]

Thou shalt love thy neighbor (that is an Israelite; *Leviticus*, xix. 18), and shalt hate thine enemy (for example the seven peoples, with whom the Israelites are forbidden to have friendship and to whom they are to show no mercy; *Exodus*, xxxiv. II; *Deuteronomy*, vii. I. To these the Amalekites are to be added, against whom the Jews are bidden to wage implacable war; *Exodus*, xxvii. 19; *Deuteronomy*, xxv. 19).

4. For the understanding of the words of Christ, however, we must once for all observe that the law given through the agency of Moses may be considered in two ways. First, it may be viewed in relation to that which it has in common with other laws customarily established by men, in so far, surely, as it restraints the graver crimes by the fear of visible punishments[43] and by this means holds the Jewish people in a state of civil society; from this point of view it is called 'the law of carnal commandment,'[44] and 'law of works.'[45] Or, in the second place, the Mosaic law may be viewed in relation to that which is peculiar to divine law, in so far, at any rate, as it demands purity of soul and certain actions which can be

omitted without a temporal penalty; from this point of view it is called 'spiritual law'[46], 'restoring the soul.'[47] The scribes and the Pharisees, contending themselves with the first viewpoint, paid small heed to the second, which is more important, and did not impress it upon the people; the truth of this statement can be shown not only from our books but also from Josephus and the learned men of the Jews.

5. Even in relation to the second point of view, however, it is important to know that the virtues required of Christians were also either commended to the Jews, or enjoined upon them; but they were not enjoined upon the Jews with the same emphasis and with so great breadth of application as upon Christians.[48] In both respects moreover Christ sets His teachings over against those of the old time; whence it is clear that His words do not embody a mere interpretation. Recognition of this fact is important not merely with reference to the point now under consideration, but many others as well, that we may not make use of the authority of the Hebraic law to a greater extent than is just.

Arguments drawn from the Holy Writ on behalf of the negative view, that war is not in conflict with the law of the Gospel:

1. Passing by the arguments, then, which seem to us untenable, the first and weightiest evidence by which we prove that the right to war was not completely annulled by the law of Christ, shall be that passage of Paul in I Timothy (ii. 1–3):

   'I exhort, therefore, first of all that supplications, prayers, intercessions, thanksgivings be made for all men; for kings and all that are in high place; that we may lead a tranquil and quiet life in all godliness and gravity. This is good and acceptable in the sight of God our Saviour, who would have all men to be saved, and come to the knowledge of the truth.'

   In this passage we are taught three things: that it is acceptable to God that Kings become Christians; and also that, having become Christians, they remain kings (the thought was thus expressed by Justin Martyr): 'Fir this we pray, that kings and princes along with their royal power may possess a sound mind'; and in the book entitled *Constitutions of Clement* the Chursh prays for 'Christian authorities,' that is, for Christians magistrates; finally, that this also is acceptable to God, that Christian kings enable other Christians to lead a tranquil life.

2. But how shall the ruler do this? Paul explains elsewhere[49]: For he is a minister of God to thee for good. But if thou do that which is evil, be afraid, for He beareth not the sord in vain. For he is a minister of God, an avenger for wrath to him that doeth evil.' By the right of the sword through a figure of speech every form of compulsion is understood, as also sometimes in the writings of the jurists; but in such a way, nevertheless, that the right to impose the extreme penalty, that is the actual use of the sword, is not excluded.

The second *Psalm* serves to throw not a little light upon this passage; for although it had its true application in the person of David, nevertheless it is more fully and more completely applicable to Christ, as we may learn from *Acts* (iv. 25; xiii. 33) and *Hebrews* (v. 5). This Psalm exhorts all kings to receive the Son of God with reverence; that is, that as kings they show themselves also His ministers, as St Augustine rightly explains.

The words of Augustine on this point I quote: 'In this way kings serve God in the capacity of kings if, just as is divinely enjoined upon them, in their kingdoms they ordain good and prohibit evil, not only in respect to matters which relate to human society but also matters that concern the divine religion.' In another passage he says: 'In what way, then, do kings serve the Lord in fear, except by prohibiting and punishing with religious severity the things that are done contrary to the commandments of the Lord? For it is one thing to serve the Lord, another to serve Him as king.'[50] 'Kings,' he says, a little further on, 'serve the Lord in the capacity of kings when in serving Him they do those things which they cannot do except as kings.'[51]

3. A second argument is furnished to us by that very passage of which we have quoted a portion, wherein the highest power, such as that of the king, is said to be from God, and is called an ordinance of God. From this it follows the inference that obedience should be rendered to it—that, too, wholeheartedly—and that he who resists it is resisting God.

If by the word 'ordinance' a thing should be understood which God merely does not will to prevent, as the attitude of God is with reference to wicked actions, there would follow no obligation to pay respect or render obedience, least of all, wholeheartedly; and the Apostle in proclaiming and in magnifying this power so earnestly would be saying nothing which would not be appropriate to acts of brigandage and thievery. It follows, therefore, that this power is understood to have been ordained by the approval of the will of God; hence, the inference, since God does not will that which is contrary to Himself, that this power is not in conflict with the will of God revealed through the Gospel and binding upon all men.

4. The force of this argument, furthermore, is not weakened by the objection that those who were in authority at the time when Paul wrote were strangers to the Christian faith. For, in the first place, the statement is not unreservedly true, since Sergius Paulus, proprietor of Cyprus, had long before professed Christ;[52] not to speak of the ancient tradition in regard to the king of Edessa, which to some extent may be tinged with falsehood, yet seems to have had its origin in truth. Then, again, the question is not whether the individuals were unrighteous but whether the function exercised by them was in itself unrighteous. That it was not, we maintain, was declared by the Apostle when, speaking even of his own time, he said that this function was ordained by God, and therefore should be honoured even in the inmost feelings of the soul, which in a proper sense are subject to God alone. Consequently, both Nero and King Agrippa, whom Paul so

earnestly urges to embrace the Christian religion,[53] could have subjected themselves to Christ and have retained in the latter case a royal, in the former an imperial power, the maintenance of which without the right of the sword and of arms is inconceivable. Just as the sacrifices in the olden time were sacred according to the law even though offered by wicked priests, so sovereign power is a righteous thing though it is held by a wicked man.

5. A third argument is drawn from the words of John the Baptist. When he was earnestly asked by Jewish soldiers (from Josephus and other writers it is perfectly clear that many thousands of this race were in the military service of the Romans) what they must do to escape the wrath of God, he did not bid them withdraw from military service, as he must have done if such was the will of God, but to abstain from extortions and deceit, and to be content with their wages.[54]

   In regard to these words of the Baptist, which clearly enough imply an approval of military service, many make answer that what the Baptist enjoined differs so greatly from the precepts of Christ that it was quite possible for the Baptist to teach one thing, and Christ another. The validity of this objection I cannot admit. The gist of the doctrine which John and Christ brought to men they set forth with the same introductory plea: 'Repent, for the kingdom of heaven is at hand.'[55] Christ himself said that the kingdom of heaven (that is, the new law, for the Jews have the custom of calling the law by the name of the kingdom) commenced to be taken by violence from the days of the Baptist.[56] It is said that John peached the baptism of repentance for the remission of sins;[57] the Apostles did the same, it is said, in the name of Christ.[58] John demands fruits worthy of repentance, and threatens destruction to those who do not bring forth such fruits.[59] He demands works of love beyond the law.[60] It is said that the law lasted until John, that is, that a more perfect doctrine began with him.[61] And the beginning of the Gospel is traced to John.[62] John himself by this title is reckoned greater than the prophets[63] since he was sent to give a knowledge of salvation to the people,[64] to announce the Gospel.[65]

   Nowhere, in fact, does John distinguish Jesus from himself by the difference in their teachings, although the things which were taught by John in a more general and vague way, as rudiments, were clearly set forth by Christ, the true Light. The difference with John recognized between them lay rather in this, that Jesus was the promised Messiah,[66] the king of the Heavenly Kingdom, whom would give the power of the Holy Spirit to them that believe on him.[67]

6. The fourth argument, which seems to me to have no slight weight, is this. If the right to inflict capital punishment and to defend citizens by arms against brigands and robbers should be taken away, there would follow a riot of crimes and a deluge, so to speak of evils, since even now, with regularly constituted courts in operation, the force of evil is with difficulty restrained. Wherefore if it had been the purpose of Christ to bring about such a state of affairs as had never been heard of, beyond doubt with the

most direct and explicit words he would have laid down the rules that no one should pass a sentence of death, and that no one should bear arms. We nowhere read that he did this; for the statements which are brought forward to that effect are neither exceedingly general or obscure. But fairness itself and the common sense teach not only that general statements should be limited, and ambiguous expressions favourably interpreted, but even that in a degree there may be a departure from the strict signification and ordinary use of words, in order to avoid an interpretation which would involve extremely grave consequences.

7. Fifth, by no argument can it be shown that the law of Moses relating to judgements ceased to be in force before the city of Jerusalem was destroyed, and with it alike the form of the Jewish state and the hope of its re-establishment. For neither in the law of Moses is any term set for this law, nor do Christ or the Apostles ever speak of the abolition of it, except in so far as this may seem to be included in the destruction of the state, as we have said. On the contrary Paul says that the high priest was appointed in order that he might render judgement according to the law of Moses.[68] Christ himself in words introductory to his teachings says that he came not to destroy the law but to fulfil.[69]

What bearing this has on the part of the law relating to rituals is not obscure; for shadowy outlines are filled out when the perfect form of the thing is shown. But in what way can this be true of the laws relating to judgements, if Christ, as some think, by his coming did away with them? If, however, the obligation of the law remained as long as the Jewish state continued to exist, it follows that Jews, even when converted to Christianity, if they were summoned before a magistrate could not escape service, and that they were bound to judge not otherwise than as Moses had commanded.

8. Weighing all the arguments deliberately I do not find even the most trivial consideration which could have influenced any upright man, who herd those words of Christ as they were spoken, to form a different opinion. I recognize the fact that before the time of Christ some things were permitted, as a matter of external freedom from punishment or even of purity of mind—we have neither need nor leisure to deal with those details more fully here—which Christ did not permit to those who favoured his doctrine; as, for example, to put away a wife for any sort of offence whatsoever, and to exact vengeance in court from him who had inflicted an injury. But while between the teachings of Christ and those permissions there is indeed a difference, there is no conflict. For the man who keeps his wife, or who renounces his right as an individual to exact vengeance, does nothing contrary to the law; he does in fact what the law above all desires. For different, on the other hand, is the case of the judge whom the law does not permit, but commands, to punish the murderer with death; if he fails in this duty, he will himself become guilty before God. If Christ

forbids the judge to punish the murderer with death, he enjoins what is absolutely contrary to the law, he destroys the law.

9. The sixth argument shall be drawn from the example of Cornelius, the Centurion. He received the Holy Spirit, an infallible sign of justification, from Christ and was baptized a Christian by the Apostle Peter; nevertheless we do not read that he gave up his military service, or was advised by Peter that he was obliged to give it up.

   Some may answer that, when Cornelius received instruction from Peter in the Christian religion we must suppose that he was at the same time instructed in regard to the abandonment of military life. These would have an argument if it were certain and beyond that any prohibition of military service is to be found among the teachings of Christ. Such a prohibition in plain words nowhere appears; but surely in case Christ wished to lay down a rule opposed to current usage, it was necessary that something be said on the subject, at any rate in this connection, where it was specifically required, in order that the age to come might not be ignorant of the rules controlling its duty. And it is not the practice of Luke, when the quality of persons required some particular change in manner of life, to pass this without mention, as may be seen in the nineteenth chapter of Acts (verse 19) and elsewhere.

10. The seventh argument, similar to the preceding, is taken from the case of Sergius Paulus, of whom we have already made mention. For in the record of his conversion there is no indication that he gave up his office, or was instructed to give it up. What is not mentioned when, as we have said, it would be of the utmost importance that mention be made, ought to be considered as not having happened.

11. The eight argument is that Paul the Apostle, understanding that there was a plot of the Jews against him, desired that this be reported to the tribune; and when the tribune had given him soldiers, under whose protection on his journey he would be safe against all violence, he raised no objection. He did not admonish the tribune, or the soldiers, that the repelling of force by force was not pleasing to God. And yet this was the Paul who himself never let slip any opportunity to point out one's duty, or wished that opportunity be let slip by others.[70]

12. The ninth argument lies in this, that the proper end of a thing that is honourable and obligatory cannot be otherwise than honourable and obligatory. The payment of taxes is honourable—it is even an ordinance binding conscience, as the Apostle Paul explains; but the purpose of taxation is to provide the public administration with funds upon which it may draw in order to protect good men and check evil-doers.[71] Quite to the point Tacitus remarks: 'The peace of the nations cannot be had without arms, nor arms without pay, nor pay without taxes.'[72] Similar is the observation of Augustine: 'We pay taxes in order that pay may be provided for the soldiery, for the necessities of life.'

13. The tenth argument is furnished by the passage in Acts (xxv. 2) in which Paul thus speaks: 'If I have wronged any one, and have committed anything worthy of death, I refuse not to die.' Paul held the view, as I infer from this statement, that even after the publishing abroad of the law of the Gospel, there were certain crimes for which justice permitted, or even demanded, punishment by death. This is also the teaching of Peter.[73] If at that time it had been the will of God that capital punishment be abstained from, Paul might, to be sure, have cleared himself, but it was his duty not to leave in men's minds the belief that it was then not permissible than previously to punish criminals with death.

    Now when it is once proved that the inflicting of capital punishment could be lawfully retained after the coming of Christ, it is, In think, proved at the same time that in some cases was is lawfully waged, as, for example, against criminals gathered in great number and armed, who must be conquered in battle in order that they may be brought to trial. For while the strength of criminals and their boldness in resistance may be taken into account in prudent deliberation, the force of the law is not thereby diminished.

14. The eleventh[74] argument is based on the fact that the law of Christ did away with the law of Moses only in respect to the separation of the Gentiles from the Jews.[75] But it by no means did away with the things which are honourable by nature and by the common agreement of the more civilized Gentiles; rather it included them in the general teaching of all that is honourbale and virtuous.[76] Now in truth the punishment of crimes, and the use of arms which prevent wrongdoing, are by nature considered praiseworthy and are referred to the virtues of justice and beneficence.

    Here in passing it is worthwhile to note an error on the part of those who maintain that the right of the Israelites to wage war came merely from the fact that God had given them the land of Canaan. This is, to be sure, a just cause, but not the only one. For before those times under the guidance of reason, righteous men carried on wars; and afterwards the Israelites themselves waged wars on account of other causes, as David did, because of the affront offered to his envoys. For the possessions which each has by human law are not less than if God had given them to him; this right, moreover, is not taken away by the Gospel.

Answering of the arguments from Holy Writ on behalf of the affirmative view, that war is in conflict with the law of the Gospel:

1. Let us now see by what considerations the contrary opinion is supported, in order that the serious-minded appraiser may be able the more easily to decide which of the two views has the weight of argument in its favour.

    First of all it is customary to bring forward the prophesy of Isaiah,[77] who says that it will come to pass that the people will beat their swords into mattocks and their spears into pruning-hooks; 'and nation shall not lift up sword against nation, neither shall they learn war any more.'[78] But this prophecy, as many others, may be taken in a conditional sense. With such an interpretation undoubtedly we are to understand that such will be the state of affairs if all peoples receive and fulfil the law of Christ;[79] to this end God will not suffer that there be any lack of assistance on His part. It is moreover certain that if all men were Christians, and were living the Christian life, there would be no wars.

Lactantius speaks of this prudently:

> 'What will happen if all men shall agree to live in perfect accord? This surely can happen, if men would only cast aside their destructive and impious fury and be willing to be innocent and just.'[80]
>
> Or, again, the prophecy can be understood literally. If it is interpreted in this way, the facts show that it has not yet been fulfilled, but that the fulfilment of it, like the general conversion of the Jews, is to be expected. But in whichever way you interpret the prophecy, no inference can be drawn from it against the justice of wars, so long as there are men who do not suffer those that love peace to enjoy peace, but do violence to them.

2. Several arguments are ordinarily taken from the fifth chapter of *Matthew*. In order to form a proper judgement in regard to them it is necessary to recall what we said a little before, that if it had been Christ's purpose absolutely to do away with capital punishment and the right to carry on war, he would have expressed this purpose with words as plain and explicit as possible, on account of the importance of the ruling, and its newness. All the more would he have been led to do this for the reason that no Jew could think otherwise than that the law of Moses relating to judicial proceedings and public administration must retain their validity in respect to all Jews so long as theit state endured. With this general observation in mind, let us discuss the bearing of the passages in order.
3. The contrary view, then, in the second place fortifies itself with these words: 'Ye have heard that it hath been said, an eye for an eye and a tooth for a tooth; but I say unto you, Resist not him that is evil' (in Hebrew, 'the wicked man,' which the Greeks translate 'him that doeth a wrong,' *Exodus,* ii. 13); 'but whosoever shall smite thee on thy right cheek, turn to him the other also.' From this some infer that no injury ought to be warded off, or made the subject of a demand for requital, whether as a public or as a private matter. And yet, that is not the meaning of the words. Christ is here addressing not the magistrates, but those who are assailed; and he is not treating of injuries in general, but of a specific sort of injury, such as a slap on the cheek; for the latter part of the statement restricts the generality of the earlier part.

4. Similarly in the precept which follows, 'And if any man would go to law with thee, and take away thy coat, let him have thy cloak also,'[81] not every appeal to a judge or arbitrator is forbidden. Such at any rate is the interpretation of Paul, who does not prohibit all lawsuits,[82] but does forbid Christians to sue one another in pagan court-rooms. In this he follows the example of the Jews, among whom the maxim was current that 'he who refers matters of the Israelites to strangers dishonours the name of God.' Now Christ, in order to train us in forbearance, wishes us not to go to law about things easy to replace, as a coat, or a cloak in addition to the coat if need be; but though our legal rights be absolutely perfect, he wishes us to abstain from enforcing them.

   Apollonius of Tyana used to say that it was unworthy of a philosopher 'to engage in a lawsuit about a small sum of money.'[83] 'The praetor,' says Ulpian 'does not disapprove that act of him who considered it worthwhile to deprive himself of property that he might not have to engage too frequently in lawsuits in regard to it. This attitude of restraint, on the part of a man who has an aversion to lawsuits, is not to be criticized.'[84] What Ulpian here mentions as approved by good men, Christ enjoins, selecting the matter of his teachings from the most honourable and universally approved examples.

   From this, however, you would not rightly infer that it would be wrong even for a parent or guardian in case of necessity to defend before a judge that which involved the means of subsistence of children or of wards. For a coat and a cloak are one thing; entire means of subsistence is quite another. In the *Constitutions* of Clement it is said of the Christian, if he has a lawsuit, 'Let him try to settle it, even if thereby he be compelled to suffer some loss.' Here also that is applicable which is customarily said of things moral, that they do not consist in a point, but have a certain latitude.
5. In like manner, in what follows, 'And whosoever shall compel thee to go one mile, go with him two,' our Lord did not speak of a hundred miles, a journey which would take a man too far from his business, but of one mile, and, if need be, of two, involving an amount of walking which would seem like nothing at all. The meaning, therefore, is that in matters which are not likely to inconvenience us very much we ought not to insist upon our rights, but to give up even more than is demanded, in order that our patience and kindness may become manifest to all.
6. There follow the words: 'Give to him that asketh thee,[85] and from him that would borrow of thee turn not thou away.'[86] If you should put this into practice without limitation, nothing could be more harsh. He who does not take care of those of his own house 'is worse than an unbeliever,' says Paul.[87] Let us then follow the same Paul, a most excellent interpreter of the laid down by the Master. In urging the Corinthians to exercise a spirit of liberality toward those that were in Jerusalem he says: 'Not that others may be eased and ye distressed, but that by equalization your abundance may be a supply for their want';[88] that is—adopting the words of Livy in

respect to a not dissimilar case—that from the superabundance of your resources you minister to the necessities of others.[89] The same point of view appears also in Xenophon's Cyrus: 'Whatever I see that I have beyond my needs I use to supply the wants of my friends.'[90] A similar principle of equalization we may apply to the interpretation of the precept which we have just quoted.

7. Just as the Hebraic law favoured freedom of divorce in order that it might mitigate the harsh treatment of wives by their husbands, so also in order to restrain private vengeance, to which that nation was specially prone, it had conferred upon an injured person the right to exact retaliation from the wrongdoer, not however, by his own hand, but before the judge. This rule the law of the Twelve Tables also followed: 'If a man breaks a limb of another, let there be like injury in turn.'

NOTES

1. Seneca, *Letters*, cxxiv [XX. Vii. II]: 'Just as in every case a nature, unless brought to its highest perfection, does not manifest its type of good, so the good of man is not found in man unless reason has been perfected in him.'

2. *Training of Cyrus*, II. iii. 9

3. Martial, *Epigrams*, III, lviii. II. Chrysostom, *On the Statues*, XI [Homily XI, iv]: 'The animals, devoid of reason, have their weapons in the body itself; thus the ox has horns, the wild boar tusks, the lion claws. To me, on the contrary, God has not furnished weapons in the organization of my body, but outside the body, showing by this very fact that man is a gentle animal, and that I do not at all times have need of such weapons. Often, in fact, I lay my missile aside, sometimes I take it up again. Weapons, therefore, he caused to be separate and apart from my nature, in order that I might be more free and unfettered, and might not be compelled always to carry them.

4. Cassiodorus, On the Soul [ix]: 'And since the body of man is able to defend itself neither with horn nor with tusk nor by means of fight' (as the other animals do), 'there were granted to him a powerful chest and arms; to the end that with the hand he might ward off attempted injury and protect himself by presenting his body—so to speak as a kind of shield.'

5. *On the Parts of Animals*, IV, 10.

6. *On Duties*, III [III. v. 22].

7. *On Duties*, I. xi. 34.

8. *Letters*, XII, iii. 1.

9. *Digest*, XLIII. xvi 1.27.

10. *Art of Love*, III. 492.

11. *Genesis*, xiv. 20.

12. *Exodus*, xvii.

13. *For Milo*, iv. 10. Seneca [Letters, XX. Iv. 18]: 'The surest means of defence in the case of each is nearest at hand; to each the protection of itself has been committed.' Quintilian, [Institutes of Oratory, VII. Ii. 21]: 'First, in every sort of case there

must be a defence, because by nature our own safety is more important to us than the destruction of an adversary.' Well does Sophocles say in the *Trachinian Women* [lines 278, 279]: For openly had he himself defended, God would have pardoned him his combat just.

14. *For Milo*, xi. 30.

15. *Digest,* IX. ii. 4.

16. *Digest*, I. i. 3.

17. *Jewish War*, III. xxv [III. viii. 5].

18. *Natural History*, VII., pr.

19. *Digest,* I. i. 5. The writer of the *Lives of Famous Men* says in *Themistocles*: 'He declared that the Athenians in accordance with his advice—as they were permitted to do by the common law of nations—surrounded with walls the gods of their state, their city, and their homes, in order that they might be able the more easily to defend these against the enemy.'

20. *Digest*, I. i. 3.

21. *Genesis*, ix. 5, 6.

22. The law of Radamanthus is stated by Apollodorus, in Book II [Apollodorus, *Library*, II. iv. 9]: 'The Law of Radamanthus: if a man has avenged himself on one who first attempted to injure him, let him go unpunished.'

23. *Controversies*, X. pr. 5.

24. *Genesis,* iv. 14.

25. *Laws*, IX, viii.

26. Pliny, *Natural History*, Book VII, chapter liv [VII. Liv. 200], relates that the first sentence of death was pronounced in the Areopagus.

27. Thucydides, *History of the Peloponnesian War*, Book III, xiv.

28. *Genesis*, iv. 24.

29. Josephus [Antiquities of the Jews, I. iii. 8]: 'I enjoin upon you that your hands be kept free from the shedding of men's blood; and if a man shall have committed murder, let him be punished.'

30. A point that Grotius seems to have overlooked is that even in the era of the Giants, c. 10,000 B.C., the concept of rightful and lawful punishment was already existent.

31. *Exodus*, xvii. 9.

32. *Genesis*, xxxviii, 24.

33. *Leviticus*, xviii.

34. *Numbers*, xxxv. 31, 33.

35. This constitutes an excellent observation of Grotius.

36. I *John*, iii, 16.

37. *Exodus*, xx. 30.

38. *Leviticus*, xxi. 21; *Numbers*, xxx. 16, 17, 30.

39. *Exodus*, xx. 30.

40. *Deuteronomy*, xxiv. I.

41. *Exodus*, xx. 7; *Numbers*, xxx. 2.

42. *Leviticus*, xxiv. 20; *Deuteronomy*. xix. 21.

43. *Hebrews*, ii. 2.

44. *Hebrews*, vii. 13.
45. *Romans*, iii. 27.
46. *Romans*, vii. 14.
47. *Psalms*, xix. 9.
48. Chrysostom, *On Virginity*, chapter xliv: Formerly, so high a degree of virtue had not been demanded of us, but it was permitted to exact vengeance of him who inflicted an injury, to return abuse for abuse, and to devote oneself to amassing riches; to swear an oath free from guile, to take an eye for an eye, and to hate an enemy. Nay, more, it had not been forbidden to live luxuriously, or to give way to anger, or to cast out one wife and take another. And not even this only, but the law permitted a man to have two wives at the same time, and both in this and other matters there was large latitude in those times. But after the coming of Christ the way of life was made much more narrow.
49. *Romans*, xiii. 4.
50. *Letters*, I. clxxxv. 19.
51. *Boniface*.
52. *Acts*, xiii. 12.
53. *Acts*, xxvi.
54. *Luke*, iii. 14.
55. *Matthew*, iii. 2; iv. 17.
56. *Matthew*, xi. 12.
57. *Mark,* i. 4.
58. *Acts*, ii. 38.
59. *Matthew*, iii. 8 and 10.
60. *Luke*, iii, 2.
61. *Matthew*, xi. 13.
62. *Mark*, i. 1; *Luke*, i. 77.
63. *Matthew*, xi. 9; *Luke,* vii. 26.
64. *Luke*, ii. 77.
65. *Luke*, iii. 18.
66. *Acts,* xix, 4; *John*, i. 29.
67. *Matthew*, iii. 2; *Mark*, i. 8; *Luke*, iii. 16.
68. *Acts*, xxiv, 3.
69. *Matthew*, v. 17.
70. 2 *Timothy*, iv. 2.
71. *Romans,* xiii, 3, 4, 6.
72. *Histories*, IV. Lxxiv.
73. *1 Peter,* ii. 19, 20.
74. The eleventh argument is that in the prophecy of the Apocalypse certain wars of the righteous are foretold, with manifest approval (*Revelation*, xviii. 6).
75. *Ephesians,* ii. 14.
76. *Corinthians,* xi, 13, 14.
77. This prophecy is interpreted by Chrysostom with reference to the peace that came to the world through the beneficent agency of the Roman Empire; in his homily that *Christ is God* [vi] he says:

It was foretold, in fact, not only that this religion would be steadfast, immovable, and unshaken, but that with it peace would come to the world, that in the different states the rule of aristocracies, yes even of kings, would cease, and that there would be one rule over all men: of that empire the greater part would enjoy peace, a condition opposite to that which previously existed. Formerly, in fact, even craftsmen and orators put on arms and stood in line of battle. But after the coming of Christ that custom fell into disuse and the practices of war were restricted to a limited class of individuals.

78. I*saiah*, ii. 4.

79. Similar is the comment of Chrysostom, *On First Corinthians*, xiii. 3 [Homily XXXII, v]: 'If there are among men such love as there ought to be, there would be no capital punishments.' This statement, however, is, in my opinion, not corresponding to the real world, in which criminal acts are committed on a number of grounds, and love on its own would perhaps not be enough to eliminate crimes and, in turn, capital punishments.

80. Of course they would need to cast aside a number of other drawbacks, such as arrogance, especially at nation level, jealousy, the vice to amass unreasonably enormous wealth and untrustworthiness.

81. *Matthew*, v. 41.

82. 1 *Corinthians*, vi. 4.

83. Philostratus, *Life of Apollonius*, II. xxxix.

84. *Digest,* IV. vii. 4. 1.

85. Seneca, *On Benefits*, Book II [II. xv. 1]: 'I shall give to the needy, but in such a way that I myself may not be in want.'

86. *Matthew,* v. 42.

87. 1 *Timothy*, v. 8.

88. 2 *Corinthians*, viii. 13.

89. Livy, VI. xv. 9.

90. Xenophon, *Training of Cyrus*, VIII. Ii. 22.

Chapter 3

Self-Defense and Modern International Law

Individual, Collective, and Preemptive Self-Defense

At the outset, it must be clarified that the legal terms *Use of Force*, *Law of War*, and *Armed Conflict* are synonymous. The *Law of War* is divided into two categories. The first category is called *jus ad bellum*. This means the justifications of war, or the legal basis on which war may be launched. It is precisely the legal basis that makes war just. The second category is called *jus in bello*, and it refers to the rules underpinning the waging of war. It is also termed *Law of Armed Conflict*, or *Humanitarian Law of Armed Conflict*, precisely because it comprises those humanitarian rules that must be complied with and respected in the course of armed conflict. This category includes rules for the protection of civilians, the protection of cultural property in times of war and peace, the protection of prisoners of war, etc.

In the present chapter, we shall examine an aspect of the Use of Force, namely Self-Defense in International Law. First, let us overview the developments with regard to the Law of War prior to 1945, viz. in the period before the enactment of the United Nations Charter.

The legality of war was occupied by the teaching of the Roman Catholic Church. Saint Augustine (354–430 AD) said: It is a custom that Just Wars are those that avenge wrongs, when the nation or the state against which warlike action is directed has neglected either to punish wrongful acts committed by its own citizens or restitute what has been wrongfully been occupied by itself. Moreover, war of that kind is undoubtedly just and is ordained by God Himself. In the seventeenth century, Grotius tried to bring back these traditional dogmas or ideas.

In the modern and contemporary periods of International Law, attempts have been made so that the Use of Force might be reduced, if not eliminated. The Hague Convention of 1907 demanded that war should be precipitated by a formal declaration or ultimatum. However, declaration of war does not presently constitute a formal prerequisite of war.

The Covenant of the League of Nations, signed in 1919, did not prohibit war altogether. Article 12 (1) provided: "the members of the League agree that, if there should arise between them any dispute likely to lead to a rupture, they will submit the matter either to arbitration or judicial settlement or to inquiry by the Council, and they agree in no case to resort to war until three months after the award by the arbitrators or the judicial decision or the report by the Council."

The three-month-delay period aimed at calming the passions down through the lapse of time.

The efforts for total prohibition of war culminated with the General Treaty of Renunciation of War, known as the Kellogg-Briand Pact (or Pact of Paris), concluded in 1928. The Treaty provided: "The High Contracting Parties solemnly declare that they condemn recourse to war for the solution of international controversies, and renounce it as an instrument of national policy in their relations with one another. The High Contracting Parties agree that the settlement or solution of all disputes or conflicts of whatever nature or whatever origin they may be, which may arise among them, shall never be sought except by pacific means."

The aforementioned Pact, which followed the First World War, constituted a serious effort on the part of the international community and of International Law to place boundaries to war and to regulate international relations. However, World War II, which followed, and other armed conflicts prove that this effort was not fruitful.

A cornerstone and groundwork of International Law is the General Prohibition of the Use of Force in the UN Charter. Article 2(4) of the UN Charter provides: "all members shall refrain in their international relations from the threat or use of force against the territorial integrity or political independence of any State, or in any manner inconsistent with the purposes of the United Nations."

Article 2(4) speaks of the use of force and not expressly of war; therefore, according to some views, some hostilities are taken as not being warlike and consequently as not falling under this provision of the Charter. However, the prevailing view is that Article 2(4) refers to every form of force.

It is noteworthy that paragraph 4 of Article 2 comprises the phrase "in any manner inconsistent with the purposes of the United Nations." Article 1 of the Charter of the United Nations states that a primary purpose of the United Nations Organization is the preservation of international peace and security, which means that any violation of international peace is automatically inconsistent with the purposes of the United Nations. The above terminology leaves open the possibility for someone to argue that force used for various purposes (for example, for the protection of human rights) is lawful. Before examining a legal exception to the general prohibition of the use of force, namely self-defense, it would be useful to provide an instance of implementation of Article 2(4).

A paradigm example is the *Corfu Channel* case. British warships were being destroyed by submarine mines while exercising the right of innocent passage in Albanian territorial waters. The United Kingdom sent off more warships to remove the mines from the area. Removing mines is not included in the right of innocent passage. In this case, which arose before the International Court of Justice, the Court held: "The Court can only regard the alleged right of intervention as the manifestation of a policy of force, such as has, in the past, given rise to most serious abuses and such as cannot, whatever the present defects in international organization, find a place in international law."

The Declaration of Friendly Relations adopted by the General Assembly of the United Nations Organization in 1970 also prohibits armed intervention and regards it as a violation of International Law.

Self-defense is a commonly accepted exception to the general prohibition of the use of force of the UN Charter.

Article 51 of the UN Charter states: "Nothing in the present Charter shall impair the inherent right of individual or collective self-Defense if an armed attack occurs against a member of the United Nations, until the Security Council has taken the measures necessary to maintain international peace and security. Measures taken by Members in the exercise of this right of self-Defense shall be immediately reported to the Security Council and shall not in any way affect the authority and responsibility of the Security Council under the present Charter to take at any time such action as it deems necessary in order to maintain international peace and security."

Four facets of the right of self-defense in International Law will be analyzed.

First, we turn to preemptive self-defense or anticipatory self-defense. When there are serious indications that an armed attack is imminent against the territorial integrity of a state, then that state reserves the right of self-defense, being able to strike first against the attacking state. The right of anticipatory self-defense has formed the basis of NATO action aiming at protecting even non-members of the United Nations. The question of whether an armed attack is imminent is obviously a matter of opinion, and any rule based on this criterion is subjective and subject to violations and abuse. This means that a state can rarely be absolutely certain about the intentions of another state. But the exclusion or abolition of the right of preemptive or anticipatory self-defense would take away from the innocent state the military advantage of striking first. During the Cold War, neither the United States of America nor the Soviet Union (as it then was) was in need of relying on anticipatory self-defense, as both of those states had the capability of striking second, that is, the capability of launching a nuclear counterattack against the opposite side, even if one of them had already suffered the consequences of a nuclear attack. Nowadays, nevertheless, it seems that Russia would definitely exercise the right of anticipatory self-defense by installing missiles in central Europe as a response to the potential installment of a missile system in Poland on the part of the United States. On the contrary, the West might, in such a case, rely on preemptive self-defense in order to prevent Russia from installing missiles in Poland, as an action of this sort would endanger the security and wider strategic interests of NATO, particularly of the United States of America and the United Kingdom.

A characteristic instance of a state relying on the right of preemptive self-defense took place in 1981, when Israel bombed a nuclear reactor in Iraq. Israel put forward the argument that the reactor would have been used for the production of nuclear bombs to be directed against its own state, and that Israel had the right to destroy the reactor by an act of preemptive self-defense. The UN Security Council condemned the Israeli action. The United States and the United Kingdom declared that preemptive self-defense was not justified upon the facts (there was not sufficient evidence leading to the conclusion that the reactor would have been used for the production of nuclear bombs). However, they did not touch upon the issue of whether Israel hypothetically had the right to act in preemptive or anticipatory self-defense, in case the reactor had, indeed, formed a real threat for Israel. Actually, they did not turn down the existence of the right of preemptive or anticipatory self-defense.

Another instance was the invocation of the right of preemptive self-defense on the part of the United States in 1986, against acts of State-funded terrorism, in order to justify the bombardment of Libya.

Second, we consider self-defense and claims over territory. When Argentina invaded the Falkland Islands (which are adjacent to Argentina and were claimed by the United Kingdom, because, *inter alia*, they are rich in oil installations) in 1982, the Security Council of the United Nations by its Resolution demanded the immediate withdrawal of all Argentinian forces from the Islands. This Resolution amounted, in fact, to a condemnation of the use of force on the part of Argentina. Irrespective of which side the scales of justice favor, it remains a rule of International Law that a state that legally occupies and has effective administrative control over a territory—in other words, has territorial sovereignty—has the right to use force on the basis of self-defense against the attacking state claiming to have rights over that territory. It must be noted that the United Kingdom had established effective control over the

Falklands, because as of the very beginning of the nineteenth century, British families had settled on the Islands and formed the aboriginal population as it were.

At this juncture, I would like to note a view expressed by Michael Akehurst, an eminent International Law jurist, who on this occasion, though, puts forward a rather absurd and dangerous opinion. In his book *Modern Introduction to International Law* (Routledge), he says that a state claiming some territory can rely on the right of self-defense and use force as a response to a military intervention by another state claiming to have sovereignty over that territory, even if that other state considers that it has (or if, as a matter of fact, it does have) a stronger case for ownership title (or territorial sovereignty) over the territory in question than the state that controls and illegally occupies it. He goes on saying that the two states that were attacked by Iraq on the basis of territorial claims in the two Gulf Wars (Iran in 1980, and Kuwait in 1990), both had the right to self-defense despite the fact that Iraq had a better and stronger claim. Against this opinion of Akehurst, let me put forward the following hypothetical question: If ever the Republic of Cyprus decides to exercise the right of self-defense as provided by Public International Law, to restore justice in the illegally occupied (by Turkish troops) areas of the Republic, would the so-called Turkish Republic of Northern Cyprus have the right to act in self-defense? In my opinion, such a "development" would bring about a distortion of the principle of self-defense itself. The invocation of self-defense as of every principle of International Law, is and must be the privilege only of states that act according to law and justice.

Third, we turn to armed reprisals. Self-defense does not contain a right to reprisals. If, for example, terrorists enter a state, that state has the right to use force, to arrest or expel the terrorists, but having done so, it does not have the right of retribution against the state from which the terrorists came. Nevertheless, a right of armed reprisal as such does exist, and this is clearly witnessed through a study of the theory of International Law. Cassese, the eminent International Law jurist, has provided a definition of *armed reprisals* in International Law that is now widely accepted by jurists, as well as the international community: "Reprisals are acts or actions in response to an unlawful act by another State. In other words, reprisals are unlawful acts that become lawful in that they constitute reaction to an illegality by another State."

Fourth, we consider the armed protection of nationals abroad. The prevailing view in International Law is that an attack against the nationals of a state who are abroad, or the failure of a foreign government to grant them the kind of help provided by International Law, gives the right to this state to use armed force to protect its nationals without securing consent of the foreign government. A paradigm example is the rescue operation of Israel in Entebbe.[1]

All the above mentioned facets of self-defense, and the right to self-defense in general, are set up under serious restrictions. The most important restrictions are those laid down by the principle of proportionality and the principle of necessity. The purpose of these restrictions and requirements is to ensure that the right of self-defense is not the subject of abuse and that undue force is not used under the pretext of self-defense. In its Advisory Opinion on the Legality of the Threat or Use of Nuclear Weapons 1996, the International Court of Justice stated the following important legal points: "the proportionality principle may not exclude the use of nuclear weapons in self-defense in all circumstances. But at the same time, a use of force that it proportionate under the law of self-defense, must, in order to be lawful, also meet the requirements of the law applicable in armed conflict which comprises in particular the principles and rules of humanitarian law."

In the notorious *Caroline* case, Mr. Webster stated: "There must be a necessity of self-defense, instant, overwhelming, leaving no choice of means and no moment for deliberation."

NOTE

1. A similar affair is the case of the US Diplomatic and Consular Staff in Tehran. On November 4, 1979, several hundred Iranian students and other demonstrators took possession of the United States Embassy in Tehran by force. They did so in protest at the admission of the deposed Shah of Iran into the United States for medical treatment. The demonstrators were not opposed by the Iranian security forces who "simply disappeared from the scene." United States consulates elsewhere in Iran were similarly occupied. The demonstrators were still in occupation when the International Court of Justice was called to give a judgment. They had seized archives and documents and continued to hold fifty-two United States nationals (women had been released). Fifty were diplomatic or consular staff; two were private citizens. In an earlier judgment, the Court had indicated interim measures at the request of the United States. In the present judgment, the Court ruled on the United States request for a declaration that Iran had infringed a number of treaties, including the 1961 and 1963 Vienna Conventions on Diplomatic and Consular Relations respectively. It also asked for a declaration calling for the release of the hostages, the evacuation of the Embassy and consulates, the punishment of the persons responsible and the payment of reparation. In April 1980, while the case was pending, United States military forces entered Iran by air and landed in a remote desert area in the course of an attempt to rescue the hostages. The United States justified its action, in a report to the Security Council pursuant to Article 51 of the UN Charter, as being in "exercise of its inherent right of self-defense with the aim of extricating American nationals who are and

remain the victims of the Iranian armed attack on our Embassy." The attempt was abandoned because of equipment failure. United States military personnel were killed in an air collision as the units withdrew. No injury was done to Iranian nationals or property (*International Court of Justice Reports* 1980, 3). The Court by thirteen votes to two decided that the Islamic Republic of Iran had violated obligations owed by it to the United States of America under international conventions in force between the two countries, as well as under long-established rules of general International Law. The Court also decided that Iran must immediately take all steps to redress the situation resulting from the events of November 4, 1979, including the release of the hostages and the return of the premises and documents to the United States, and that Iran was under an obligation to make reparation to the United States. Iran, which declined to participate in the proceedings, did not comply with the judgment of the Court in any respect. The hostages were ultimately released in January 1981 as a result of a negotiated settlement with the United States.

Chapter 4

Self-Defense

A Thorough International Law Analysis

NATURAL LAW AND SELF-DEFENSE

For the natural lawyer, the right of self-defense was not an independent problem, but rather a part of the problem of defining the just war. It illustrated but one of the just causes of war, and a war *propulsare hostes* was recognized as a just war by the early theologians and schoolmen. As adopted, and to some extent secularized, by later writers, it became an integral part of the concept of the *bellum justum*, but it was still essentially based upon natural law. Grotius stated:

> The right of self-defense, it should be observed, has its origin directly and chiefly in the fact that nature commits to each his own protection.[1]

Suarez refers to self-defense as the result of the innate tendency to preserve one's own life and one's own being, and both inclinations are common to men and to other animals. Gentili,[2] Victoria, Wolff,[3] and Vattel were equally of the opinion that natural law sanctioned the right of self-defense. Indeed, with some writers the right was not merely sanctioned, but commanded; self-defense was a duty imposed upon the state by natural law and owed to the subjects of the state by virtue of the social contract. Wolff states that:

> Each nation is bound to preserve itself . . . the whole is bound to the individuals to provide for them those things which are required as a competency for life, peace and security.[4]

There is, however, no unanimity as to the precise rights or interests of the state that may protected by self-defense. In the extreme statement of Vattel, it is available to protect the state against any injury, any violation of its rights.

More moderate formulations limit the scope of the right to the protection of the property of the state, and the lives and property of its subjects.[5] It is not, according to Grotius and Victoria, justified merely to extend state territory or to weaken a neighbor, nor for the sake of differences of religion or glory of the princes. The essential requirement, common to most writers, is that self-defense lies only for an injury received or threatened, and it is to be used only against the state inflicting such injury.[6]

Regarding the insistence upon fault on the part of the state against which self-defense is directed, the *propter aliquam culpam impugnationem mereantur* of Aquinas, is, perhaps, the most important contribution to the concept of self-defense made by these early writers. It is an essential condition of the lawful exercise of self-defense today. There was some measure of agreement that fault might exist where conduct merely threatens another state, for the right was conceded against an imminent or threatened injury, provided the danger was "immediate and imminent in point of time."[7] Yet in doubtful cases, the state must abstain from anticipating injury, and it must exercise care not to act upon vague and doubtful suspicions lest it should run the risk of itself becoming the aggressor.

Since self-defense is only one aspect of the larger concept of *bellum justum*, little distinction is drawn between self-defense and the use of force for securing redress or inflicting punishment. Admittedly, Grotius distinguished self-defense and punishment as different just causes of war. For other writers, this distinction is only relevant in characterizing a just war as defensive or offensive.

Bowett's view is that under these circumstances, it is believed that natural law concepts can, by themselves, provide no satisfactory answer to the question of the basis and character of self-defense. The preferable view, he submits, is one that involves an empirical examination of the rights for which International Law has sanctioned the use of self-defense as a means of protection.

SELF-HELP

The distinction between self-defense and self-help is important, not solely because it is necessary to know precisely the scope of the right reserved to members under Article 51 of the UN Charter, an express exception to the obligation not to resort to force or the threat of force, but also because the right of self-defense is only available against a use or threat of force that is deemed contrary to International Law.

THE RIGHT OF TERRITORIAL INTEGRITY

The most obvious substantive right for which the right of self-defense serves as a means of protection is the right of territorial integrity, and it is in the defense of state territory that the right of self-defense is most clearly invoked. The analogy between natural persons and states, drawn by natural lawyers of the Middle Ages, was used to identify the territory of the state with the body of the individual and thus recognize the assault upon state territory as the clearest example of a situation affording to the territorial state a right of self-defense. The right of territorial integrity is founded in the duty imposed on all members, and possibly non-members of the United Nations, by Article 2(4) of the UN Charter:

> All Members shall refrain in their international relations from the threat or use of force against the territorial integrity or political independence of any State, or in any other manner inconsistent with the Purposes of the United Nations.

It has, therefore, been regarded as axiomatic that the right of territorial integrity was the right *par excellence* that might be protected by the right of self-defense. The indictments against the Major War Criminals of the Axis Powers, heard at Nuremberg, show how predominantly the concept of a crime against the peace was based upon the violation of the right of territorial integrity, and though this was not in issue and consequently never a direct finding, it is implicit in the judgments of the International Military Tribunal at Nuremberg that the violation of this right afforded to the victim state the right of self-defense.

There might conceivably be circumstances in which one state is justified in action that, *prima facie*, constitutes a violation of the territory of another state, and this is particularly relevant to the situation in which a state acting in self-defense is forced to take action within the territory of another state. This illustrates the double aspect of the right of territorial integrity; on the one hand, it is a right that may be protected by the exercise of self-defense, and on the other, it may be subject to the right of self-defense of other states. It is a right that is never absolute in character, but relative to the rights of other states. This principle of the relativity of rights must necessarily impose a qualification on the statement, normally true, that the right of territorial integrity may be defended by the exercise of self-defense.

It seems clear that by territorial integrity it was never meant to acknowledge an absolute right to inviolability. Certainly President Wilson, the author of Article X of the Covenant in the sense that he foresaw the guarantee contained therein as the very backbone of the whole Covenant, seems to have regarded the expression territorial integrity as meaning immunity from armed invasion but from forcible annexation. In the Corfu Incident of 1923 the whole question was raised by the bombardment Corfu by Italy without any intention of annexation. It is not suggested that Italy's action could be characterized as self-defense, but that action did raise the question whether the guarantee involved literal inviolability, as Greece contended, or only freedom from annexation or invasion with that intent.

THE RIGHT OF PROTECTION OF NATIONALS

It cannot be doubted that the state may defend its nationals or any person within its territorial jurisdiction from hostile attack. Insofar as such hostile attack emanates from groups within its own territory, the state may rely on the procedures of its own administrative and legal system to justify the necessary defensive measures. Where, however, the attack emanates from a foreign state, or from groups outside the defending state's own territorial jurisdiction, the defensive measures can be taken in the exercise of a right of self-defense recognized in International Law.

The more difficult problem arises when the state purports to intervene within the territory of another state to protect its nationals. It is our present purpose to examine how far the protection of nationals abroad can be said to fall within the concept of self-defense.

The Protection of Nationals Abroad

The right of the state to intervene by the use or threat of force for the protection of its nationals suffering injuries within the territory of another state is generally admitted, both in the writings of jurists and in the practice of states.

In the arbitration between Great Britain and Spain in 1925, one of the series known as the *Spanish Moroccan Claims*, Judge Huber, as rapporteur of the Commission, stated:

"However, it cannot be denied that at a certain point the interest of a State in exercising protection over its nationals and their property can take precedence over territorial sovereignty, despite the absence of any conventional provisions. This right of intervention has been claimed by all States; only its limits are disputed."

Oppenheim states in similar terms:

> The right of protection over citizens abroad, which a State holds, may cause an intervention by right to which the other party is legally bound to submit. And it matters not whether protection of the life, security, honor or property of a citizen abroad is concerned.[8]

In certain cases, where diplomatic protection in the sense of diplomatic interposition or of the presentation of a claim on behalf of a national by his state has either failed or is inadequate to prevent an immediate danger to life or property that would otherwise be irremediable, states have resorted to the threat or use of force as a means of protection. It is with this form of protection that we are here concerned. We now envisage action by the protecting state that involves a *prima facie* violation of the independence and territorial inviolability of the territorial state. Insofar as this action takes effect in derogation of the sovereignty of the territorial state, it must necessarily be exceptional in character and limited to those cases in which no other means of protection are available. It presupposes the inadequacy of any other means of protection against some injury, actual or imminent, to the persons or property of nationals, and, moreover, an injury that results either from the acts of the territorial state and its authorities or from the acts of individuals or groups of individuals that the territorial state is unable, or unwilling, to prevent.

In most cases, the protecting state, to intervene in this way, is occasioned by a breach of a duty imposed on the territorial state under general International Law to use due diligence in safeguarding the lives and property of aliens within its territory from unlawful infringement. To this extent, the notions of state responsibility and protection are supplementary; both depend on the failure of the territorial state to conform to minimum standards based upon general International Law, to a standard of justice, very simple, very fundamental, and of such general acceptance by all civilized nations as to form part of the International Law of the world.[9]

Nevertheless, it is conceivable that, even where due diligence has been exercised by the territorial state, there may be a threat to the lives and property of these aliens originating from groups of individuals for which the territorial state can bear no responsibility "for mob violence," but only that it is feasible for this to occur in circumstances where the territorial State has nevertheless acted with due diligence.

It is of interest to note the developments envisaged by the Draft Code of Offences against the Peace and Security of Mankind, Article 2(9), which provides that the following will be criminal acts under International Law:

Acts by the authorities of a State or by private individuals, committed with intent to destroy, in whole or in part, a national, ethical, racial or religious group as such, including

i. Killing members of the group;
ii. Causing serious bodily or mental harm to members of the group;
iii. Deliberately inflicting on the group conditions of life calculated to bring about its physical destruction in whole or in part;
iv. Imposing measures intended to prevent births within the group;

v. Forcibly transferring children of the group to another group.

In these circumstances, where the protective action is not based upon a breach of an obligation by the territorial state, such action as the protecting state may take must in no way be directed against the territorial state.[10] The territorial state is legally bound to submit to such action as is reasonably taken, and the principle of relativity of rights prevents the territorial state from asserting its right of territorial integrity to the extent of obstructing the action of the protecting state. This is so even though the measures of protection are not due to the territorial state's fault, but are due to circumstances in which the protecting state must insist on the precedence of its right of protection over the rights of the territorial state.

The Defense of Nationals as the Defense of the State

Political theories of the social contract gave rise to the view that protection, as the duty of the state, afforded the consideration of the *pactum subjectionis*, and that protection of the nationals of the state was, in effect, protection of the state itself. Within the definition of the state, the requirement of a community is essential, and without nationals, without the community, the state ceases to exist. On this reasoning, it is feasible to argue that the defense of nationals, whether within or without the territorial jurisdiction of the state, is in effect the defense of the state itself.

Indeed, it may reasonably be argued that the defense of members of the community of a state, of its nationals, is as much a part of the defense of the state as the defense of any portion of its territory or of its political independence. A too-ready acceptance of this view leads to a ready acceptance of the proposition that the defense of the interests of nationals is, *ipso facto*, the defense of the interests of the state. In practice, it cannot be said that a threat to the safety of nationals abroad constitutes a threat to the security of the state. Obviously, to imperil the safety of a single national abroad is not to imperil the security of the entire state. And yet there may be occasions when the threat of danger is great enough, or wide enough in its application to a sizable community abroad, for it to be legitimately construed as an attack on the state itself.

This is also demanded by the requirement of proportionality that is common both to reprisals and to self-defense. It follows therefore that action in self-defense must be conditioned by respect for the equal rights of other states and that it must not be, in the words of Mr. Webster, "unreasonable or excessive . . . but justified by the necessity of self-defense . . . limited by that necessity and kept clearly within it." The principle of relativity of rights and the notion of proportionality involve a strict adherence to the measure of proportionality the occasion demands, so that a state may not lightly violate the independence and integrity of another state in defense of its own right to the treatment of its nationals according to established standards.

The Conditions of Protection

The normal condition precedent to the protection by the state is the allegiance of the person protected to that state. In the absence of this condition, it is difficult to see how the act of protection can be brought within the concept of self-defense, for the nexus of nationality, essential if this assimilation between state and community is to be well-founded, is absent.

Given the nationality of the subject, it is commonly supposed that the state has not only a right but a duty to extend its protection to that subject. This notion has its support in the writings of the earlier jurists and been put in the following terms by the Supreme Court of the United States in the case of *Luria v. the US*:

> Citizenship is membership of a political society and implies a duty of allegiance on the part of the members and a duty of protection on part of the society.

On the other hand, it has been denied that the subject has any absolute right of protection. Whatever the position may be in Constitutional Law, and clearly in both England and the United States, the right is conditional on the fulfilment of the duties of allegiance. There can be no doubt that the state, in exercising its right to protect, is asserting its own right, a right recognized by International Law, and, it is submitted, a right that emanates from the more general right of self-defense.

The imminence of danger to life or property is another condition. Clearly, insofar as the state taking measures of protection is motivated by factors other than the need for protection, they cease to be within the concept of self-defense. The practice of the United States affords the greatest source of instances of action in protection of the lives and property of its citizens. In a memorandum published in 1912 by Mr. Clarke, solicitor for the Department of State, we find the statement that:

> no nation, it would seem, has with more frequency than this government used its military forces for the purpose of occupying temporary parts of foreign countries in order to secure adequate safety and protection for its citizens and property.[11]

In fact, from 1813 to 1899, US military forces were employed on at least forty-six occasions to protect American citizens abroad,[12] and between 1900 and 1927, on at least twenty-four occasions.

After the intervention of the United States in Cuba, during the revolution of 1895–1898, President McKinley, in his special message of April 11, 1898, justified the intervention on the ground that, *inter alia*:

"We owe it to our citizens in Cuba to afford them that protection and indemnity for life and property which no government there can or will afford, and to that end to terminate the conditions that deprive them of legal protection."

Again, in Haiti, in 1915, although in this case a prominent American has found it "extremely difficult to reach an unbiased conclusion concerning the propriety of acts committed on behalf of the U.S. in Haiti in 1915," one ground of intervention was the imminent danger to American lives and property. Moreover, Secretary Lansing on that occasion specifically stated that "in so acting that U.S. has no design upon the political or territorial integrity of Haiti."[13]

It is interesting to note that on only one occasion has the US government refused its approval of the decision of a local commander to use armed force to protect US citizens abroad. The Regulations for the Government of the Navy of the United States, under which action has been taken on many occasions, are of interest insofar as they set out the basis upon which intervention is justified in these terms:

> The right of self-preservation, however, is a right that belongs to States as well as to individuals, and it includes the protection of the State, its honor, and its possessions, and the lives and property of its citizens against arbitrary violence, actual or impending, whereby the State or its citizens may suffer irreparable injury. . . . It (the use of force in time of peace) must be used only as a last resort, and then only to the extent which is absolutely necessary to accomplish the end required. It can never be exercised with a view to inflicting punishment for acts already committed.

It is believed that this accurately states the conditions upon which the right of self-defense may be exercised in the protection of nationals and their property, the question of the protection of the honor of the state apart. For in these terms, protection is seen as an exceptional measure, available as a last resort to prevent irreparable injury, and never as an act of reprisal for acts already committed.

By these tests it is possible to distinguish self-defense in the protection of nations from measures of reprisals.

There are, of course, instances of the use of force in the protection of the lives and property of nationals to be found in the practice of other states. The Don Pacifico Incident in 1850, in which Great Britain laid an embargo on all Greek merchant vessels in Greek ports to secure the protection of the rights of a British subject (the right in this case being one to compensation for damage done by rioters), is an extremely controversial instance. It is doubtful whether Great Britain would be prepared legally to maintain the same position today. Recent examples of the use of force in the protection of the lives of nationals are found in the claims of Israel to justify military operations outside the territory subject to its jurisdiction. Israel similarly stated that its own action was in order to protect the Jewish population, traffic, and economic life, including the protection of the Jewish settlements where . . . life and property are in imminent danger. There was, so far as can be ascertained, no categorical ruling by the Security Council that these claims were inconsistent with the right of self-defense recognized by the Charter.

It is submitted that the protection in the sense of the use of military force or the threat of such use can rarely, if at all, be extended to the property of rights of nationals abroad. This is not to imply that other forms of protection by way of diplomatic protest or the taking up of the national's claim before an international tribunal are prohibited. What is suggested is that an actual or threatened injury can seldom meet the requirement that it may injure the security of the state.

It is a wider view of the limits of self-defense than that advocated in the proposals of the USSR (as it then was) delegation that justification for attack cannot be found in possible danger to life or property of foreign residents in that it concedes that right to protect the lives of nationals. On the other hand, it may be narrower in that the USSR delegation's proposals reject "possible danger" as a sufficient cause, but do not eliminate *actual* danger. Fitzmaurice, the United Kingdom delegate to the Sixth Committee of the General Assembly in 1952, stated the recent Soviet proposal defining *aggression* in similar terms to the 1933 definition and similarly excluding the mistreatment of foreigners as a justification for action otherwise defined as aggression, that:

> by mistreating foreigners on its own territory, a State committed an act of aggression against the country of which the foreigners were nationals: and in defending itself, the State concerned was exercising its right of self-defense.

In many cases, the injury to property rights is capable of being satisfactorily met by compensation from the territorial state.

Recently the problem was posed by the Iranian Nationalization Laws of 1951 directed at the expropriation of the property of the Anglo-Iranian Company in breach of concessionary rights. The question that arose, and that was posed to the foreign secretary of the United Kingdom, Mr. Morrison, in the House of Commons, was whether the UK was in a position to protect the lives of British subjects in Iran, and also to protect the oil installations belonging to the AIOC from seizure or sabotage. Mr. Morrison replied that the Government certainly took the view that they had every right, and indeed the duty, to protect British lives. In fact a cruiser was dispatched to Abadan, later supported by seven other vessels, and the debates show exactly how narrowly the decision to avoid the use of force was avoided. The omission by Mr. Morrison to reply to the question in identical terms—that is to say to include the right to protect property—might well be significant. It might, however, possibly be explained on the assumption not that the UK had no right to protect British property by the use of force, but that the injury to the property of AIOC was neither remedial nor irrevocable.

An even more recent example from the British state's practice, of the view that the use of force in the protection of lives and property of nationals is to be justified in self-defense, is to be found in the statements made in Parliament by a government spokesman on the intervention in Egypt in October 1956. The Lord Chancellor stated on November 1:

> we have three good grounds for intervention: the danger to our nationals, for example those at Ismalia; the danger to shipping in the canal . . . ; and the danger to the enormously valuable installations in the canal itself.[14]

Mr. Butler, the leader of the House, stated on the same day that there was no doubt that their action was in accordance with customary international law and Art. 51 of the Charter.[15] The defect of this argument lay not in the principle it assumed, but in the application of the principle to the facts. There was, prior to the intervention of United Kingdom and French forces, no evidence that the Egyptian government had failed to protect foreign nationals from acts of violence. Moreover, the action taken involved the use of force, not against the Israeli forces that, by their advance, threatened to bring hostilities to the Canal Zone, but solely against Egypt.

It is inevitable that this exercise of the right of self-defense, being initially based on subjective evaluation of the interests of the protected, should be subject to the abuses so often involved in an individual measure for the protection of rights.

The fear that lies behind a refusal to recognize the defense of nationals abroad within the concept of self-defense is that this recognition would permit large-scale intervention totally unrelated to the danger to which the nationals are exposed. This cannot be so if the requirement of proportionality is complied with, and this requirement is essentially part of the lawful exercise of a right of self-defense.

SELF-DEFENSE UNDER THE U.N. CHARTER

We have seen that under the Covenant of the League and the Paris Pact, the prohibitions against war were, by general consent, never taken to preclude the right of self-defense. In San Francisco, the view of Committee I in dealing with the effect of this prohibition was that the "use of arms in legitimate self-defense remains admitted and unimpaired."

The Interpretation of Article 51

The correct interpretation of Article 51 is, it is submitted, only to be achieved by a full appreciation of its relation to Article 2(4). It is incontestable that prior to the Charter, a right of self-defense was recognized by general International Law, so that the question that must be posed is whether the Charter contains a prohibition of action that would normally be legitimate as the exercise of self-defense, a right admitted and recognized by the general law. As Goodhart has rightly said:

> The Members of the United Nations when exercising their inherent powers do so not by grant but by already existing right. The Charter limits the sovereign rights of the States; it is not a source of those rights.

It is, therefore, fallacious to assume that members have only those rights that the Charter accords to them; on the contrary, they have those rights that general International Law accords to them, except insofar as they have surrendered them under the Charter. Kelsen, writing of the right of self-defense, says the right has no other content than the one determined by article 51; this is a fundamentally erroneous approach that produces a restricted interpretation of the article not warranted by the Charter.

Now all the relevant obligation assumed by members is, *prima facie*, that contained in Article 2(4): All Members shall refrain in their international relations from the threat or use of force against the territorial integrity or political independence of any State or in any manner with the purposes of the United Nations.

As we have seen, the view of the Committee I at San Francisco was this prohibition that left the right of self-defense unimpaired; in the word of its rapporteur, the use of arms in legitimate self-defense remains admitted and unimpaired.[16]

Action taken for the purpose of, and limited to, the defense of a state's political independence, territorial integrity, and the lives and property its nationals (and even to protect its economic independence) cannot, by definition, involve a threat or use of force 'against the territorial integrity or political independence' of any other state.

Nothing in the Present Charter Shall Impair the Inherent Right of Individual or Collective Self-Defense

Goodhart's opinion is that it "need not have been included in the Charter at all if it is correct to say, as I believe it is, that the individual State are only deprived of the exercise of those powers which have been specifically forbidden to them." The reference to an inherent right suggests something of the philosophy of natural law, a tendency to regard the right as established by natural law rather than positive law, and this view is certainly a useful and important theoretical opinion of the legislator. Its significance lies in its indication that the right is an existing right, independent of the Charter, and not the subject of an express grant.

If an Armed Attack Occurs

Kelsen argues that:

> this article applies only in case of armed attack. The right of self-defense must not be exercised in case of any other violation of the legally protected interests of a Member.[17]

The reasoning behind this view is that the Charter forbids any use of force on the part of the individual members except for the exercise of the right of self-defense against an armed attack. With respect, this statement is inaccurate and misleading, for the relevant prohibition is Article 2(4), which contains no prohibition of the exercise of self-defense as permitted under the general law; moreover it is quite certain that under the general law, the right was not limited to cases of an armed attack. This restrictive interpretation, if accepted, would involve two propositions: firstly, that action in self-defense may not be 'anticipatory,' but must await an armed attack, and secondly, that self defense is only legitimate where the measures used to violate the state's interests take the form of an armed attack.

In the discussions of the General Assembly's Sixth Committee in 1952 in connection with the definition of *aggression*, the representatives of Belgium, Greece, the United Kingdom, and the United States all considered that a state threatened with an impending attack might be justified in attacking first in self-defense. A writer, Waldock, has also deduced from the judgment of the International Court of Justice in the Corfu Channel Case in 1949[18] the proposition that, so far as the right of self-defense is concerned, it is enough if there is a strong probability of armed attack—an imminent threat of armed attack—and considers that at any rate, it is clear that the Court did not take a narrow view of the inherent right of self-defense reserved by Article 51.

The judgment is not free from ambiguity, but with respect to this writer, it is difficult to deduce from the judgment anything quite so definite. So far as the passage through the straits was concerned, the UK argument rested on the view that the passage was in the exercise of a right recognized by International Law, and as the right of innocent passage, it did not cease to be innocent because of the precautions taken to meet the event of an attack by Albanian shore batteries. Neither the UK argument, nor the Court's judgment, expressly rested on the basis of self-defense. The Court did state that the mission was designed to affirm a right that had been unjustly denied. It also stated that:

> The intention must have been, not only to test Albania's attitude but at the same time to demonstrate such force that she should abstain from firing again on passing ships. Having regard, however, to all the circumstances of the case . . . the Court is unable to characterize these measures taken by the United Kingdom authorities as a violation of Albania's sovereignty.[19]

Against a Member of the United Nations

The view has been expressed that the literal interpretation of this phrase would limit the members' right of self-defense to situations where the attack has been made on a member state.[20] On this interpretation, members would have no right to assist non members under the right under the right of collective self-defense; the matter is of some importance since organizations in self-defense may, and do, contain non-members of the United Nations as, for example, with Italy's original membership of NATO.

Of this argument, Goodhart has rightly said:

> Such a limitation on the rights of sovereign States would, however, have to be expressed in clear terms and cannot be supported by the doubtful rule of construction that expression *unius est exclusio alterius*.[21]

The situation that arose in Korea when the Republic of South Korea, a non-member of the UN, was attacked by forces from north of the 38th parallel on June 24, 1950, was undoubtedly one in which South Korea was placed under the necessity of acting in self-defense. The resolution of the Security Council on June 25 implied this in noting an "armed attack" upon South Korea and in determining that the action of the North Korean authorities constituted a "breach of the peace." The reference to an "armed attack" might be an indication that the Security Council considered Article 51 applicable so as to warrant assistance to South Korea by virtue of members' rights of collective self-defense; indeed, this is the only basis upon which the US decision to authorize the intervention of US air and sea forces on the side of South Korea, prior to the recommendation of the Security Council on June 27 that members furnish assistance, can be justified. However, the practice on this occasion is inconclusive, for the US authorities sought another justification.

Until the Security Council Has Taken the Measures Necessary to Maintain International Peace and Security

This clause illustrates the essentially provisional nature of action in self-defense under the centralized system. Such a system presupposes that the right is inevitable as an interim measure of protection, but that it should cease when the machinery of the centralized system itself operates as an effective protection the individual members' rights. Accordingly, under the Charter, such action by the individual state, or even by a number of states acting under the collective right, is envisaged as a temporary measure and in no way a substitute for the collective action of the Organization. This view is supported by the fact that all members have conferred primary responsibility for the maintenance of peace and security on the Security Council. There would seem, therefore, to be a legal obligation to suspend individual or collective self-defense once the Security Council has taken these measures. The paramount difficulty here lies in the question of competence to decide whether the Security Council has, in fact, taken "the measures necessary to maintain international peace and security." If this competence rests exclusively with the Security Council, then the decision of the Security Council, that such measures has been taken, would of itself deny to the defending state its right to continue in its interim protection of its interests. Yet the decision of the Council without more cannot, one would suppose, terminate action in self-defense,[22] for the phrase "measures necessary" implies positive action. Whether such positive action by the Council, or by member states pursuant to its decisions or recommendations, does, in fact, constitute the necessary measures must be decided on the facts of the individual situation.

On the other hand, to allow the defending state to be the sole judge of whether the Council has taken the necessary measures, opens up the possibility of unilateral action ousting collective action in matters relating to international peace and security, and this would plainly contravene the very spirit of the Charter. On balance, therefore, it is suggested that the preferable view, and one that is not excluded by the Charter, is that whether the necessary measures have been taken must be determined objectively, as a question of fact, and that both the Security Council and the defending state are able to reach their own decisions on this. Should these decisions conflict, then the individual member admittedly runs the risk of its continued action being characterized as a "threat to the peace, breach of the peace, or act of aggression" under Article 39.

Measures Taken by Members in the Exercise of the Right of Self-Defense Shall Be Immediately Reported to the Security Council

This phrase imports a legal obligation to report immediately to the Security Council any measure actually taken by the members in self-defense. In contradistinction to Article 54, which imposes on members of regional arrangements and regional agencies an obligation to report "activities undertaken or in contemplation," this Article does not involve any obligation to report preparatory measures. The information members supply under this Article will afford a basis, though not the only basis, upon which any subsequent action of the Council relating to the taking of provisional measures under Article 40, or to a determination under Article 39, or even enforcement action under Articles 41 and 42, may be made.

COLLECTIVE SELF-DEFENSE

The use of the phrase *collective self-defense* in Article 51 of the UN Charter has been the subject of criticism on the ground that it embodies a contradiction in terms. Kelsen argues that, since self-defense involves action that is, by definition, unilateral in character, to speak of a collective "unilateral" right is to indulge in self-contradiction: for him the right of self-defense "is the right of the attacked or threatened individual or State."[23] For similar reasons, other authors have preferred to call the right not that of self-defense, but defense of another state. Whatever are the merits of these criticisms, it is clear firstly that the provision was intended to cover the sort of collective action in self-defense that regional arrangements might wish to take and for which their constitutive treaties made provision.

Baty states:

> That self-defense, when legitimate, need not be limited to one's own defense, but may extend to the defense of States unjustly attacked, appears to follow from the analogy of private law.[24]

A survey of the provisions of some of the main systems of law on this point would seem to bear out the analogy this writer seeks to draw. The English

Common Law clearly recognizes self-defense as going beyond the defense of one's own person or property, although the cases suggest there must be some relationship between the person attacked and the person who assists in this lawful defense. The American Re-statement on the Law of Torts again both recognizes the right and limits it to the defense of those who are members of one's household, or those whom one is under a legally or socially recognized duty to protect.

There would seem little question that, on the analogy of private law, the right is both individual and collective, and since "general principles of law" may be regarded as a legitimate source of Public International Law, the analogy serves to support the theory of the collective right of self-defense. Of immediate interest, however, is the fact that the right is limited to those cases where there exists some sort of proximate relationship; the right extends to the defense of one's family, to one's servants, and to those persons whom one is under a recognized duty to protect. These cases seem to presuppose an interest in the integrity and well-being of his family and his servants. In Roman law, the interest was confined to those cases where the protector had rights of dominion over the persons he sought to protect in self-defense.[25] It is this element that distinguishes self-defense from actions taken to defend some complete stranger in whose well-being the protector has no special interest, for in the latter case, of the protector intervenes to defend the stranger, it is generally by virtue of some duty imposed by the law to prevent a breach of the peace or grievous wounding; it is not by virtue of a right of self-defense, either individual or collective. Even in the absence of a duty of positive action, assistance rendered to the stranger is legally distinct from self-defense, for its purpose is the maintenance of the public peace and not the protection of the intervener's substantive rights. For self-defense to apply, there must be a violation of the intervener's own rights against which he may act in self-defense, but in those cases in which the law recognizes a proximate relationship between the intervener or protector and the actual victim such that the attack violates the protector's legally recognized interests in the security of the victim, the right of self-defense will be collective. If this analysis is correct, then, when we carry the analogy into the international sphere, it follows that the collective right will exist where the state invoking the right can show some interest of its own that is violated by the attack launched upon another state. We must similarly presuppose a proximate relationship, though not necessarily in terms of geographical contiguity, which makes a direct violation of the rights of one state an indirect, but nevertheless real, violation of the rights of another state that comes to the former's aid by virtue of the latter's right of collective self-defense.

The second theory is one that is based upon the concept of a duty to maintain international peace and to redress a violation of the rules of International Law.[26]

This theory meets with certain difficulties, for the existence of such duties in International Law is highly questionable, and it appears to be a concept that goes far beyond what the actual relationships of state would justify. Moreover, as Stowell has pointed out,[27] so long as the duty of vindicating the law depends on the sovereign decision of each state as to how and when this obligation shall be fulfilled, the content of such a "duty" is problematic. The provisions of Article 16 of the Covenant and of the Kellogg-Briand Pact of 1928, can scarcely be held to have imposed a duty on signatories to vindicate a breach of the obligation contained in the Covenant and the Pact. Nor is it considered that the present development of the law justifies the assertion that each state has an interest in the general preservation of world peace, if by the term *interest* we mean a legally recognized interest a state may protect by the exercise of self-defense. Lauterpacht has said of the concept of collective self-defense:

> Such an extension of the notion of self-defense is a proper expression of the ultimate identity of interest of the international community in the preservation of peace.[28]

In fact, however, this interest is no more than the general interest (and the term is being used without legal significance) that members of any community have in the preservation of peace within that community. Bowett's view is that the danger in admitting that, by virtue of an interest in the maintenance of international peace and security, any state can assist another state deemed to be acting in self-defense, is that it opens up the possibility of unlimited action under a system of defensive alliances that would be quite contrary to the Charter system.[29]

Similarly, although it has been suggested that collective self-defense is the best means of fulfilling one of the primary purposes of the United Nations, namely to take effective collective measures for the preservation and removal of threats of the peace, and for the suppression of acts of aggression or other breaches of the peace (UN Charter Article 1 [1]), this function is equally clearly one quite distinct from self-defense; the identification of the two arises from a failure to distinguish the protective right of self-defense from collective sanctions. Stone has rightly said:

> So far is the inherent right of self-defense under Article 51 from being a means of taking the collective measure for the prevention of threats to the peace and

> the suppression . . . of aggression under Article 51, paragraph 1, that large-scale resort to it would be rather the clear sign of the defeat of that principle.

The third theory provides by far the most satisfactory explanation of the collective right, for it demands that each participant in the collective action has an individual right of self-defense; the existence of its individual right, which is largely a question of fact in the circumstances, is a condition precedent to the state's participation in its collective enforcement. There are, in final analysis, three possible situations:

1. State A violates the legally protected interests of State B. Here A is in breach of an established duty, and B may exercise the right of individual self-defense.
2. State A violates the legally protected interests of States B and C. Here A is in breach of an established duty vis-à-vis both B and C and both may exercise their rights of individual self-defense, in which case the position is as in (1) above, or may exercise these in concert; this is the position that is properly termed *collective self-defense*. The essence of this position is that the participants base their action on a violation of their own legally protected rights or interests, and this remains true whether they are two or twenty-two in number.
3. State A violates the legally protected interest of State B only; B exercises its right of self-defense, and C joins in collective action. Here the participant C cannot base its action on a breach of its own rights but falls back upon the different concept of a duty to maintain international peace and security.

State Practice Prior to the Charter

The practice of certain states prior to the Charter affords evidence that they considered a proximate relationship to exist between themselves and certain other states so that an attack upon those other states would constitute a threat to their own security. The classic example of this practice is, of course, the Monroe Doctrine, and it is proposed to deal with the Monroe Doctrine and certain similar doctrines advanced by Great Britain.

The Monroe Doctrine

The reactionary policy of the Allied Powers in Europe after 1815, directed toward the suppression of any revolutionary regime, and in particular from Troppau in 1823, produced a special anxiety in the United States. It had been made known to the United States by Mr. Canning, the British foreign secretary, that the Powers of the Holy Alliance contemplated this policy of reaction to the Western Hemisphere, in particular to the Spanish colonies in South America.[30]

The attitude of the United States was publicly declared by President Monroe in his annual message of December 2, 1823, the critical part of which stated:

> We should consider any attempt on their part to extend their system to any portion of this hemisphere as dangerous to our peace and safety.[31]

In pursuance of this principle, the United States protested against the European interventions in Mexico from 1825–1860 and even more strongly after the withdrawal of the English and Spanish naval forces from Vera Cruz in April 1862, against the French occupation of Mexico under Archduke Maximilian. A later and important illustration of this attitude was seen in the interposition of the United States in the controversy between Great Britain and Venezuela over the boundary dispute of 1895, the United States maintaining not only that the dispute was a serious and direct menace to its own integrity, tranquility, and welfare, but that the refusal of Great Britain to arbitrate amounted to an appropriation of territory contrary to the principles of the Monroe Doctrine.

Under this same principle, the United States opposed even the indirect acquisition of control of American territory by non-American states through the medium of public agencies. In 1912, the Senate adopted a resolution that:

> When any harbor or other place in the American continents is so situated that the occupation thereof for naval or military purposes might threaten the communications or the safety of the United States, the government of the United States could not see without grave concern the possession of such harbor or other place by any corporation or association which has such relation to another government, not American, as to give that government practical power of control for naval or military purposes.

The fear on which this resolution was founded was that Japan might indirectly acquire footing in territory adjacent to Magdalena Bay.

These examples suffice to show that from the point of view of the United States, her security was so dependent on the security of the American continent as a whole that any attack upon that continent would jeopardize her interests to such an extent as to afford to the United States the right of self-defense. There is ample evidence that for many years the United States maintained this view as a matter of unilateral policy and that its essential basis was the right of individual self-defense.[32] It was only gradually that the United States sought to secure the agreement of other American States in the essentials of the policy and their pledge of active cooperation so as to make the Monroe Doctrine not merely a policy of self-defense of the United States but of collective self-defense of the continent as a whole. The culmination of this change, inevitable due to the growing independence of the other American States and their resentment of the professed right of intervention in their affairs by the United States, came at the Eighth International Conference of American States on December 24, 1938, when there was approved, unanimously, a Declaration of the Principles of Solidarity of America, more commonly known as the Declaration of Lima. It was probably only at this stage that the Monroe Doctrine ceased to be a purely unilateral policy of the United States, and the true process of collectivization begun. While the Declaration contained nothing more than an obligation of consultation at the initiative of any one of the signatory states, the implication as to the character of the Monroe Doctrine in the future was unmistakable. At the first meeting of the foreign ministers of the American Republics at Panama, on October 3, 1939, this shift from a unilateral to a collective right was further emphasized by a resolution providing for consultation should any region of America subject to the sovereignty of a non-American state be obliged to change its sovereignty and thereby produce a danger to the security of the American continent. It declared, *inter alia*, that:

> Any transfer, or attempted transfer, of the sovereignty jurisdiction, possession or any interest in or control over any such region to another non-American State would be regarded by the American Republics as against American sentiments and principles and the rights of American States to maintain their security and political independence,and that this community has international juridical capacity to act in the manner provided for in the Convention.

It is at this stage that the Monroe Doctrine becomes a collective doctrine and not an assertion of unilateral policy by the United States.

Hyde states:

> The basis of the claim would be that the proper defense of the nation is rendered more difficult and its safety jeopardized by the transfer generally of non-American territory to non-American States . . . a moderate and reasonable enunciation of the principle of self-defense.[33]

The British Doctrines

It would be erroneous to assume that the United States has, alone of the world powers, maintained the principle that her security demanded a claim of special interests in parts of the world not within her territorial jurisdiction.

Great Britain has made similar claims in relation to Afghanistan, Persia, and Egypt.[34] It was to enforce recognition of these claims that the British note of May 19, 1928, was sent to the United States government in connection with the Treaty for the Renunciation of War, or as it is more commonly known, the Kellogg-Briand Pact of 1928. The British government therein stated:

> There are certain regions of the world the welfare and integrity of which constitute a special and vital interest for our peace and safety. . . . Their protection against attack is to the British Empire a measure of self-defense.

The reference to certain regions of the world was not, on this occasion, further specified; to the extent that these regions included parts of the British Empire, subject to the sovereignty of Great Britain, the claim was perfectly legitimate. To the extent that these claims referred to regions under the sovereignty of other states, the claim could not be justified as self-defense except upon proof that, in fact, an attack upon these regions would jeopardize Britain's security and violate her own rights.

THE CHARTER AND COLLECTIVE SELF-DEFENSE

Since the term *collective self-defense* is not defined in the Charter, it is necessary to resort not only to general principles of law and the practice of states prior to the Charter, but also to the *travaux preparatoires* to clarify the meaning of the term under the Charter.

The connection between Article 51 and the need to safeguard the freedom of action in self-defense contemplated by regional arrangements has already been stressed. The Act of Chapultepec of March 3, 1945, had stated:

> That any attempt on the part of a non-American State against the integrity or inviolability of the territory, the sovereignty or the political independence of an American State shall be considered as an act of aggression against all American States.

With this view the Latin American representatives agreed.

The basis of the Act of Chapultepec was that an attack against one is an attack against all; this may be intended as a statement of fact or as a legal fiction. Whether it would be true as a statement of fact would depend entirely upon the extent and gravity of the attack. In Bowett's submission, the term *collective self-defense*, as used in the Charter, does no more than recognize that members may exercise collectively what is their individual right.[35]

The view that this is a possible construction of Article 51, is, in Bowett's submission, based upon a misconception not only of the character of any action in self-defense, but also of the whole system of the Charter in which Article 51 finds its place.[36] It is a view that derives from the assumption that, since states were formerly free to conclude any defensive treaty or alliance and to act on the obligation of assistance contained therein, that freedom or right is still preserved to member states under Article 51. There are, however, several grounds for disagreeing radically with this view. Firstly, there is the notion of freedom to conclude and act upon a defensive treaty of alliance developed in an age that knew no prohibition of the state's right to resort to war or to use force, or in that (as under the Covenant) the system of collective security was decentralized. The system under the Charter is radically different, for the Charter contains not only a prohibition of the right to use force or the threat of force, but also a system of collective security in which primary responsibility for the maintenance of international peace and security is vested in the Security Council (Article 24), and in which members agree to accept and carry out the decisions of the Security Council (Article 25). This degree of centralization was never found under the League, and it is, therefore, a false analogy that lies at the basis of an argument that because states were free to aid any other state in self-defense under the Covenant, they are therefore free to do the same under the Charter.[37] Admittedly, it may be a more convenient view at the present time in view of the frustration of the Security Council by the lack of unanimity amongst the permanent members.

The relative importance of Article 51 in the general scheme of the Charter increased tremendously with the frustration of the centralized machinery for maintaining international peace and security. The lack of agreement between the permanent members of the Security Council, demonstrated in the application of the veto and the absence of any agreements under Article 43 whereby members would place armed forces and facilities at the disposal of the Council, combined to bring about a measure of decentralization quite unforeseen in an organization distinguished from the League by its increased centralization of enforcement machinery. The emphasis shifted, therefore, from Chapter VII of the Charter, and especially Articles 39, 40, 41 and 42, to those other provisions of the Charter that provided for decentralized but collective action. In the first place Article 51, as we have seen, provided for collective self-defense, and a number of treaty arrangements based upon this right of collective self-defense have developed, arrangements of which the North Atlantic Treaty Organization is the prime example. The essential difference is really twofold; firstly, states organized for collective self-defense may exercise their rights without the prior authorization of the Security Council, whereas regional arrangements may take enforcement action only with that authorization, and, secondly, under Article 51, members are bound to report to the Security Council only measures taken in the exercise of the right of self-defense, whereas regional arrangements under Article 54 must keep the Security Council fully informed of activities undertaken or in contemplation. These differences, measured against the background of the antagonism between the Eastern and Western powers, suffice to make the issue an important one, and we suppose, therefore, to discuss the arguments in relation to NATO, although it must be borne in mind, they are of general application and not necessarily limited to the nature of that particular organization.

Collective Self-Defense and Regional Arrangements

The principal exposition of the view that NATO is an organization based on Article 51 and not Chapter VII of the Charter is to be found in the book entitled *The North Atlantic Treaty* by the former legal advisor to the British Foreign Office, Sir W.E. Beckett. In the main, his argument is threefold:

1. Article 53 envisages the use of regional arrangements for enforcement action under the Security Council's authority, and this term, as evidenced by its use in Articles 2(5) and 50, refers to action ordered or authorized by the proper organ of the United Nations. Such action, he maintains, is essentially different from action in self-defense which under Article 51 clearly does not require the prior authorization of the Security Council.
2. The matters with which regional arrangements are intended to deal are defined in Chapter VIII and do not include action in self defense. To this Kelsen replies that it would have been superfluous to specifically include this, since Article 51 already states that 'nothing in the present Charter shall impair the inherent right . . . ,' and presumably this means nothing in Chapter VIII could do so; hence the superfluity of a specific mention of this matter. In Kelsen's view the phrase 'such matters relating to the maintenance of international peace and security are appropriate for regional action' is perfectly apt to include self-defense, for 'there can be no doubt that the organization of collective self-defense is a matter relating to the maintenance of international peace and security.'
3. The hall-mark of a regional arrangement is that it contemplates measures in case of a conflict between members of an arrangement, whereas organizations in collective self-defense contemplate only measures against threats of from outside the organization. Whereas this might be the normal situation, on a strict interpretation of the Charter this is not necessarily so, and Kelsen rightly maintains that this particular argument has no basis in the Charter. Indeed, the US Secretary of State, Dean Acheson, in a press conference on NATO on March

18, 1949,when questioned about the scope of Article 4 of the treaty, expressed the opinion theta members of N.A.T.O. would, under that article, act together against a threat to a member's political independence coming from within that member's own territory, this is difficult to reconcile with the view that N.A.T.O. operates only against external threats. As Kelsen has said:

> the wording of the Charter does not exclude organization of collective self-defense through regional arrangements as a substitute . . . for collective security . . . and the rule of Article 53, that no enforcement action shall be taken without the authorization of the Security Council does not apply to the exercise of the right of collective self-defense organized in the regional arrangement because this rule is restricted Article 51.[38]

It may also be added that it is perfectly possible for an organization primarily designed for collective self-defense to be used for enforcement action if the members agree to carry out the recommendations or decisions of the Security Council so as to undertake action that is not action in self-defense.

If, therefore, we can assume that organizations of states can exercise their rights of individual or collective self-defense regardless of whether they are formally designated organizations in collective self-defense or regional arrangements, the only relevant question is whether these organizations purport to claim to exercise a right of self-defense in any way inconsistent with the Charter.

Treaty Arrangements Contemplating the Use of Force without the Prior Authorization of a Competent Organ of the UN

In the main, these arrangements claim expressly to be based upon Article 51 of the Charter; Article 5 of the North Atlantic Treaty refers to action that parties will take in the exercise of the right of individual or collective self-defense recognized by Article 51 of the Charter of the United Nations, and there are similar provisions in other treaties.[39]

In most of these treaties, there is an obligation on Members to consult together in certain circumstances; Article 4 of the North Atlantic Treaty may be taken as a typical example:

The Parties will consult together whenever, in the opinion of any of them, the territorial integrity, political independence or security of any of the Parties is threatened.

The question of inconsistency with the Charter really only arises when they contemplate action involving the thereat or use of force. Action of this nature must be in conformity with Article 2(4) (which, it will be noted, brings in the general question of consistency with the Purposes of the United Nations), and Article 51; the latter article imposes certain positive obligations on Members in respect of their right of individual or collective self-defense. When action *prima facie* within the terms of the prohibition of Article 2(4) is contemplated under these treaties certain questions arise; they are, namely, whether the circumstances in which such action is contemplated correspond with the circumstances in which that action is permitted by the Charter, whether in the execution of such action any inconsistency with obligations under the Charter is involved and finally, whether such action is correctly and necessarily characterized as action in self-defense, individual or collective.

The Question of Consistency with the Special Obligations Imposed under Article 51

There are, apart from thc limitations and conditions imposed by general International Law, certain special obligations imposed by Article 51 relating to the exercise of the right of self-defense by members of the United Nations. These are the obligation to report immediately to the Security Council measures taken in the exercise of the right, and also the obligation to cease action in self-defense when the Security Council has taken the measures necessary to maintain international peace and security. Certain of the treaties faithfully repeat these obligations in express terms: Article 5 of the North Atlantic Treaty states:

> Any such armed attack and all measures taken as a result thereof shall immediately be reported to the Security Council. Such measures shall be terminated when the Security Council has taken the measures necessary to restore and maintain international peace and security.

Article 4 of the Warsaw Pact contains a restatement of these obligations, but the bilateral security treaties concluded by the USSR do not contain similar provisions, and it has been suggested that for this reason these treaties are to that extent illegal. There is, in my submission, no basis for this view; the obligations to report measures undertaken, and to cease such measures once the Security Council has taken the measures necessary to restore and maintain international peace and security, arise from the Charter and a restatement of them in unnecessary. It would, of course, be illegal to stipulate in these treaties conduct inconsistent with these obligations, but the mere omission to restate the duties imposed by the Charter is not in itself illegal.

The Legal Character of the Action Contemplated under the Treaties

The final, and perhaps most substantial, question is whether the action contemplated under these treaties, whether of the simple bilateral type or of the more complex form, is correctly characterized as action in self-defense, individual or collective. If, as suggested, the right of self-defense is available only to a state that defends its own substantive rights, and the difference between the individual and the collective right lies in whether states exercise their right of self-defense individually or in concert, then the question arises whether the action contemplated by these treaties is necessarily of that character.

These treaties are based upon the principle that an attack against nay one party is an attack against the other party or parties to the treaty; the principle is the same whether the operative phrase is armed attack, aggression, or aggressive policy. As an abstract statement, this must be a legal fiction; in the concrete suggestions envisaged by these treaties it may also be a statement of actual fact. It is not difficulty to envisage a direct attack against a state in Western Europe that, in view of the magnitude of the attack and the evidence of a wider aggressive intention that it affords, in fact, threatens the security of all the states in the northern part of the Western Hemisphere. The interdependence of the securities of a number of states may, in this age, be stated without real fear or contradiction; it would result in an attack against one constituting in fact, and not merely as a legal fiction, a violation of the right to independence and security of other states. On the other hand, it would be ludicrous to suppose that merely by the conclusion of a treaty, any two states could bring mutual assistance within the concept of self-defense—at least if this is to be a juridical concept and not a term of diplomacy. To state, for example, that an attack upon Chile, say by one of its South American neighbors, is an attack upon the United Kingdom would be a possible statement, but it would belong to the realm of fiction rather than fact. Consequently, should the United Kingdom afford military assistance to Chile in those circumstances, its action would only by a twist of terminology be collective self-defense. It is not believed that the juridical concept of a right of self-defense can be stretched to an extent that is so far removed from fact by using this fiction of an "attack against one is an attack against all."

It is for this reason, it is believed, that these treaties are concluded between states in some geographical proximity to each other. Many of them are restricted in their application to defined regions. Whether it be the "North Atlantic area" defined in Article 6 of the North Atlantic Treaty, the European area of the Brussels Treaty or the Warsaw Treaty, the region defined in Article 4 of the Rio Treaty, or the "Pacific area" defined in Article 8 of the Manila Treaty, the regional nature of these treaties suggests an interdependence in fact of the security of the member states. It approximates to the proximate relationship of kinship that in private law justifies assistance by one person to another within the concept of self-defense. Within the defined area of the statement that an attack against one state is an attack against all must be taken to be a statement of the belief of the parties that the security of each is so dependent on the security of every other party, that a violation of the rights of one party would, in fact, also constitute a violation of the rights of all other parties. The treaties therefore establish a means by which these states, each having the right of individual self-defense, may exercise their rights collectively. It is significant that the declaration by the governments of the United States, the United Kingdom, and France, recorded at the London Conference in October 1954, these governments stated that:

> They will regard as a threat to their own peace and safety any recourse to force which in violation of the principles of the United Nations Charter threatens the integrity and unity of the Atlantic Alliance or its defensive purposes.

And in these circumstances they considered Article 4 of the North Atlantic Treaty would be applicable. This declaration, with its insistence on a threat to their own peace and safety, implies that each one of the three states would deem itself to be in a state of individual self-defense and the North Atlantic Treaty would provide the means of exercising these individual rights collectively. Similarly, Article IV of the Anzus Pact states:

> Each Party recognizes that an armed attack in the Pacific Area on any of the Parties would be dangerous in its own peace and security.

Yet even with the restriction implicit in the limiting of membership to states within a defined region, it is not necessarily true that every armed attack would, even within the region, in fact constitute an attack on each party so as to allow to each party the right of self-defense. And yet without this individual right, they can scarcely claim to participate in a collective exercise of the right of self-defense.[40] In such a case, intervention by states like the United States, Canada, or Norway could not really be justified on the basis of the right of self-defense, individual or collective, if that right is to retain a juridical connotation and not dissolve into a description of political affiliations. It is not suggested that it is only geopolitical proximity that can constitute that interdependence between states that is essential before an attack upon one is also an attack upon the other. Though the nexus between states that have such an interdependence is normally of a geographical kind, it is not permissible to assume that only this kind of link is sufficient to afford an adequate basis for the exercise of the right of collective self-defense. Interdependence can be of a political character; for example, the link between members of the British Commonwealth is political rather than geographical, and it may be perfectly proper to treat an attack upon any one member of the Commonwealth on any considerable scale as an attack upon the Commonwealth as a whole. There may also be ties of an economic or strategic character that make the security of one state dependent upon the security of another. Indeed, the British interests in the Middle East may be of this character, and reference has already been made to the British reservation in signing the Pact of Paris in 1928. It is perhaps more the reality of the independence than the kind of interdependence that is vital here, and the important question is always in final analysis, whether an attack upon one state in fact threatens the security of the other. The existence of geographical proximity, political, economic, or even cultural ties relates really to the question of proof of interdependence. The difficulty is, of course, to distinguish real interdependence that can alone afford a legal basis for the right of collective self-defense from a mere claim to spheres of interests that ranks as a political rather than a legal doctrine. It is a distinction that must, however, be drawn if collective self-defense is to retain a juridical connotation.

Each member of a collective security arrangement, whether regional in character or not, would, therefore, in each case have to decide whether in the light of the conditions imposed on the exercise of the right of self-defense by general International Law, the state had the right of self-defense to exercise according to the treaty arrangements for the collective exercise of such a right. Reliance on the treaty is not enough, for the obligations contained in the treaty are subject to the overriding obligations contained in the Charter, and Article 2(4) is categorical. Unless the states using force or the threat of force in pursuance of their obligations under a collective security treaty can show that their action was authorizes by a competent organ of the United Nations, they must show their action is justified as being the exercise of the right of individual or collective self-defense, and this right is governed by general International Law, not by these collective security treaties, whether bilateral or multilateral. Moreover the requirement of proportionality would exclude a general right of intervention by all parties to the treaty, if the effect of that general intervention would be with a disproportionately large amount of force.

The other possible explanation of the nature of the action contemplated under these treaties is that, where the conditions governing the exercise of the right of self-defense are not satisfied, participation in collective action by members not satisfying those conditions is still justified as action taken for maintaining international peace and security within a particular region. This is not the avowed nature of the action. The Western treaties and the Warsaw Treaty at least avowedly claim their juridical basis in the right of self-defense, but as a purpose of the organization, it is sometimes stated that the organization will take such action as it deems necessary, including the use of armed force, to restore or maintain the security of the North Atlantic area, or whatever the appropriate region is.

Article 5 of the Rio Treaty suggests this alternative basis for action taken by providing for the reporting of action taken in contemplation to the Security Council in the exercise of the right of self-defense or for the purpose of maintaining inter-American peace and security. However, it is possible the latter alternative refers to the action the Organization of American States would take as a regional arrangement pursuant to an authorization of the Security Council. The North Atlantic Treaty does not expressly contemplate the Organization being used as a regional arrangement, although there is nothing to prevent its members taking action to maintain or restore international peace and security pursuant to a request of the Security Council. To the extent that the automatic or literal application of these treaties could warrant action not strictly within the concept of self-defense, at least for some of the members of the organization, this other basis would seem to be the only one available. The action taken would be in the nature of collective security action rather than action in collective self-defense. It would be, within the region, a substitute for the kind of collective security, which, under the Charter, the Security Council was designed to take. The phrase "to restore or maintain the security of the North Atlantic area," is, literally, a regional definition of the functions relating to the maintenance of international peace and security for which, on a global basis, the Security Council has been given primary responsibility.[41] The Warsaw Treaty, in Article 4, is even wider in phrasing. These phrases bear close analogy to the phrasing used with reference to the Security Council's powers in Articles 24, 39, 42, and 43 of the Charter. To regard the action of these treaty organizations as a regional substitute for the action that, under the Charter, it was contemplated that the Security Council would take is consistent with the fact that in the main they developed after 1946 and after the Security Council had begun to demonstrate the lack of real unanimity amongst the permanent members and, as a result, the unlikelihood of its fulfilling this function. It is also consistent with the attitude of the United Kingdom, France, and the United States in relation to the situation in the Middle East. The Tripartite Declaration of May 25, 1950,[42] states that these powers have a deep interest in the establishment and maintenance of international peace and security in the area . . . and should they find that any of these states (the Middle East states) was preparing to violate frontiers or armistice lines, would, consistently with their obligations as members of the United Nations, immediately take action, both within and outside the United Nations, to prevent such violation. Kunz, writing of NATO, says:

> But the Treaty certainly had in view the fact that the Security Council is paralyzed by the veto; here as in the United Nations as a whole Article 51 is being used more and more as a substitute, as Ersatz for the non-existing general collective security and sanctions. But self-defense under Article 51 gains, under such conditions, a very different meaning and become s a technique pretty much near to the old-fashioned right to resort to war, especially as there is no juridical control over the exercise of self-defense.[43]

This is not to suggest that such collective security action is necessarily illegal. But, not being self-defense, its legality depends on considerations different from those governing the legality of action in collective self-defense. The other considerations are, firstly, that until the Charter is amended or abandoned, it is the Security Council that is vested with primary responsibility for collective security, whether regional or global. It follows that normally the prior authorization of the Security Council is a condition precedent to the right of members to take collective security action. This is borne out by Article 52, which prevents regional arrangements from taking such action except with prior authorization from the Security Council. Secondly, since the responsibility of the Security Council is primary and not exclusive, and since the Security Council may well be prevented from fulfilling its responsibilities due to a lack of unanimity among the permanent members, there is a secondary responsibility on the totality of the UN members. Yet this responsibility lies on the totality of members acting collectively; the reference to "collective measures" in Article 1(1) of the Charter must mean measures taken on the authorization of the totality of the members as represented by the General Assembly, and not to groups of members as represented by a regional arrangement or collective security organization. There is, since the General Assembly Resolution on Uniting for Peace of November 3, 1950,[44] a specific procedure set up whereby the General Assembly may recommend or authorize members to take action of this kind when the Security Council fails to fulfill its primary responsibility due to the lack of unanimity of the permanent members. It is submitted, therefore, that before individual members or groups of members can take collective security action (as opposed to action in collective self-defense), it must clearly be shown that both the Security Council and the General Assembly have failed to take the necessary action. Only then can it be said that members have a residual responsibility in the matter. Moreover, whereas the Security Council's failure may be explicable by reason of the power of veto, this cannot be said of the General Assembly. The failure of the General Assembly can only be attributed to a refusal of the necessary two-thirds majority of members to take or authorize collective measures in the circumstances. In identical circumstances, the action of a number of states, parties to a collective security arrangement, in arrogating to themselves the right to take collective action when the General Assembly itself is not prepared to recommend such action, would be extremely suspect.

It is for the foregoing reasons that this author rejects the plea that the intervention of British and French forces in Egyptian territory in October 1956, was justified in self-defense. It is submitted that the alternative plea that the action was aimed at the separation of the Israeli and Egyptian forces and the maintenance of international peace and security in the Middle East must also be rejected. This latter construction of the intervention was stated in the prime minister's speech in the Commons on October 31, in his broadcast to the nation on November 4, and again in the House of Commons on November 1 It also figured repeatedly in government statements subsequent to those dates.

It may be doubted, whether, on the facts, the action taken was wholly consistent with this aim, for, even accepting the argument that a landing was only militarily feasible in the Canal area, this does not explain the absence of any kind of forceful measures to compel the withdrawal of Israeli forces from Egyptian territory. The mere fact that Israel had, and Egypt had not, accepted the ultimatum issued jointly by Britain and France on October 30, is not a sufficient explanation, for that begs the question of the right of those states to issue such an ultimatum involving, as it did, the threat of force. However, the crucial issue is not so much one of the consistency of this construction with the facts, but of the legality of a state action involving the use or threat of force, other than self-defense, unauthorized by the United Nations.

There can be no question but that this action was not authorized by the Security Council or the General Assembly. The resolution introduced by the United States in the Security Council on October 30, calling on all states not to use force or threat of force, was vetoed by the United Kingdom and France against an otherwise-majority vote of seven members. This was not a case of action desired by the Council but which the Council itself was unable to recommend because of a single veto. The General Assembly's resolution of November 2 also, by a majority of sixty-four votes to five, with six abstentions, urged an immediate ceasefire and a halt to the movement of military forces into the area. Despite this, the first actual landings of British and French troops took place three days later.

The danger of conceding to individual states or even groups of states the right to take collective security action, unauthorized by the competent organs of the United Nations, lies in the possibility that antagonistic groups may each reach a decision that action is necessary to maintain or restore international peace and security, and under a claim of right, plunge the world into war. It was for this reason that the Royal Institute of International Affairs Study Group in 1938 considered that, in order to prevent regional pacts from degenerating into alliances of the prewar pattern, an essential condition of their right to take action for the maintenance of international peace and security was that they should act only with the prior authority of the Council of the League or the Permanent Court of International Justice. It was a realization of this danger that at San Francisco led to the rejection of the Australian proposal that in the event of the Security Council failing to act, each member state retained the right to take such action as it deemed necessary in the interest of international peace and security.[45] For similar reasons, writers have urged neutrality rather than intervention in a conflict in which the aggressor has not been determined by a competent organ of the United Nations.[46] The General Assembly resolution on the Duties of States in the Event of the Outbreak of Hostilities provides that a state engaged in hostilities should take all steps practical in the circumstances and compatible with the right of self-defense to bring the armed conflict to an end at the earliest possible moment. A general right of intervention conceded to the allies of the immediate participants could scarcely be regarded as consistent with the aim of this resolution. For the concession of a right to decide upon action in the interest of international peace and security (and against which state or states) to every state brings about a potentially anarchical situation. It is, therefore, an additional reason for rejecting the concept of collective self-defense.

It is readily admitted that once we assume the impotency of the competent organs of the United Nations, this view has serious disadvantages. To oppose all collective action (other than that which is strictly self-defense) not sanctioned by a competent organ of the United Nations, would open the way for piecemeal aggression.[47] Each victim would fall in turn with no hope of assistance from friendly nations. There are, however, weighty reasons against accepting these serious disadvantages of the view as conclusive arguments against it. Firstly, these practical disadvantages stem from the system or right and duties with which members surrounded themselves on signing the Charter. The restrictions in the Charter on the freedom of unilateral action, of action involving force unsanctioned by the competent UN organ, were really feasible only on the assumption that the Security Council would fulfill the responsibilities assigned to it. In fact, it has not done so, but the consequences of this, however disadvantageous, are reasons for questioning the political wisdom of the Charter scheme. They are not reasons for extending and distorting the legal concept of self-defense.

There does, however, remain the final problem inherent in any system of collective security of the legality of action to assist a State pending the decision of the competent organ. Even under the Acheson Plan, although an emergency meeting of the Assembly may be called within twenty-four hours, the necessary investigation of the facts or even the formal procedure for taking a decision may take time. As Kelsen has stated:

> Between the moment the illegal attack starts and the moment the centralized machinery of collective security is put into action, there is, even in case of its perfectly prompt functioning, a space of time, an interval, which may be disastrous to a victim.[48]

During the interim period, pending a decision of the competent organ of the United Nations, the victim state is not devoid of assistance, for those of its neighbors who are themselves placed under the necessity of self-defense by the illegal attack, whose own right of self-defense is activated by the attack, may exercise the right of self-defense in concert with the original victim. If prior provision has been made for this occasion in collective self-defense by treaty so much the better. Moreover, the greater the scale of the attack, the wider the range of neighboring states imperiled by the attack and able to invoke their right of self-defense. The right would not justify a general right of intervention at this stage. States not individually in a state of self-defense would have no right to take action or join in collective action. To allow them to do so would, at this stage, completely nullify the whole system of collective security and signal a return to the very anarchy that the system of collection security is designed to prevent. The right of states that are not acting in self-defense to intervene must await the authorization of the competent organ of the centralized machinery, and this obligation cannot be avoided by perversion of the concept of collective self-defense.[49]

If it should still be contended that in an age of nuclear warfare, the destructive power of an initial attack could completely destroy a state entitled only to assistance from other states placed under the necessity of exercising their right of self-defense, then it is only possible in reply to suggest that the technological advances of modern warfare might well have made any system of collective security archaic. The only real solution to this problem lies either in combining the system of collective security with some means of depriving all the individual states of the kind of armaments that, by their immediate destructive power, make the system unworkable; or in moving toward a system of world federation in which component states would be completely disarmed.[50]

The intention is not to ignore these difficulties, but only to state the conviction that they are not solved by distorting the concept of self-defense, individual or collective, beyond all legal recognition.[51]

It is conceded that these views are based upon the assumption that the system of rights and duties imposed by the Charter is still binding upon members. The position might arise in which, due to the frustration of the machinery envisaged in Chapter VII for the maintenance of international peace and security and in particular the failure to implement Article 43, members take the view that the Charter no longer represents the fundamental law of international society or even the literally binding treaty. This view, which implies invoking the doctrine *clausula rebus sic stantibus*, would perhaps enable the members to assume a greater freedom of action based upon a right to take such action as is necessary to maintain or restore international peace and security. It is not believed that states have yet taken that view,[52] a view that involves substantial repudiation of the Charter, and the inauguration of the Acheson might well have forestalled the necessity for taking such a view. If, in the future, the necessity for taking that view should arise, then members would fall back upon the system of rights and duties imposed by general International Law, apart from the Charter, and the legality of their actions would have to be determined exclusively by that law.

NOTES

1. Grotius, *De Jure Belli ac Pacis*, Book II, chapter I, s. iii, 172 of translation in Classics of International Law, ed. J.B. Scott, Publications of Carnegie Endowment.

2. *De Jure Belli*, Book I, chapter XIII ()—"All laws and all codes allow the repelling of force by force. There is one rule which endures for ever, to maintain one's safety by any and every means."

3. *Jus Gentium*.

4. *Jus Gentium*, 22–23 trans.

5. Grotius, *De Jure Belli ac Pacis*, Book II, chapter I, 172–73, trans.

6. See Victoria's fourth proposition, relying on Augustine: "there is a single and only just cause for commencing a war, namely a wrong received."

7. Grotius, *De Jure Belli ac Pacis*, Book II, chapter I, 173 trans.; Pufendorf, *De Jure Naturae*, Book II, chapter V, 275–76 trans.

8. *International Law*, Vol. I (8th ed., London: Longmans, 1955), 309.

9. Elihu Root, 'The Basis of Protection to Citizens Residing Abroad,' Presidential Address to the 10th Meeting of the American Society of International Law; cited in Stowell, *Intervention in International* Law (J. Bryne & Company, 1921), 159.

10. See Article 7 Harvard Draft Convention on International Law, which draws a clear distinction between cases where the alien suffers injury inflicted by an individual or group of individuals for which the state is not responsible, and where the injury results from the act of an authority of the state.

11. Right to Protect Citizens in foreign countries by landing forces, 1912 (revised ed., 1929).

12. Milton Offutt, Protection of Citizens Abroad by the Armed Forces of the U.S. (1928), chs. II, III.

13. Report of the Senate Investigating Committee, Senate Docs. No. 794, 315.

14. Speech in House of Lords, *Manchester Guardian*, November 2nd, 1956.

15. Speech in the House of Commons, ibid.

16. *Recent Trends in the Law of the United Nation* (Cambridge: Cambridge University Press, 2014), 914.

17. *Law of the United Nations* (The Lawbook Exchange, 2000), 269, 797–78.
18. I.C.J. Reports (1949), 5.
19. I.C.J. Reports (1949), 31.
20. See Stone, op. cit., 246, fn 20.
21. Op. cit., 202.
22. *Contra* Waldock, *op. cit.*, 496. Stone, *op. cit.*, 244, regards the competence as exclusively within the S.C., apparently on the basis *nemo iudex in sua causa.* And see British Commentary on the Charter, Cmd. 6666, 9: 'It will be for the S.C. to decide whether these measures have been taken and whether they are adequate for the purpose.' For a contrary view, see Goodrich and Hambro, op. cit., 300, who suggest it is for each defending state to decide both when and how long conditions exist that justify the exercise of the right.
23. *Law of the United Nations* (1950), *op. cit.*, 792.
24. *Canons of International Law*, 99.
25. Sohm, *Institutes of Roman Law*, 3rd ed., 224. Wrongs to persons or their property under the *potestas* of the paterfamilias were considered to be wrongs to the paterfamilias; Buckland, *Textbook of Roman Law* (Cambridge: Cambridge University Press, 1921), 104.
26. The conclusion is almost inescapable that any postulation of a duty to maintain international peace, as a basis of the right of self-defense, is based upon the theory of the just war. Until any particular act of force by a state can be classed as either a delict or a sanction the postulate of such a duty seems an anomaly in the legal system. The existence of such a duty would make all treaties of assistance merely declaratory of existing International Law; it cannot be supposed that, at least prior to the Charter, this was the case.
27. *Intervention in International Law*, *ante*, 48.
28. Oppenheim, *International Law*, Vol. II, 7th ed., *ante*, 155.
29. Bowett's view goes on that this decision is delegated to the Security Council, which is invested with primary responsibility for the maintenance if international peace and security, and whose decisions the member states are bound to accept. The duty to vindicate the law is conditional upon a decision of the Security Council, which may, subject to certain provisos, legally oblige a member to fulfill such a duty. I do not agree with Bowett's view at this point as defensive alliances, at least to a limited extent, are and should be an important and inseparable part of the international system.
30. Mr. Canning to Mr. Rush, August 23rd, 1823, cited Moore, *Digest*, Vol. IV, 392.
31. *Ibid.*, 285.
32. Hughes, 'Observations on the Monroe Doctrine,' *American Journal of International Law*, Vol. 17 (1923), 616; Clark, Memorandum on the Monroe Doctrine, Department of State Publication No. 37, 1930.
33. *International Law*, Vol. I, 288.
34. Pearce-Higgins, 'The Monroe Doctrine,' *British Yearbook of International Law*, Vol. 5 (1924), 114.
35. See Derek Bowett, *Self-Defense in International Law* (New York: Praeger, 1958), 216.

36. *Ibid.*, 216.

37. See Derek Bowett, *Self-Defense in International Law* (New York: Praeger, 1958), 218: The individual members cannot on the one hand delegate primary responsibility for the maintenance of international peace and security to the Security Council (Article 24), and on the other claim this right of unilateral action to support any state they consider to be acting in self-defense. This sort of freedom of alliance cannot stand together with a system of collective security as centralized as the United Nations Charter.

38. *Op. Cit.*, 164.

39. For example, Article 3, Rio Treaty; Article IV, Brussels Treaty (Treaty of Economic, Social and Cultural Collaboration and Collective Self-Defense, Brussels, March 17, 1948).

40. Bowett states: "It is possible to imagine an armed invasion of Greece, for example, arising out of difficulties on her northern frontiers and taking the form of a limited invasion into Greek territory by forces of a neighboring State though technically within the terms of Article 4 of the North Atlantic Treaty, could not possibly be said to constitute in fact an armed attack on every NATO member." With great respect, I do not agree with this view: Why should an invasion of Greece form an exception to the general rule?

41. Bowett, *Self-Defense in International Law* (New York: Praeger, 1958), 240.

42. *Times*, May 26th, 1950. See also the debate in the Commons on February 13, 1950, in which the U.K. prime minister seems to suggest 'action' involves the use of force; reported in the *Manchester Guardian*, February 14, 1956; but see the report in the *Manchester Guardian*, February 15, 1956, of the statement by a Foreign Office spokesman that forces would not be used without the consent of the countries to which they would be sent.

43. See Bowett, *Self-Defense in International Law* (New York: Praeger, 1958), 241: With that analysis of the reasons for the development of NATO we would agree; we would not, however, agree that either the political conditions of post-war, or these treaties, can alter the concept of self-defense. To distort that concept to cover collective action by states, some of which may have no right of self-defense, may produce a politically desirable result; it does not produce a legal basis for which such action recognized by International Law. If the juridical concept of self-defense is to have any meaning it must, in our view, be distinguished from collective action for the purpose of maintaining international peace and security within a defined region. The latter we would characterize as collective security action.

44. Off. Rec. G.A., Fifth Session, Plen. Meeting. 341–37. The legal character of action taken pursuant to a recommendation of the General Assembly under this resolution is, in our view, that of collective measures for the purpose of maintaining international peace and security (Article 1 [1]). This seems to follow from the resolution itself which refers to recommendations with a view to making appropriate recommendations to Members for collective measures . . . to maintain or restore international peace and security. For a similar similar construction, see Kelsen, *Recent Trends*, 975. Also Mc Dougal and Gardner, 'The Veto and the Charter: An Interpretation for Survival' Yale L.J., Vol. 60 (1951), 258, 288–91. Also Woolsey,

'The Uniting for Peace Resolution of the U.N.,' *American Journal of International Law*, Vol. 45 (1951), 129, at 137. The view has been taken that this Resolution is itself based upon the right of collective self-defense preserved under Article 51. See Stone, *Legal Controls of International Conflict*, at 275: 'The Uniting for Peace Resolution A is thus seen to fit into the anarchic self-defense derogation from the Charter far more naturally than it can be forced (if it can be forced at all) into its collective peace enforcement provisions.' Various delegates have, in the debates on the Resolution, also attempted to argue its validity on the basis of Article 51. See Off. Rec. G.A. Fifth Session, 360th, 361st, 364th Meetings of First Committee. This view is, in our opinion, mistaken; the Resolution contemplated action for collective security, not collective self-defense. See Waldock. 'The Regulation of the Use of Force by Individual States in International Law,' R.C. 1952, 505, for a rejection of the view that the Acheson Plan is based on self-defense rather than on the General Assembly's secondary responsibility for the maintenance of international peace and security.

45. Bowett, *Self-Defense in International Law* (New York: Praeger, 1958), 244.
46. Jessup, *Modern Law of Nations* (Read Books, 2007), 205.
47. Bowett, *Self-Defense in International Law* (New York: Praeger), 245.
48. *American Journal of International Law*, Vol. 42 (1948), 785.
49. Bowett, *Self-Defense in International Law* (New York: Praeger, 1958), 247.
50. *Ibid.*, 247.
51. *Ibid.*, 247.
52. *Ibid.* 248.

Chapter 5

Armed Reprisals

THE CONCEPT OF DEFENSIVE ARMED REPRISALS

Reprisals constitute countermeasures that would be illegal if not for the prior illegal act of the state against which they are directed. While most reprisals are non-forcible—that is, unarmed—we shall focus in this context on armed reprisals. These ought to be distinguished from belligerent reprisals, namely reprisals resorted to by Belligerent Parties in the midst of hostilities after an armed conflict has begun.

Armed reprisals are measures of counterforce short of war, undertaken by one state against another in response to an earlier violation of International Law in peacetime.[1] To be lawful, recourse by Utopia to armed reprisals, like other unilateral uses of force, against Arcadia—without the authorization of the Security Council—is prohibited unless it comes under the rubric of self-defense, as per Article 51 of the UN Charter, customary International Law, and the writings of those learned in International Law. Therefore, Utopian armed reprisals would be illicit if they are instigated in response to ordinary violations of International Law by Arcadia. However, if an Arcadian armed attack occurs, Utopia can invoke the right of self-defense in a multifaceted fashion. One permissible form of self-defense is that of defensive armed reprisals. This does not, as it has been contended,[2] subvert the structures of the UN Charter. On the contrary, since defensive armed reprisals are a subcategory of self-defense, they are carried out in conformity with Article 51.

A juxtaposition of defensive armed reprisals and on-the-spot reaction discloses points of convergence as well as divergence. In both cases, the use of counterforce is limited to measures short of war. But on-the-spot reaction postulates a temporal and geographic relation to the original armed attack. When activating defensive armed reprisals, the responding state strikes at different times and regularly in a different place. A reset of time and place may be dictated by the circumstances of the incident. A Utopian patrol under fire by Arcadian troops may be taken out of action, and there may be no other Utopian units nearby to return fire. A Utopian submarine attacked by an Arcadian destroyer may be sunk when sailing on a solidary mission. In addition to the time element, the specific location may be unsuitable for effective Utopian response. Even if Utopian units are available nearby, it may prove militarily disadvantageous for Utopia to respond with counterforce at the exact geographic limits from which the Arcadian attack was launched.

The availability of the option to resort to defensive armed reprisals at another time and place—compared to the Arcadian armed attack—enables Utopia to weigh where, when, and how to strike a blow that would be most efficacious. The assertion that the target of any defensive measures must have directly contributed to the occurrence of the armed attack is,[3] in the view of the present author, wrong. In fact, the Utopian counteraction need not mirror the earlier Arcadian attack.[4] The target selected by Utopia may be entirely dissimilar to the original object of the Arcadian attack, and it may be located far away from the initial flashpoint. What Utopia must keep in mind is the need to respect the rights of third states. This is particularly pertinent if the defensive armed reprisals are likely to endanger international shipping at sea.

THE INTERCONNECTION BETWEEN DEFENSIVE ARMED REPRISALS AND BELLIGERENT REPRISALS

When states carry out defensive armed reprisals, their operations must be guided by the rules of the *jus in bello*. This is true of all uses of force, even short of war, and defensive armed reprisals form no exception. However, the interaction between the *jus ad bellum* and the *jus in bello* is complicated by a number of treaty stipulations on the subject matter of reprisals.

The four 1949 Geneva Conventions forbid certain acts of reprisals against protected persons, such as prisoners of war, and objects. A similar provision appears in Article 4 (4) of the 1954 Hague Convention on the Protection of Cultural Property. Protocol 1 of 1977, additional to the Geneva Conventions, goes a lot further in banning a whole range of acts of reprisals. Thus, attacks against the civilian population or civilians by way of reprisals are prohibited under Article 51 (6) of the Protocol. Article 60 (5) of the Vienna Convention on the Law of Treaties makes it clear that provisions prohibiting any form of reprisals against protected persons, contained in treaties of a humanitarian character, are not subject to the application of the general rules enabling termination or suspension of a treaty as a consequence of its material breach by another Party.

In essence, the measures of reprisals interdicted in the instruments cited amount to belligerent reprisals—i.e., *jus in bello* reprisals carried out in the duration of hostilities. By their nature, the strictures of the Geneva Conventions or the Hague Convention are germane to defensive armed reprisals as a form of conduct under the *jus ad bellum* no more than they are in other situations in which inter-state force is employed. If prisoners of war are captured in the course of defensive armed reprisals, they must be protected as in all other types of hostilities, and the protection comprises an immunity from belligerent reprisals. But even if a prisoner of war is unlawfully exposed to belligerent reprisals during a military operation characterized as a defensive armed reprisal, the legality of the whole operation as an act of counterforce in response to an armed attack is not compromised by that breach.

A different outcome is apparently produced by the broader prohibitions of reprisals incorporated in Additional Protocol I. Although the injunctions of the Protocol, like those of the Geneva and the Hague Conventions, were intended to cope with the problem of the *jus in bello* belligerent reprisals, it may be inferred from their language that the discretion of a state contemplating defensive armed reprisals pursuant to the *jus ad bellum* is also curtailed where the choice of objectives for counterstrikes is concerned.

If the original armed attack by Atlantica was directed against the Patagonian civilian population, Patagonia might wish to requite the wrongful action with defensive armed reprisals aimed equally at civilians. Nonetheless, under Article 51(6) of the Protocol, should Atlantican civilians be the target of the Patagonian armed reprisals, the whole retaliatory operation would be illegal.[5]

While Additional Protocol I introduces a considerable change in the potential application of defensive armed reprisals, it must be appreciated that its provisions on the subject of reprisals are controversial.[6] Although the Protocol is binding on most States, due account must be taken of the fact that the United States issued a formal announcement in 1987 that it would not ratify the Protocol since that instrument is "fundamentally and irreconcilably flawed."[7] The United States of America is not alone in objecting to these provisions of the Protocol.

Non-contracting Parties to the Protocol are still by customary international norms of the *jus in bello*. In the *Kupreskic* case of 2000, a trial chamber of the ICTY held that the prohibition of belligerent reprisals against civilians has emerged as customary International Law subsequent to the adoption of the Protocol in 1977.[8] This is an extravagant claim endorsed neither by state practice nor by the majority of International Law scholars. In any event, in the *Martic* case of 2007, an ICTY trial chamber took it for granted that belligerent reprisals are permitted by customary International Law, provided that they meet prescribed conditions.[9] In 2008, the ICTY Appeals Chamber in the same case confirmed this line of approach. Consequently, the strict limitations of the Protocol do not impinge on the freedom of non-contracting Parties to resort to defensive armed reprisals.

THE CONDITIONS OF NECESSITY, PROPORTIONALITY, AND IMMEDIACY

As in other circumstances in which self-defense is invoked, defensive armed reprisals must meet the conditions of necessity, proportionality, and immediacy. Proportionality is the quintessential factor in appraising the legality of defensive armed reprisals. This was highlighted in the 1928 Arbitral Award, rendered in a dispute between Portugal and Germany, in the *Naulilaa* case.[10] The proceedings related to an incident that had taken place in 1914, shortly after the outbreak of World War I (at a time when Portugal was still a neutral state), on the border between the German colony of Southwest Africa (present-day Namibia) and the Portuguese colony of Angola. In that incident, three German nationals (one civilian official and two army officers) were shot dead. In retaliation, the German forces attacked and destroyed a number of Portuguese installations in Angola over a period of several weeks. The arbitrators held that these measures were excessively disproportionate.

It is unrealistic to expect defensive armed reprisals to conform strictly and literally to the tenet of an eye for an eye. A precise equation of casualties and damage caused by both sides in the course of armed attack and the defensive armed reprisals is neither a necessary nor a possible condition. All the more so, since in every military entanglement there is an element of chance, and defensive armed reprisals can unpredictably give rise to more casualties and damage than anticipated. However, the magnitude of armed reprisals must be adapted to the scale and effects of the armed attack. A calculus of force, introducing some symmetry or approximation between the dimensions of the lawful counterforce and the original unlawful use of force, is imperative. The main consideration is that counterforce must not be excessive, according to the language employed by Mr. Webster in the aforementioned notorious *Caroline* case, compared to the original use of force.

A good modern example may be drawn from the *Oil Platforms* judgment. Although the International Court of Justice dismissed an American contention of an exercise of self-defense short of war (in effect, defensive armed reprisals) in response to an armed attack by Iran, it added:

> the Court cannot assess in isolation the proportionality of that action to the attack to which it was said to be a response; it cannot close its eyes to the scale of the whole operation, which involved, *inter alia*, the destruction of two Iranian frigates and a number of other naval vessels and aircraft. As a response to the

> mining . . . of a single United States warship, which was severely damaged but not sunk, and without loss of life, neither . . . [the operation] as a whole, nor even that part of it that destroyed the . . . platforms, can be regarded, in the circumstances of this case, as a proportionate use of force in self-defense.[11]

It is plain that the legal position would have been utterly different had there been loss of life, and *a fortiori* if the American warship had been sunk. Undoubtedly, proportionality in this context must be assessed on the basis of the damage actually caused by the other side, rather than what might have happened had things gone really wrong.

With regard to necessity, considering that defensive armed reprisals postdate the initial armed attack, reliance by the victim state on counterforce is contingent on its first seeking in vain an amicable solution to the dispute. This is another condition pronounced by the arbitrators in the *Naulilaa* case. If the attacking state is ready to discharge its duty of making adequate reparation to the victim state—in conformity with the general rules of state responsibility—defensive armed reprisals would be illicit. But the need to consider alternatives to the exercise of counterforce does not mean the injured state must embroil itself in prolonged wheel-spinning negotiations. If no redress is offered within a reasonable time, a state confronted with an armed attack is entitled to put in effect measures of defensive armed reprisals.

The right of the victim state to avoid dilatory stratagems is tied in with the rule that defensive armed reprisals must also meet the requirement of immediacy. It is unlawful to engage in these measures of counterforce in response to an armed attack that occurred in the remote past.

If armed reprisals do not meet the three requirements of proportionality, necessity, and immediacy, they cannot be deemed defensive.[12]

NOTES

1. Yoram Dinstein, *War, Aggression and Self-Defense* (Cambridge: Cambridge University Press, 2017), 264.

2. Darcy, 'Retaliation and Reprisal,' *The Oxford Handbook of the Use of Force in International Law* (Oxford: Oxford University Press, 2015), 895.

3. See Kaye, 'Adjudicating Self-Defense: Discretion, Perception, and the Resort to Force in International Law,' 44 *Columbia Journal of Transnational Law* 134, 162 (2006).

4. *Nicaragua* Case (Merits), ICJ Reports [1989] note 24, at 379 (Dissenting Opinion of Judge Schwebel).

5. See Hampson, 'Belligerent Reprisals and the 1977 Protocols to the Geneva Conventions of 1949,' 37 *International and Comparative Law Quarterly* 818, 837 (1988).

6. Dinstein, *War, Aggression and Self-Defense* (Cambridge: Cambridge University Press, 2017), 267.

7. Message from the President of the United States to the Senate, 1987, 26 International Legal Materials, 562.

8. *Prosecutor v. Kupreskic* et al. (ICTY, Trial Chamber, 2000), paras. 527–33.

9. *Prosecutor v. Martic* (ICTY, Trial Chamber, 2007), paras. 263–67.

10. Naulilaa case (1928) 2 *Reports of International Arbitral Awards*, 1011, 1026.

11. *Case Concerning Oil Platforms* International Court of Justice Reports [] 198–99.

12. Dinstein, *War, Aggression and Self-Defense* (Cambridge: Cambridge University Press, 2017), 269.

Chapter 6

The Politics and Ethics of Humanitarian Intervention

The pivotal question to be analyzed in the present chapter is the following: Is there a right of (unilateral) humanitarian intervention?

Humanitarian intervention may be defined as the proportionate use of force by governments to prevent serious violations of fundamental human rights of individuals in another state who would readily consent to such a military operation. According to Oppenheim, *when a state commits cruelties against and persecution of its nationals in such a way as to deny their fundamental human rights and to shock the conscience of mankind, intervention in the interests of humanity might be legally permissible.*[1] The vexed question of humanitarian intervention will now be thoroughly examined in the light of state practice, relevant rulings of the International Court of Justice (if any), and the theoretical approach to the matter as presented by academic debates and the writings of those learned in the law in general.

HISTORICAL EVIDENCE OF HUMANITARIAN INTERVENTIONS

In the massive material on humanitarian intervention that I have gone through, the contribution of Thucydides to the subject matter has been unduly neglected.[2] Even Grotius scarcely makes mention of him.[3]

The Thucydidean historical work, a masterpiece of political philosophy and science, sets an authoritative example of humanitarian intervention in international relations. The affairs that follow should be seen in the light of the fact that Greek cities in ancient times were states themselves.[4] First, Book IV of *The History of the Peloponnesian War* may at first sight be said to pose an example of humanitarian intervention; on its way to Sicily, the Athenian fleet was met with a sea storm, which forced the ships to seek refuge in the

Peloponnese (Pylos).[5] As the war between Athens and Sparta was at its apex, the Athenian navy members were arrested by the Lacedaemonians. Cleon, the Athenian demagogue, forcefully urged the Athenian Assembly for a military campaign to prevent their fellow citizens from being massacred. Although the incident might be better described as an operation to save nationals abroad (since the Athenian prisoners of war were not subjects of the Spartans), it has generated the criteria for a legitimate humanitarian intervention as these were formulated in the speech of the Athenian general Demosthenes only a while before the commencement of the military rescue operation: *Men who have gathered in this venture, let no one of you wish to be esteemed a man of rationality; but, instead, with plain courage, which leaves no moment for deliberation, let him attack the opponents and even be optimistic that he will eventually be victorious. When matters reach a point of overwhelming necessity, as the present case is, crude reflection is least needed in view of the instant danger.*[6] Secondly, in Book I, an account is given of a clear instance of humanitarian intervention. The Island of Lesbos (member of the Athenian Empire–Commonwealth or Confederation of city-states) revolted from Athens.

The Athenians set sail against the Mytilenians (the inhabitants of Lesbos) and warned them that if they were to refuse an order to surrender, they would demolish their fortifications. An embassy of Mytilenians seeked the help of Sparta thus: *Come to the help of Mytilene. It is our lives that we are risking; an even more general calamity will follow if you will not listen to us.*[7] The very basic criteria for humanitarian intervention were in this case fulfilled: (i) the Mytilenians were subjects of a state (Athens), (ii) they consented to the military intervention undertaken for their own sake, and (iii) they faced the imminent danger of a humanitarian catastrophe. The Spartans, indeed, dispatched a fleet that reached the coast of Lesbos but never engaged in fighting. The conservative foreign policy of Sparta dictated that the military forces of the state were to keep an eye on a possible revolt of the Helot population in the Peloponnese. This affair serves, if nothing else, as an instance clearly showing that humanitarian disaster might, indeed, be the outcome of non-intervention, as it eventually was with the Mytilenians. Therefore, humanitarian intervention in cases of instant necessity is a must.

STATE PRACTICE

Pre-Charter Unilateral Humanitarian Interventions

Intervention of Great Britain, France, and Russia in Aid of Greek Revolutionaries

The joint intervention of Great Britain, France, and Russia in support of the Greek insurgents against Turkish oppressive rule is said as being the earliest example of true humanitarian intervention.[8] The treaty between the three powers, signed in London on 6 July 1827,[9] lays down in its preamble the grounds on which they justified their intervention.[10] According to paragraph 1 of the Preamble, of concern was "all the disorders of anarchy caused by the struggle, which both impede the commerce of the states of Europe and gave opportunity to pirates which not only expose the subjects of the High Contracting Parties to grievous losses, but also render necessary measures which are burdensome for their observation and suppression."[11] Further, by paragraph 2 of the Preamble, two of the powers (Great Britain and France) "had received from the Greeks an earnest invitation to interpose their Mediation with the Ottoman Porte,[12] and together with the Emperor of Russia, animated with the desire of *putting a stop to the effusion of blood, and of preventing the evils of every kind,* had resolved to combine and regulate their efforts with a view to re-establish peace-efforts demanded *no less by sentiments of humanity, than by interests for the tranquillity of Europe.*"[13] The treaty was primarily an offer of mediation in the transition to Greek autonomy.[14]

The Navy Battle of Navarino took place on the 20th October 1827 and ended with a serious defeat of the Turkish forces, and the withdrawal of the Egyptian army from the Morea. Ian Brownlie dismisses the characterization of the action as an instance of humanitarian intervention as "ex post factoism,"[15] saying that the governments of the day did not refer to a legal justification for intervention[16] and that jurists and historians have ascribed numerous motives to the action.[17] He concludes that the substantial motive was the prevention of racial extermination in the Morea, but this cannot be discussed "in terms of a legal concept which probably did not exist at the time."[18] At this point, Professor Brownlie manifestly contradicts himself. Earlier (in the very same publication), he acknowledged that a majority of nineteenth-century publicists recognized a right of humanitarian intervention.[19] More important perhaps is his assertion that Great Britain and France might have participated in the action due to fears of unilateral intervention by Russia. This may throw some light on the diplomatic background to the London Treaty. There is evidence that Ibrahim's plan to commit genocide in Greece was only a pretext for an alliance between Britain and Russia against

Turkey.[20] Nevertheless, during the middle stages of the Greek Revolt, support for Greece was explained more on in the context of Europe's emotional interest. This was reflected in the orders from Lord Bathurst, secretary of state for the colonies, to Sir Harry Neale, commander in chief of the Mediterranean Station, in February 1826:

> *His Majesty has long had reason to lament the atrocities which have disgraced the contest in which Greece has been for many years unhappily involved. . . . When it is understood, that, whether with the consent of the Porte or not, designs are avowed by Ibrahim Pacha to extirpate systematically a whole community, to seize upon the women and children of the Morea, to transport them to Egypt, and to re-people the Morea from Africa and Asia, to change, in fact, that part of Greece from an European State, into one resembling the States of Barbary; His Majesty cannot, as the Sovereign of an European State, hear of such an attempt without demanding of Ibrahim Pacha, either an explicit disavowal of his ever having entertained such an intention, or a formal renunciation of it, if ever entertained.*[21]

Simon Chesterman[22] argues that "the incident is at best a questionable precedent for the doctrine of humanitarian intervention. Russian involvement had little to do with humanitarian concerns and—despite the public statements of British officials—it was this that served as the catalyst for intervention."[23] Also, before embarking on an analysis of the incident, he cites[24] *Historicus*, obviously in an attempt to support his view: "*The emancipation of Greece was a high act of policy above and beyond the domain of law*."[25] Unquestionably, the joint intervention of the Great Powers was, indeed, a high act of policy. Anyone denying this reality would simply do injustice to the actual facts. To deny the underlying strategic expediencies or commercial interests of the intervening Powers would certainly be a mistake, but to assert that these have been the primary motives, let alone the only ones, to the joint military action undertaken would amount to a distortion of history. Such an assertion would unjustifiably put into doubt the humanitarian sentiments of the highly civilized Europeans. It would also minimize the decisive role played by the Great Powers in the celebrated liberation and independence of Greece, that since the conquest of Constantinople by the Ottomans in 1453, it had undergone the most onerous and disgraceful (albeit eventually glorious) period of her history. Further, it would marginalize the ingenuity and magnanimity shown by brilliant British leaders, especially that of George Canning, then–prime minister. The contribution of Canning to the freedom of Hellas has been duly respected and honored by the Greeks. The joint intervention of Great Britain, France, and Russia in aid of the Greek insurgents (1827) remains a paradigm example of humanitarian intervention, which put a halt to a major humanitarian catastrophe, thus affirming the sanctity of human life.

French Occupation of Syria, 1860–1861

In 1860, thousands of Maronite Christians were killed by Muslims on Mount Lebanon, then part of Syria but within the Ottoman Empire. After a meeting of the ambassadors of Great Britain, France, Prussia, Russia, and Austria, a convention was signed.[26] Under the terms of the Convention, the sultan, wishing to stop, by prompt and efficacious measures, the effusion of blood in Syria, and to show his firm resolution to establish order and peace among the populations placed under his sovereignty, agreed to the dispatch of twelve thousand troops to Syria to contribute toward the reestablishment of tranquility.[27] France was to provide half the number. A French force was sent, but it came across the restoration of order by the Ottoman local government. Despite that, the French troops occupied parts of Syria, and warships remained in the area from August 1860 to June 1861. Brownlie includes this as the most likely exception to his general statement that international practice in the nineteenth century discloses no genuine case of humanitarian intervention.[28] However, it has been said that the measures taken by the Ottoman sultan made foreign intervention unnecessary and suspicious in view of the various interests of European states in the declining Ottoman Empire. It has also been asserted that the Christians were responsible for the strife.[29] Nevertheless, a crucial aspect of the incident that renders it an instance of humanitarian intervention is the absence of interest on the part of the parties to the action taken. Although it took place in the context of French colonialism in the area, the occupying force departed when the mandate came to a conclusion. In a protocol signed before the adoption of the Convention Between Great Britain, Austria, France, Prussia, Russia, and Turkey, the powers declared "in the most formal manner" that they would not seek any territorial advantage, exclusive influence, or concession under the pretext of the occupation. There should be no doubt that the concerns of the powers, especially France, for the Christian populations were purely humanitarian.

United States Intervention in Cuba, 1898

The US intervention in Cuba 1898 seems to be another instance of humanitarian intervention in state practice preceding the adoption of the UN Charter. Stowell refers to it as "*one of the most important instances of humanitarian intervention*."[30] Chesterman, on the other hand, citing Fonteyne, says that "the action was but the flashpoint of the broader war with Spain. In a matter of months, the Spanish navy was defeated. Spain had relinquished the remnants of its empire, the United States had established herself as a world power, and

Cuba was an American protectorate."[31] Atrocities were committed by Spanish authorities in Cuba attempting to control the insurrection of 1985. Beyond doubt, the Spanish policy of forcing the population into concentration camps in order to identify revolutionaries instigated genuine outcry in the United States. According to the estimations of Ferrell, about two hundred thousand Cubans perished while in the concentration camps.[32] Another factor leading to the US intervention was the destruction of the US battleship *Maine*, probably by a Spanish submarine mine.[33]

In his special message to Congress on 11 April 1898, President McKinley outlined three justifications for US intervention in the conflict: "the cause of humanity, protection of US citizens, and self-defense."[34] A resolution was then passed, authorizing intervention because of "abhorrent conditions which have shocked the moral sense of the people of the United States, have been a disgrace to Christian civilization, culminating, as they have, in the destruction of a United States battle ship."[35] The goal of the intervention was to secure the independence of Cuba.

Fonteyne, cited again by Chesterman, does not include the intervention in Cuba as an instance of humanitarian intervention, as in his view it lacks a clearly humanitarian motive.[36] But such a view, it seems to me, could not stand as valid argument militating against the characterization of the intervention as humanitarian. True, states may be driven to interventions by "mixed" motives. This does not mean that interventions under these circumstances may not be described as humanitarian.

It is interesting that Teson concludes his brief survey of pre-Charter practice by stating that the most important precedent for a right of humanitarian intervention is the Second World War itself.[37] Citing Michael Walzer's just war analysis of the conflict,[38] he argues that the "Allies fought Fascism not just because Hitler and Mussolini engaged in military aggression, but to defend dignity, reason, human rights, and decency . . . against degradation, authoritarianism, irrationality, and obscurantism."[39] This view is also endorsed here, and, as Teson put it, the example of World War II is the "paradigm of a just war."

Post-Charter Unilateral Humanitarian Interventions

Let us now turn to some instances of the post-charter state practice.

Belgian and US intervention in the Congo, 1964

In 1964, one-third of the Congo came under the control of a rebel group based in Stanleyville. The rebel forces took a thousand or so foreign residents hostage and threatened to kill them. Peaceful efforts to free the hostages having failed, Belgian forces intervened with United Kingdom logistical assistance and United States aircrafts. The troops were withdrawn after a successful operation. In the 1970s, the mission was characterized as one of the clearest modern instances of true humanitarian intervention and one that should be viewed as lawful in character.[40] In a note to the address to the Security Council, Belgium spoke of the mission as being "*a legal, moral and humanitarian operation which conforms to the highest aims of the United Nations: the defence and protection of fundamental human rights.*"[41] The United States, in a letter to the Security Council, stated that "the sole purpose of this humanitarian mission was to liberate hostages whose lives were in danger."[42] However, as Harris[43] observes, the rescue operation was undertaken under the consent of the Congolese government and hence was not dependent upon any right to humanitarian intervention.[44] Another reason for the doubtful description of the intervention as a humanitarian one is that it took place in the context of colonialism.[45]

Indian Invasion of Bangladesh, 1971

Until 1971, Pakistan consisted of East and West Pakistan, with India between the two parts. In March 1971, East Pakistan declared itself independent under the name of Bangladesh. Although the Pakistan army was initially successful in suppressing the rebellion, rebel guerrilla forces launched a general offensive with considerable success. As there was evidence to suggest that India, which had taken into its territory about one million refugees from East Pakistan,[46] had given the guerrillas military assistance, Pakistani and Indian troops clashed in the border area (the Indian prime minister, Indira Gandhi, having first declared war). Eventually Pakistan surrendered, and Bangladesh has since received recognition (that of Pakistan included!) as an independent state. The Indian intervention in East Pakistan is commonly held up as one of the more promising examples of humanitarian intervention. Teson calls it "*an almost perfect example*";[47] Fonteyne says that "*it probably constitutes the clearest case of forceful individual humanitarian intervention in this century*";[48] and Bowett includes it as the only possible illustration of the practice in the period 1945–1986.[49] In the Security Council, India's representative stated that "we have on this particular occasion absolutely nothing but the purest of motives and the purest of intentions: to rescue the people of East Bengal from what they are suffering."[50] India's prime minister, when appealing to foreign governments for help, said that the general and systematic nature of inhuman treatment inflicted on the Bangladesh population was evidence of a crime against humanity.' It is not surprising that Lillich stated that the intervention was *morally* justified.[51]

Tanzanian Intervention in Uganda, 1978–1979

Tanzania's intervention in Uganda has been a clear case, and indeed is, of humanitarian intervention. Long years of animosity between the Ugandan dictator Amin and the president of Tanzania Nyerere culminated in 1978, when Ugandan forces occupied part of Tanzania invoking self-defense. The Tanzanian president stated that this was an act of war, and went on to say that he had the capacity and determination to hit Amin. The latter offered to withdraw his forces. However, there was serious evidence that the Ugandan occupation had resulted in acts of massacre, destruction, and rape. So the Tanzanian armed forces penetrated into Uganda, as Amin could not be "let off." Consequently, the dictatorial regime of Amin in Uganda's capital, Kampala, was defeated and deposed. Tanzania's president stated: "Those who say that Tanzania created a bad precedent are liars. What we did was exemplary at a time when the OAU found itself unable to condemn Amin. I think we have seta good precedent inasmuch as when African nations find themselves collectively incapable of punishing a single country, then each country has to look after itself."[52] The international community approved of the intervention.[53] This is clearly attested by the fact the new regime in Kampala was immediately recognized. There was no debate on the matter either in the Security Council or the General Assembly. Teson pointedly concludes that "on the whole the Tanzanian action was legitimized by the international community,"[54] which "virtually approved the Tanzanian intervention."[55]

Assessment of State Practice

In view of the post-Charter State practice, there is evidence strongly suggesting the existence of a customary international law right of unilateral humanitarian intervention. We try to impose order on diplomatic history. Humanitarian intervention is the best explanation of the Tanzanian action, for example; in the relevant words of Dworkin, "it is the one that interprets that piece of history in its best light."[56]

It is noteworthy that the emergence of a customary international law right of humanitarian intervention was further endorsed in the Nicaragua case,[57] which here deserves some elaboration. The Court held that reliance by a state on a novel right or an unprecedented exception to the principle of non-intervention might, if shared by other states, tend toward modification of customary international law.[58] Although the Court found that the argument derived from the preservation of human rights in Nicaragua cannot afford a legal justification for the conduct of the United States, went on to make a critical observation: "no doubt the provision of strictly humanitarian aid to persons or forces in another country, whatever their political affiliations or objectives, cannot be regarded as unlawful intervention, or in any other way contrary to international law."[59] This dictum clearly paved the way for the establishment of a post-charter international custom of unilateral humanitarian intervention. The ICJ, having reaffirmed the criteria for the formation of new rules of customary international law as laid down in the *North Sea Continental Shelf* cases, provided a definition of *opinio juris*, essential requirement to the creation of international custom: "either the states taking such action or other States in a position to react to it, must have behaved so that their conduct *is evidence of a belief that this practice is rendered obligatory by the existence of a rule of law requiring it*."[60]

It seems that even the best cases of humanitarian intervention, such as *Bangladesh* (1971) and *Uganda* (1978–1979), lack the necessary *opinio juris*. The UK Foreign Office Policy Document No. 148 on *Humanitarian Intervention* is illuminating: "often the humanitarian benefits of an intervention are either not claimed by the intervening state or are only put forward as an *ex post facto* justification of the intervention. . . . State practice, especially since 1945, at best provides only a handful of genuine cases of humanitarian intervention, and on most assessments none at all." The FCO Policy Document concluded, in a rather ambiguous language, that *the best case that can be made in support of humanitarian intervention is that it cannot be said to be unambiguously illegal.*

However, a widespread argument in favor of a right of humanitarian intervention is that it survived the passage of the UN Charter. It is noteworthy that in *Nicaragua*, the ICJ noted that the Charter does not cover the whole area of the regulation of the use of force in international relations. Particularly, Article 51 refers to the "*inherent* right of self-defense." Bowett writes: "It is fallacious to assume that members have only those rights which the Charter accords them; on the contrary they have those rights which general international law accords to them except in so far as they have surrendered them under the Charter." The prohibition in Article 2(4), Bowett continues, "left the right of self-defence unimpaired." Thus, it is hereby proposed that a customary right of humanitarian intervention is a legitimate form of self-defense or self-help. Michael Reisman says: "*because rights without remedies are not rights at all, prohibiting the unilateral vindication of clear violations of rights when multilateral possibilities do not obtain is virtually to terminate those rights*."[61] However, this statement does not interpret the scope of the right of self-defense as a justification for unilateral humanitarian intervention.

If, however, this last argument finds no support, then an argument based on the hierarchy of international law sources may be put forward. Treaties and custom are of equal authority.[62] In the present case, there is obviously a conflict between Article 2(4) of the UN Charter (itself an International Treaty) and an alleged emerging post-charter customary law right of humanitarian intervention. In deciding this conflict, a basic principle (in fact, a general principle of law) may be applicable; namely *lex specialis derogat legi generali* (a special law prevails over a general law). "Special law," in the present conflict, is the customary right of humanitarian intervention, whereas "general law" is the UN Charter Article 2(4) provision laying down a *general* prohibition of the use of force. It may thus be argued that the former (humanitarian intervention being a *special kind* of forceful action) prevails over the latter. For the purposes of the present analysis, it should be clear enough by now that pre- as well as post-Charter state practice indicates, at least as far as I can see, the existence of a customary international law right of *unilateral* humanitarian intervention. Additionally, UN practice has in recent years witnessed a trend toward humanitarian intervention or aid and needs to be looked at in passing.

Post-Charter UN Humanitarian Interventions

The end of the Cold War has transformed the situation in the UN Security Council, so that the way has been paved for humanitarian interventions by this political institution.[63] The approach of the past, that the United Nations is not authorized "to intervene in matters which are essentially within the domestic jurisdiction of any state,"[64] is not the international position anymore. As the former UN secretary general Perez de Cuellar stated, "we are witnessing . . . the belief that the defence of the oppressed in the name of morality should prevail over frontiers and legal documents."[65]

Iraq, 1991

The period after the defeat of Iraq in the Kuwait crisis witnessed risings of the Kurds in the northern part of the country, which were brutally repressed by the Iraqi Army in disregard of the relevant Geneva Conventions provisions or human rights international instruments. The international community was particularly moved by the fate of hundreds of thousands of Kurdish refugees abandoning their homes. Security Council Resolution 688 (1991) stated that the Council condemned the repression of the Iraqi civilian population in Iraq. The UK, the United States, and other states brought forces into Iraq in aid of the Kurdish refugees. The UK foreign secretary spoke thus about the military operations purposes: "*We are vigorously pursuing this proposal for safe havens. Our aim is to create places and conditions in which the refugees can feel secure. We are not talking of a separate Kurdistan or a permanent UN presence.*"[66] The objectives of the intervention were humanitarian. As Professor Greenwood very well put it:

it is difficult to resist the conclusion that the intervening states were in practice asserting a right of humanitarian intervention of some kind.[67] This conclusion is reinforced by the statement of the Minister of Defence in the House of Commons when a "no fly" zone was imposed in southern Iraq: "the zones were established to meet situations of *severe humanitarian need.*"

Liberia, 1990

In 1990, a civil war between different factions brought about anarchy in the country. A declaration issued by the Economic Community of West African States (ECOWAS) Heads of State, following the despatch of peacekeeping forces, read as follows: "first and foremost to stop the senseless killing of innocent civilian nationals and foreigners and to help the Liberian people to restore their democratic institutions."[68] It is unclear whether the government of Liberia gave its consent to the intervention.[69] Again, as Greenwood observes "the intervention seems to involve the assertion of some kind of right of humanitarian intervention."[70]

Kosovo, 1999

The situation in Kosovo[71] involved serious violations of human rights, and there was an impending humanitarian catastrophe well before the NATO action (undertaken to put a stop to the ethnic cleansing of Albanians) began. The Security Council Resolution 1160, adopted a year before the NATO operations, referred to "intense fighting in Kosovo and in particular the excessive and indiscriminate use of force by Serbian Security forces and the Yugoslavian Army which have resulted in the displacement of over 230,000 persons from their homes"[72] and dictated immediate steps to avert the "*impending humanitarian catastrophe.*" The UK Representative to the UN justified the NATO military intervention, undertaken without express authorization of the Security Council, on the ground that a right to take military action in case of overwhelming humanitarian necessity is recognized by international law.[73] In my view, the use of force by NATO was *prima facie* not contrary to international law, and was justified on a right of humanitarian intervention.[74] However, the historical background to the conflict should also have been taken into consideration in the first place, in which case the intervention ought most probably to have been rendered unlawful.

Conclusively, as Greenwood stated, quite pointedly, "it is no longer tenable to assert that whenever a government massacres its own people . . . international law forbids military intervention altogether."[75]

The argument can be made, however, that the carrying out of humanitarian intervention authorized by the Security Council may militate against the existence of a right to humanitarian intervention on part of states.

Nevertheless, a counterargument would be that in case a state makes use of its veto power in the Security Council, thus disabling the latter from taking military action where human rights are clearly violated, states may then be capable of intervening unilaterally to prevent the occurrence of gross violation of human rights.

LEGAL AND POLITICAL THEORY ON HUMANITARIAN INTERVENTION

This subsection (of the second Part of the present chapter) will address the fundamental issue of the moral justification of humanitarian intervention (*bellum*). An inquiry into the ethical foundations of the international legal system. Indeed, the link between international law and political (and therefore moral) philosophy is consistent with the Grotian tradition in international law that regard the Law of Nations as founded upon universal moral values.

Sovereignty versus Human Rights

At first sight there is a legal duty to refrain from the internal affairs of other states. Each state is bound to respect the sovereignty of its neighbour states. This view has its roots in legal positivism. The German philosopher Wolff was the first to separate the international law principles from the ethics of the individual. De Vattel, along similar line of argument said: "The duties of a nation towards itself are of purely national concern, and no foreign power has any right to interfere."[76] Great academic debate has erupted over the general prohibition of the use of force as stipulated in Article 2(4) of the UN Charter,[77] especially the wording "against the territorial integrity or political independence of any State."[78]

It is necessary to show that a right of unilateral humanitarian intervention is compatible with Article 2(4) of the UN Charter.[79] The only exceptions to the general prohibition of the threat or use of force are the "inherent right of individual or collective self-defence in the face of an armed attack against a State in Article 51 of the UN Charter, and enforcement actions by the Security Council or by a regional organization or group of States authorized to use force by the Security Council under Chapter VII of the Charter." Neither of these provisions is applicable to unilateral humanitarian intervention. Two arguments may be employed: that a genuine humanitarian intervention would not be a use of force against the "territorial integrity or political independence" of another state, or that it would not be "inconsistent with the Purposes of the United Nations." It is noteworthy that in their commentary on the Charter, Goodrich and Hambro observed that it is possible to construe the language as allowing certain limited uses of force, such as a temporary intervention for protective purposes.[80] Teson, noting that the promotion of human rights is as important a purpose in the Charter as the control of international conflict, concludes that to argue that humanitarian intervention is prohibited by Article 2(4) is a distortion.[81]

Article 2(4) must be read and interpreted in conjunction with the purposes of the United Nations, one of which is the promotion of human rights. The Preamble to the Charter reads as follows: "We the peoples of the United Nations determined . . . to reaffirm faith in fundamental human rights, in the dignity and worth of the human person, in the equal rights . . . of nations large and small." Article 1(3) states: "To achieve international co-operation in solving international problems of an economic, social, cultural, or *humanitarian* character, and in *promoting* and encouraging *respect for human rights and for fundamental freedoms for all*."[82] Further, Article 55(c) of the Charter declares that the United Nations shall promote "universal respect for, and observance of human rights and fundamental freedoms for all without distinction as to race, sex, language, or religion." More importantly, by Article 56 "all members pledge themselves to take joint *and separate action* in *co-operation* with the Organization *for the achievement of the purposes set forth in Article 55*."[83] Further, Professor *Greenwood*, in a memorandum submitted in response to a request from the UK House of Commons Select Committee on Foreign Affairs in connection with its hearings on the NATO intervention in Kosovo 1999, quite pointedly states:

> The development of international human rights law since 1945, through global agreements such as the Genocide Convention and the International Covenant on Civil and Political Rights and regional instruments such as the European Convention on Human Rights, has reached the point where the treatment by a State of its own population can no longer be regarded as an internal matter. In particular, widespread and systematic violations of human rights involving the loss of life on a large scale are well established as a matter of international concern.

The clear deduction from the above should be that the right of unilateral humanitarian intervention is clearly not incompatible with Article 2(4) of the UN Charter.

Apart from the legal debate, however, I would suggest, from the moral standpoint, that the rights of states under international law derive from individual rights. The proper role of the state is to ensure protection of the rights of the individuals.[84] As Hersch Lauterpacht very well put it, "states are like individuals; it is due to the fact that states *are composed* of individual human beings. . . . The dignity of the individual human being is a matter of direct concern to international law."[85] This is the true meaning of the Grotian analogy of states and individuals. Therefore, in my opinion, state sovereignty must give way to the protection of human rights whenever these are flagrantly violated.[86] In view of the preceding theoretical discussion in this section, which is hoped not to have been at a high level of abstraction, I strongly submit that states have *a moral right*, to say the least, to *unilaterally* intervene in cases of overwhelming humanitarian necessity. The writings of learned jurists should, in my submission, be taken much more seriously into account, and perhaps cease to be seen merely as subsidiary sources of public international law (despite Article 38(1)(d) of the ICJ Statute). Further, State practice of ancient times cannot be neglected.[87] The adoption of the UN Charter is not meant to suggest that pre-charter international customary law has automatically been abrogated. Instead, customary law can, indeed, be considered as part and parcel of a unified international law tradition; as living international custom, living law, which may still find appeal in the modern world.

Just War (*Bellum* Justum)

The justification for humanitarian intervention must be seen in the context of whether it is ever lawful to wage war.

War Is Not in Conflict with the Law of Nature

Cicero has presented: "What can be done against force without force?"[88] In Ulpian we read: "Cassius writes that it is permissible to repel *force by force*, and this *right* is bestowed by nature. From this moreover it appears that it is permissible to repel arms by means of arms."[89] That war is not in conflict with the law of nature is proved from general agreement among natural lawyers.[90] The jurist Gaius says: "Natural reason permits defence of oneself against danger."[91] "For there is," says Josephus, "that law of nature which applies in the case of all creatures, that *they wish to live;* and therein lies the reason why we consider those as enemies who clearly wish to rob us of life."[92]

Biblical Texts Arguments That War Is Compatible with the Law of the Gospel

Despite the divine commandment given to Moses, "Thou shalt not kill,"[93] two other commandments of the Old Testament that seem to conflict with the former ones, to say the least, are hereby quoted: "An eye for an eye, a tooth for a tooth."[94] Despite the call for love in the New Testament, these provisions could still be held valid. In my humble opinion, Moses (as well as mankind) has been given the authority of God to enforce divine law on earth.

On this rationale, transgressors of law may, if necessary, be put to death. Indeed, a comparison may be made between the right to wage war and the death penalty. Being fervent exponent of the latter, I would argue that war may be justified on the same grounds as is the penalty of death. If the right to inflict capital punishment and to defend citizens by arms against criminals should be taken away, there would follow a riot of crimes, and illegality among nations. Paul thus speaks: "If I have wronged any one, and have committed *anything worthy of death*, I refuse not to die."[95] There are certain crimes for which justice permits, or even demands, punishment by death. I strongly submit that it is in the *love of innocent men* that both capital punishments and *just wars* have their origin. The words of Chrysostom on human punishments become here relevant: "men do such things not in cruelty but in kindness."[96] There is, on the other hand, the consideration that we are bound to love our enemies by the example of God. But the same God inflicts punishments upon some wicked men, even in this life. Further, a counterargument may be phrased as follows: "God is called gracious, merciful, and long-suffering."[97] Yet, it is Christ himself who inflicts severe punishments upon disobedient Jews, and uncovers their hypocrisy.[98] The occasional wrath of Jesus Christ was imitated by the apostles, who used the power which had been given them by God for the punishment of wrongdoers. Chrysostom, on First Corinthians, iv. 21 states: "Shall I kill. . . . For as there is a spirit of gentleness, so there is a spirit of severity."

War as Punishment

Grotius, drawing on the ideas advanced by Gentili,[99] admitted a right to wage war for the purposes of punishment.[100]

Furthermore, I should like to submit a proposition by no means original, yet, as it will be shown, of everlasting value. The moral justification for a just war lie primarily in a deep feeling of *anger.* Aristotle, in his masterpiece *Rhetoric*, made the point explicitly: "anger is the human feeling which makes a man exact *revenge* upon someone who is thought *to deserve it.*"[101] Anger, though according to some views the ugliest passion, forms proof of the fact that human beings are moral agents. It is evidence that people, being members of a moral community, by no means approve of instances of violation of moral and legal principles.[102] Therefore a just war may be implemented as a measure of *just retribution* and deterrence, both theories of punishment being applicable; such a proposition directly fits the case of humanitarian intervention.[103] On the one hand, intervention of this kind can be launched as a means of retribution against the state that violates the fundamental human rights of its own nationals; on the other, it may serve as a vehicle for deterring humanitarian catastrophe from taking place in a given situation.

War in the Name of the Oppressed

Saint Ambrose had written that "he who does not keep harm off a friend, if he can, is as much in fault as he who causes it."[104] Grotius and Gentili, who quoted Saint Ambrose, entirely share this view. However, Grotius's position differs from that of Gentili, in that, according to Grotius, the justice of war waged on behalf of oppressed subjects is clearly a legal right rather than a moral duty. In *De jure belli ac pacis*, II, xxv, para.8, it is stated:

> *If, however, the wrong is obvious, in case some Busiris, Phalaris, or Thracian Diomede should inflict upon his subjects such treatment as no one is warranted in inflicting, the exercise of the right vested in human society is not precluded. In conformity with this principle Constantine took up arms against Maxentius and Licinius, and other Roman emperors.*

Hersch Lauterpacht refers to this as the "first authoritative statement of the principle of humanitarian intervention."[105]

NOTES

1. *Oppenheim's International Law* (9th ed. Sir Robert Jennings and Sir A. Watts, Longman 1996) p.442; H. Lauterpacht's rationale for humanitarian intervention is that "ultimately peace is much more endangered by tyrannical contempt for human rights than by attempts to assert, through intervention, the sanctity of human personality" (*International Law and Human Rights*, London: Stephens & Sons, 32).

2. See Phillipson, Coleman, *The International Law and Custom of Ancient Greece and Rome* (London: Macmillan, 1911).

3. Here is what he mentions: "In Thucydides the Corinthians find it just that 'each party should punish its own subjects'"(*De jure belli ac pacis, ante*, II, xxv, 1). Even this reference ignores the context in which these words have been spoken, and may therefore be misleading as regards the era's state practice on intervention.

4. It is precisely because of the fact that the Greek cities were themselves recognized as States—albeit with common origins of blood, language, and religion—that the Peloponnesian War, though often described as the greatest "Civil War" in antiquity, was in fact an international conflict.

5. Coincidently, more than two thousand years later, the Navy Battle of Navarino, described above, was to take place on the same spot, Navarino being the contemporary name of ancient Pylos.

6. Thucydides, *History of the Peloponnesian War* (Cambridge: Harvard University Press, 1972) Book IV, para. XXXVIII. (emphasis added). Note the striking similarity between the terminology used in this text, and the one employed in the *Caroline Case* 1840: "It will be for Her Majesty's Government to show a necessity of self-defence, instant, overwhelming, leaving no moment for deliberation." It makes one wonder

whether Mr. Webster was a fervent reader of Thucydides. In fact, research I have done into his biography have revealed that indeed he studied Thucydides to a significant extent. A criterion is that humanitarian intervention must correspond to the dictates of the proportionality principle. The *Caroline* case principle may be seen as one that sets limits to the use of force in general and calls for adherence to proportionality. The classic formulation of Mr. Webster may in this context be quoted: "did nothing unreasonable or excessive; since the act is justified by the necessity of self-defence, must be limited by that necessity, and kept clearly within it."6.

7. Thucydides, *History of the Peloponnesian War, ante*, Book II, para.14.

8. See Stowell, *Intervention in International Law* (Washington, DC: John Byrne & Co, 1921), 126–27; Anthony D' Amato, 'The Invasion of Panama was a Lawful Response to Tyranny' (1990) 84 *A.J.I.L.* 516, 519.

9. This was the formalization of a protocol signed at Petersburg, 4 April 1826, by the Russian chancellor, the Russian ambassador to London, and the Duke of Wellington. It was then communicated to Paris, where it gained support.

10. Treaty between Great Britain, France, and Russia, for the Pacification of Greece, signed at London, 6 July 1827 (Edward Hertslet, *The Map of Europe by Treaty*, London: Butterworths, 1875, vol. 1, 769–70).

11. See extensively John Westlake, International Law (2nd edition, Cambridge: Cambridge University Press, 1910), 319, n 3.

12. Chesterman, in his *Just War or Just Peace: Humanitarian Intervention and International Law* (Oxford: Oxford University Press, 2001), 29, n 167, says that "as the intervention took place within what was then Turkish territory, it is not an instance of intervention by consent." With great respect, this view seems to be rather absurd. Who should have been expected to give consent to the joint humanitarian intervention of the Great Powers other than the insurgents themselves? Is it conceivable that the Ottoman Porte could have consented to an intervention by European States in the territory of its Empire for the purpose of liberating its own oppressed subjects? But, see below, at page 55, the particular circumstances under which the Sultan's consent was given to the French intervention in Syria, 1860–1861.

13. Emphasis supplied.

14. On this, see CW Crawley, *The Question of Greek Independence: A Study of British Policy in the Near East, 1821–1833* (Cambridge: Cambridge University Press, 1930), 79.

15. Brownlie, 'Humanitarian Intervention,' in John N Moore (ed.), *Law and Civil War in the Modern World* (Baltimore, Maryland: Johns Hopkins University Press, 1974), 220.

16. Brownlie, *ibid.*, 220–21; Brownlie, *International Law and the Use of Force by States* (Oxford: Clarendon Press), 339.

17. Brownlie, 'Humanitarian Intervention,' *supra*, 339.

18. Brownlie, *ibid.*, 339.

19. Brownlie, *ibid.*, 338.

20. Crawley, *ante*, 49, 54.

21. See Woodhouse, *The Battle of Navarino* (London: Hodder & Stoughton, 1965), 35–36.

22. Clearly adopting a Brownlie approach to the subject matter.

23. Chesterman, *Just War or Just Peace, ante*, 32.

24. *ibid.*, 28.

25. William Vernon Harcourt, *Letters by Historicus on Some Questions of International Law: Reprinted from 'The Times' with Considerable Additions* (London: Macmillan, 1863), 6.

26. Convention Between Great Britain, Austria, France, Prussia, Russia, and Turkey, respecting measures to be taken for the Pacification of Syria, signed at Paris, 5 September 1860, in Hertslet, *ante*, 1455, Preamble paragraph 1.

27. *Ibid.* Art. 1.

28. Brownlie, *International Law and the Use of Force by States, ante,* 340.

29. See Thomas Frank and Nigel Rodley, 'After Bangladesh: The Law of Humanitarian Intervention by Military Force' (1973) 67 *A.J.I.L.* 275, 282, citing the Minute of the British Commissioner to Syria, who remarked that 'the original provocation proceeded from the Christians.'

30. C. Stowell, *Intervention in International law, ante*, 481. It is also cited by Michael Reisman and Myres McDougal, 'Humanitarian Intervention to Protect the Ibos' in Lillich (ed.) *Humanitarian Intervention and the United Nations* (Charlottesville: University Press of Virginia, 1973), 182–83. Oscar Straus, an American commentator, states that one would search in vain the records of the world's history to find a more striking example of a war undertaken by any nation from motives singularly humane and free from selfish interests and purpose (Humanitarian Diplomacy of the United States, 1912, 6, *Proceedings of the American Society of International Law*, 50).

31. Apparently, a similar view was put forward by Michael Walzer in his *Just and Unjust Wars: A Moral Argument with Historical Illustrations* (New York: Basic Books, 1992), 103–34.

32. Robert Ferrell, *American Diplomacy: A History* (New York: Norton, 1975), 350.

33. See Moore, *A Digest of International Law* (Washington, DC: Government Printing Office, 1906) vol. 6, 181–84 (Report of Senate Committee on Foreign Relations).

34. President McKinley, Special Message to Congress, 11 April 1898, in Moore, *ibid.,* vol. 6, 219–20.

35. *Ibid.*, vol. 6, 226.

36. Fonteyne, 'The Customary International Law Doctrine of Humanitarian Intervention: Its current Validity Under the UN Charter,' (1974) 4 *California Western ILJ* 203, 210–11.

37. *Ibid.*, pp. 178–79.

38. Michael Walzer, 'World War II: Why Was This War Different?' (1971), 1, *Philosophy and Public Affairs*, 3.

39. Teson, *Humanitarian Intervention, supra*, 178; Chesterman, on the contrary, says that although it may be argued that humanitarian concerns played a part in the Allied involvement in the war, they were nevertheless subsidiary to more traditional motives such as self-defense (*Just War or Just Peace, ante*, 28).

40. See Lillich, 'Forcible Self-Help by States to Protect Human Rights' (1967), 53, *Iowa Law Review*, 325

41. S/6063 (1964).

42. S/6062 (1964).

43. See Harris, *Cases and Materials on International Law* (London Sweet & Maxwell, 1998), 919.

44. Evidence of this is the letter of Prime Minister Tshombe of the Democratic Republic of the Congo to the American ambassador in Leopoldville dated 21 November 1964 (in Whiteman, *Digest of International Law*, *ante*, Vol. 12, 213).

45. On this point, see Thomas Frank and Nigel Rodley, 'After Bangladesh: The Law of Humanitarian Intervention by Military Force' (1973) 67 *AJIL* 275, 288.

46. The International Law Commission summarized events as follows: 'The principle features of this ruthless oppression were the indiscriminate killing of civilians, including women and children and the poorest and the weakest members of the community; the attempt to exterminate or drive out of the country a large part of the Hindu population; the arrest, torture and killing of students, business men and other potential leaders among the Bengalis; the raping of women; the destruction of villages and towns.

47. Teson, *Humanitarian Intervention, ante*, 207.

48. Fonteyne, *The Customary Law Doctrine of Humanitarian Intervention: Its Current Validity Under the UN Charter,' ante*, 204.

49. Derek Bowett, 'The Use of Force for the Protection of Nationals Abroad,' in Antonio Cassese, ed. *The Current Regulation of the Use of Force* (Dordrecht: Martinus Nijhoff, 1986), 50.

50. S/PV 1606 (1971) para. 186.

51. See Lillich, *Humanitarian Intervention, ante*, 114

52. *Keesing's Contemporary Archives: Record of World Events* (hereinafter cited as *Keesing's*) (1979), 29673.

53. The US secretary of state Cyrus Vance stated: 'Our position is very clear; we support President Nyerere's position that according to which Ugandan troops must withdraw immediately': *ibid.*, 29669.

54. Teson, *Humanitarian Intervention*, ante, 187.

55. It is necessary, at this stage, to mention quickly some incidents in which humanitarian motives were indeed marginal; these very incidents should be viewed in the context of the Cold War.

(i) In 1968, Warsaw Pact forces purported to aid the people of Czechoslovakia. The humanitarian motives were rejected by the Security Council. Initially the USSR asserted that the Czech government leaders had requested its assistance in dealing with opponents of the regime. Afterward, it put forward that the socialist community had a duty to intervene whenever socialism came under attack in a socialist state. This was to be called the 'Brezhnev Doctrine.' In 1956, the USSR invasion of Hungary (on which see S/PV.754, 1965 para.53) was condemned by the international community.

(ii) The 1964 intervention in Vietnam and 1965 intervention in the Dominican Republic fall within the same category of interventions.

(iii) The US interventions in Grenada 1983, and Panama 1989, though frequently cited as cases of humanitarian intervention or as pro-democratic interventions, the US never invoked humanitarian intervention as justification for these actions.

56. Ronald Dworkin, *Law's Empire* (London: Fontana, 1986), 87–113.

57. *I.C.J.* Reports 1986, 14.

58. *Nicaragua (Merits)* [1986] ICJ Reports p. 109, para.207.

59. *Ibid.*, 114 para.242.

60. *Ibid.*, 109 para.207.

61. Michael Reisman, 'Sovereignty and Human Rights in Contemporary International Law' (1990) 84 *AJIL* 866, 875.

62. See Michael Akehurst, 'The Hierarchy of the Sources of International Law,' 47 (1974–1975) *B.Y.B.I.L.*, 273.

63. Instances of humanitarian intervention include, inter alia, the UN intervention in the former SFRY 1992, Somalia 1992, and Sierra Leone 1997–1998.

64. UN Charter, Article 2(7).

65. (1991) 22 *Diplomatic World Bulletin.*

66. *H.C. Debates*, Vol. 189, Col. 21; 15 April 1991.

67. Greenwood, 'Is there a Right of Humanitarian Intervention?,' (1993) 49 (2) *The World Today*, 36.

68. UN Doc. S/21485.

69. For a detailed account of the facts, see Greenwood, 'Is there a Right of Humanitarian Intervention?' *ante,* 37.

70. *Ibid.*, 37.

71. For a brief account of the origins of the conflict, see Chesterman, '*Just War or Just Peace*?' *ante,* 207.

72. SCR 1199, 6th paragraph of the Preamble.

73. See S/PV.3988 (1999), 12.

74. See further, the truly excellent memoranda submitted by Professors Christopher Greenwood QC and Vaughan Lowe before the House of Commons Select Committee on Foreign Affairs,*http://www.parliament.the-stationery-office.co.uk/pa/ cm199900/ cmselect/cmfaff;* Hoffmann, *Humanitarian Intervention* (1977).

75. Greenwood, 'Is there a Right of Humanitarian Intervention?' *ante*.

76. de Vattel, 'The Law of Nations' (Washington DC, Carnegie Institution, 1916) I, iii, para.37.

77. See, generally, Brownlie, *International Law and the Use of Force by States, ante*; Schachter, 'The Rights of States to Use Armed Forces' (1984) 82, *Michigan Law Review*, 1620.

78. Walzer proposed that 'any use of force by one state against the political independence of another constitutes aggression and is a criminal act'(*Just and Unjust Wars, ante*, 61.

79. UN Charter Article2(4): 'All Members shall refrain in their international relations from the threat or use of force against the territorial integrity or political independence of any state, or in any other manner inconsistent with the Purposes of the United Nations.'

80. Goodrich and Hambro, *Charter of the United Nations: Commentary and Documents* (Boston: World Peace Foundation, 1946), 68–69.

81. Teson, *Humanitarian Intervention, ante*, 151.

82. UN Charter, Article 1(3) (emphasis added).

83. UN Charter, Article 56 (emphasis added).

84. This presupposes a kind of social, what Rawls has called 'hypothetical' consent in his *Theory of Justice*.

85. H. Lauterpacht, '*The Grotian Tradition in International Law,' ante*, 27 (emphasis original).

86. Most legal scholars who are opposed to humanitarian intervention emphasizing the danger of abuse, are putting forward a policy objection rather than a principled argument. As Professor Greenwood very well put it in his *Memorandum, ante,* 5 'all rights are capable of being abused. The right of self-defence has undoubtedly been the subject of abuse but it is never seriously suggested that international law should not include the right of a State to defend itself.'

87. Thucydides, having detected the unchangeable character of human nature, ably predicted: 'My work is not a piece of writing designed to meet the taste of an immediate public, but was done to last for ever' (*History of the Peloponnesian War, ante,* Book I, para.22).

88. *Letters*, XII, iii 1.

89. *Digest*, XLIII, xvi. 1. 27 (emphasis supplied).

90. Cicero, in regard to force used in the defense of life, wrote: 'There is this law which is not written, but born with us; which we have not learned, have not received, have not read, but which we have caught up, have wrung out from nature herself; a law regarding which we have not been instructed, but in accord with which we have been made; the law that if our life has been placed in jeopardy by any violence, or weapons of enemies, every possible means of securing safety is morally right' (*For Milo*, iv. 10).

91. *Digest*, IX. ii. 4.

92. *Jewish War*, III, viii. 5.

93. *Exodus*, xx. 30.

94. *Leviticus*, xxiv. 20; *Deuteronomy*, xix. 21; see also: 'Thou shalt love thy neighbour (that is an Israelite), *Leviticus*, xix. 18, 'and shalt hate thine enemy, against whom the Jews are bidden to wage implacable war' [*Exodus*, xxxiv. ii, Exodus, xxvii. 19; *Deuteronomy*, xxv. 19].

95. *Acts* xxv. II (emphasis added).

96. *On First Corinthians*, iii. 12; see also Seneca, *On Clemency*, Book I. Chap. ii.

97. *Exodus*, xxxiv. 6.

98. *Matthew,* xxii. 7.

99. Alberico Gentili, *De jure belli* [1612], (Classics of International Law; Oxford: Clarendon Press, 1933).

100. Grotius, *De jure belli ac pacis*, (Kelsey ed. London, 1964) II, xx; Grotius also cites Augustine: 'They think that they should decree the commission of crimes of such sort that if any state upon earth should decree them, or had decreed them, it would deserve to be overthrown by a decree of the human race' (On Benefits, VII, xix, 9). Augustine's statement may qualify as a powerful argument for humanitarian intervention.

101. The element of 'Anger' appears in the Homeric Epics, too (hence the wrath of Achilles in the *Iliad*).

102. This argument is not dissimilar to the one expressed above at page 78 that love of the innocent is the motive for waging war.

103. It is submitted that only in this way can moral order be restored and international legality be preserved.

104. St Ambrose, *De Officiis*, I, xxxvi, para.179.

105. Hersch Lauterpacht, 'The Grotian Tradition in International Law' (1946) 23 *British YBIL* 1, 46.

Chapter 7

The Joint Intervention of the Great Powers in Aid of the Greek Revolutionaries

This chapter serves to indicate that certain powerful British politicians (and certainly Philhellenes such as Stratford Canning) at the time aimed at containing, if not dismembering, the Ottoman Empire. This forms another ground to suppose or assert that the British intervention in Greece—Navarino 1827—was not launched merely as a check upon Russia.

DIPLOMATIC BACKGROUND TO THE INTERVENTION

In March 1821, when the Congress assembled at Laibach, Alexander I had Metternich on his side and, at the same, time, he offered some prospect of mediation if order were restored, and showed some sympathy for Greek hopes which made his letter to Ypsilanti's far from reassuring to the Sultan.

At Constantinople, the Russian ambassador, Stroganov, openly but not officially favored the Greek cause for independence. As soon as the news from Moldavia reached the city, he repudiated the revolt and persuaded the Greek bishops to pronounce the anathema upon it. But the Russian consul the Bucharest did his best to conceal the fact. The Turks, hardly restrained from declaring war on Russia at once, sent about thirty thousand men to the Principalities and took some violent measures ending with the interruption of commerce, the imprisonment of the Russian Embassy's banker, and the execution of the Greek Patriarch. This last step, especially the ill-usage of the body by the mob, did more than anything else to sanctify the cause in the eyes of every Greek. The Patriarch was of course no enemy of the *Hetaireia* and probably knew its secrets, but he had done the most that the Sultan could expect in publicly denouncing the revolt. The Porte quoted the example of Peter the Great, who put his own son to death and abolished the office of Patriarch in Russia. The wholesale massacre of Turks at the beginning of the revolt in the Morea roused the fury of the people in Constantinople the, Stroganoff brought to a head of the unsettled disputes arising out of the Treaty of Bucharest and demanded fulfilment of the treaties in general. Early in June, relations were broken off, the Ambassador retired to Buyukdere and then on board a Russian frigate; in July a new ultimatum of four points was presented, which to the points covered by the treaties, demanded a change of system regarding the Greeks generally. Storganov, without waiting for a written answer, left Constantinople, and war seemed certain. Russia claimed her right to protect the Greeks as Christians: The Sultan asserted his right to deal with them as rebels.

From this moment for the next two years the efforts of Metternich, were devoted to separating the Russo-Turkish dispute from the Greek question, and so to preventing war. The danger was real; Alexander returned home in June and the scale at once began to turn. Society and the army clamored for war. The voice of legitimist and even of common prudence seemed faint. Russia appealed to the Powers to prevent the specter of a religious war by supporting her demands.

The only extermination so far had been that of the Turks in the Morea, followed by isolated reprisals in Constantinople.

The Powers were not prepared to do anything in concert with so suspected an ally as Russia. Austria could never be sincerely her ally in the Eastern Question until it should be time for an undisguised partition. Metternich steadily refused to do the one thing which the war party in Russia desired—to make the Greek revolt an excuse for a war of conquest, a war in which Austria to take part in the Eussei in dispute he would only agree to urge the Sultan to withdraw his troops from the Principalities and to concede the other points of strict treaty right. As to the Greeks, he independently pressed the Sultan to subdue the revolt without delay, to offer pardon on submission and to promise, for the future, privileges like those already granted to the Serbians; even if unsuccessful he wished to delay any general congress until the separate Russo-Turkish dispute should be settled. Above all he was anxious not to appear to countenance the rebels. Prussia, on the other hand, refused to join a secret pact with Austria to support the Russian view. Aiming at the role of mediator, he tried to appease Metternich's anger at the sympathy for the Greeks which had been cautiously expressed in a *Memoire* by Ancillon, a Prussian official, and reproved the Philhellenic excesses of the German Courts.

The British Government was on different grounds opposed to any action by the Allies. Regarding the Russian appeal Castlereagh told Lord Strangford, the British Ambassador at Constantinople, not to act with the Allies, but to prevent if possible, a rupture between Russia and Turkey.

> Castlereagh looked upon the revolt only as one more example of the unaccountable restlessness of Europe. The Porte was at least exempt from the revolutionary danger. Strangford was told that 'whatever the merits of the case you are accredited to the Porte, and you must awaken it to the necessity of asserting its authority over an infuriated people.' But here as elsewhere in Europe Castlereagh refused to act merely on the ground of legitimacy. Strangford had proposed to summon the Greeks, on behalf of the Powers, to conditional surrender; but Castlereagh made difficulties of form to avoid signing the joint declaration in that sense: it was consequently dropped, Russia refusing too.[1]

He also rebuked the ambassador for telling the British admiral to assist the Turkish fleet.

He lost no time in defining the British policy as one of strict neutrality,[2] but this did not at first imply any recognition of the Greeks as belligerents. The High Commissioner of the Ionian Islands, like most of the officials on the spot, was strongly contemptuous of the Greeks. He had already issues proclamation forbidding any interference by Ionians. Despite this, more than three thousand Ionians found their way to the Morea, and the Turks complained that, although this was allowed, the Government asked for return of a few Ionians serving in the Ottoman fleet. At first the insurgent flag only was excluded from Ionian ports, but after October 29, 1821, armed vessels of both parties were refused admittance. Lord Strangford was loud in echoing the complaints of the Turkish ministers, whom he encourages to summary measures in suppressing the revolt. He was a brilliant but somewhat erratic diplomatist, with a great knowledge of the East and a reputation of something too much of Eastern suppleness. He seems at least never to have been fully trusted either by the Foreign Office or by his colleagues. The Russians complained much of his conduct on this occasion. On the other hand, he was lifted as a devoted admirer of Metternich's principles and as a person in whom the Turks had confidence, to undertake the charge of the obtaining concessions which would avert was with Russia

Russia tried every means of turning the opportunity to account. The Tsar, unable to hope for a collective interference, first addressed to France a tempting offer of alliance with the ultimate prospect of a French protectorate in the Morea. The French Government had already declared against taking any part. The Tsar's overture was not taken very seriously by Paris because his mood was changing from day to day. But, France, in her existing state of weakness and isolation, could not ignore the possible value of a Russian Alliance and the old lure of a revived prestige in the Levant under new conditions.

In September, the Tsar talked once more of an alliance of all the Powers. Such projects met with little response, but he made another attempt to angel for French, for Prussian and even for English co-operation. The French Government would take no active part for fear of Austria but might be tempted to oppose a congress and to promote Russian interests by excluding other Powers from the settlement at the end of a Russo-Turkish war. But Castlereagh would not listen. On being told that, if Russia intervened, the first step would be the occupation of the Principalities, Castlereagh exclaimed: "that would be a new partition and repetition of Poland."

Having found no encouragement, and fortified by the continuous exhortations of Metternich, the Tsar did his best to restrain the war party in the army and in the Cabinet.

In the first weeks of 1822 the scales turned more sharply against war, and the campaigning season began instead with a special mission from the Tsar to Vienna. The Russian Government agreed to modify the four points in which its ultimatum had been defined, and not to seek the promise of the other Powers to recall their ambassadors from Constantinople unless the amended demands were rejected. But although the ultimatum was modified, the Greek question was reintroduced. The Powers were to take measures in common, first to end the war and assure tranquil possession to the Porte.

Metternich objected to the measures as implying something more permanent than a single act of amnesty and he rejected altogether a provision which hinted at something less than full Turkish sovereignty over the Morea. The Russian envoy spoke with two voices, being furnished with divergent instructions from the Chancellor and from the Corfiot, Capodistria. He explained that the Tsar did not desire for the Greeks autonomy like the Serbians.

The war party in Russia was for the time defeated or diverted thoughts of intervention in Spain. The Tsar himself calculated that a Spanish crisis must either separate England again from Austria or at least keep the Alliance busy in the West. Capodistria offered to resign in May when he saw the instructions drawn up for the coming congress. His resignation was not formally accepted, but in August he was given unlimited leave of absence. He retired to Geneva and there became the center of a large correspondence on behalf of the Greeks.

England, as Metternich undoubtedly expected, refused to take part in these proceedings, and used much stiffer language toward Russia. Castlereagh was determined not to interfere, if he could avoid it, in the Greek Question: the arrangements proposed for the Greeks would have to be guaranteed by all the Powers concerned, binding England by new ties to the Alliance. This was just the course which he could never propose to Parliament. He had no desire to see a Greek state, but the aloofness of England was in fact the best chance for the Greeks. Strangford at Constantinople, to whom the chief part of the negotiation was now entrusted, acted practically under Metternich's instructions, and renewed the conferences. His orders were not to meddle with the Greek Question.

Metternich was not in a hurry to withdraw his ambassador: the whole question was adjourned to the coming congress of all the Powers. With the fall of Capodistria, Metternich's ascendancy over the Tsar was complete. Nesselrode, the Chancellor, had professed a warm admiration for Capodistria. But the two men were rivals, and since the revolt Capodistria had naturally inclined to the war party in Russia. Metternich believed that he had been in correspondence with Ypsilanti's. Nesselrode was an experienced German official, by nature cautious and opposed to violent measures. But his influence alone, without that of Metternich, could not have kept the Tsar in check.

When the Congress met at Verona, the Greek Question was quietly and completely ignored. Russia demanded that plenipotentiaries should meet for the pacification of Greece, or else that the Porte should prove its sincerity—a Turkish pacification being a pleasant euphemism for a retaliatory slaughter as the massacre at Chios had just proves to the world. Salomon Rothschild, satisfied that the Tsar no longer intended war in the East, concluded at Verona the arrangements for a large loan to Russia, and was rewarded with the Order of Vladimir.

If the Greeks could hold their own, they might be glad one day that their affairs had not been settled for them at Verona. Castlereagh and Canning took the only possible line, that of absolute neutrality. But Canning showed at once that he was even more suspicious than was Castlereagh of any settlement by congress, and therefore in appearance even less favorable to the Greeks. Castlereagh, in his instructions to Wellington, said that in view of the paralysis of the Turkish forces by land and sea and the progress made by the Greeks toward the formation of a Government, it will be difficult if a de facto government shall be established in the Morea, to refuse it the ordinary privileges of a belligerent. Wellington might offer his good offices for succession upon condition of amnesty or of the creation of a qualified Greek government. But was also to make no engagement or guarantee. Canning's supplementary instructions, when he came to Foreign Office on Castlereagh's death, rejected interference in any form whatever. 'The Turks now appear to have the upper hand; in any case we cannot further interfere between Russia and the Porte or between the Porte and the Greeks.' Supposing the Greeks first violated a settlement guaranteed by England, we could not help the Porte against them, and therefore in the opposite case we could not help them against the Porte.[3]

But there was soon a general impression that England favored the Greek cause. The formal recognition of Greek blockades in March 1823 merely endorsed a practical measure already in force on the spot for the protection of commerce. Nevertheless, it was a step further than the other Powers would go toward conceding the rights of a belligerent to the rebel subjects of a legitimate sovereign.[4] Strangford admitted that the Turkish minister made a thrust home when he asked whether Canning would allow the right of America to recognize the Irish rebels as belligerents—a reference to Ireland.

In March 1823, the other Powers were disturbed by rumors of conversations between the English authorities and the Greek leaders. Gentz feared a fateful decision by England to separate from the Alliances. This might not mean intervention against the Turks, but, if it did, Austria could do nothing against the English fleet. At St. Petersburg it was thought that Canning would be restrained by his colleagues, and it was even stated that he had been censured in Cabinet on April 30 for authorizing such negotiations. The truth was that Lord Strangford, on his return in January from Verona to Constantinople, found reason to believe that a large party in the Divan was ready to concede some privileges to the Greeks like those granted to the Serbs, and even to allow the guarantee of any Power other than Russia. Without waiting for the consent of his government he wrote to Sir Thomas Maitland, asking him to make use of the information as he thought fit. Maitland, on his own responsibility, asked Mavrocordato to send a delegate, and deputed Captain Hamilton, of the frigate Cambrian, to explain the situation, without making any promises, to Mavrocordato and to the leaders of other Greek parties. Some of the islanders were at that time anxious to place themselves and their trading vessels under the protection of the Ionian flag, in fear of a descent by the Turkish fleet. The overture failed. Constantine Metaxas describes an interview with Captain Hamilton at which Theodore Negris and another were present. According to this account, Hamilton spoke of a mediation by England for a status like that of the Principalities but refused to put the suggestion in writing. The deputies refused to give an answer, and the provisional Government approved their action. The people were furious at the news of a possible compromise. A few weeks later, the British consul at Patras sent on to Corfu an appeal, emanating from Petrobey of Maina and offering to place the Morea under the protection of the United Kingdom. Sir Adam, Maitland's deputy, and successor at Corfu, returned the same answer as before, a refusal.[5] The whole episode was over before it was known to the Foreign Office in London. It was really an effort to discover on what terms the Greeks would submit, but it was differently interpreted by Greek hopes and by the fears of other Powers.[6] After the autumn of 1821, British neutrality had been enforced overall in very difficult circumstances by the Ionian Government. But Canning insisted that it should be a real neutrality on equal terms and complained that British subjects have been active in the Levant in their exertions on behalf of the Turks.[7]

These were indications of change in English foreign policy.

Meanwhile, Strangford returned from Constantinople and renewed his efforts to reach a settlement between Russia and the Porte. He claimed that

Canning's policy had lost him the confidence of the Turks, but by September 1823 he had succeeded that the Tsar, after a meeting with the Austrian Emperor agreed to send a representative at Constantinople and to do nothing further about Greece without consulting hi allies. Russia invited all the Powers to a conference at St. Petersburgh in spring and promised a Memoire about Greece. Metternich accepted the proposal but intended to delay as much as he could as the Turks were expected to make great effort to subdue the revolt the next year. Canning replied to the Tsar's invitation.

In January the promised Memoire, proposing the division of Greece into three Principalities, with a status like those of the Danube. The Turks would have an annual tribute and garrisons in specified fortresses. This very proposal, though far short of what the Greeks demanded, was a great advance on anything that had been achieved before. It was the first definite scheme proposed. It gave the Greeks much greater territory than they were ever likely to regain by their own efforts and struggle, because the risings in Boeotia and Epirus had entirely failed. From their perspective the scheme was not despised as it were, but it was not welcomed by the 'European' Greeks who saw in it the domination of Fanariot families with Byzantine traditions, instead of the Western constitutional monarchy to which they visualized. The Constitution of Epidaurus had proclaimed the complete independence of Greece in January 1822. The effect of the Memoire was to complete the disillusionment of many Greeks who had once staked their faith upon Russia. One of them wrote:

> I learn the real policy of the European Powers, particularly that of the Russian Court. I ask you a thousand pardons, Brother, for having hitherto disagreed with you in opinion. I now put faith in and humble myself in the name of Christ to England while I damn Russia from one end to the other, with all its inhabitants and noblemen.[8]

It would have been better if the Greeks had expected less from any of the Powers and had concentrated their attention on presenting Europe by their own efforts with a *fait accompli*. The Memoire was ill-received by the Powers, to whom it seemed a mere device for securing the predominance of Russia. Metternich answered cautiously in favor of the scheme three months later. Metternich was only waiting for the end: the Sultan's treaty with the Pasha of Egypt was already rumored, giving him the Morea and Candia if he could subdue the revolt. in May, Strangford wrote to Gentz: "If Mehmet Ali Pasha does his duty, we shall I doubt not escape from the infernal question at least in its present formidable shape."[9]

Canning still refused to have anything to do with a congress. To account for his horror of congresses, we must not forget Spain and South America. He was already in disgrace with the Alliance, and for that reason with the King and the Troy members of the Cabinet. The King complained that the Jacobins of the world (now calling themselves the Liberals) saw the peace of Europe secured by this great measure and have therefore never ceased to vilify the principle of the Quadruple Alliance. The Tories could reasonably argue that the concern of Britain was not with the constitutions of other states but with the peace of Europe. It was precisely in these two points that the Alliance failed. It was based, in Metternich's view, on the principle of interference, and it chose to forego the best prospect of peace for the sake of a theory. The countries of South America, Spanish thought they were in sentiment and civilization, had little reason now to profess an obstinate loyalty to the King of Spain: to insist upon the abstract assertion was not ta make for peace but to prolong civil war. Still less could the Greeks be expected to acknowledge again the absolute sovereignty of conquerors of different faith and of inferior intelligence. It needed no enthusiasm for the idea of nationality to see that, after the massacres of 1821, Turks and Greeks could never live peacefully together in the Morea of the Peloponnese. It was no business of the British Government to stir up national or constitutional movements abroad, but it was equally no concern of England to prolong civil wars by refusing to recognize accomplished facts. Canning's policy was inspired not by Liberal Ideas but by plain common sense.[10] But his strength in the Cabinet rested upon the outside support of Liberal public opinion, to which he at times appealed to secure his object. For this reason, he was branded as an opportunist alike by ultra-Tories and by Whigs, and the suspicion that he was among those who use sentiments to promote interests lay like a shadow across his career. His policy was attacked by Tories merely because it was approved by Liberals abroad and denounce by Metternich. It was disliked by the Whigs, who felt that he was infringing their patent on false pretenses.

Metternich, the mainspring of the Alliance, was the known enemy of any settlement which should seem to legitimize the revolt. But there was another special feature in the case of Turkey which made even the strictest Tories less inclined to co-operate with the Alliance. Castlereagh himself had given it as his opinion that collective threats had no effect upon the Turks and only made them suspect an alliance of Christendom against Islam. Wellington agreed that "our hands at Constantinople will be much weakened by becoming parties to this negotiation with other Powers."[11] Yet, he pronounced in favor of attending the Congress, and alluded in his correspondence with Metternich to the Cabinet's distrust of Canning. Wellington, however incautious, was too loyal to be suspected of a foreign intrigue to overthrow his colleague. But his prestige must have led Metternich to underrate Canning's power in the United Kingdom.

Failing a congress there remained isolation for England. It was for the present the strongest position. It did not preclude, if necessary, forcible resistance to Russian conquest, nor even isolated intervention on behalf of the Greeks. This possibility, tempting as it seems in retrospect, did not perhaps occur to Canning at this time. It would have been a simple matter for a British squadron to have prevented the Egyptian fleet from leaving Alexandria for the Morea. Although the Pasha of Egypt was nominally a vassal of the Sultan, it might have been successful without a rupture with the Porte, considering what was afterward done at Navarino with impunity. And if it would have been done without war, it would have gone far toward settling the Greek Question, for Metternich could not have delayed longer, with no prospect of the revolt being crushed. It would have been a stroke characteristic of Canning, but if it crossed his mind, it must have been dismissed as impracticable. The Cabinet, already restless, could never have consented to such an enterprising policy.

Canning's ideas at this stage may be gathered from an interview with Sir John Bowring, the disciple and afterward executor of Bentham, the editor of the Whig *Westminster Review,* and a leading member of the newly formed Greek Committee.[12] To Bowring's suggestion that it would be a sound argument to create in Greece a barrier against Russia, Canning replied: "Yes, that would be a proper argument for English policy, but what language could we hold to Russia to obtain her consent, knowing as we do that she can conquer Greece and Turkey when she pleases?" Interference might involve the mediator in war. Canning then asked about the condition of the Greek Provisional Government and the prospects of the loan. Bowring said that the Greeks would reject the status of a Principality or of a tributary state but might be willing to pay to the Porte a capital sum in compensation if a loan could be raised for this purpose. (This was in fact the issue eight years later.) He complained of the conduct of the English consuls in the East and argues that the Government should recover control by dissolving the Charter of the Levant Company as was done in the following year for that and other reasons.[13]Canning thanked him for evidence about a consul having supplied the Turks because they could quote this fact at Constantinople where they speak of the indifference of Englishmen on behalf of the Greeks. Bowring came away with a very favorable impression of Canning's disposition toward the Greeks.

The Greeks repudiated the Memoire and appealed to Canning for aid: that they should do so shows the reputation which he had already acquired abroad. His answer was not encouraging, but the mere fact of his answering at all implied another stage in the recognition *de facto* of the Greek Government (though not of independence quite yet). He denied any official knowledge of the Russian *Memoire* and proclaimed once more the neutrality of England:

> Since we know that the two parties are equally decided to reject every conceivable agreement, the hope of successful intervention becomes absolutely inadmissible at the present moment. . . . Bound as we are to the Porte by established relations of friendship and by ancient treaty obligations which the Porte has not violated, it certainly cannot be expected that England should engage in hostilities unprovoked by this Power in a quarrel which is none of ours.

A *Hatti-Sherif* (September 16) appointing the new Grand Vizir exhorted him to new efforts against the Greeks. Lord Byron's arrival in Greece was the high-water mark of the Philhellene enthusiasm. In June, the first instalment of the ill-fated loan arrived at Zante.[14]

Austria, on the other hand, complained that British naval officers showed decided partiality to the Greeks. Throughout the revolution, England was hampered in both framing and in executing a consistent policy by her delicate position in the Ionian Islands. But Philhellenes in England took little notice of these difficulties. The descent of the Ottoman fleet upon the island of Psara on July 4 had upon wide circles of opinion an effect like that of the destruction of Chios two years before, which had brought to birth the first Greek Committees in Europe. On July 19, Ibrahim sailed from Alexandria with twenty-five ships of war and one hundred transports, carrying the Egyptian army which was to conquer the Morea.

The Russians knew that without England conferences were of very little use. Each country felt that it could not tackle singly the question of the Greeks. Alone, Russia dared not break form the Alliance and make war upon the Turks. Alone, the English Cabinet would never have consented to risk a war by naval intervention. Both were tired of Metternich's delays, and each was reluctant to make the first advances. In September, Nesselrode wrote suspending all further communication with England on the Greek Question, in the hope that Canning would be drawn out by the fear of being forestalled. But Canning was not anxious yet to 'talk Greek.' In October, he was doubtful whether to join a news conference at St Petersburgh early in the next year. The prime minister, Lord Liverpool, was overall in favor of doing so, with no commitment to military intervention. But, on November 4, the Greek letter arrived, and its uncompromising tone convinced him that even mediation would be very difficult. Canning made this letter the chief ground for withdrawing after all form the conference, but the old condition for taking part in it was repeated with a new one added; not only must the Russian Ambassador be back in Constantinople, but, further, Russia must make a previous and public disavowal of any intention to use force. Stratford Canning, sent to St. Petersburg to watch the conference and on other business, drew up, at his cousin's request, a *Memoire* in which it was said that England would welcome Greek independence if won by the Greeks' own efforts.[15] The sentiment was less of a mockery than it might seem. Putting aside the possibility of separate English intervention, it was certain that the conference would never do anything effective before Ibrahim's army should arrive in Greece. The Greeks, on the other hand, although none of their ships were large, could arm an almost unlimited number. If they could have been united in a scheme of defense, they might have made it very difficult for Ibrahim to land. Even when their commander, Miaoules, was left with only twenty-five sails, the rest having departed home, he succeeded once in turning back the expedition and in capturing several transports. It was only through the indifference or the quarrels of the Greeks that Ibrahim was able to reach Crete in safety at the beginning of December.

Metternich was watching the expedition with some anxiety. He was committed to a conference, and it would be difficult to restrain Russia much longer. The Russian plan was out of the question. The Greek repudiation of it left only two alternatives—either intervention to subdue the Greeks, which public opinion made impossible, or a threat to recognize the independence of Greece as the only way to a settlement without war. But there is ample evidence to suggest that Metternich's proposal was not seriously made even as a weapon of negotiation, and it contained an obvious flaw. The Turks were to be forced to offer a settlement themselves. But what of the Greeks should refuse the terms so offered, just as they had repudiated the Russian *Memoire*? Either the Great Powers must fall back on the forcible mediation which Austria had wished to avoid, or the Greeks must be quickly subdued. This was in fact Metternich's expectation. On the day that the conference opened (February 24), Ibrahim landed in the Morea the first division of his army of ten thousand Egyptians; and it seemed as if the end could not be far off.

Soon it was clear that this second conference would fall like the first. Prussia, as before, tried to hold the balance between Russia and Austria. France gave positive support to the Russian proposals, already fearing a separate Anglo-Russian agreement in the event of failure. The conference dragged on for weeks, and then merely instructed the ambassadors at Constantinople to make a verbal preliminary attempt to persuade the Porte to invite mediation. The Turks rejected these 'good offices' of the Great Powers. The Russian Cabinet did not even wait for the result but sent a circular insisting on the necessity of coercive measures. Metternich would not admit this, foreseeing in practice coercive measures would be aimed against the Turks alone. He was thoroughly satisfied with the result of the conference. All that was necessary was to humor the Tsar a little longer.

The Egyptians had by the end of July, overrun the whole of the Morea, although the armed bands of the Greeks kept up desultory attacks from the mountain districts. Missolonghi had been regularly besieged since April. But the Greeks when they could assemble and pay enough ships for a short expedition, kept some control of the sea and were able to supply the town from that side. The islands kept up the spirit of insurrection, but only the only the incompetence of the Turkish fleet prevented the complete collapse of the revolt.

Discussion with England on the Greek Question, already suspended in September 1824, already had been closed by Nesselrode (to Lieven on November 30).

The King and some of the Cabinet were alarmed at this new evidence of English isolation. George IV required his ministers to sign a joint profession of faith toward the Alliance and noted on the document: "I am satisfied that with these assurances provided they are faithfully fulfilled." Canning, at whom all this was aimed, offered to resign, but the King could not afford to lose him, and from this time made the best of it and showed him much more confidence.[16]

Canning's two conditions were therefore fulfilled. But Nesselrode was full of compliments from Canning and recommended him to place the entire confidence in Lieven. Stratford, having departed from the capital, met the Tsar in May at Warsaw, where there may have been some hints of a separate understanding in the future.

Lieven was to wait for confidential proposals on Canning's part. Canning was sick to death of congresses and was nearly ready for a new move. A small Committed at Zante told the English Resident of General Roche's plans, and with the knowledge, but with the direct authorization of the High Commissioner, set on foot a rival appeal for English protection.[17] This Act of Submission, drawn up, says Trikoupis, in a foreign tongue and badly translated into Greek, announced that the independent Greeks of their own accord solicit the Illustrious Protection of Great Britain for all their several provinces to be comprehended under one permanent system administration. It did not at first find much support. But at the end of June, Ibrahim was advancing on Nafplion, the last fortified place in the Morea left to the Greeks. He met with a string show of resistance at the mills of Lerna, hut his sudden retirement may have been partly due to the approach of Captain Hamilton, who landed next day to confer with the Greek leaders. As to the appeal of Protection Hamilton reported to the High Commissioner that he "told them I had no power to say anything about it, that it was out of my line, but that I would inform you of all they had said."[18] He was given a copy of the Act of Submission, dated June 30 and signed by Kolokotronis and about one hundred chieftains of the Morea.

The Greeks hoped not only for political recognition but for the aid of the British fleet in stopping reinforcements from Egypt. Captain Hamilton acknowledged the Greek right to lawful prizes, but he was equally prompt to blockade dccc hydra to obtain the surrender of captains guilty of piracy.

In August, possibly on his advice, but at the instigation of the Greek Committee in London, an agreement was signed for the services of the famous Lord Cochrane, on terms which promised a rich reward to the adventurer.[19] Spaniolacki, with the London deputies Orlando and Luriottes obtained an interview with Canning to discover what his attitude would be. The idea of a Protectorate was dismissed, and, in case of any doubt, a new proclamation of neutrality was published. Canning told the deputies that there might be a point in the contest when Britain would promote a fair and safe compromise. The deputies replied that the Greeks would have independence or death.

But the way was now clear for England to offer mediation, preferably alone, of if that failed, with Russia for an ally, Canning, who was embarked on a complicated voyage of diplomacy and wished to keep both course open, dispatched his cousin Stratford Canning to Constantinople with instructions to urge the Porte to accept mediation before Russia should force the issue.[20] If this separate intervention was successful Canning hoped to win prestige for England and still more for himself, leaving Russia with no excuse to make new demands. But the chances of success with either party in the struggle were mall at best, and he did not neglect the second possibility, the daring policy of controlling Russian aggression by joining her as an ally.

The news there on 25th October, Lieven told Canning that the Court of Russia had positive information that Ibrahim was to keep whatever part of Greece he should conquer and that his plan for disposing of his conquest was to remove the whole Greek population, carrying them into slavery in Egypt or elsewhere and to re-people the country with Egyptians and others of the Mahometan religion. Afterward Stratford Canning heard a rumor on his way to Constantinople, and reports of it appeared in the press. Even if no good evidence of this outrageous plan was ever forthcoming, it was true that Ibrahim had begun a new system of terrorization. Such a positive statement of the rumor was perhaps made by the Russian minister to act as a spur upon the English Cabinet.[21]

Not only Lieven and the French but even the Austrian ambassador professed to look to England for the next step. From the tone of Canning's private letters, it is abundantly clear that he was influenced by the alluring prospect of a personal triumph in a field where hi rival Metternich had failed, of a national triumph where the Alliance had failed.

Wellington began to feel alarmed about the probable consequences of war:

> The establishment of a new Power in Europe which must be founded on the principles of modern democracy and therefore inimical to this country, which must be continental at the same time and maritime . . . would under any circumstances be no small a subject for consideration. . . . But the establishment of a Greek Power in Europe by means of . . . a Russian army is quite a different case

> from that of Greek Power established by its own unassisted exertions against the Turks. . . . I would recommend you then to connect yourself with Austria and France as the best mode of preventing the Emperor of Russia from carrying out his supposed measure.

He recommended a joint declaration of the Powers against the Russian aggrandizement, thus dividing the unpopularity if saving the Turks.[22]

During December the Lievens and Canning stayed once more at Seaford and there the project of a separate and secret understanding with Russia took shape. The only account of the discussions is from the Russian reports, which said that Canning was the first to make the proposal.

Canning explained his policy to Granville in a single sentence: "I hope to save Greece through the agency of the Russian name upon the fears of Turkey without a war."[23] Canning was therefore prepared for either issue, for peace or war between Russia and Turkey. England in any case would use her navy only. He was supposed to have been won over by the prospect of personal glory and by the persuasive tongue of Princess Lieven to this course of action. Yet, he pretended that an Anglo-Russian alliance for a special object was desirable or easy in execution. The chances for successful intervention without war were doubtful at best: intervention which appeared to be based on religious grounds would be doomed to failure from the first.[24]

On January 10, 1826, on the way to his post, Stratford Canning had a discussion with Mavrocordato and Zographo on board a ship near Hydra. They admitted in private conversation that many leading Greeks were ready to accept an arrangement which should secure autonomy and removal of all the Turkish population, without releasing them from tribute and the sovereignty of the Sultan. But the only answer which they were authorized by the Government to make was still death or independence.

Meanwhile, Stratford had no concessions to offer to the Turks, who would certainly never grant independence unless compelled by force. Ibrahim exclaimed:

> I am determined to put them down . . . everything shall be destroyed and the inhabitants in the mountains must perish whether of cold or hunger.

Yet, he received very few submissions.

The Turks were meanwhile irritated by the Stratford's defense of the action of the Philhellenes;[25] and their leisurely habits were outraged by his haste to arrive at a result for Wellington's benefit. The personal influence of the Sultan, always opposed to concession, was stronger than ever. Finally, they daily expected news of the fall of Missolonghi, the last garrison apart from Athens left in Continental Greece, and the focus for months past of sympathy in Europe. The Greeks were in a desperate position; their agents and sympathizers fed the newspapers of Europe with comfortable lies, but the same people confessed in private letters that the Peloponnesians behave as if war no longer existed: the government is powerless outside Nafplion, and anarchy is unchecked. The fall of Missolonghi was partly encouraged by Austria: soon after Stratford visited Hydra, the Austrian consul at Prevesa was dining with Ibrahim and discussing his plans: "As soon as Missolonghi has fallen, Ibrahim and the Capitan Pasha will attack Hydra and then Nafplion by land and sea."[26]

Nothing was to be expected in Greece or at Constantinople. The only ray of hope left was at St Petersburg. Wellington's mission could not pass unnoticed in political circles. The general impression in England was that he had gone to negotiate for the independence of Greece, but Gentz doubted any result from the overtures of the Greeks. Wellington himself was at last convinced that general conferences were useless and that the British must aim at qualified independence. Lord Strangford approvingly wrote: "the young Emperor Nick does not care a straw for the virtuous and suffering Greeks. He considers armed intervention or indeed any intervention at all as little better than an invitation to his own subjects to rebel."[27]

Afterward, Wellington accepted the Tsar's assurance s and concentrated on toning down the language of the new Russian ultimatum to be sent to Constantinople. It was drafted and shown to him on March 10 and sent off with one or two changes on March 17, but he was informed of this until four days later. On the same day (21st), Lieven arrived upon the scene of action and the Greek Question was suddenly brought forward once more. Being the prime mover of the affair, he had come on leave from London at the Tsar's command to complete the work. Having dispatched the ultimatum, Nesselrode asked for Wellington's proposals about Greece. The knowledge of the ultimatum made Wellington anxious to get an agreement signed.

A Protocol was concluded on April 4, 1826, which, taken by itself, was a very tentative document. But unlike the protocols of the Allies, it was the work of two parties who meant to act upon it. The offer of mediation was grounded, not on Ibrahim's proceedings, as Canning had suggested (for there was yet any confirmation of them), but on the Greek invitation to England.[28] The Protocol proposed to make Greece a tributary dependency of the Turkish Empire, autonomous but allowing the Sultan a certain share from the nomination of its rulers: all the Turks were to be removed from the territory concerned and the Greeks to buy out their properties. Nothing was said about the Turkish fortresses or about boundaries, except that the tow Powers would settle the details to be proposed. The Greek letter of April 29 did not define the boundaries which they expected to obtain but made a general claim to all the districts which had been under arms, whether subdues or not, referring especially to Euboea and Crete. The full claim would have included most of Thessaly and Epirus and territory even farther north, where risings were suppressed during the first months of the insurrection in 1821. But, about the same time, Trikoupis, afterward foreign minister of Greece and historian of the Revolution wrote for Stratford a memorandum on the possible boundaries. He pleads first for a territory.

The point in which the Protocol fell short of the Greek offer was the latter gave no share to the Turks in the nomination of the governors and said nothing about compensation to the Turks for their properties.[29] It also demanded the guarantee of Great Britain as indispensable. The other differences were not unbridgeable. The whole offer was of course based not on their desires but on what the leaders thought practicable after their interview with Stratford. The Protocol made it quite clear that mediation was to be offered to, not forced upon, the Turks—the agreement to be proposed to the Porte if that Government should accept the preferred mediation. There was in the Protocol no mention of force. But although both parties clearly disclaimed any views of aggrandizement, the possibility of a Russo-Turkish war was not definitely excluded:

If the mediation offered by H.B.M. should not have been accepted by the Porte and whatever may be the nature of the relations between H.I.M. and the Turkish government, Great Britain and Russia will still consider the terms of the arrangement specified in this la first article of the Protocol as the basis of any reconciliation to be effected by their intervention whether jointly or separately between the Porte and the Greeks.

The Protocol therefore contained by implication an effective threat of the use of force on part of England, but in conversation the idea of a pacific blockade was mentioned in connection with Ibrahim's proposed plan.

THE TREATY OF LONDON

It is difficult to interpret the real intentions of Canning, but at least he made it appear that he would not be altogether sorry if Russia made war after all. He wrote to Granville: "I do not know any more than you do on what the Duke of Wellington grounds his hopes that the peace between Russia and Turkey will not be interrupted."[30] It is likely that Canning disappointed at the apparent abandonment of the Greek Question, wanted to make the agency of the Russian name upon the fears of Turkey so formidable as to secure the success of Stratford's negotiations.

For the moment, he was to delay the execution of the Protocol until he could persuade France to take part, and perhaps even Prussia, which was more and more inclined to escape from subservience to Austria. The French

Government was offended at being left out but made the best of it in the hope of taking part later.

Metternich poured scorn upon the Protocol, done to save Wellington face and impossible to execute without war. The Russians on their side were in no hurry to carry out the Protocol until their own demands were satisfied. The Tsar spoke of it apologetically as signed merely to humor England and as unlikely to come too much. The Russians assured the Turks that in any case the Protocol contained an absolute disavowal of force. Their object was to obtain through the Greek Question an excuse for war. For this purpose, it was necessary to have a promise from England of resorting to force if necessary, and, if possible, to throw upon England the lead in negotiation.

Lieven returned to London in August, and at once addressed to Canning several questions, to which he did not reply for a month and then only with great caution. There was no evidence for Ibrahim's plans. Stratford Canning, having failed alone, was to tell the Turks that he expected Russian support. Finally, if this joint mediation failed too, they would resort with the consent of the other Allies to a withdrawal of Ambassadors and a threat of recognizing Greek independence. Canning was forced to make this concession by the opposition of the rest of the Cabinet. He told Granville:

> We must proceed in this Greek business with caution and good heed, for I have considerable difficulty in my way: not the least of which arises with the signer of the Protocol himself. I see my way, however, and will get through to the end, but it must be as old Lord Chatham used to say, *gradatim*.

He wrote to Stratford promising instructions. "I shall have more difficulty in Grecizing them with others than with Lieven." The first step was merely to communicate the Protocol to the French ministry (August 20), which gave a general approval. Lord Bathurst (Colonial Secretary) complained to Wellington: "I know it has long been a great object with the Foreign Office to take a part for the Greeks as being a very popular cause among a large description of well-meaning people, as well as with all democrats."[31]

Despite these difficulties with his colleagues Canning did not change his attitude toward the struggle in Greece. During the summer, the Greek pirates became more active than ever. Neutrality became more than ever difficult in execution: orders were sent to deal sternly with pirates, but not to follow the practice of the French and Austrian admirals by refusing recognition to the Greek flag altogether. Canning ingeniously made the principle of legitimacy recoil upon itself by arguing that the Powers which denied a national existence to the Greeks should seek compensation for piracy from the Porte, which was responsible for keeping its subjects in order. It was certain that the

Turkish fleet could never "pacify' the Archipelago and there was no reason why England should do so on its behalf.[32]

Wellington wanted to arrest Lord Cochrane, who was notoriously fitting out a steamer to join the Greek service. But Canning successfully contested the point of law, and Cochrane was tacitly allowed to sail. But, although Cochrane was a bold adventurer, he did not achieve against the Turks what was expected from his reputation in Chile, and certainly did no damage to any European merchants.

Forced by the Cabinet to take this step-in retreat, Canning escaped from the difficulty by enlisting the aid of France. As soon as the Cabinet dispersed, he traveled to Paris and remained there for nearly six weeks (September 18–October 25). Charles X was enthusiastically anxious to co-operate in naval measures. He was determined not to be left out and wanted to outbid Russia for the alliance of England.

These were the words of Canning a year before: "If we act, we must finish what is to be done." He hoped still to restrain Russia from war, but he was ready to run the risk for the sake of a settlement. Russia was pressing for a promise of force if necessary. Canning was ready for a strictly limited coercion, but the Cabinet was uneasy. The question of sending troops to Portugal was a new cause of division. Wellington wrote to him: "your refusal to go to war cannot be too peremptory" and complained that Lieven was already going beyond the terms of the Protocol.[33]

On November 19 Lieven wrote to Canning assenting in the first place to the promised plan of co-operation with other Powers by a threat of withdrawing ambassadors and of recognizing the Greeks as independent. In a separate letter of the same date, he wrote: "the emperor only enters the Greek Question with the firm determination of deciding it. . . . He has authorized me to concert with your Excellency the ulterior measures which it would become indispensable to adopt."[34]

Wellington wrote:

> I did everything I could to prevail on Mr. Canning not to enter the treaty and he certainly negotiated it as far as negotiation went before the secession of Liverpool (February 1827) without the knowledge of any of his colleagues except myself. But they and we all are highly blamable for having suffered the negotiation to move at all.[35]

It appears that Wellington might have threatened to resign when it came to signing a treaty if other events had not already thrown him out of office. The Whigs, on the other side, were getting impatient. Russia had just declared war on Persia, and Lord Grey wrote to Princess Lieven: "I congratulate you on your Persian successes and on your peace with the Turks."

These overtures revealed that not much force would be needed to drive Ibrahim out of Greece.

On November 26, Gentz felt confident that the whole edifice of the Protocol was collapsing. Two days later, the other Powers received a formal invitation to take part in the work, but Metternich was very suspicious, and said that Canning was trying to bring them into a new Alliance on his own terms: Austria must beware of a Concert which would belie its true function by putting Turkish suzerainty for full sovereignty. He addressed to Russia and to England several questions designed to find out exactly what was the settlement in which he was invited to take part.

At the end of the year, Austria refused to take part in the Greek settlement in view of the coercive measures proposed but promised to bring pressure upon the Turks. For the present, Metternich contended himself with advising the Sultan to forestall mediation by offering a plan of his own. The Sultan's 'pacification' was to take the form of a new expedition from Egypt, the form which Metternich welcomed most.

At the beginning of 1827, Canning had passed the blind alley of a settlement under the auspices of the Alliance and had little to fear from Metternich. Nesselrode was bound to follow Stratford's lead and confirmed the right of Russia to settle the Greek Question by herself if necessary, according to very stipulations of the Protocol.

But he succeeded in making the exasperated Turks believe that England was leading the way: he described Great Britain as the sworn enemy of the Porte," Stratford wrote, "and me a little better than a Greek."[36]

The negotiation in London proceeded slowly. On January 19, 1827, France offered a draft treaty but without any mention of how it was to be enforced except the sending of consuls to Greece. Before it had been fully considered, Lord Liverpool's sudden illness and retirement threw everything into confusion. The struggle long impending between Wellington and Canning was fought out, and on April 10 Canning became prime minister with Lord Dudley at the Foreign Office. Wellington resigned his seat in the Cabinet and his command of the army. Canning's triumph had come at last: momentous issues hung on the result, not least among them the fate of the Greek treaty. The reputation of Canning in Greece is illustrated by the following statement: "The new English Government is for the nations in general and not for Aristocracy alone."[37] In March, the Russian draft appeared, proposing a naval blockade if the Turks would not yield, and in the background ulterior measures, presumably a Russo-Turkish war. Wellington objected to the whole of this article. Canning added the words "without taking part in hostilities." He seems to have hoped even now that Austria would come in on his terms. But Metternich would agree to no sanction except a threat of rupture in the name of the five Powers, refusal not necessarily to imply an actual rupture. In his view, the Turks must retain their fortresses in the Morea and full sovereignty over Greece, and the Turkish dominions must be solemnly guaranteed for the future. The best comment on this is a letter of Gentz to Metternich a fortnight earlier: "why not draw up a fourth plan and so increase the confusion?"[38] At the beginning of May, an amended draft was submitted by France, including this time an additional article. Yet, another draft was produced by England and Russia.

Finally, the Treaty of London was signed.[39] Its terms were ostensibly almost the same as those of the Protocol of 1826, with one or two amendments introduced at the desire of France. In the Preamble, the Greek invitation to France as well as to England was made a ground of intervention, besides commercial interests, and the spread of piracy. England no longer refused to guarantee the settlement but did not promise to do so. A step toward recognizing the claims of the Greeks to be heard was made in the provision that the boundaries should be negotiated between the Allies and the two contending parties. By the Protocol the Allies were simply to have decided what boundaries they would propose to the Porte.

The important part of the Treaty was the additional article, which provided that in case the Porte should not after one month accept the mediation, the Allies would at once send consuls to consuls to Greece if either party should refuse the preliminary armistice, "the High Powers will jointly exert all their efforts to accomplish the object of such armistice, without, however, taking any part in the hostilities between the two contending parties." Conditional instructions to this effect would be sent to the admirals. In case of obstinate refusal, the Powers "will nevertheless continue to pursue the work of pacification as the Conference in London might decide." These expressions were vague enough; and they were made little clearer by the instructions sent to the ambassadors and the admirals a week later. The armistice was first to be notified to both parties; if the Turks should refuse, the admirals were to treat the Greeks as friends, and to unite their squadrons for intercepting supplies from Egypt or the Dardanelles. But they must take "extreme care to prevent the measures which you shall adopt against the Ottoman marine from degenerating into ppm p and not to make use of force unless the Turks persist in forcing the passages which they [the admirals] had intercepted." It was obvious that no effective force could be used against either party by land. The Treaty was, perhaps inevitably, a compromise between a strictly impartial mediation and an open intervention on behalf of the Greeks. But it led to a great deal of sophistry and puzzled the admirals not a little. What were they to make of their instructions "to watch over the maintenance of the armistice without taking part in the hostilities?" But the general sense was clear enough: to cut off Ibrahim's supplies and to set the Greek Government on its legs.

France signed the Treaty to keep England and Russia in check, just as England had signed the Protocol to restrain Russia. The French had delayed the signature and the execution of the Treaty in every possible way. It suited Austria to exaggerate the jealousies and to minimize the good will of the new allies. In a sense the mutual suspicion of the Powers was the Greeks' best security: each of them was not so much concerned with making Greece an independent state but each was driven in that direction by the fear of allowing the other an excuse for further interference. The native Greeks cared little for their diplomatic status if the Turks were excluded from their midst; the interests of the Powers more than the enthusiasm of the people eventually made Greece into an independent kingdom. National sentiment was the very lifeblood of a people which from the first laid claim to some further extension, and already dreamed of almost a definite expansion in the future. The Greeks living in Europe with ambitions for the future recognized this and built upon it; Metternich saw it too, but without the same satisfaction. He ridiculed the Treaty's lack of precision and prophesized that the naval squadrons could not follow their instructions without hostilities.

THE NAVY BATTLE OF NAVARINO

The Treaty was published, including the secret additional article, in the *Times* of July 12. This, with the Russian Memoire of January 1824 and the Protocol of 1826 was the third document which found its way prematurely into the press in the last two cases at least to the advantage of the Russian policy. The Turks of course would know of the Treaty officially before long, but the knowledge of the forcible methods threatened in the secret article would make the risk of desperate resistance even greater. The news in Greece, though long expected, accused the greatest joy and excitement. Even in Corfu—an island under British protection and officially discouraged from taking too much interest in the fate of Greece—"men went mad with joy. The bells were rung, the Christians gave thanks to God, old men danced . . . a day of resurrection"[40]; Greece, indeed, seemed very nearly dead. At the meeting of the National Assembly in April, the party feuds had been composed only by the appearance of Lord Cochrane and Sir Richard Church, who were thereupon elected as commanders-in-chief by land and sea. Capodistrias was elected President for seven years in the face of some opposition from the islanders, who did not want national union. There were some fears of the disapproval of England, but Stratford, despite doubts, the Greeks to choose him. Kolokotronis was at first opposed but having resigned his own command in favor of Church, he told the politicians that they in turn ought to give way to Capodistrias. These were high-sounding appointments, but outside the Assembly and even within it the Greeks were losing heart. The new commanders were not easy partners. Cochrane was a strong adventurer, imperious and too impatient of Greek indiscipline, and intrigue to judge coolly the chances of success. Church, who had some experience of suppressing brigands in the kingdom of Naples, understood and won the affection of the Greek irregular bands, but he was too impulsive and not strong enough to impose his will upon Cochrane.

Their attempt to relieve the Acropolis of Athens failed: the Greek troops were demoralized by the disgraceful scene at the Monastery of St. Spyridon when a party of Turks who had surrendered were put to death. Church, who saw it all from the harbor, makes it clear that it was not a cold-blooded massacre, but the outcome of an attempt to disarm one of the prisoners, whose pistol went off in the process. A Greek shot him dead, and the leaders were unable to prevent a general fight. The Greek chief Karaiskaki was opposed to Cochrane's plan of attacking across the open ground. He wished instead to cut off from the north the supplies of the besieging force. General Church agreed with him, but when Cochrane threatened to depart if his own plan was not followed, they surrendered their judgment. Finally, on the eve of the attack, Karaiskaki was killed in a chance encounter, and the camp was thrown into confusion by his loss. The attempt next day was a complete fiasco, and on June 5 the garrison capitulated, although the state of their supplies hardly warranted the surrender of this, the last fortress north of the Isthmus.

Church's camp was soon broken up, and he remained with a small force holding the Isthmus. The *capitani* on the borders began to think of making terms with the Turks. In the Morea, some of the long-enduring peasants were driven for the first time to submission. The islanders made no effort to prepare against the new Egyptian fleet which was coming to destroy Hydra and Spezzia. The Government, according to an English observer, consisted of a boy, a sailor, and a cuckold. The editor of the Greek Gazette wrote to a friend: "If I knew that by telling untruth I could be useful to the country, I would not have written truth to anybody; but our situation is known to all the world."[41]

Btu the Greek leaders' inactivity was due partly to their hopes of foreign intervention. If the Powers were going to save them, there was no need to bestir themselves.

Canning's advent to power was very welcome to the Russians, who dreaded the hostility of Wellington.[42] Their belief that he would allow England to be used for Russian objects was mistaken: he had entered the alliance for a definite and limited purpose; if he had lived to see that accomplished, Russia might have found in him thenceforth an opponent less irritable but more formidable than the Duke. If a Russo-Turkish war became inevitable, there is little doubt that he would have replied by promoting the full independence of

Greece. He was moving, as he said, *gradatim*. The duke himself was driven in the end to the same course, but in a moment of panic and without conviction. The Cabinet took many weeks to form, but at last Canning was free of that suspicion from colleagues under which he had suffered so long. The King was quite reconciled to his policy, and indignant at Wellington's behavior in the crisis. He told Esterhazy that he never expected that the duke would look to be Prime Minister. Or resign his command rather than serve under Canning. The attacks upon Canning from Whigs and ultra-Tories alike were more violent than ever, but he was able to meet them. A month later, Canning was dead, because of serious deterioration of his health. Princess Lieven wrote: "We have just lost Canning. The Mercantile class is in dismay, the people in tears, everybody who is not Metternichish is in despair."[43] Metternich did not conceal his joy and prophesized the return of Wellington after an interval of confusion. The makeshift government of Goderich and Dudley was in doubt about the Eastern and most other affairs. Lord Grey, a possible successor to power, was decidedly hostile to the Treaty, as his letters to Princess Lieven show: "What you say does not satisfy me as to the expediency of a combined naval operation. . . . I must view with considerable jealousy any arrangement which may have a tendency to place Greece in a state of dependency upon Russia."[44] Wellington was now commander-in-chief once more, and reserved a very questionable right of differing publicly from the Cabinet upon political matters. But Bathurst wrote to hi: We cannot recall our stipulations with France and Russia, and it seems therefore desirable that this crusade should be executed by those who have advised it."[45]

When Canning died, the Treaty was fairly launched. Stratford was ready to act on August 3, but he had to wait for his colleagues' instructions. On the 16th 1827, the ambassadors delivered their first declaration to the Reis-Effendi, who refused to read it in their presence. They were supported by a note from Prussia, but the Austrian Internuncio withheld even the unofficial support which had been promised. Although his action was afterward disavowed by Metternich, he can hardly have mistaken his instructions on so important a point. The term for acceptance had been shortened to a fortnight in view of the violent manifesto published by the Turks before the Treaty was even signed.

On the 31, the second declaration was presented, and final instructions to the admirals followed. The limits of the blockade were important, as they would inevitably be taken by the Greeks as the minimum boundary approved by the Powers. They were fixed by the ambassadors to extend from the Gulf of Volo on the East to the mouth of Aspropotamos on the West, with the contiguous islands—and in addition Samos, and perhaps Candia. A month later, Codrington was told not to blockade Candia for the present. Stratford was at this time in favor of excluding Acarnania to leave a large portion of the coast opposite the Islands in Turkish hands. This was the very cause of Wellington's anxiety afterward. But the fact that a year later the Greeks had reestablished themselves in the province rightly outweighed Stratford's mind the doubtful objection of policy. It was another instance of awkwardness "of combining our protection over the Ionian Islands with our Greek policy."[46]

The blockade was to prevent neutral as well as the Turkish vessels from bringing supplies to the Turks. But, in deference to Austria, Dudley relaxed this provision on October 16. Her ships did a brisk trade with the Turkish armies under convoy of her men-of-war. Her position was that, having no special convention with the Greek rebels, she must observe a position of neutrality. In other words, Austrian subjects must commit no acts of war for either side and could only pas an effective blockade at their own risk. But the Austrian naval commanders were told to give convoy whenever possible to vessels trading with the Turks, and in that case not to submit to any right of search. Dudley's concession was made because the Law Officers could find no legal ground for interfering with such convoys of a neutral power when the allies were themselves not belligerents.

The Turkish and Egyptian transports were to be encouraged by the allied commanders to return home. A to those who had already been in Navarino, "may persist in staying there, and they must, like the fortresses, incur all the chances of war." In private, Stratford Canning wrote to Admiral Codrington that "although the measures are not adopted in a hostile sprit, yet the prevention of supplies is ultimately to be enforced, if necessary, and when all other means are exhausted by cannon-shot." Codrington repeated this phrase to all his captains: "I have never felt a wish to see another war until now, and I really think it might prove a more humane way of settling affairs here than any other. One strong act of coercion would place the Turks at our mercy, and we could then settle the whole matter as we chose and take Candia ourselves into the bargain. . . . How can we coerce the Turks without hostilities?"[47]

Codrington's first duty was to persuade the Greeks to accept the armistice, but meanwhile his opinion was that "the Greeks should work hard to do all that is possible before the armistice."[48] The French admiral, de Rigny, was a man of steady judgment, without any Philhellenic sympathies. His attitude toward the Greeks was mid-way between the decided partiality of Codrington and of Captain Hamilton, and the animosity of the Austrian naval commanders.[49] After much discussion, the Greek Government formally accepted the armistice on September 3. But the Rumeliot troops, backed by Church, Cochrane, and Kolokotronis, tried to prevent it and, in fact, took very little notice of it. Having failed all through the summer to act, Cochrane was able, now that an armistice had been accepted, to organize without difficulty an expedition to the west coast. As the Turks refused the armistice, and the

Powers could only enforce it by sea, the Greeks could not be expected to fold their arms while Ibrahim ravaged the Morea. But, in any case the Government at Nafplion had to check on the activities of the chiefs. A last effort to prevent the new Egyptian fleet from sailing had failed. As soon as Stratford had unofficial news of the Treaty, he had written to Codrington suggesting that his appearance off Alexandria might stave off the blow, but the French ambassador objected.

At the end of August, Codrington left Smyrna and sailed the island of Hydra, which the Egyptian fleet was expected to attack first. He did not receive until September 8 the instructions authorizing him to act on the Turks final refusal. The French admiral was nowhere to be found, having mentioned three different appointments. He had returned to Smyrna, writing that he proposed to stay there until the Russian fleet should arrive. He showed the greatest reluctance to risk an encounter with the Egyptians, who had several French officers among them. The Egyptians were equally anxious not to force an issue; their fleet, having left Alexandria, sailed first to Rhodes, and then to the north coast of Africa. It was not until September 10, when news came that it was on its way to Navarino, that de Rigny at last left Smyrna. In the same day, Codrington sailed from Hydra to intercept the Egyptians with his squadron alone; but when he came in sight of the bay on the twelfth, he found them already anchored there beside the Turkish fleet. This was straining the letter of his orders in favor of the Greeks. Stratford at Constantinople was getting impatient too. Sir F. Adam asked Codrington for advice, defined the position in cryptic words: "The Greeks having accepted the armistice and the Turks refused it, the Greeks are at liberty to commit hostilities, but we are not at liberty to allow hostile collisions."[50]

Here were sophistries enough to bemuse even a diplomatist, and the temper of the fleet was impatient of such subtleties. On September 19, Codrington served a notice to Ibrahim, inviting him to return under convoy to Egypt. No answer was given, but on the 21st the Egyptian fleet put out to sea, probably for Hydra. Codrington determined to oppose it alone, although his flagship *Asia* was badly manned, and his tackle was poor. But at this moment, the French admiral appeared, and the two commanders now sent a joint letter to Ibrahim pointing out the consequences of resistance. They said that their orders were such that they would go to any extremities rather than abandon the object. If then a single cannon-shot were fired against their flags, it would be fatal to the Ottoman fleets. A warning was also sent to the Austrian transports in the harbor that they could not be treated otherwise than as Turkish vessels. In face of the two squadrons, the Ottoman ships all returned to the Harbor by the evening of the twenty-fourth. The French admiral had a separate interview with Ibrahim and professed to be convinced of his good faith;

but it was harder to count on the Turkish admiral, who was disposed to resist, and suspected Ibrahim's loyalty.

On the twenty-fifth, there was a conference between all the four commanders. Three accounts exist, by Codrington, de Rigny and Ibrahim. But no written agreement was signed. Ibrahim promised to remain in the harbor, and to suspend operations on lands until a courier should bring orders from Constantinople within twenty days. Ibrahim says that he only promised not to attack Hydra, and that he was given permission to provision Patra, but the other accounts deny this. Ibrahim may have lied or may have misunderstood, but it is hard to believe that Codrington, after his expressed intention to the contrary, should have given leave for the supplies to a Turkish fortress.[51]

Next day, a dragoman came from Ibrahim, asking leave to stop Cochrane from entering the Gulf of Patras, but Codrington answered that the Gulf was not, like Albania, beyond the existing theatre of war. "Within it, the Greeks having accepted our mediation, I had no authority for interfering with their operations."[52] It was the Philhellene volunteer, Captain Hastings, who had entered the Gulf, and on September 29 he sank nine Turkish ships in the Bay of Salona. Hastings was an ex-officer of the Royal Navy, who now commanded the steamboat *Karteria*, and had trained there the most disciplined and effective gunners in the Greek service. Ibrahim, when he heard of this, was furious, and sent out Turkish fleet to provision Patras. The allied squadrons had departed, leaving no guard-ships to watch the bay. Codrington met the Turks on October 2 and turned them back. Two days later they set sail again, and due to stormy weather passed to the mouth of the Gul, but on the sixth, Codrington reappeared and warned them to return. He fired several shots across their bows, and towed away one boat which was carrying provisions ashore. When the wind allowed, they began to return. On the tenth, the Russian fleet was at last sighted, and they all, blockaders and blockaded, proceeded back to Navarino. The time agreed for Ibrahim to get his orders from Constantinople expired on the 15th. Austria advised Ibrahim to follow whatever orders the Porte should give and assured him that the admirals had no authority to fire.

But now there was little doubt about the issue. Despite Ibrahim's promise, his captains went on ravaging the country, especially round Patras and Vostitza. The Egyptian fleet had brought more than five thousand men and four hundred cavalries. After burning and cutting down the olive trees, they enslaved the Greeks who fell into their hands. It seems that Ibrahim, on the 17th of October, after the arrival of a courier from Constantinople, had led a column in person toward Messenia. His proclamation to the Messenians was intercepted and sent to the admirals by Kolokotronis. A frigate was sent sailed down the coast to inspect, and returned next day having observed by the clouds of fire and smoke that Ibrahim's work of destruction was still going on. The allied officers had landed and distributed bread among some of the starving people.[53]

Codrington made no secret of his intention to fight. He wrote to Wellesley in Vienna: "There His Highness' fleet will terminate its hostile career."[54] The Russian Admiral Heyden was too ready to go all lengths. He told Codrington that, in his opinion, the emperor had already declared war.[55] Only de Rigny was less keen, for France was already cultivating the friendship of Mehemet Ali. It was, indeed, a curious situation. Inside the bay, the Turkish and Egyptian fleets, mutually suspicious, together with many French officers and several Austrian transports. Outside, the three allied squadrons. The coast infested with Greek boats, so that the admirals could not even promise safety to Ibrahim's courier. And cruising not far off, Lord Cochrane, commander-in-chief of the Greek navy, once an admiral of the British fleet against the French.

The admirals held a conference on the 18th and laid down three possible courses. First, to maintain the blockade; but this would be expensive and difficult in winter. But this would be expensive and difficult in winter; secondly, to anchor in Navarino and remain there; but such a situation could not last long in a confined space; or, thirdly, to proceed to take a position with the squadrons in Navarino in order to renew to Ibrahim propositions, which entering into the spirit of the Treaty were evidently to the advantage of the Porte itself.[56] Codrington afterward explained that these propositions were simply that Egyptian fleet should return home, but they were never actually made before entering the harbor, because Ibrahim, was nowhere to be found, and no sooner the squadrons inside than the battle began.

Codrington seems to have originated this plan of sailing into the harbor; Heyden at once agreed, and de Rigny acquiesced without much trouble. The British Admiral, who was the senior, took command and allotted positions. On the day before the battle, he wrote in ambiguous oracles to his wife: "Well, this day had gone by with all preparation and no fight . . . we must now take the chance of what tomorrow produces. My own squadron will think it a pity if it all ends in smoke. Such, however, is my own expectation." The allied fleets were inferior in actual numbers but had far more guns than the Turks. It was common prudence to enter the harbor absolutely prepared, but there is little doubt that the admirals meant to fight on the smallest pretext.[57] The Order of Battle, issued on the nineteenth, contained this sentence: "If time allows, the allied squadrons will, before the Turkish fleet takes any hostile action, cast anchor with spring cables. No shot must be fired before a given signal, so that it may be the Turks who open fire."[58]

Codrington's account of the way in which the battle began next day (October 20) is confirmed by the log of the *Dartmouth*, the vessel which was chiefly concerned. At 12:30 her captain answered the signal to prepare for battle, at 1 o'clock the signal to close. At 1:23 a Turkish boat came alongside the Asia as she entered the narrow mouth of the bay, to ask (as Codrington reported) that the fleets should not come in. Meeting with a refusal the Turkish officer went ashore to a tent on the hill, where a gun was fired, and a red flag hoisted. The fleets entered and anchored without firing a shot. A fireship was lying near the mouth of the harbor, and men were seen actively at work on board. Daertmouth was ordered to remove it, and a boat was manned to carry out the order; as they rowed up, bearing a flag of truce, they were fired upon, and several men were killed. Dartmouth returned the fire with musketry, and the French flagship joined in. This French ship was in turn greeted with cannon-shot from the nearest Egyptian, and thereupon the action became general. Before the nightfall, the Ottoman fleet was destroyed.

It is worth quoting the important Circular Letter of Sir Richard Church, sent from the Headquarters of Diakophto on the 28th of October 1827 to the Generals and Officers commanding troops, which manifests, among other things, the humanitarian sentiments upon which Great Britain acted in the case of the intervention at Navarino, in aid of the Question and cause of Greek Independence:

> The tremendous roar of the artillery of hundreds of ships of war, and the continual lightning of consuming fire, blazing awfully to announce the repeated peals of bursting like thunder from thousands of heavy cannon will have already announced to many the glorious event of the destruction of the Turko-Egyptian fleet in the harbor of Navarino by the allied fleet of England, France and Russia under the supreme direction of His Excellency Admiral Sir E. Codrington, and his noble supporters Admiral De Rigny and De Heyden. To those who from distance from the shores of Navarin could not have had the extreme delight of hearing the thunder of the Battle I have now the pleasure to communicate this signal interposition of divine Providence by the chastising hands of three Christian Powers in favor of Greece in favor of the Hellenic race. I need say no more I think to tell you to redouble your efforts in the service of your Country—Ibrahim Pasha who makes war even on your fruit trees and who avoids the serious and bloody combat with men, to make slaves of your helpless children of both sexes for brutal purposes—whose most sacred and most secret asylums are assailed by his ferocious bands whilst he keeps aloof from manly warfare—this Pasha this ferocious Pasha now contemplates with dismay the remains and wrecks of that late mighty Turko-Egyptian fleet which had brought so many thousand Turks and Arabs to your shores and which had so amply provided them with all their wants—It is with a truly joyful heart that I communicate to you this great event, and desire you to make it known—to all the troops and inhabitants in your vicinity—I salute you.[59]

NOTES

1. Castlereagh to Strangford, 28 October, in Foreign Office [F.O.] Turkey, 97.

2. Castlereagh to Strangford, 20 November, in Foreign Office [F.O.] Turkey, 97.

3. Castlereagh's instructions to Wellington, in *Despatches*, I, 284.

4. See Crawley, *The Question of Greek Independence* (Cambridge: Cambridge University Press), 26. I am not agreed with this view, which has no foundation in International Law. The Porte had no legitimate sovereignty over Greece as conquest was by no means a lawful means of acquiring sovereignty at the time.

5. Strangford to Canning, 10 February 1823 (No. 8) in Foreign Office [F.O.] *Turkey*, 114.

6. See Crawley, *The Question of Greek Independence* (Cambridge: Cambridge University Press, 1930), 29.

7. Letter to Levant, 29 April 1823. The interruption of British trade with the Morea was negligible compared with the disturbance to trade, in Smyrna and elsewhere, threatened by the Greek unrest (Public Records Office, [PRO], *Archives*, 125).

8. Turturi to Gerostathi, 8 March 1824, in Colonial Office [C.O.] *Ionian Islands* 27.

9. On 4 March Consul Salt at Cairo reported Ibrahim's preparations, see Foreign Office [F.O.] *Turkey*, 126.

10. Crawley, *The Question of Greek Independence* (Cambridge: Cambridge University Press, 1930), 33. I am not entirely agreed with this view, because, as it shall appear later in this analysis of political events, Canning in his decision to conclude the Treaty of London was much influenced by the Philhellenic sentiments of some of his colleagues.

11. Wellington to Canning, 10 February 1824, in *Despatches*, 2, 204.

12. See Bowring's *Autobiographical Collections*, 1877, 281–88.

13. On the dissolution of the Levant and the reorganization of the consular service, see an important memorandum by Consul-General Cartwright.

14. The good faith of the Greek deputies who negotiated the loan in London may be measured by this extract from their letter to the 'Venerable Greek Government': "With regard to the appropriation of the land [as security] we are of opinion the Government should not agree to it, or if it does, to allot them barren unhealthy and mountainous parts, giving them ancient and renowned names to make an impression on the Commissioners. Hume deserves such treatment; he alone having insisted on that article: by which means the Government fully satisfies all their demands" 13 August 1824 (excerpted) in *Colonial Office* Ionian Islands 27.

15. Instruction to Stratford Canning, 8 December, in Foreign Office [F.O.] *Russia*, 144

16. King's letter, 27 January; Cabinet minute, 29 January; Canning to King, 1 February; interview of Sir W. Knighton with Canning, 27 April, in Stapleton, *Canning and his Times*, (Kessinger, t1831) 437.

17. Trikoupis, III, 267. Adam to Buthurst, 22 June, in *Colonial Office, Ionian Islands* 33: the substance is—Count Roma (one of the Committee) is going too far in his proposals to Miaoules and Kolokotronis; Adam has warned him not to speak for the British Government.

18. Hamilton to Adam, 9 July (enclosed in Adam's report, 4 August), in *Colonial Office, Ionian Islands*, 33. The usual account, that Hamilton induced Ibrahim to retire by turning his guns on the town, cannot be true, for he says himself that Ibrahim had already retreated. The American Philhellene S.G. Howe, noted in his *Journal* Ibrahim's retreat on 28 June, and on the 29th, the *Cambrian* and another frigate beating up the Gulf of Argolis.

19. S.G. Howe's Journal, 19–24 July, Mavrocordato to Hamilton, 1 September (enclosed in Adam's report, 17 September), in *Colonial Office, Ionian Islands* 33. Later, Hamilton was disgusted with Lord Cochrane: to Stratford Canning, 19 April 1827, in *British Museum, Add MSS* 36461–36566. Correspondence relating to Cochrane in *British Museum, Add. MSS* 36462–36464 (*Broughton Papers*).

20. Stratford Canning had made his name at Constantinople in negotiating the Treaty of Bucharest in 1812 between Russia and the Porte. He began with an ardent sympathy for Greece, tempered by doubts: "Are terms of accommodation recommended by other Powers likely to embrace the independence of the Greeks, which could never be won from the Porte without a war? I speak of probabilities . . . as a matter of humanity, I wish with all my soul that the Greeks were put in possession of their whole patrimony, and that the Sultan were driven bag and baggage into the heart of Asia" (September 1821), Instructions, 12 October 1825, in Foreign Office [F.O.], Turkey, 133.

21. Memorandum of Conference, 25 October, in Wellington's Despatches, II, 547. See also Canning and his Times, 474. The same report attributing the plan to Soleiman Bey is mentioned in a dispatch from the Russian consul at Corfu to Nesselrode [*Colonial Office, Ionian Islands*, 33].

22. To Canning, 22 November, in Wellington's Despatces, II, 568–70.

23. Canning to Granville, 13 January in *Canning and his Times*, *op. cit*. 471.

24. See Crawley, *The Question of Greek Independence* (Cambridge: Cambridge University Press, 1930), 54.

25. Crawley, *The Question of Greek Independence* (Cambridge: Cambridge University Press, 1930), 56.

26. Intercepted letter from the Austrian consul, 26 February, after a conference at Missolonghi, *Colonial Office, Ionian Islands*, 37.

27. Lyttleton to Bagot, 31 January, in Bagot, *Canning and his Friends*, (1909, reprinted, Nabu Press, 2010), II, 328.

28. This was not yet strictly true; but Stratford's interview (10 January, 56) gave reason to expect that the Assembly would make the invitation, which was sent in fact on 29 April, Protocol 4 April in Temperley, *The Foreign Policy of Canning* (London 1926), Appendix VII.

29. This, of course, in contemporary International Law would be out of the question, as 'property' of illegal foreign settlers cannot possibly be compensated.

30. 18 April, in *Canning and his Times*, 473–74.

31. Canning to Granville, 7 August, in *Canning and his Times*, 477; to Stratford 4 August (private) in *Stratford Canning Papers*, 12, and see *Foreign Office* [F.O.] *Turkey*, 141.

32. See draft letters to Stratford Canning, 2 August, with Wellington's objections in Wellington's *Dispatches,* III, 355. The Turkish fleet left the Dardanelles in July and returned in November, having done nothing: Stratford Canning, 29 November, in *Foreign Office* [F.O.] *Turkey*, 145.

33. Wellington to Canning, 8 November, *Despatches*, III, 446. Canning to Granville, 12 November in Canning and his Times, 486 and 22 November in *Foreign Office* [F.O.] *France*, 347.

34. See Crawley, *The Question of Greek Independence* (Cambridge: Cambridge University Press, 1930), 70.

35. Wellington's *Despatches*, VI (8 September 1829).

36. Stratford Canning, 15 March 1827 in *Foreign Office* [F.O.] *Turkey*, 152.

37. Archbishop Ignatius to Capodistria, 25 May, in *Colonial Office, Ionian Islands*, 43.

38. Revealed in the correspondence of Canning to Stratford Canning, 19 February, in *Foreign Office* [F.O.] *Turkey*, 151.

39. For the Text and Drafts, see Temperley, *Foreign Policy of Canning, ante*, Appendix VIII.

40. Capodistria to his brother, 218 July, in *Colonial Office, Ionian Islands*, 43.

41. May 1827, in *Colonial Office, Ionian Islands*, 43.

42. Princess Lieven, *Letters*, 98.

43. Princess Lieven, 10 August, in *Letters*, 104.

44. Grey to Princess Lieven, 2 September, in *Correspondence (paperback edition, 2018)*. He also spoke against the Treaty in Parliament.

45. 12 August, in Wellington's *Despatches*, IV, 81.

46. See Stratford Canning's Despatches in *Foreign Office* [F.O.], 155–57.

47. Codrington to his wife, 28 July, in *Life of Codrington*, I, 395.

48. Codrington to his wife, 20 August, in *Life of Codrington*, I, 242.

49. Crawley, *The Question of Greek Independence* (Cambridge: Cambridge University Press, 1930), 85.

50. Sir F. Adam to Codrington, in *Life of Codrington*, I, 464.

51. See accounts for the interview by Codrington and de Rigny in *Parliamentary Papers*, 1830, XXXII.

52. *Life of Codrington*, II, 126.

53. See extensively Church's *Narrative.*

54. Codrington to Wellesley, 11 October, in Life of Codrington, II, 45.

55. Codrington to Wellesley, 11 October, in *Life of Codrington*, II, 56.

56. Crawley, *The Question of Greek Independence* (Cambridge: Cambridge University Press, 1930), 90.

57. *Ibid.*, 91.

58. A very good account of the battle itself is in Clowes, *The Royal Navy* (London, 1903) IV, 251–62.

59. Copies in Greek and English in *British Museum,* MSS 36554.

Chapter 8

National Liberation Wars or Wars in Aid of Self-Determination

PHILOSOPHY OF LAW AND MODERN INTERNATIONAL LAW ON NATIONAL LIBERATION WARS

In Thermopylae, one may observe the well-known ancient Greek inscription "O stranger, let the Lacedaemonians know that here we lie dead obeying their commands." In the Periclean Oration of Thucydides, the reader comes across the phrase "having considered that happiness means freedom and that freedom is valor, do not disregard warlike operations." It is these and similar sayings that inspired Hellenism to launch a national liberation war in the beginning of the nineteenth century, not because Hellenism was or is warlike, but because necessity dictated war, in order that Hellenism might survive and preserve the elements of its national identity in the context of a free country.

In this chapter, my aim is, in the first part, to prove that International Law and fundamental Philosophy of Law allow or recognize the use of military force, that is, war, in aid of self-determination. In the second part, the aim is to lay down the neglected (by modern historiography) diplomatic background that led to the Navy Battle of Navarino, the most critical battle of the Greek Revolution, and to approach the issue critically from the legal point of view. In the third part, my aim is to generally explore philhellenism and its role in the above war incident.

There have been various efforts for reduction or diminution of the phenomenon of war as a means for settling international disputes, for example, the Covenant of the League of Nations 1919, the Treaty of Renunciation of War, known as Kellogg-Briand Pact or Pact of Paris 1928. The most important step in that direction is the General Prohibition of the Use of Force embodied in the Charter of the United Nations. Article 2, paragraph 4, provides: "All members shall refrain in their international relations from the threat or use of force against the territorial integrity or political independence of any state, or in any manner inconsistent with the purposes of the United Nations." This provision is accompanied by exceptions.

The Concept of International Law, particularly the Law of War permits the use of force in four cases: (a) individual and collective self-defense. Article 51 of the UN Charter says: "Nothing in the present Charter shall impair the inherent right of individual or collective self-defense if an armed attack occurs against a member of the United Nations, until the Security Council has taken the measures necessary to maintain international peace and security. Measures taken in the exercise of this right of self-defense shall be immediately reported to the Security Council and shall not in any way affect the authority and responsibility of the Security Council under the present . . ." (b) humanitarian intervention, (c) collective action under Chapter VII of the UN Charter, following decision of the Security Council, in cases when regional or international security is at stake, and (d) national liberation war.

The concept of the political and legal principle of self-determination means the freedom of peoples to frame internally their own government without any external interference (internal self-determination) and in the external sphere to ordinate their own fate and international position (external self-determination). The Charter of the United Nations, in Article 1, paragraph 2, states that *one of the purposes of the United Nations is to develop friendly relations among nations based on respect of the principle of equal rights and self-determination of peoples*. Of great importance is the International Covenant on Civil and Political Rights 1966,[1] but mainly the Declaration of Independence of Colonial Territories and Peoples, adopted by the General Assembly of the United Nations Organization.

Paragraphs 1 and 2 declare that subjugation of peoples to foreign rule and sovereignty constitutes violation of fundamental human rights, is against the UN Charter and forms an obstacle to the development of international peace and cooperation. *All peoples have the right of self-determination. By virtue of that right they freely determine their political status and freely pursue their economic, social and cultural development.*

If a people of a specific territory are considered by International Law that it holds the legal right of self-determination, but the state that administers or occupies that territory denies the people to exercise that right, the people may launch war in aid of self-determination or national liberation war, terms that are synonymous and are used interchangeably.

There is general agreement with regard to the above rule of customary International Law. It is noteworthy that the states of the West do not disagree as to the validity of this rule. The use of force for deterrence of exercise of the right of self-determination is unlawful.

Of great importance is General Assembly Resolution 2105 (XX), consecrated in 1965. It recognizes the legitimacy of the struggle by peoples under colonial rule to exercise their right to self-determination and independence and invites all states to provide material and moral assistance to the national liberation movements in colonial territories.

The General Assembly also regarded that the right to self-determination refers not only to the peoples that under colonial rule, but also to the Palestinians and the inhabitant populations of South Africa.

An alternative legal basis of the rule that third states are called to assist peoples that wage war in aid of self-determination is collective self-defense. This presupposes that the rules of self-defense, which are in force in case an attack is launched against a state, apply by mutatis mutandis to national liberation wars.

Here, is must be stressed that some national liberation movements or organized peoples who wage war for self-determination are sometimes called as terrorists. I personally have no inclination to support terrorism—quite the opposite. International Law, in these cases, not only does not regard these peoples as terrorists, but grants them specific rights: (1) all rights stemming from Humanitarian Law of Armed Conflict, therefore the peoples are protected from war crimes committed against them, (2) rights and obligation stemming from the Law of Treaties, for example, to decide about boundaries disputes and to negotiate the establishment of an independent state, (3) the right to demand that respect is shown toward their official representatives, precisely because the national liberation movement functions as a *sui generis* international personality.

Philosophy of Law, and medieval philosophy in particular, based on Greek Philosophy, grounded just war theory on natural law, the principles of which are not necessarily written down, but must constitute the foundations of every legislation and corresponding political practice. More specifically, what is Natural Law? It is imperative that a definition is provided in the context of the present analysis. Natural Law is (i) all the basic practical principles which indicate that the kinds of human well-being must materialize in the form of goods, and they are somehow necessary for every reasonable man, (ii) all the basic methodological criteria of practical reasonableness, which demarcate reasonable and unreasonable thought, (iii) a general corpus of moral values.

Natural Law is Divine Law, which is composed of objective moral values, crystallized through human logic, enforceable on human life, so that well-being and excellence may be implemented.[2] A question of primary importance is whether one should rely on these principles because some divine apocalypse so dictates or because of hypothetical reasoning. The expressions *Natural Law* and *Divine Law* should not lead to a differentiation among the two concepts, and to the conclusion that Natural Law is an attribute of the material world distinct from a metaphysical principle. Plato and more intensely Aristotle do not regard the existence of God or Gods as an argument to support their position that truly there exist objective values of well-being (or objective goods). However, their reasoning and argumentation drives them to the conclusion of acceptance of the real existence of a superior being. *God holds the beginning and end of the whole*, says Plato. Aquinas, in a similar way, in his political philosophy work *Summa Theologica*, defines Natural Law as the taking part of Eternal Law in human reasonable beings.

Therefore, through Jurisprudence legal and political philosophers, such as Aquinas as well as the Roman jurists previously, tackled the issue of just war. Aquinas, much based on Aristotle, whom he often quotes in his work *Summa Theologica*, having referred to loci of the Old Testament, pursuing a logic of juristic principles, lays down the cases, in which (according to his view) war can be considered as just.

Firstly, when national liberation war is waged. This must go through the approval of the sovereign Executive.[3] In the same way that a state needs to face internal threats, Aquinas argues, it may wage war to protect its territorial sovereignty. Secondly, war is imperative, when the attacking states deserve to be punished or avenged for mistakes or misfortunes which they have caused against another states. It is stressed that such a war must essentially be launched when a state refuses to provide restitution for the illegalities that it has caused or refuses to restore an illegally occupied territory. It is also emphasized that the motives of this war must be genuine. According to a true religion or theory of the world, the medieval theorist goes on, lawful is that war which is declared on the basis of noble and genuine intentions, for the purpose of punishing wrongful acts, and aiming at restoring legal order, views shared by St. Augustine, too. This is the philosophy of law which formed the legal basis of the war waged by Greek insurgents, in an era when there was not even a League of Nations nor an organization of collective security.[4]

Modern just war theory, following the medieval one, is expressed in a nutshell as it were in the Harvard scholarly journal *Foreign Affairs*, where leading American International Law and Politics scholars, including Michael Walzer (author of *Just and Unjust Wars*), put down their position on the subject matter. In analyzing the criteria of war in aid of self-determination, and especially of intervention on part of a third state in favor of a people, the following is stressed: if a people is not prepared to spend time and energy on the national liberation movement, to place its property in its service, to risk even its own life, it should expect foreigners to come to its help. This is the primary criterion. The second criterion is need. This means that a people cannot be substantially succored by any means other than war. The third, criterion is the strong possibility that the war will be successful and that success will not be achieved to the detriment (or with heavy cost) for the people that is destined to be liberated. Nevertheless, let me submit that most national liberation wars in the history of International Law have witnessed a large number of casualties on part of those conducting the war in aid of self-determination. It is practically almost always the case that this kind of war requires human sacrifices, if the purpose, that is liberation, is to materialize.

THE POLITICAL CONTEXT OF THE BATTLE AT NAVARINO AND INTERNATIONAL LAW ON THE USE OF FORCE RAMIFICATIONS

Let us now enter the second part of the chapter. Few things have been written by Greek authors—even in scholarly series concerning the history of the Greek Nation—on the diplomatic background to the Navy Battle of Navarino. Many elements of what I shall now present are based on genuine official papers that I have studied in the context of further studies on the Use of Force in the Archives of the United Kingdom Foreign Office.

In 1818 a secret Protocol was signed by Great Britain and Russia, on which surprisingly enough Greek bibliography remains almost silent. This Protocol provided three things: (a) the possibility of a Russian-Turkish war was not precluded, (b) an effective threat of the use of force on part of Russia and (c) even if Russia decided to lead things to war against the Ottoman Empire, the agreement would not be dissolved and Great Britain would consequently be able to take part in the war.

The Protocol is revealed in the Archives of Lord Walden.[5] Lord Walden was appointed undersecretary of Foreign Affairs at the age of twenty-four. The aforementioned Protocol played an important role in the subsequent diplomacy of Great Britain and Russia.

Divine blessing was the appointment of George Canning to the United Kingdom Ministry of Foreign Affairs in 1822. He was determined to implement the secret Protocol gradually. He hoped, on the one hand, to contain Russia, that was promising the use of force in favor of the Greeks if need be, on the other hand, he was prepared to use limited controlled force on part of Great Britain to the benefit of the Greek Question of Independence, despite the opposite view of the Westminster Parliament, as he reveals in his memoirs in a letter to his friend Granville. He intended, at first instance, to remove the Turks from the Peloponnesian Morea and the islands. Toward this direction, he struggled to disentangle France and Prussia from the policy of the Great Powers of the day, that is, the policy of the Holy Alliance (to which Austria,

Prussia, France, and Great Britain belonged) with regard to the Anatolian Question. What was (or is) the Anatolian Question? Briefly, it was the effort of the Great Powers of Europe of that day to suppress liberation movements and keep friendly inter-state relations with the Ottoman Empire, to be the heirs as it were of the Ottoman Empire in case the latter ended up divided (evidently after intervening wars). At the same time, it was the effort of these very Great Powers to prevent Russia from coming down to the Aegean region and the Eastern Mediterranean, where important economic and geopolitical interests were (and pretty much are) at stake. However, Canning made it clear that he would ensure that his aims would materialize with or without the cooperation of the Holy Alliance.

Canning suggested that negotiations take place in London between Great Britain, Russia, France and Austria as regards the Question of Greek Independence. Russia and France proposed a settlement plan, which was turned down. A proposal on part of Metternich's Austria, aiming at bringing about further uncertainty, was also turned down. In the Foreign Office File titled Russia, Metternich appears saying "why do not we propose another plan so that we may intensify confusion?"

In 1827, April 10, Canning was elected Prime Minister of Great Britain. That the issue was of decisive significance is indicated by the statements of the Russian diplomat Nesselrode, who, according to the Foreign Office File *Turkey* 152, said: "Great Britain is has declared that it is an enemy of Turkey, and Canning is a little bit better than a Greek man." Archbishop Ignatius, a member of the intelligentsia of that time, wrote to Capodistrias: "the new British government is meant to be a fighter for the sake of nations and not only of aristocracy."[6] It is noteworthy that the collaborators of Canning were very much pro-Greek. Among them was the Minister of Foreign Affairs, Lord Dudley, and his Irish nephew and close coordinator, Stratford Canning. Also, the Duke of Wellington, who shared the views of the Holy Alliance, resigned from Cabinet.

Eventually, on July 6, 1827, through the decisive role of Canning, the Treaty of London was concluded. The Treaty of London, as it was called, was signed by Great Britain, Russia and France.

This Treaty was based on the application for protection that the Greeks had made to Great Britain and France, on humanitarian grounds, on the need to protect commercial activity, and on the need to fight piracy. The first terms of the Treaty formed a repetition of the provisions of the secret Protocol between Russia and Great Britain. The Great Powers would demand from the Turks and the Greeks to make truce. If this was accepted, the Great Powers and the opponents would immediately commence negotiations in Constantinople. Greece would gain its autonomy and independence and her borders would be the subject of negotiations among the allied Powers and the opposing sides.

The most important part of the Treaty was the additional article, which stated that in case the Ottoman Porte did not accept mediation within a month, the Allies would instantly send ambassadors to Greece. If any of the two opponent parties did not accept the initial truce, the Great Powers would exert all their influence, so that the aim of truce would be successful, without though taking part in the hostilities among the two sides.

In case truce would be totally turned down, the Great Powers would continue the peace making measures in accordance with steps that would be determined at a Conference, which would start its proceedings in London a week later, so that it might observe developments and guide the action of the Navy.

The article goes on, if meanwhile the Turks do not accept the truce, the admirals would consider Greeks as their friends and would unify their fleet, in order to cut down provisions and ammunition of the Turks form Egypt or the Dardanelles. But the admirals should be particularly careful, so that they may prevent measures taken against the Ottoman fleet to develop into hostilities, and should not use force, unless the Turks insist in breaking the blocks which the admirals would pose.

It was clear that the use of force could not be easily avoided. The commands to the admirals were at the end very clear and certainly did not preclude the use of strong military force. The most reliable text of this very important Treaty of London may be found in the excellent work *The Foreign Policy of Canning 1830.*

In the Commands or Guidance Rules that were sent from London by Admiral Codrington, who was in charge of the allied fleet due to his long military experience, what was further regulated was the coasts that were to be peacefully secured. And this was because the commission of mistakes must be avoided.

The From the coast of Volos in the East to the river Aspropotamos in the West, and the islands Euboea, Salamis, Aigina, Hydra, Poros, Spetses, and the rest of the adjacent islands, except Rhodes, Samos and Crete the line was demarcated, which was to be the territory of the future independent Greek State.

Canning had triumphed over every opposition to his policy expressed by the majority of Westminster Parliament, by both great parties, Tories and Whigs. He succeeded in attracting to his side public opinion, which was very much in favor of the Greek case. Meanwhile, Capodistrias was elected governor of Greece. But, totally unexpectedly, Canning died, after serious deterioration of his health. Princess Lieven, the wife of the Russian Ambassador in London, and a very active member of the social and cultural life of the British Capital, wrote: “We have just lost Canning. The Mercantile class is full of sorrow, people are in tears, anyone who is not Metternichish is in despair.” His death was characterized by the Porte as a "Prophet's Miracle," and the re-ascent to power of Wellington gave hope to the Sultan that the Treaty of 6 July would remain dead letter. If the unpredictable death of Canning had occurred five weeks earlier, that is, prior to the ratification of the Treaty of London, this fact could have had fatal consequences for the history of Greece. His people and collaborators though still held command and were determined to implement and enforce the provisions of the Treaty. On August 16, Stratford Canning gave a note to Reis Ephent by which he demanded acceptance of the terms of the Treaty within fifteen days, whereas Codrington and the French Admiral de Rigny officially announced the Treaty to the Greek Government.

The Turks, after the successes of Ibrahim and Kioutahis, as well the fall of the Acropolis of Athens, believed that the Revolution was doomed. But, they were proved wrong within the next few weeks. Stratford, wrote privately to Admiral Codrington, in a letter kept in the Foreign Office File titled *Stratford Canning's Papers* (152): "although the measures are not taken with hostile intentions, nevertheless, the interception of provisions of the Turkish fleet must eventually be imposed, if need be, and when all other measures are exhausted, through gun-shot."

In a letter to his wife. as attested in his autobiography, Admiral Codrington said: "I have never felt the need to see war, but I really believe that this could prove the most humanitarian way than any other through which we could solve this question. A strong use of force should place the Turks in our mercy."

Military acts ensued.

Kolokotronis, a few days later, sent a report to Codrington regarding the terrible and disastrous acts of Ibrahim, and requested the immediate protection of the Greek population.

The Turco-Egyptian fleet, which had already anchored in Navarino, was composed in all by eighty-nine vessels carrying 2240 firearms, whereas the allied fleet only had twenty-seven warships (twelve British, eight Russian and seven French) with 1324 firearms. The 8th of October was supposed to be the day of the great Navy Battle. The pretext was the assassination of Petros Mikelis, the messenger of Codrington. Late in the evening, everything was over. The ships of the Turkish fleet were utterly destroyed and the allied fleet lost not a single vessel. Six thousand Turco-Egyptians were killed, whereas 650 allies were killed or wounded. All three allied Powers fought with bravery and admirable collaboration. The soul of the Navy Battle though was Admiral Codrington. The immediate result of the Battle was the withdrawal of the Turco-Egyptian army from the Morea. The conclusion of the apocalyptic Navy Battle was stamped by the letter of Sir Richard Church, Commander in Chief of the Army, sent to the Greek Generals and army men:

> The Navy Battle of Navarino was clearly a just war in aid of self-determination of the Greek insurgents and simultaneously the first humanitarian war or humanitarian intervention in the modern history of International Law and International Relations. It put an end to a humanitarian catastrophe and confirmed the sanctity of human life.

Occasionally, the term "intervention" is mistakenly translated in Greek as an interference in the sovereignty of Greece. The result of this translation is very often misleading. In this case, the term "intervention" in International Law, in the nineteenth century, meant exactly what it means nowadays, that is, *armed* intervention. Those who make the translation are usually non-lawyers, without in-depth knowledge of the historical background, and hence they translate wrongly, the implication being that the intervention of the Great Powers was an illegal interference in the sovereign rights of Greece. This mistaken translation does injustice to the unquestionable historical fact. The Navy Battle of Navarino, was not merely an illegal act, but was a fully justified legal action, which was accepted and greeted by the Greek people. It must be stressed that the Greeks themselves requested the intervention and it was the constant calls for help (especially toward London) of the Greek insurgents that led, among other factors and reasons, to the Navy Battle. Hence, the first paragraph of the Treaty of London expressly states that the allied Powers received form the Greeks an earnest invitation to mediate with the Ottoman Porte.

On the other hand, some writers of International Law do not regard the Navy Battle of Navarino as a humanitarian intervention, they reject the proposition that it can be regarded as humanitarian war. Their view is based on the supposition that the intervention took place on a territory that was then under Turkish sovereignty, therefore it does not form an example of intervention which is launched with the consent of the government of a state. With respect, this view does not seem to be logical. Who was supposed to give consent to that joint humanitarian intervention of the Great Powers other than the Greek insurgents themselves? Is it conceivable that the Ottoman Porte could ever have consented to an intervention of European Powers on the territory of its Empire with the sole aim of liberating its own subjects? In essence, this view expressed by some International lawyers, fortunately a tiny minority of them, constitutes distortion one of the prerequisite of humanitarian intervention. Consent to humanitarian intervention is as a norm given by the oppressed people of a country and not by a belligerent occupant.

Furthermore, the learned and excellent late Chichele Professor of International Law in the University of Oxford, Ian Brownlie, in his book *International Law and the Use of Force by States*,[7] submits that in the case of Navarino the characterization of the intervention as "humanitarian" constitutes ex post factoism, an act which was preceded by motives and intentions other than humanitarian. He says that the writers of that era, attribute various motives to the intervention. At page 339, he concluded that the substantial motive was the prevention of the racial extermination of the Morea, but this, according to his expression, cannot be discussed in the light of a legal concept which probably did not exist at the time. Brownlie, in this case, clearly and unexpectedly contradicts himself, because in the immediately previous page of his book, namely 338, he accepts that the majority of the nineteenth-century international lawyers and writers recognized a right of humanitarian intervention. Simon Chesterman, a student of Brownlie, in his doctoral dissertation published in 2001, entitled Humanitarian Interventions and International Law, argues at page thirty-two that the military episode at Navarino is at best a questionable incident in the context of the doctrine of humanitarian intervention. The Russian involvement, he submits, had little to do with humanitarian motives and sentiments, and this had been the catalyst for the British intervention. In an attempt to support his view, he quotes a newspaper columnist, called Historicus, who, in the middle of the nineteenth century, wrote in the *Times* of London that the liberation of Greece was an act of high policy far from any province and notion of law, and that the plan of Ibrahim to commit genocide in Greece was only the pretext for the alliance between Britain and Russia against the Ottomans.

In spite of the above, in the midst of the Greek Revolution, support of Greece on the part of the Great Powers was interpreted more in the context of the sentimental interest of Europe. This is evidenced and well-documented by the commands of Lord Bathurst, then secretary for the colonies, to Sir Harry Neale, commander of the Mediterranean Station, in February 1826: "His Majesty has long has reason to lament the atrocities which have disgraced the contest in which Greece has been for so many years unhappily involved. . . . When it is understood that, whether with the consent of the Porte or not, designs are avowed by Ibrahim Pacha to extirpate systematically a whole community, to seize upon the women and children of the Morea, to transport them to Egypt, and to re-people the Morea from Africa and Asia, to change, in fact, that part of Greece from an European State into one resembling the States of Barbary; His Majesty cannot, as the Sovereign of an European State, hear of such an attempt without demanding of Ibrahim Pacha, either an explicit disavowal of his ever having entertained such an intention, or a formal denunciation of it." This confidential letter, it is noteworthy, did not see the light until many years after the Navy Battle of Navarino, and it may at least be inferred that it was not compiled for any purpose that had to do with the internal politics of Britain at the time. What is more, George Canning, when informed about the genocidal murder committed by Ibrahim in the Peloponnese, wrote to his cousin Granville: "I am beginning to believe that the time is fast approaching when we must do something about this issue."

Further, the second paragraph of the Treaty of London deserves a very careful reading: "*the allied Powers animated with the desire of putting a stop to the effusion of blood, and of preventing the evils of every kind, had resolved to combine and regulate their efforts with a view to re-establish peace-efforts demanded no less by sentiments of humanity [emphasis supplied], than by interests for the tranquility of Europe.*"

In this critical appraisal of the humanitarian intervention of the Powers in Greece it would be essential to mention that the right of humanitarian intervention exists in the Philosophy of International Law already since the beginning of the sixteenth century. Grotius, commonly referred to as the father of modern International Law, in his famous book entitled *De Jure Belli ac Pacis [On the Law of War and Peace]*, expressly writes that in cases whereby the rights of the subjects of a state are violated to a degree that the conscience of mankind is shocked, intervention in the interest of the values of humanism is legally permissible. The right of humanitarian intervention is also confirmed by customary International Law and related decisions of the International Court of Justice.

So, unquestionably, the intervention of the Great Powers in Greece was a high act of policy. Anyone denying this reality would do injustice to the actual facts. To deny the strategic and economic interests of the Powers that intervened would be a mistake, but to assert that these interests constitute the primary motives, let alone the only ones, of this military action, would amount to a distortion of international political and legal history. Such an assertion would unfairly disregard the genius and humanity exhibited predominantly by British politicians and military officials in favor of the cause for independence of Greece, which, since the fall of Constantinople underwent the most onerous and disgraceful, albeit eventually glorious, period of her history.

This brings us to the final part of the present chapter. The decisive Battle of Navarino did not come about from nowhere. It was to a great extent the result of the efforts of a brilliantly constructed network of Philhellenism, which put systematic pressure upon European political leaders through its committees, particularly in London. It is also true to say that it was the result of the intense mobilization of forces by the Greeks of the diaspora, notably by the exile classicist Coraes and the diplomat Capodistrias, who had international connections in his capacity as Foreign Minister of the Tsar. It is amazing how the Greeks combined diplomatic efforts with war, and the manner in which they succeeded in urging Britain and Russia to combine their forces for the liberation of Hellas.

Once again, I cannot but emphasize the genius and magnanimity of George Canning and his close collaborators who. He read Law at Oxford and was saturated by the principles of justice. As reported by the Oxford Dictionary of National Biography, Canning was, at his youth, a very able orator at Oxford

University, hated oligarchy, and was a firm supporter of liberal movements. He constitutes an example of the important role that political personalities can play in international relations when they hold power at the right time. Also, Admiral Codrington was undoubtedly a Philhellene. The book by Crawley, entitled *The Question of Greek Independence*, published by Cambridge University Press in 1930, which is perhaps one of the best monographs on the issue of the liberation of Greece and the fundamental role played by Britain in this regard, is full of references on the pro-Greek sentiments of Codrington.

Broadly, the affection and inclination toward classical studies and the Greek culture, the fast-growing interest of Europeans toward the descendants of the ancient Greeks and the admirable struggle of those people were among the factors that moved international public opinion, particularly the intelligentsia, favorably toward the Greek revolution and cause for independence. Everett, professor of the classics at Harvard, gave all his property to the service of the Greek revolutionaries. The British naval officer, Hastings, strengthens the struggle of the Greeks by providing his knowledge to Greek native sailors.

Lord Byron, the poet and classicist of Trinity College, Cambridge, is remembered as the paramount figure that expressed philhellenism. His sacrifice in Greece at age thirty-six was an important factor that moved and instigated the British Government in acting in favor of Greek independence.

NOTES

1. *International Covenant on Civil and Political Rights 1966*: All peoples have the right of self-determination. By virtue of that right they freely determine their political status and freely pursue their economic, social and cultural development.

2. See Iacovos Kareklas, Philosophy of Law: Ancient Greek and Modern (in Greek, ΦΙΛΟΣΟΦΙΑ ΤΟΥ ΔΙΚΑΙΟΥ: ΑΡΧΑΙΟΕΛΛΗΝΙΚΗ ΚΑΙ ΝΕΩΤΕΡΑ, Athens: NOMIKI BIBLIOTHIKI, 2012).

3. However, in my opinion, this position may not always be true, because it can be the case that a people or peoples are under sovereign rule, in which case there is no executive to approve the launching of war in aid of self-determination. Political history does, indeed, indicate and prove the validity of this legal and political proposition. A typical instance is the Greek Revolution, more of which in a moment.

4. This is only an indication of the great importance of international legal theory in the determination of most crucial questions such as war in International Law.

5. F.O. 360, United Kingdom Foreign Office.

6. C.O. [Colonial Office], *Greek Revolution*, 43.

7. Brownlie, *International Law and the Use of Force by States* (Oxford: Oxford University Press, 1963).

Chapter 9

Pro-Democratic Intervention and International Law

UNILATERAL PRO-DEMOCRATIC INTERVENTION

There is a considerable literature on the emerging right to democratic governance, arguing in essence that the democratic entitlements spelt out in human rights treaties are at last achieving some status.[1] For the greater part of the twentieth century, the relatively small number of actual democracies and uncertainty as to the precise content of such a right precluded general endorsement of a principle of democracy.[2] Moreover, as James Crawford argues, the manner in which classical International Law conceptualized sovereignty and the state was deeply undemocratic.[3]

In the course of the 1980s, however, democracy came to assume far greater importance. The number of states legally committed to open, multiparty, secret ballot elections; new discourses in International Law and International Relations stressing democracy as a value emerged and the international community showed greater willingness to encourage to apply pressure upon a state to hold or recognize the results of elections, or take part in electronic monitoring.[4] Although the right to democratic governance remains, at best, inchoate, the crucial questions that will be addressed in this chapter are whether and how such right may be legally enforced.

A preliminary distinction must be made between a unilateral right of pro-democratic intervention, and situations where the Security Council makes a determination that disruption to democracy constitutes a threat to international peace and security within the meaning of Chapter VII of the UN Charter. The fact that the Security Council authorized cation in such circumstances provides support for the view that the right to democratic intervention that the right to democratic governance may be acquiring some substance, but a finding that its absence may constitute a threat to the peace does not establish a unilateral right of intervention. It is also necessary to distinguish the more general questions of intervention by invitation[5] or in time of civil war.

This chapter will first consider the theories of International Law that have been said to support a doctrine of unilateral pro-democratic intervention. Several modern writers have adopted positions that recall Grotius's right to wage war on behalf of the oppressed. This view fell from favor with the emergence of a principle of non-intervention. Such a right of intervention is premised upon the entitlement of A to assert and enforce B's rights as against C—a doctrine of self-help that violates cardinal principles of the international legal order. A more extreme position asserts that an undemocratic regime loses the protection of International Law by effectively voiding its sovereignty. If taken literally, such a rule would render up to a third of the world's states susceptible to intervention on this basis. More realistically, it opens that way to selective application of a principle that is prone to abuse. The argument presented here is that such a norm is neither legally accurate nor politically desirable—both conclusions being drawn from the two major examples of unilateral intervention sometimes characterized as pro-democratic: the US interventions in Grenada in 1983 and in Panama in 1989–1990. The US intervention in the Dominican Republic in 1965 and US actions in Nicaragua in the early 1980s are occasionally referred to as additional examples of pro-democratic intervention, but have been considered and rejected elsewhere.[6]

Discussion of the democratic entitlement in terms of eternal enforcement is fundamentally to misconceive its nature. Popular sovereignty may well represent the aspirations of many peoples around the globe, but the only vehicle in which this particular human right may find meaningful expression remains sovereignty of a more traditional kind.

Theories on Unilateral Pro-Democratic Intervention

Popular Sovereignty

In an editorial comment published in 1990, Michael Reisman argued that the term sovereignty constituted an anachronism when applied to undemocratic governments or leaders, and that traditional concepts of sovereignty were being replaced by a popular sovereignty vested in the individual citizens of a state.[7] This meant that unilateral intervention in support or restore democracy did not violate sovereignty—and therefore International Law—but instead upheld and vindicated it.

Such a justification of unilateral intervention to promote democracy depends on a radical reconceptualization of sovereignty. Much has been written on the decline of sovereignty as the defining concept of International Law and International Relations. At its most extreme, popular sovereignty is said to have displaced the traditional notion of sovereignty as the critical new constitutive policy of International Law. On this view, the Austinian conception of the sovereign as by definition the repository of legal authority has been supplanted by the state authorized to represent and protect the individuals from which it derives its reason to exist. Reisman, cited above, concluded that it was anachronistic to say that the United States violated Panama's sovereignty in 1989 by launching an invasion to capture its head of state. This is not so much a logical conclusion. No matter what role the concept of popular sovereignty plays in modern International Law, it does not follow that the illegitimacy of one regime entitles a foreign government or any foreign state to use military force to install a more "legitimate" regime. Although similar positions are adopted by Anthony D'Amato and Fernando Teson, who dismiss any defense of the principle of non-intervention as examples of the rhetoric of statism and the Hegelian myth respectively, what they and Reisman do not appear to consider is the possibility that both Noriega's voiding of the 1989 election and the US invasion violated Panamanian sovereignty in various ways.

Within any normative system, rights will inevitably conflict. It is not enough to assert that the rights of Panamanians are being violated and that this must trump a conflicting right that prohibits the unilateral use of force in international relations. Despite the fact that sovereignty has to some degree been transformed since the adoption of the UN Charter, democracy has not displaced peace as the principal concern of that instrument, and of the international legal system more generally.[8] A comparison may be made with the right of self-determination: enshrined in the major human rights instruments and numerous resolutions of the General Assembly, it is nevertheless that any right of secession to which it might give rise is limited or nonexistent—as a result of Articles 2(4) and 2(7) of the Charter—to the colonial context. This view finds support in the International Court of Justice's judgment in *Nicaragua*. The Court held that, regardless of what the United States thought of Nicaragua's Sandinista regime:

> Adherence by any state to any doctrine does not constitute a violation of customary International Law; to hold otherwise would make nonsense of the fundamental principle of state sovereignty, on which the whole of International Law rests, and the freedom of choice of the political, social, economic and cultural system of a state. Consequently, Nicaragua's domestic policy options, even assuming that they correspond to the description given of them by the Congress finding, cannot justify on the legal plane the various actions of the Respondent complained of.[9]

The Reagan Doctrine

The closest that a state administration has come to articulating a foreign policy consistent with a right of pro-democratic intervention is the Reagan Doctrine:

> Mirroring the basic American constitutional principles, the Reagan Doctrine rests on the claim that legitimate government depends on the consent of the governed and on its respect for the rights of citizens. A government is not legitimate merely because it exists, not merely because it has independent rulers, Nazi Germany had a de facto government headed by Germans; this did not make it legitimate.[10]

Leaving aside the obvious question of whether Nazi Germany's illegitimacy in 1945 derived from the treatment of its civilian population or its campaign of aggressive war, the implication appears to be that legitimacy under President Ronald Reagan was linked to the consent and the rights of the governed. In fact, however, the Reagan's Doctrine application was much more limited. Writing in 1989, Jeane Kirkpatrick and Allan Gerson (US permanent representative to the United Nations and counsel to the US mission respectively from 1981 to 1985), went on to emphasize that the Reagan Doctrine had been developed primarily as a response to the Brezhnev Doctrine, countering the perceived Soviet objective of global empire.[11] As such the legal basis for the support—including military support—for insurgencies was justified ion the ground of self-defense. This was made clear by Reagan himself in the 1985 State of the Union address that came to be seen as a significant articulation of the doctrine:

> We must not break faith with those who are risking their lives—on every continent, from Afghanistan to Nicaragua—to defy Soviet-supported aggression and secure rights which have been ours from birth. . . . Support for freedom fighters is self-defense.[12]

The doctrine was criticized in its day and its applications in Grenada and Nicaragua were condemned by the General Assembly and the ICHJ respectively.

The Copenhagen Document

It has been argued that some support for the democratic intervention thesis may be found in the document adopted by the CSCE in its 29 June 1990 meeting in Copenhagen.[13] One of a series of documents elaborating the non-binding Final Act of Helsinki, the Copenhagen Document contains broad provisions concerning respect for human and minority rights. Here of particular interest are its provision on the link between human rights, representative government, and the responsibility of states to defend and protect these institutions.

The participating states declare that the will of the people, freely and fairly expressed through periodic and genuine elections is the basis of the authority and legitimacy of government. As quoted by Malvina Halberstam,

> they recognize their responsibility to defend and protect . . . the democratic order freely established through the will of the people against the activities of persons, groups or organizations that engage in or refuse to renounce terrorism or violence aimed at the overthrow of that order or of that of another participating state.[14]

Halberstam thus asserts that a strong argument can be made that the Copenhagen Document authorizes one state to intervene including the use of force to protect a freely elected government in another state: "While paragraph 6 does specifically authorize the use of force," she states, "neither does it prohibit the use of force."[15] Such pedantry is correct but misleading. It is instructive to quote in full the words omitted by the ellipsis in Halberstam's extract: "the participating state recognize their responsibility to defend and protect, in accordance with their laws, their international human rights obligations and their international commitments, the democratic order freely established."[16] By implication, this would make such a defense and protection subject to Article 2(4) of the UN Charter.[17]

In some circumstances, a request from the legitimate regime in time of crisis may justify intervention. Halberstam extends this, however, to cover a freely elected government that does not request assistance. Citing the justification presented by D'Amato and Abraham Sofaer for the US invasion of Panama, she argues that such an intervention would not contravene Article 2(4) of the UN Charter. At the same time, Halberstam suggests that the document in fact provides evidence of a new emerging right of intervention independent of Article 2(4). Referring to Franck's analysis of another international instrument, she argues by analogy that the provisions of the Copenhagen Document are also weighted with the terminology of opinion juris and are deliberately norm creating. Franck was, however, discussing the UN Charter. There is some dispute as to the extent to which CSCE documents are to be considered evidence of customary International Law. Although not enforceable in themselves, that they provide evidence or will influence the development of customary International Law. Nevertheless, her case for this influence is surely overstated.

Although she notes that the right she interprets as being created or recognized in the Copenhagen Document is more limited that that proposed by Reisman or the Reagan Doctrine, the fact that she implies that it would have provided a legal basis for the US invasion of Panama suggest its probable scope of operation. Moreover, such an interpretation is inconsistent with the Moscow Document adopted by the CSCE in 1991. Once again, the participating states condemned forces that seek to take power from a representative government of a participating state, and committed themselves to

> support vigorously, in accordance with the Charter of the United Nations, in case of overthrow or attempted overthrow of a legitimately elected government of a participating state by undemocratic means, the legitimate organs of a state.[18]

Although Halberstam's analysis of the Copenhagen Document is footnoted by a number of writers in support of a right of pro-democratic intervention,[19] her conclusions do not stand up to much scrutiny. Except for the Reagan Doctrine, there is no state practice to support her interpretation.

Legitimacy, Recognition, and Intervention

Underlying the various approaches to the external consequences of the installation of particular regimes is the more basic question of the international legal status of governments. It is important to note that in the years immediately preceding the period currently under discussion, both the United States and the United Kingdom abandoned the practice of granting formal recognition to regimes that came into power by unconstitutional means. This position is consistent with the practice of the majority of states, which formally recognize states rather than governments.

For the United Kingdom, Lord Carrington explained that this change in policy occurred because the previous practice of recognition had been misunderstood as implying approval of a new regime, particularly where there might be a public concern about human rights violations or the manner in which the regime came to power:

> We have therefore concluded that there are practical advantages in following the policy of many other countries in not according recognition to Governments. Like them, we shall continue to decide the nature of our dealings with regimes which come to power unconstitutionally in the light of our assessment of whether they are able of themselves to exercise effective control of the territory of the state concerned and seem likely to continue to do so.[20]

Actually, the United States under President Rutherford Hayes (1877–1881) had required a demonstration of popular support as a criterion for political recognition of a government. This was part of an elaborate set of criteria for recognition that developed over the nineteenth century. In 1977, the State Department explicitly deemphasized the use of recognition in favor of focusing on whether the United States wished to have diplomatic relations with new governments. The establishment of such relations, according to the State Department, 'does not involve approval or disapproval but merely demonstrates a willingness on our part to conduct our affair with other governments directly.'[21]

Nevertheless, reports of the death of recognition of governments as a meaningful practice in International Law are rather exaggerated. In spite of modification of the practice of recognition—the abandonment of formal public statements of recognition—legal consequences continue to flow from dealing or not dealing with particular regimes. State practice continues to demonstrate for formal recognition. The Security Council has occasionally called upon states not to recognize any regime set up by an illegitimate occupying power, and decided, acting under Chapter VII of the UN Charter that members states shall refrain from recognizing the illegal regime of Ian Smith in Southern Rhodesia.[22]

The recognition or non-recognition of regimes depending on their commitment to democracy may well prove the most effective means of fostering a right of this form of polity. There is some evidence from the breakup of the USSR and the former Yugoslavia that a regime's respect for democratic and other human rights may be required as a precondition for the recognition of a state. There is, however, no evidence that states generally withhold recognition from non-democratic regimes; such regimes are occasionally allowed to participate in intergovernmental organizations and to enjoy the benefits and protections of International Law—notably, a large proportion of the international community supported military action in defense of Kuwaiti sovereignty in 1990–1991, though it had no pretensions to democracy. An exception to this is the Organization of American states, which in 1997 amended its Charter to permit suspension of a member whose democratic government is overthrown by force.[23] However, it is not argued that the failure to recognize a particular regime deprives that State of the protection afforded by Article 2(4) of the UN Charter.

There is also a certain question of consistency here. If one accepts that non-democratic states are international legal persons capable of acting as such (for example, in their capacity to conclude binding treaties), it seems odd to argue that their international legal right does not extend to the basic principle prohibiting the use of force. This inconsistency is exacerbated by the fact that the prohibition of the use of force is widely regarded as having achieved the legal status of a *jus cogens* rule. A Treaty providing for an illegal use of force would thus be void under Article 53 of the Vienna Convention on the Law of Treaties. Contrary to this legal situation, even the most fervent supporters of the right to democratic governance do not claim that this right has achieved a *jus cogens* status.

STATE PRACTICE ON PRO-DEMOCRATIC INTERVENTION

This section sub-chapter considers the two major examples of unilateral intervention characterized as pro-democratic: the US intervention in Grenada (1983) and Panama (1989).

US Intervention in Grenada, 1983

On October 1983 a force of about four hundred US Marines and fifteen hundred paratroops, together with three hundred soldiers from neighboring Caribbean states, landed in Grenada, where a violent coup d'état had been staged by radical Marxist opponents of the leftist Maurice Bishop regime. The newly self-appointed Revolutionary Military Council was deposed after three days of fighting. US troops withdrew by 15 December, leaving only a small number of US and Caribbean support personnel on the island. Precise casualty figures were disputed, but appear to have numbered in the low hundreds (including up to forty-seven in the accidental bombing of a hospital).

The Reagan administration provided three justifications operations Urgent Fury. First, it cited an in an invitation form the Governor-General of Grenada, received on 24 October 1983. According to Deputy Secretary of State Kenneth Dam, the legal authorities of the Governor-General remained the sole source of governmental legitimacy on the island in the wake of the tragic events. As a point of Constitutional Law, this is open to question.[24] Moreover the invasion was already in an advanced stage of implementation by the time the request was supposedly received—just one day before the troops landed. Although the proximity of the request to the invasion is not determinative of its legality, it does indicate clearly that even the United States did not regard it as decisive.[25] The *Economist* (which strongly supported the action) concluded that the request was almost certainly a fabrication concocted between the Organization of Eastern Caribbean states and Washington to calm the post-invasion diplomatic storm.

Secondly, the United States cited a request to intervene from the OECS. On 2 November 1983, Dam refereed to Articles 3, 4, and 8 of the OECS Treaty, which, he stated, deal with local as well as external threats to peace and security.[26] This reference was misleading—the threat does refer to such threats but not in terms that could possibly justify the use of force against a member state. Three months later, State Department Legal Adviser Davis Robinson presented a modified position, relying instead on Article 6, which grants plenary authority to the heads of government of the OECS states.[27] He then referred to Article 3(2) which, he stated, 'expressly empowers the heads of government to pursue joint policies in the field of mutual defense and security, and such other activities calculated to further the purposes of the Organization as the member states may from time to time decide.' He omitted to mention that Article 3(2) merely states the fields in which member states will endeavor to co-ordinate, harmonize, and pursue joint policies. The Major Purposes listed in Article 3(1) include the defense of member states sovereignty, territorial integrity, and independence.[28] In both statements the United States relied upon Chapter VIII of the UN Charter in a manner that conflated pacific means of dispute settlement under Article 52 with enforcement actions under Article 53—measures that require Security Council authorization. Only the former Article was cited by the United States to justify an action that was clearly not pacific.

Thirdly, the United States invoked the protection of nationals abroad as a legal justification. The facts supporting this thesis have been contested—in particular, the United States asserted that Grenadian officials refused to let US citizens leave the island, although Canada claimed to have flown a chartered plane to and from the island on the very day of the intervention. It was acknowledged by US officials that the scale of the operation went beyond the limits of this narrowly drawn ground for the use of force.

A Security Council resolution deploring the intervention as a violation of International Law was vetoed by the United States.[29] The General Assembly did, however, pass a resolution that deeply deplored the US-led intervention as a flagrant violation of International Law.[30] Subsequent events also undermined the US legal position. None of the Eastern Caribbean states involved referred to the humanitarian motives initially stressed by the United States. Instead, they claimed that the action was to help stabilize the country to restore law and order, but above all to block the Russians and the Cubans, to prevent Marxist revolution from spreading to all the islands. They described the landing as a preemptive defensive action.

In the attempt to find support for a unilateral right of pro-democratic intervention, Grenada is a strained example. The United States itself did not seek to raise this justification, or any justification that could be seen to imply a right of pro-democratic intervention. In a letter to the American Bar Association, a State Department Legal Adviser stressed that the United States specifically did not rely on an expanded view of self-defense, new interpretations of Article 2(4) or a broad doctrine of humanitarian intervention. As Chesterman observes, even if it had invoked the restoration of democracy as a justification, "the preponderance of opinion juris in this instance is to be found in the negative reaction of other states, and thus supports the contrary view."[31]

US Intervention in Panama, 1989[32]

Supporters of a right of unilateral pro-democratic intervention rely most heavily on the US invasion of Panama in 1989 as a paradigmatic example of their theory at work. Close examination confirms, however, that the case of Panama supports precisely the opposite conclusion.

On 20 December 1989, twenty-four thousand US troops begun an operation to overthrow the government of Panama and capture its head of state, General Manuel Noriega. President George Bush explained and justified the action on four grounds: "to safeguard the lives of Americans, to defend democracy in Panama, to combat drug trafficking and to protect the integrity of the Canal Treaty." Having rendered Noriega fugitive, the United States recognized the rightful leadership of the likely victors of elections held earlier that year; diplomatic relations would resume immediately, and steps would be taken to lift economic sanctions imposed against the Noriega regime.[33] US forces would be withdrawn as quickly as possible. Bush added that he would continue to seek solutions to the problems of this region through dialogue and multilateral diplomacy.

Analysis of the legal basis of the action—code-named 'Operation Just Case'- is made difficult by the amalgamation of policy and legal reasoning in such statements. Of the four grounds outlined above, the exercise of an inherent right of self-defense safeguarded under Article 51 of the UN Charter and the protection of nationals abroad surely could amount to a legal argument. But it was the claim that intervention may be justified in support of democracy that won the strongest support from legal academics, coming predominantly from the United States. D'Amato described US actions in Panama and previously Grenada as milestones along the path to a new non-statist conception of International Law. Reisman similarly heralded a new era in which "the people, not governments, are sovereign."[34] In a rather isolationist conception of customary International Law each regarded the invasion as a significant and positive development, apparently ignoring the broad condemnation of the intervention by the international community. A Security Council Resolution was blocked by the American veto.[35] The General Assembly condemned the action. Professor Sir Elihu Lauterpacht was a rare non-US voice in support of the invasion, stating that the only justification offered by the United States with any merit was that it had "acted in support of the democratic process—a concept of internationally recognized relevance."[36]

The Bush administration invoked democracy in support of the invasion in two ways: as the exercise of a right to act unilaterally to promote democracy in another state, and as a legitimate assistance to a democratically elected head of state, Guillermo Endara, who, it was claimed, had consented to that action. In accordance to Abraham Sofaer, Legal Adviser to the State

Department at the time of the invasion, when Endara was informed of the impending arrival of US troops on 19 December 1989, he

> decided to be sworn in as President. He welcomed the US action, presented his views as to the proper objectives of US efforts and immediately begun to co-operate fully in their implementation. He appealed to the Panamanian forces not to resist the US action, which he said was unavoidable and seeks to end the Noriega dictatorship and reestablish democracy, justice, and freedom.[37]

Even if one accepts the legitimacy of Endara and his colleagues, the United States never claimed that he actually requested the invasion. Although President Bush stated that Endara welcomed the assistance of the United States[38] and there was some reference to his being consulted,[39] he was informed of the plans for a military intervention only when troops were already in the air. Endara was sworn in at Fort Clayton, a US military base in the Canal Zone, less than an hour before the invasion begun.

There is, in fact, some evidence that Endara was not entirely happy about the invasion, which he later described as a 'kick in the head,' stating that he would have been happier without it.[40] In a profile on him written in January 1990, he explained his reaction to the news from US officials that an invasion was imminent and that they wanted him to take the oath as president:

> It would have been very easy for me to say, 'I'm not going to take this job under occupation by American forces'. . . . But I knew that I couldn't do that. I had to assume the responsibility of Government—the people chose me to be President. I couldn't simply tell the US: 'You pick the Government. You are the occupying power and you do what you want.'[41]

This raises the question of what might have happened had he refused to take an oath as president. Sofaer argues that one reason Endara's consent was not secured prior to the invasion is that it would have exposed him to unjustifiable political and physical risk.[42] But, as the New York Bar Association observes, the claim that unilateral intervention is justified in support of democracy is weakened when elected leaders are unable to ask openly for such intervention for fear of popular disapproval.[43] It might have been such concerns that led Endara claim initially that he was sworn in on Panamanian territory—an assertion contradicted by witnesses and uniformly disregarded by the press.

After noting that Endara'a consent would have been sufficient to justify the invasion had he controlled the territory of Panama and been able to exercise governmental powers prior to 19 December 1989,[44] Sofaer asserts that the fact that he lacked such control does not deprive his consent of legal significance.[45] It is not clear what Sofaer intends by this, but it may indicate an argument that a new government may retrospectively validate the action that brought it to power. This appears to be the import of Lauterpacht's comment that

> What matters in law is not the technical propriety of the United States action at its inception but whether the Government of Panama itself now regards that action as lawful.[46]

The implication is that a newly installed regime may pardon violations of International Law committed against its predecessor. Regarding their obligations under the rules of state responsibility, this may be the case, although if the norm breached was one of *jus cogens*, then it is extremely doubtful that any *ex post facto* waiver would be effective.[47] There is now very considerable support for the view that the prohibition of the unlawful use of force constitutes a peremptory norm of International Law. As already indicated, a treaty violating this norm would be void according to the Vienna Convention on the Law Treaties.

Also, international Courts and Tribunals are not bound to accept such a waiver. In the *Barcelona Traction Case,* the ICJ held that certain rules of International Law entail obligations *erga omnes*, with all states having a legal interest in the protection of the rights involved. By way of illustration, the Court referred to the obligations outlawing acts of aggression.[48]

If an intervention were to violate such an obligation, other states may be considered individually as injured parties.[49]

In the event, most Latin American states withdrew their ambassadors from Panama after the invasion and refused to recognize the Endara Administration, stating that diplomatic relations would be normalized when the US troops returned to pre-invasion levels and some of form of plebiscite demonstrated popular support for the new regime. The Permanent Council of the OAS initially refused to accept the credentials of the ambassador dispatched by Endara to represent Panama. Noriega's ambassador remained and participated in the vote criticizing the invasion.[50] Over the course of the following months, however, most governments extended recognition to the Endara regime.

STATE PRACTICE EVALUATION

The immediate obstacle to adopting the arguments advanced favoring a right of unilateral pro-democratic intervention is that they are simply not accepted by even a significant minority of states.[51] Despite the fact that there is evidence of support on part of the United States and certain US legal scholars,[52] upholding or restoring democracy has not previously been asserted as an independent basis for intervention. It was not raised by Tanzania when it deposed Idi Amin in Uganda in 1979, nor by France when it helped overthrow 'Emperor' Bokassa in the Central African Republic in 1979. On those occasions when it has been invoked by the United States to justify its actions in Grenada, Nicaragua, and Panama (expressly or by comments of its advisers and legal commentators), the action has been condemned by the international community and by the ICJ, when the issue came it before it.

Also, there is a wealth of evidence supporting exactly the opposite conclusion. The Declaration on Friendly Relations, adopted without a vote by the General Assembly in 1970, affirms that every state has an inalienable right to choose its political, economic. Social and cultural systems, without interference in any form by another state.[53] General Assembly Resolution 45/150 (1990), adopted by a large majority recognizes that.

> The efforts of the international community to enhance the effectiveness of the principle of periodic and genuine elections should not call into question each state's sovereign right freely to choose and develop its political, social, economic, and cultural systems, whether they conform to the preferences of other states.[54]

Apart from the doctrinal problems that such an argument poses, it is also questionable that such a doctrine would be really desirable. In the *Nicaragua* Case, the Court refused to contemplate the creation of a new rule opening a right of intervention by one state against another on the ground that the latter has opted for some ideology or political system.[55] Such a rule would be exercised, *ex hypothesi*, arbitrarily. It is noteworthy that Thomas Franck, an exponent of aright of pro-democratic intervention, in a landmark paper on the right to democratic governance, argued that for such a right to be meaningful, the opposite approach should be pursued:

> Steps should be taken to meet the fear of some smaller states that election monitoring will lead to more Panama-style unilateral military intervention by the powerful, perhaps even for reasons less convincing than those which provoked the 1989 US military strike against the Noriega dictatorship. That a new rule might authorize actions to enforce democracy still conjures up just such chilling images to weaker states, which see themselves as the potential objects of enforcement of dubious democratic norms under circumstances of doubtful probity.[56]

Reisman disputes this position. He argues that a commitment to democracy coupled with an unwillingness to allow for its unilateral enforcement (if that is the only feasible option) produces anomalous results such as sanctions regimes that severely punish the victims while enriching the villains.

There are other ways for one state to manifest its concern at the undemocratic behavior of another. The most common manner of doing so is to refuse to recognize a regime's representative authority, or at least refuse to deal with it in some—particularly economic—ways.

Further, pro-democratic intervention violates the right of internal self-determination, that is, the unfettered right of peoples to choose freely their own governmental system without any external interference. Therefore, it is very difficult for a state to impose as it were a democratic government in another state, particularly if that other state's population would not concur to such a political development. On the other hand, should not the international community legitimately intervene in cases whereby one is faced with flagrant violation of human rights of the subjects of an oppressive regime, especially in view of the fact that democracy is in itself a significant and fundamental human right?

It may be the case that the political conditions globally are gradually moving towards the establishment of a right of pro-democratic military intervention.

NOTES

1. See Thomas Franck, 'The Emerging Right to Democratic Governance' (1992) 86 *American Journal of International Law* 46; Gregory Fox, 'The Right to Political Participation in International Law' (1992) 17 *Yale International law Journal* 539, Gregory Fox and Brad Roth (eds.) *Democratic Governance and International Law* (Cambridge: Cambridge University Press, 2000).

2. James Crawford, 'Democracy and International Law' (1993) 44 *British Yearbook of International Law*, 113–16.

3. James Crawford, 'Democracy and International Law' (1993) 44 *British Yearbook of International Law*, 113–16.

4. See Agenda for Democratization, UN Doc A/51/761 (1996); Support by the United Nations System of the Efforts of Governments to Promote and Consolidate New or Restored Democracies, UN Doc. A/50/332.

5. See Ian Brownlie, *International Law and the Use of Force by States* (Oxford: Clarendon Press, 1963), 317–27.

6. See Brad Roth, *Government Illegitimacy in International Law* (Oxford: Clarendon Press, 1999).

7. Michael Reisman, 'Sovereignty and Human Rights in Contemporary International Law' (1990) 84 *American Journal of International Law*, 866.

8. Simon Chesterman, *Just War or Just Peace: Humanitarian Intervention and International Law* (Oxford: Oxford University Press, 2001), 92.

9. *Nicaragua* (*Merits*) [1986] ICJ Reports 14, 133 para. 263.

10. Jeance J Kirkpatrick and Allan Gerson, The Reagan Doctrine, Human Rights, and International Law, in Louis Henkin (ed) *Right v Might: International Law and the Use of Force* (New York: Council on Foreign Relations, 1989), 19, 23.

11. *Ibid.*, 23.

12. President Reagan, State of Union Address, 6 February 1985, in [1985] *Reagan Papers* 135.

13. Rein Mullerson, 'Self-Defense in the Contemporary World' in Lori Fisler Damrosch and David Scheffer (eds), *Law and Force in the New International Order* (Boulder: Westview, 1991), 13, 15–16. See further Christopher C DeMuth, *The Reagan Doctrine and Beyond* (Washington, DC: American Enterprise Institute for Public Policy Research, 1988).

14. Copenhagen Document, para. 6.

15. Halberstam, 'The Copenhagen Document: Intervention in Support of Democracy' (1993) 34 *Harvard International Law Journal* 163.

16. Copenhagen Document, para 6.

17. Simon Chesterman, *Just War or Just Peace: Humanitarian Intervention and International Law* (Oxford: Oxford University Press, 2001), 95.

18. Conference on Security and Co-operation in Europe: Document of the Moscow Meeting of the Conference on the Human Dimension, Emphasizing Respect for Human Rights, Pluralistic Democracy, the Rule of Law, and Procedures for Fact-Finding, 3 October 1991, reprinted in *International Legal Materials* 1670, para. 17.

19. See e,g. Michael Reisman, 'Humanitarian Intervention and Fledgling Democracies' (1995) 18 *Fordham International Law Journal* 794, 802 n 26.

20. UK Parliamentary Debates, Lords, 28 April 1980, cols 1121–2, reprinted in (1980) 51 *British Yearbook of International Law* 367.

21. Diplomatic Recognition: A Foreign Relations Outline (1977) 77 (1998) *Department of State Bulletin* 462, 463.

22. SC Res 277 (1990) para 2 (Rhodesia) adopted 14-0-1 (Spain)

23. OAS Charter (1948) article 9, as amended by the Protocol of Washington, adopted on 14th December 1992 by the Sixteenth Special Session of the General Assembly of the OAS, amendment entered into force 1997. For US ratification see (1994) 88 *American Journal of International Law* 719.

24. See Michael Levitin, The Law of Force and the Force of Law: Grenada, the Falklands, and Humanitarian Intervention (1986) 27 *Harvard International Law Journal* 621, 646–47.

25. Robert J Beck, 'International Law and the Decision to Invade Grenada: A Ten-Year Retrospective' *Virginia International Law Journal* 765, 789–90.

26. Dam, Statement before the House Committee on Foreign Relations.

27. Robinson, Letter addressed to Professor Edward Gordon, Chairman of the Committee on Grenada of the American Bar Association's Section on International Law and Practice.

28. OECS Treaty, n 73, article 3(1)(b).

29. [1983] *UNYB* 211. The draft resolution was voted down 11-1-3 (US against; Togo, UK, and Zaire abstaining).

30. GA Res 38/7 (1983) adopted 108-9-27.

31. Simon Chesterman, *Just War or Just Peace: Humanitarian Intervention and International Law* (Oxford: Oxford University Press, 2001), 102.

32. See generally Simon Chesterman, 'Rethinking Panama: International Law and the US Invasion of Panama, 1989,' in Guy Goodwin-Gill and Stefan A Talmon (eds), *The Reality of International Law: Essays in Honour of Ian Brownlie* (Oxford: Oxford University Press, 1999), 57.

33. See Memorandum Terminating Economic Sanctions Against Panama, 20 December 1989, in [1990] 2 *Bush Papers* 1726 (lifting economic sanctions imposed by Executive Order No 12635).

34. Reisman, *Ante*, n 18; Panel Discussion,' The Panamanian Revolution: Diplomacy, War and Self-Deytermination in Panama: I Self-Determination and Intervention in Panama' (1990) 84 *American Society of International Law Proceedings* 182, 192 (Teson).

35. [1989] *UNYB* 175. The draft resolution was voted down 10-4-1 (Canada, France, UK, and US against; Finland abstaining).

36. Elihu Lauterpacht, 'Letter to the Editor: Legal Aspects of the Panama Invasion,' *Times*, 23 December 1989.

37. Abraham Sofaer, 'The Legality of the United States Action in Panama' (1991) 29 *Columbia Journal of Transnational Law* 281, 289.

38. Letter from President Bush to Speaker of the House Thomas Foley, 21 December 1989, in [1989] 2 *Bush Papers* 1734, para 5.

39. See Letter from Mr. Pickering, Permanent Representative of the United States to the United Nations, to the President of the Security Council, 20 December 1989, S/21035 (1989) para 2: The United States undertook this action after consultations with the democratically elected leaders of Panama.

40. Philip Geyelin, 'Noriega Was Only Part of the Problem,' *Washington Post*, 1 January 1990.

41. David Pitt, 'To Many in Panama, the New President is an Enigma Wrapped in a Smile,' *New York Times*, 28 January 1990.

42. Sofaer, *Ibid.*

43. Association of the Bar of the City of New York, *Ibid.*, 82.

44. Sofaer, *Ibid.*, n 94, 290 (citing Lassa Francis Lawrence Oppenheim, *International Law* (Hersch Lauterpacht ed); 8th edn; Longmans, 1955), 305.

45. Sofaer, *Ibid.*, n 94, 290.

46. Lauterpacht, *Ibid.*, n 93.

47. Simon Chesterman, *Just War or Just Peace: Humanitarian Intervention and International Law* (Oxford: Oxford University Press, 2001), 105. See also Ronzitti, 'Use of Force, *Jus Cogens* and State Consent,' in Cassese, *Ibid.*, n 80, 147.

48. *Barcelona Traction Case* [1970] ICJ Reports 3, 32.

49. See Yoram Dinstein, *War, Aggression and Self-Defense* (2nd ed. Cambridge: Cambridge University Press, 1994), 112.

50. Tom Farer, 'Panama: Beyond the Charter Paradigm' (1990) 84 *American Journal of International Law* 503, 510.

51. See generally Oscar Schachter, 'The Legality of Pro-Democratic Invasion' (1984) 78 *American Journal of International Law* 645, 649; Louis Henkin, 'The Use of Force: Law and US Policy' in Henkin, *Ibid.*

52. The UK has also provided support for the US invasion in Panama. In a statement on the subject, the Secretary of State for Foreign and Commonwealth Affairs, Mr. Douglas Hurd, observed in part: 'We fully support the American action to remove General Noriega, which was undertaken with the agreement of the leaders who clearly won the elections held last May. Noriega's arbitrary rule was maintained by force. We and many others have repeatedly condemned Noriega and called for the election result to be respected. Every peaceful means of trying to see the results of the democratic elections respected have failed.'

53. Declaration on Friendly Relations, GA Res. 2625 (XXV) (1970).

54. GA Res 45/151 (1990 para 3 adopted 111-29-11.

55. *Nicaragua (*Merits) [1986] ICJ Reports 14, 133.

56. Thomas Franck, 'Legitimacy and the Democratic Entitlement,' in Fox and Roth, *Ibid.*

Chapter 10

Military Intervention by Treaty Right

The Turkish Military Intervention of Cyprus

The present chapter examines the diplomatic and legal context to the Turkish intervention in Cyprus 1974. On the one hand, the main legal argument put forward by Turkey to justify the intervention, which was based on the Republic of Cyprus Treaty of Guarantee, is put under scrutiny; international legal theories on the legality of intervention envisaged by Treaty are judiciously presented. On the other, the diplomatic background to the Treaty in question is explored in the light of available Foreign Office Files, UN documents, UK Parliamentary Debates to verify whether a right to military intervention was expressly provided for. Then the conduct of Turkey is tackled on the hypothesis that she did have a right to intervene. Finally, it is stressed how the preceding discussion can be useful for security arrangements in the context of the current negotiations for a settlement to the pending Cyprus question.

At dawn of the 20th of July 1974, Turkey, following the coup d'etat of the 15th of July 1974 engineered by the Greek military junta (then ruling Greece) to overthrow the democratically elected President Archbishop Makarios,[1] proceeded to an armed attack[2] by air and by sea against the independent and sovereign Republic of Cyprus.

TURKISH JUSTIFICATIONS FOR THE INTERVENTION AND CLAIMS REGARDING THE TREATY

Various justifications were given by the Turkish leadership for the purposes of the intervention. The then Prime Minister of Turkey Mr. Ecevit made the following official statement according to the statement of the Permanent Representative of Turkey Mr. Olcay at the meeting of the Security Council of the 20th of September 1974:

> The Turkish armed forces started this morning an operation of peace in Cyprus to put an end to struggle of decades of years brought about by extremist elements. During the last steps of the Cyprus tragedy, these extremist elements started massacring their own people, the Greeks. It is admitted by everybody that the last coup has been staged by the dictatorial regime of Athens. As a matter of fact, it was more than a coup: it was a violent and flagrant violation of the independence of the Republic of Cyprus and of the international treaties on which the Republic was founded. Turkey is co-guarantor of the independence and the constitutional order of Cyprus. Turkey acting is fulfilling her legal responsibility. The Turkish Government has not resorted to the armed action until after all the other means were tried and proved unsuccessful. This is not an invasion but an act to put an end to invasion. The Turkish armed forces will not open fire unless being fired at. I am addressing all the Greeks in Cyprus who have been the victims of atrocities, of terrorism and dictatorship: bury in the past the dark days of inter-communal enmities and strife which were resorted to by the terrorists themselves. Join hand in hand with your Turkish brothers to speed up the victory and together build up a new free and happy Cyprus.[3]

In other statements he said that the objective of the operation was to overthrow the regime which toppled Archbishop Makarios; when, however, he was asked to say whether the intention was to restore Archbishop Makarios to power he declined to answer, as he declined to state whether Turkey intended pulling out its forces after gaining control of the island.

In a Turkish government communiqué issued immediately after the intervention by the Turkish Embassy in London it was stated that Turkey as one of the guarantor powers had decided to carry out its obligations under article IV (2) of the Treaty of Guarantee with a view to safeguarding the security of life and property of the Turkish community and even that of many Greek Cypriots.[4]

The main argument put forward by Turkey to justify the 1974 military intervention in Cyprus is based on the Treaty of Guarantee of the Cyprus Republic. The Treaty, signed on 16 August 1960 between the United Kingdom, Greece, Turkey, and the Republic of Cyprus, forms an integral part of the constitutional order of the Republic.[5] By Article I, the Republic of Cyprus undertook the obligation to maintain its independence, territorial integrity, and security as well as respect for its Constitution. Under article II, Greece, Turkey, and the United Kingdom guaranteed the independence, territorial integrity, and security of the Republic of Cyprus and the situation established by the basic articles of the Constitution. Article IV, which constitutes the strongest basis of the Turkish argument provides the following:

> *In the event of a breach of the provisions of the present Treaty, Greece, Turkey, and United Kingdom undertake to consult together with respect to the representations or measures necessary to ensure observance of those provisions. In so far as common or concerted action may not prove possible, each of the three guaranteeing Powers reserves the right to act with the sole aim of re-establishing the situation created by the present Treaty.*

Turkey first declared that intervention had been to guarantee the independence of the island. According to Turkey, the coup government of Mr. Sampson was no more than a puppet regime under orders from Greece, ready to rule the end of the island's independence and to annex it to Greece. In a Turkish government communiqué of 20 July it was stated that "the Turkish community in the island can no longer tolerate this situation which offends human dignity and threatens the lives and the very existence of its greater majority, and they, therefore, anticipate Turkey *as a Guarantor Power*, to liberate them as soon as possible."[6] The Turkish government went on to state that "*Turkey as one of the guarantor powers had decided to carry out its obligations under article IV(2) of the Treaty with a view to safeguarding the security of life and property of the Turkish community and even that of many Greek Cypriots*".[7] The Turkish Cypriot leader Rauf Denktash wrote that "Turkey, as one of the guarantors of the Cyprus Republic, could not accept the *fait accompli* against the independence and sovereignty of the republic, nor could it stand by and watch Turkish Cypriots being killed."[8] He also says that Turkey was left with no alternative but to move alone under Article 4 (2) of the Treaty of Guarantee to protect the independence of the island and to put an end to the terrible destruction of life and property.[9] Denktash further alleges that the Turkish villages were being attacked throughout the island by mobile units of the National Guard, the pattern of the onslaught resembling that of 1963.[10]

TREATY OF GUARANTEE AND INTERNATIONAL LAW

What is of crucial importance and need be examined is whether *unilateral military* intervention may be conferred by *treaty right*. In other words, whether such a right (even if expressly stipulated) is in accordance with the principles of Public International Law.

Theories on the Legality of Military Intervention by Treaty Right

It is commonly accepted in academic theories that armed intervention is legal when is done based on a right provided for by treaty. The legality of such an intervention finds support in most academic writings, at least before the passing of the UN Charter.[11] Vattel is one of the advocates of such a view. Although he supports the principle of non-intervention, which he considers as flowing from Sovereignty—"the most precious principle that states ought to safeguard"—accepts the exception of intervention provided for by treaty.[12] Phillimore, also writing in the nineteenth century, considers intervention legal, in case this is guaranteed by treaty right.[13] Diena, while is of the view that intervention violates the sovereignty and territorial integrity of states, regards intervention provided for by treaty as an exception to the rule of non-intervention.[14] The preceding views are also shared by Oppenheim,[15] Lawrence,[16] Hodges,[17] and Westlake[18] among others. Greek writers also hold the views. Seferiades, having said that states have no right to intervene in the internal affairs of other states, conceded that intervention under a treaty is legal.[19] Tenekides, though, who states that the well-established principle of non-intervention has been considerably strengthened by the United Nations Charter, writes the following: "International Law exceptionally accepts intervention if this is based upon agreement freely entered into or treaty providing for intervention in special circumstances."[20] Professor Brownlie wrote that states may lawfully confer by treaty a right to intervene by the use of armed force within the territorial or other legally permitted limits of their jurisdiction. They may also give *ad hoc* consent to the entry of foreign forces on their territory, to the passage of foreign forces and to operations by foreign forces on their territory.[21] Therefore, the charge of aggressive war against Thailand was disregarded by the International Military Tribunal at Tokyo on the ground that consent was given to the passage of Japanese forces through Thailand.[22] Brownlie gives some examples indicating that a right to intervene by force on the territory of another state could properly be conferred by treaty. Article 3 of the Treaty of 22 May 1903, between Cuba and the United States provided: "*The government of Cuba consents that the United States may exercise the right to intervene for the preservation of Cuban independence, the maintenance of a government adequate for the protection of life, property, and individual liberty.*"[23] The Treaty of Friendship between Persia and the R.S.F.S.R., signed on 26 February 1921, provided as follows in Article 6:

> *If a third party should attempt to carry out a policy of usurpation by means of armed intervention in* Persia, or if such Power should desire to use Persian Territory as a base of operations against Russia, or if a Foreign Power should threaten the frontiers of Federal Russia or those of its Allies, and if the Persian Government should not be able to put a stop to such menace after having been once called upon to do so by Russia, Russia shall have the right to advance her troops into Persian interior for the purpose of carrying out the military operations necessary for its defense. Russia undertakes, however, to withdraw its troops from Persian territory as soon as the danger has been removed.[24]

Another example is the General Treaty of Friendship and Co-Operation signed by the United States and Panama on 2 March 1936. Article 10 provided:

> *In case of an international conflagration or the existence of any threat of aggression which would endanger the security of the Republic of Panama or the security of the Panama Canal, the Governments of the United States of America and the Republic of Panama will take such measures of prevention and defense as they may consider necessary for the protection of their common interests.*

An identical provision in Article 7 of the Treaty of 1903 was the basis for the United States armed intervention in Panama in 1904 for the purpose of restoring order.[25] Further, the Agreement signed between Egypt and the United Kingdom on 19 October 1954,[26] provided for the evacuation of British forces from the Suez Canal area. The United Kingdom was given the right to reenter the area with military forces given an attack was made by a state which was a member of the Arab Collective Security Pact, or Turkey.

Despite the above, the principles of self-determination[27] and equality of states[28] as stipulated in the U.N. Charter have put into doubt the right of military intervention conferred by Treaty. Several jurists have denied that such a treaty is valid. Nevertheless, in Brownlie's view, the right of forcible intervention on the territory of a state may still be lawfully conferred by treaty.[29]

Arguments for the Legality of Intervention Envisaged by Treaty.

Legitimate Limitation of a State's Sovereignty

It has been said that military intervention, constituting involvement in the internal affairs of a state, violates the principle of sovereignty. However, if intervention is done based on a treaty right, the sovereignty of the state against which the intervention is launched is not violated, because the *treaty* right of intervention suggests legitimate and legal limitation of the state's sovereignty.[30] Given that the state itself has *accepted* the diminution of its sovereignty, the intervention must be legal. Under such circumstances the state is obligated to accept the intervention. Contrary to the above argument, it has been asserted that a treaty envisaging a right to intervene is illegal, because it is in violation of general principles of law. Since international law acknowledges the principle of independence of states, it comes that a state has the obligation of self-preservation. The treaty envisaging intervention deprives a state from the exercise of self-preservation and administration.[31] But those who advocate for the legitimate limitation of sovereignty of the state conceding a right of military intervention, say that there is no such thing as obligation to self-preservation.[32] In the *Austro-German Customs Union Case*, Judge Anzilotti, in a separate Opinion, went so far as to assert that according to general international law each state is free to deny its independence, also described as sovereignty (*suprema potestas*), and even its own existence.[33]

Volenti non fit injuria

Most authors base the legality of intervention by treaty right upon the consent of the state agreeing to the grant of a right of intervention to another state. The legal axiom *volenti non fit injuria* is not only a theoretical construction, but has constituted the legal basis of interventions in state practice.[34] Proponents of this legal axiom also suggest that entering into treaties is a right of independent states, which may by way of treaty confer a right of intervention to another state in the same way as they may by international agreement concede part of their territory to a third state.[35] Thus, a state not only gives away its sovereign rights, but, on the contrary, exercises its sovereign right of concluding a treaty. In the *Wimbledon Case*, the Permanent Court of International Justice held that "the right of entering into international engagements is an attribute of state sovereignty."[36] In the *Perry Case*, which appeared before the Supreme Court of the United States, Chief Justice Hughes stated in his judgement: "the right to make binding obligations is a competence attaching to sovereignty."[37]

Pacta sunt servanda

One view dictates that since the intentions of two or more states coincide in an International Agreement, so that a right to intervention of one of the contracting parties into the internal affairs of the other may be agreed, law regulating their relations is therefore created. This law is binding. In accordance with the principle of *pacta sunt servanda*, the contracting parties are obliged to fulfil the terms of the Agreement.[38] Interventions are illegal, unless the intervening state acquires special right to intervene according to public international law principles. Thus, it could be argued, the binding force of international treaties may be said to sufficiently form the basis of the legality of intervention accorded by treaty.

Furthermore, the legality of intervention of this sort may be grounded upon the relevant principle of *modus et conventio vincunt legem.* The rationale behind this very legal principle is that, given the lack of a unified international legislature, the creation of legal rules governing relations between members of the international community depends to a great degree on international conventions, which do create legal relations among the parties to a convention. *Modus et conventio vincunt legem*, like *pacta sunt servanda* is a generally recognized principle, on condition that the content of the treaty is in conformity with legitimacy.

Upon the three arguments mentioned so far, a strong case for the legality of military intervention provided for by treaty right may be built up. Consequently, we could assert, at this stage, that Turkey's military intervention in Cyprus 1974 was a legal act according to international law principles; that Article IV (2) of the Cyprus Treaty of Guarantee, even if expressly authorized unilateral armed intervention, would be perfectly lawful. Nevertheless, in the subsection to follow, I shall attempt to present views going against this assertion.

Arguments Against the Legality of Intervention Provided for by Treaty Right

General Principles of Law

A valid treaty presupposes lawful provisions. It is true that states have the capacity, by virtue of sovereignty, to conclude treaties on any matter whatever. It is equally true, however, that in the international legal order there exist legal rules, which states -parties to a treaty—cannot, and should not, ignore. This view is pointedly expressed by the legal maxim *privatorum conventio juris publico non derogat*. The rationale underlying this axiom is that the international community, like every well-ordered society, should see to the lawful and moral coexistence of its members. As Lauterpacht very well put it, "*the parties conclude a treaty not in a legal vacuum, but against a background of existing rules of international law.*"[39] It may be true that the treaty must be interpreted by reference to the intention of the parties. But the intention of the parties must be interpreted by reference to rules of international law, in so far as their application has not been expressly excluded.[40] Along similar lines, Verdross wrote that "*no juridical order can admit treaties between juridical subjects which are obviously in contradiction of the ethics of a certain community.*"[41]

According to these *general principles of law*, a treaty comprising unlawful provisions is void (*turpes stipulationes nullius esse momenti*).[42] Unquestionably, *general principles of law* are in force under international law;[43] customary law, the history of international arbitration and Article 38(1) of the Statute of the International Court of Justice attest to their legal validity.[44]

The question which naturally follows is *which* are those international law principles violation of which renders a treaty void? Answer: the *peremptory norms of international law* otherwise known as *jus cogens*. The basis of these principles may be found in Natural law. Article 53 of the Vienna Convention on the Law of Treaties, signed at Vienna in 1969,[45] provides as follows: "A treaty is void if, at the time of its conclusion conflicts with a peremptory norm of international law. For the purposes of the present Convention, a peremptory norm of general international law is a norm accepted and recognized by the international community of states as a norm from which no derogation is permitted and which can be modified only by a subsequent norm of general international law having the same character."[46] The definition of a peremptory norm is more skillful than appears at first sight. A rule cannot become a peremptory norm unless it is "accepted and recognized (as such) by the international community of states as a whole," a requirement which is too logical to be challenged. At present very few rules pass this threshold.[47] There is considerable agreement on the *prohibition of the use of force*, of genocide, slavery, of gross violations of the right of peoples to self-determination, and of racial discrimination. Others would include the prohibition of torture.[48] The International Law Commission, in its commentary on the draft of the Vienna Convention, identified the Charter's prohibition of the use of inter-state force as a "conspicuous example" of *jus cogens.*[49] The Commission's position was quoted by the International Court of Justice in the Nicaragua case.[50] In his Separate Opinion, President Singh underscored that "the principle of non-use of force belongs to the realm of *jus cogens*."[51] Judge Sette-Camara, in another Separate Opinion, also expressed the firm view that the non-use of force can be recognized as a peremptory rule.[52] Despite some reservations, this position seems to be the prevalent one at present.[53] In the relevant draft of the International Law Commission, it is indicated that treaties providing for use of force in violation of the principles of the UN Charter, treaties for the commission of acts which constitute crimes under international law, treaties providing for slave trade, piracy *jure gentium*, and genocide, may be cited as examples of treaties that conflict with peremptory norms of general international law. Another view appears to be that a rule of *jus cogens* can be derived from custom.

In view of the above, it could be argued that the rule of general international law prohibiting the unilateral use of force, especially as laid down by

Article 2(4) of the U.N. Charter, constitutes *jus cogens*.[54] The International Law Commission observes that the prohibition of the threat or use of force undoubtedly constitutes peremptory norm of international law "from which states cannot derogate by treaty arrangements."[55] Thus, this legal rule cannot be invalidated by an international treaty. A pact of aggression concluded between Arcadia and Numidia against Utopia will not only be stigmatized as a violation of the Charter, as well as general international law, but it will also be void *ab initio*.[56] Authors such as *Guggenheim*, who see international law as dependent upon the consent and agreements of states, reject the peremptory nature of international customary law rules. Contrary to this position, *McNair* writes that states are not capable of evading peremptory norms of international law by the conclusion of special treaties.[57] Article 103 of the UN Charter may be cited as evidence of the existence of a peremptory norm of international law going against the conclusion of treaties providing for unilateral military intervention.[58]

From the above discussion it may be inferred that article IV (2) of the Cyprus Treaty of guaranteed conflicts with *jus cogens* and is legally invalid. As a result, one could argue that Turkey may not claim a right for unilateral military intervention conferred by the Treaty of Guarantee. Even if the Treaty expressly provided for such a right (which is not the case), this would again be in plain violation of peremptory norms of international law. On the other hand, a possible counterargument could be that Cyprus was not a member of the United Nations at the time when the Zurich and London Accords were signed, and so the rules of *jus cogens* as embodied in the UN Charter could not have been applicable to the newly born Cyprus Republic. In answer to such possible allegation, it may be asserted that the peremptory rules of international law laid down by the UN Charter were nevertheless applicable to all other signatory states to the Treaty of Cyprus; Turkey, Greece, and the United Kingdom were already members of the United Nations Organization at the time, clearly bound by its principles. Of course as soon as Cyprus became a UN member state (in fact long before the 1974 Turkish intervention), the principles of the United Nations—including *jus cogens*—were to be directly applicable.[59] Another objection to the applicability of *jus cogens* in the case of Cyprus may be phrased as follows: Article 65 of the Vienna Convention relates to the procedure to be followed with respect to invalidity, termination, withdrawal from, or suspension of the operation of a treaty. The Convention, which incorporates the principle of *jus cogens* into the law of treaties, makes it mandatory to refer a dispute to the International Court of Justice for a decision. Article 66 states that if, under paragraph 3 of Article 65 no solution has been reached within a period of twelve months following the date on which the objection was raised, any of the parties to a dispute concerning the application or the interpretation of articles 53 may, by a written application, submit it to the International Court of Justice for a decision unless the parties by common consent agree to submit the dispute to arbitration. On this basis, one line of argument is put forward (in fact by Necatigil),[60] that in the absence of a ruling of the International Court, a treaty, such as the Treaty of Guarantee, should not be presumed to be invalid as being against a peremptory norm of international law. In other words, the presumption should be in favor of the validity of a treaty until there is a judicial ruling to the contrary. This procedure has not been invoked by the Republic of Cyprus.

Treaties Reached under Duress or Inequitable Treaties

The legal position of the Cyprus Government, as later expressed in the United Nations by Mr. Kyprianou, then Foreign Minister, was that the "Constitution was foisted on Cyprus. . . . The combined effect of the Constitution and the Treaty of Guarantee is that a situation has been created whereby the constitutional and political development of the Republic has been arrested at its infancy and the Republic as a sovereign state has been placed in a strait jacket."[61] The Minister of Foreign Affairs also argued that the treaties "were imposed on the Cypriot people (thus) making the international legal doctrines of unequal, inequitable and unjust treaties relevant." The resulting legal conclusion, according to Mr. Kyprianou, was that the 1960 Agreements were "unequal and inequitable treaties, as a result of which they cannot be regarded as anything but null and void."[62]

According to Oppenheim, real consent is a condition of the validity of a treaty.[63]An expression of consent procured by the coercion of its representative through acts or threats directed against him is generally agreed to be without legal effect, and Article 51 of the Vienna Convention on the Law of Treaties so provides: the Treaty is void not merely voidable.[64] Any treaty signed by a state under pressure exerted by another state is void.[65] Article 32(a) of the Harvard Draft Convention on the Law of Treaties states:

> Duress involves the employment of coercion. . . . If the coercion has been directed against a person signing a Treaty on behalf of a state, and of with knowledge of this fact the treaty signed has been ratified by that state without coercion, the treaty is not to be considered as having entered by the state in consequence of duress.[66]

The argument of the Cyprus government implies that unequal treaties—agreements imposing burdens on states in unequal bargaining positions—are in themselves void. However, the Cyprus Government representatives never pressed this position to its logical conclusion, that the 1960 settlement was void.[67]

Sovereign Equality

Article 2(1) of the Charter of the United Nations declares that "the Organization is based on the principle of sovereign equality of all its members." It has been stated that the obligation of the Treaty of Guarantee "to keep unalterable in perpetuity the constitutional structure and order' purports to deprive Cyprus of one of the fundamental requirements of a state as an integral person, internal independence and territorial supremacy."[68] This point is further elaborated; article IV of the Treaty of Guarantee conflicts both with customary international law and with article 103 of the UN Charter by violating the principle of 'sovereign equality' as laid down in article 2(1).[69]

Indeed, the Republic of Cyprus does not have the capacity to amend the fundamental or so called 'Basic Articles' of its Constitution. However, absence of power of a state to change its constitution may not affect its sovereign equality. Also, absence of such power is not regarded as being incompatible with the concept of independence, a necessary requirement for statehood.[70]

By now, there should be no doubt that unilateral military intervention provided for, even expressly, by treaty right is not in accordance with public international law principles.

DID THE TREATY OF GUARANTEE PURPORT OR AUTHORIZE MILITARY ACTION?

The proper interpretation of certain expressions in the wording of Art. 4 is the subject of great controversy. "Representations" may simply be a request to comply with a duty, but they could also take the form of a threat of violence, as and when the duty bound does not behave as it should.[71] The word *measures* is also ambiguous; as Articles 41 and 42[72] of the United Nations Charter demonstrate, it may mean actions of a peaceful although coercive nature, as well as those which involve the use of force.[73]

Terminological differences culminate over the interpretation of the right of each of the guaranteeing powers *to act*. A vexed question remains whether the phrase *to act* may also imply military action. The Greek side, as one would easily guess, answers in the negative. The Turkish side, of course, in the affirmative. The former is of the view that nothing in the Treaty warrants a forcible intervention by Turkey. Criton Tornaritis Q.C., formerly Attorney-General of the Cyprus Republic holds that irrespective of the validity of the Treaty of Guarantee, from the preamble and the provisions of which it appears that the guaranteeing powers were aiming at the protection of their own interests than the interests of the Republic of Cyprus, its Article IV invoked by Turkey does not grant the right to armed intervention to the guaranteeing Powers.[74] Necatigil says that the second paragraph of the article in question, by providing for the right of any of the guaranteeing powers *to take action*, is stronger in terms than the first paragraph. If only unilateral intercession was envisaged, then there was no reason why the second paragraph should not expressly speak of the right to unilateral intercession or diplomatic representation. Upon this rationale, one could conversely say that neither a right to unilateral military action is *expressly* provided for by Article IV (2).[75]

Thus, great difficulty arises over ascertaining the intentions of the Treaty drafters which becomes even more acute in view of the very limited sources of information on the matter. The Treaty of Guarantee was initialed at the end of the Zurich Summit between Greece and Turkey of 5–11 February 1959; its content, however, was disclosed only after the London Conference.[76] The participants did not draw up an official record of the summit and the information available is unfortunately little. However, Stephen Xydis, shades light to the events. His account is the outcome of interviews with the Greek representatives.[77] According to Xydis, Turkey submitted a draft to the Greek counterpart, probably after consulting the United Kingdom. The draft allowed the right to take unilateral action, without having previously determined if a common or concerted action was in fact possible. "At a certain point of the negotiations," Xydis goes on,

> the Turkish side wanted specific reference to the right of resort to 'military' action for the purpose of restoring the situation established by the treaty. The Greek side, however, contended that resorting to military action was prohibited by the U.N. Charter and was permissible only under a decision of the Security Council, if at all. Finally, the text was drawn up in its present form, with the Turks always having possible resort to force as the *ultima ratio* in mind, in contrast to the Greeks who did not.[78]

More illuminating perhaps is the Security Council Debates of 1963 and 1974. In 1963, Turkey militarily intervened in Cyprus allegedly to protect the lives of the Turkish Cypriots who had engaged in a bloody conflict against the Greek Cypriots.[79] A Joint Peace-Making Force under British command (to its credit) operated in Cyprus towards the end of 1963 and the beginning of 1964. It was composed of contingents from the three guarantor states. This peace-making force had the task of helping the Cypriot Government in its efforts to bring about peace between the two communities. In critical debates of 1964 on the Cyprus question, representatives of Turkey at the United Nations repeatedly stated that their government's freedom of action derived from the Treaty of Guarantee, whose validity was incontestable.[80] The Cypriot Government position was stated by the then Foreign Minister,

Mr. Spyros Kyprianou. He said that his government firmly rejected Turkey's interpretation of article 4 of the Treaty of Guarantee.[81] More interesting is the view of the Greek representative. In answer to the Cyprus representative, who demanded a declaration from the guarantor states on the question whether the treaty gives the right of unilateral military intervention, he said: "Do we—the Greek government—think that this article gives us the right to intervene militarily, and unilaterally without the authorization of the Security Council? The answer is "no".'[82] Even more interesting and, indeed, revealing was the statement of the British government representative. Firstly, he said that "it was not under article IV of the Treaty of Guarantee that the United Kingdom Government sent its troops to Cyprus. We sent our troops because they were asked for and because they were generally considered to be necessary and helpful in preventing further serious strife."[83] Furthermore, he emphasised:

> the action provided for in article IV(2) of the Treaty of Guarantee can only be taken in the event of a breach of the provisions of the Treaty, that is, in circumstances in which there is a threat to the independence, territorial integrity or security of the Republic of Cyprus as established by the Basic Articles of its Constitution; a right of intervention for this purpose, and for this purpose alone, is provided for in the Treaty. But the question of *military* intervention under article IV of the Treaty of Guarantee *would never arise if all concerned played their part as they have undertaken to do* (emphasis added).[84]

This very statement is quite clear. If the attitude of all the states concerned was in accordance with the commitments undertaken, resort to force would not be necessary. In case this should not happen, the problem arises of restoring the situation created by the Treaty of Guarantee, if need be, by measures which might comprise the use of force.[85]

However, it is, I consider, necessary to refer in this regard to the legal advice given by Sir Elihu Lauterpacht to the Cyprus Government after a consultation in London on 25 January 1964. Lauterpacht considers that the Treaty of Guarantee is valid. He does not, however, consider that the Treaty of Guarantee gives the right to *armed* intervention.[86]

On 20 July 1974, during the debates before the Security Council, the Greek Cypriot representative put forward that Turkey's action contravened the treaty itself, as well as the UN Charter. He argued that the right *to take action* denotes only the application of peaceful measures and, furthermore it does not include armed aggression, which is forbidden to member states, except in case of self-defense.[87] The Turkish representative, on the other hand, stressed that the Treaty of Guarantee gave Turkey the right to take military action, aiming at establishing constitutional administration in the island and protecting the rights of the Turkish Cypriots.[88] The Greek government's attitude was less clear and partly contradicted the 1964 declaration. It did not maintain that Article IV (2) did not allow the right of intervention. Instead, the Greek representative pointed out that for unilateral action to be considered lawful, it would have to take place only after the collapse of negotiations between the three guarantor states, and would have to have the sole aim of re-establishing the status quo ante.[89] One could therefore allege that it would seem the Greek government did not deny existence—under Article VI (2)—of a right of military intervention, but, rather, that it contested its vindication in the particular case.[90]

The United Kingdom did not take up a position with regarding the content of Article IV (2) of the Treaty of Guarantee. Nevertheless, great light is shed on the British position by the debates before the House of Commons, particularly by a report prepared by the Select Committee appointed to conduct an examination of the Cyprus situation.[91] The Foreign Secretary replied in the following manner to the Members of Parliament who asked him whether, under Art. IV (2), the United Kingdom had the right to use force as and when there was a breach of the Treaty of Guarantee: "I dare say legally we had."[92] From a careful reading, though, of the Select Committee's records, the Foreign Minister seemed to hesitate; not because he was not of the opinion that Article IV of the Treaty of Guarantee gave a right to military intervention, but because he doubted if it was wise from a political standpoint to use such a right.[93] The parliamentary Committee stated: "Britain had a legal right to intervene, she had a moral obligation to intervene, she had the *military capacity* to intervene. She did not intervene for reasons which the government refuses to give."[94] In a recent House of Lords Debate on the Cyprus question, Lord Caradon referred to article IV of the Treaty of Guarantee and said these:

> Having signed the treaty with the authority of Her Majesty's Government I have naturally watched subsequent events in the island of Cyprus with dismay and shame that we should have given an undertaking and have failed so shamefully to carry it out.[95]

Apart from the United Nations debates and the United Kingdom Parliamentary Papers so far considered, the available travaux preparatoires are of little help on ascertaining the intentions of the Treaty drafters concerning whether intervention must be by peaceful means alone or it may consist of measures amounting to the use of force. Even so, there exist documents of considerable gravity regarding this point. During discussions by the London Joint Committee[96] of one annex, namely, Annex C on the status of forces, the Greek delegation proposed the inclusion of a provision dealing with the settlement of disputes. The Cyprus Official Committee, in which the views of Whitehall Departments are coordinated, considered the matter, and concluded that the most satisfactory proposal was that a disputes article covering the whole Treaty and its Annexes should be included in the Treaty of Establishment.[97] The following is the crux of the said article:

> Any question of difficulty as to the interpretation or application of the provisions of the present Treaty shall be settled as follows: Any question or difficulty that may arise over the application or operation of the military requirements of the United Kingdom, or concerning the provisions of the present Treaty in so far as they affect the status, rights and obligations of United Kingdom forces or any other forces associated with them under the terms of this Treaty, or of Greek, Turkish and Cypriot forces, shall ordinarily be settled by negotiation between the tripartite Headquarters of the Republic of Cyprus, Greece and Turkey and the authorities of the armed forces of the United Kingdom.[98]

So, if any such controversy came about (and did come about in the subsequent years) the interested parties would be under an obligation to settle their differences by means of peaceful negotiation and therefore resolve any difficulty regarding interpretation of Treaty provisions on armed forces rights and obligations. It may be deducted that the need for proper interpretation of Art. IV (2) should be resolved in this context. Further, the above-mentioned article provides a mechanism by which a tribunal is set up, to decide on matters which negotiation cannot settle.[99] Unfortunately, the provisions of this article have not been complied with by Turkey either before the events of 1963–1967 or her intervention in Cyprus 1974.

Furthermore, since the textual or teleological methods of interpretation do not seem to be that helpful in the present case, the principle of effectiveness may be applicable. According to the principle of effectiveness (*et ret magis valeat quam pereat*), the words 'take action' should logically be interpreted in such a way as not to conflict with the UN Charter provisions and be likely to cause practical difficulties to the Constitutional structure, thus making it unworkable.

Be the case what it may, it must be noted at this stage that a cardinal mistake[100] was committed by the Greek side at the preliminary discussions in London between the Foreign Ministers of Greece, Turkey, and the United Kingdom, prior to the signature of the 1959 Accords. Had the Greek side supported the view of the British side that Article 2 of the Treaty of Guarantee was incompatible with the UN Charter, it would have been possible to define the term *act* in such a way as clearly to exclude military intervention. This would have been necessary to make the treaty compatible with the UN Charter.[101] In fact, the Legal Department of the UN, when the Treaty was subsequently deposited with the UN Secretariat, gave an opinion that the term *act* could not be interpreted to mean military action. Such an interpretation would make the Treaty compatible with the UN Charter, and by virtue of its provision that in the event of a conflict between the provisions of the Charter and any article of the Treaty, the Charter prevails, military intervention would be ruled out.

President *Clerides* summarized the matter quite pointedly and need be cited:

> Legally, a definition excluding the meaning of military intervention was not necessary, but politically it was imperative. The political history of the world shows that all aggressors attempt to allege a justifiable right for their act of aggression. A treaty which granted the right of unilateral 'action' could be used to create confusion, and during that confusion temporarily justify actions which otherwise would have been manifestly an undisputed act of aggression. This is exactly what happened in 1974, when the Turkish forces invaded Cyprus, after the military coup of the Greek junta, which destroyed the constitutional order of the Cyprus Republic.[102]

CRITERIA SET BY THE GUARANTEE TREATY AND THE CONDUCT OF TURKEY

An answer to the crucial question whether Turkey could, indeed, justify her military intervention based on Art. IV (4) of the Cyprus Treaty of Guarantee is now imperative. Let us assume that the Treaty of Guarantee did purport to authorize military action (though this may not be the case).

By Art. 4, the Treaty of Guarantee expressly provides for joint consultations between Greece, Turkey, and the UK, before any action is taken following such a Treaty. The machinery of joint consultations should have been put in practice and only on a failure of such consultations could unilateral action have been undertaken. Obviously, this machinery was not initiated. As a matter of undeniable fact, the Turkish Premier, Mr. Bulent Ecevit, flew to London on 17 July 1974 to seek British coordination under the Guarantee Treaty. It was made clear that if Britain was unwilling to act (which was the case) Turkey was able to intervene on her own.[103] As Mr. Callaghan, the British Foreign Secretary, said at the Geneva Conference, before Greece could be brought into the picture as guarantor, Turkey undertook unilateral action in Cyprus.

The communication of views between the Turkish and Greek Governments via the mediation initiative of Mr. Sisco, the US Under-Secretary of State, cannot be alleged to amount to the consultations envisaged by Art. 4.

On another point, in these terms spoke the United Kingdom representative during a Security Council debate on the situation in Cyprus, February 1964, in answer to the question of the Cyprus government delegate: "Is it the view of the Governments of Greece, Turkey and the United Kingdom that they have a right of military intervention under the Treaty of Guarantee in view, in particular, of the Charter?"[104] Here is what he said:

> I should like to draw the attention of members of the Council to the nature of the right provided for in article IV (2) of the Treaty of Guarantee and the limitations placed on the exercise of that right by that article. The right which is reserved to the guarantor powers is not an unlimited right of unilateral action but—and here I quote—'the right to take action with the sole aim of re-establishing the state of affairs created by the Treaty.'[105]

It follows that the extensive nature of the Turkish intervention was itself in contravention to the Treaty of Guarantee provisions, particularly Article IV (2).[106] It may also be said to have been contrary to Article II, by which Turkey, Greece and the United Kingdom undertook "to prohibit activity aimed at promoting directly or indirectly either union of Cyprus with any other state or *partition* of the island." The de facto military occupation and division of Cyprus until nowadays clearly violates the above provision.

Even if there was initial justification for military intervention by Turkey (and, indeed there could have been), such justification had faded away on Mr. Clerides's accession to power in Cyprus (and the dismissal of the dictatorial regime). Clerides represented the reestablishment of legality and Constitutional Order. But, even if such a proposition is objected to, not least because of the manner in which he took over the presidency which was not without ambivalence, once the Geneva Conference of the Guarantor Powers was convened on 25th July 1974, and diplomatic initiatives were engineered in the context of the Treaty of Guarantee itself for the re-establishment of constitutional government, the Turkish armed intervention should perhaps have come to an end. Further, at the second round of the Geneva talks, when the United Kingdom was satisfied with the assurances given by the Greek Cypriot delegation for fair resolution of the Cyprus problem, and security of the Turkish Cypriots, the Turkish military forces should have terminated their operations.[107]

Further, it would not be a paradox to classify the Treaty of Guarantee as a Regional Arrangement for the maintenance of peace and security, which is first among the purposes of the United Nations Organization.[108] So Turkey could rely upon this argument for unilaterally using force in Cyprus 1974. A counterargument lies in Article 53 of the UN Charter, which provides that "no enforcement action shall be taken under regional arrangements or regional agencies without the authorization of the Security Council." Security Council authorization for Turkish intervention was never given.[109]

THE SUBSEQUENT ACTIONS OF TURKEY

Mention has already been made to the extensive nature of the Turkish intervention.[110] However, it is necessary to explore a bit more whether Turkey's subsequent actions may be justified, even if the initial Turkish intervention was rendered lawful by the Treaty of Guarantee. The answer to this question seems to be in the negative because of the following.

Firstly, even though the Turkish Government was assured at the Geneva Conference for the reestablishment of constitutional government and the safety of the Turkish Cypriots, Turkey proceeded to a second round of military action. Explaining the reasons, which, in his view, necessitated the second operation, the Turkish Premier said:

> Having reached the conclusion that there is no use but only harm in maintaining the appearance of continuing a conference that is being internationally obstructed and the deliberations of which are unilaterally violated, Turkey has considered it her duty to fulfil by herself her prerogatives and duties as a guarantor power, and her responsibilities concerning the independence of Cyprus as well as the rights and security of the Turkish Cypriot people.
>
> The action now undertaken by Turkey is at least as rightful and legal as the action she started on the 20th of July, as a guarantor power and strictly within the bounds of her authority as such power, for the same conditions exist today as on the 20th of July—conditions that formed the basis of the rightfulness and legality of her action. This new Turkish action is as legitimate as Turkey's initial move and is its logical conclusion.[111]

In view of the preceding discussion in this section, the second phase of the armed campaign of Turkey was not *as rightful and legal as* her action of the 20th of July. The Third Report of the UK House of Commons Foreign Affairs Committee 1987 attests to the validity of this assertion.[112]

Secondly, the mass killing and brutal treatment of innocent Greek Cypriot civilians during the hostilities, the uprooting of others from their homeland and subsequent reduction to the tragic status of refugee, the unascertained fate of missing persons, the destruction of cultural property, and the occupation until nowadays of large part of the Cyprus Republic territory rather seem to argue against a valid invocation of the Treaty of Guarantee Article VI (2) by Turkey. Whatever the answer to the question whether the Turkish intervention was rendered lawful by the Treaty of Guarantee, it needs saying that humanitarian law of armed conflict as well as the European Convention on Human Rights still apply to the Turkish invasion and subsequent military presence in Cyprus.

Thirdly, the subsequent establishment of the so called Turkish Federated State of Cyprus (TFSC) in 1975, and of the "Turkish Republic of Northern

Cyprus" (TRNC) in 1983, both acts condemned by the international community,[113] rather suggest that the real aim of the Turkish intervention was not so much the restoration of constitutionalism or the protection of the Turkish Cypriot community;[114] it could most probably be the case that the intervention was also dictated by other considerations.

STANCE TAKEN BY THE INTERNATIONAL COMMUNITY

It is noteworthy that the Parliamentary Assembly of the Council of Europe, by Resolution 573 of 29 July 1974, affirmed that the Turkish military intervention was the exercise of a right emanating from an international Treaty and the fulfilment of a legal and moral obligation. However, the member states did not maintain this view after the second round of military operations.

The Resolutions of the UN Security Council and General Assembly indicate that the Turkish invasion was an illegal act. Mention shall be made only to some of them which characteristically stress the unlawfulness of the military intervention.[115] Security Council Resolution 353 (1974), passed on the 20th of July 1974, reads as follows:

> "*1.* Calls upon all states to respect the sovereignty, independence, and territorial integrity of Cyprus.
> 2. *Calls upon all parties to the present fighting as a first step* to cease all firing;
> 3. *Demands an immediate end to foreign military intervention in the Republic of Cyprus that is in contravention of paragraph* 1 above;"

Subsequent Resolutions of 1974 have confirmed Resolution 353. In Resolution, the Security Council, having referred to Res. 353, stated "*that all states have declared their respect for the sovereignty, independence and territorial integrity of Cyprus.*"

The Security Council by Resolution 365 (1974) adopts General Assembly Resolution 3212[116], and by 367 (1974) reaffirms 365 of the Security Council and General Assembly's 3212. Resolution 367 includes the following:

> Calls once more on all states to respect the sovereignty, independence, territorial integrity, and non-alignment of the Republic of Cyprus and urgently requests them, as well as the parties concerned, to refrain from any action which might prejudice that sovereignty, independence, territorial integrity and non-alignment, as well as from any attempt at partition of the island or its unification with any other country;

It is noteworthy that, although the United Nations Resolutions do not expressly *go against* the *Turkish invasion,* they amply illustrate that the intervention was an illegality. Further, it should be stressed that the words "calls upon," used in the Resolutions, have, according to some scholars, binding force.[117]

CONCLUSION

Despite the above, it seems difficult to me to overlook the, admittedly, strong arguments advocating for the legality of armed intervention accorded by treaty right, especially the ones premised upon the principles of *pacta sunt servanda* and, perhaps more importantly, *volenti non fit injuria.* The latter surely indicates the vital role played by states themselves in the determination of their own fate and the development of international relations. Simultaneously, one should not overlook the particular and complex circumstances surrounding the 1960 Zurich-London Agreements, mainly the various interests of the parties to the Cyprus Treaty. Nevertheless, having regard to the equally powerful arguments militating against unilateral armed intervention envisaged by treaty, it may be *concluded* that Turkey should not have exercised a right of intervention in Cyprus, 1974; such a proposition could remain subject to criticism, in view of the peculiarities of the Cyprus issue.[118] However, even if military action can occasionally be provided for by treaty, a stipulation of this kind must essentially be in harmony with moral values and the political context of a given society. In my opinion, and according to an objective historicopolitical appraisal, the circumstances of Cyprus are such that a treaty right of unilateral military intervention could not be provided for Turkey.

It should be noted finally that the above discussion is especially important in view of the contemporary effort to reach a peaceful settlement to the Cyprus issue. In what way is it useful?

One of the most important aspects of the Cyprus problem is that of *Security.* Would the Cyprus people like Greece and Turkey to guarantee the independence and integrity of the Cyprus state within the framework of a settlement? This, I think, given the unhappy past would not be a good idea. If, however, it would be deemed necessary that these two states play a significant role in the security of the island, then I would propose that a regional arrangement be reached along the lines of the existing Treaty of Guarantee, but expressly excluding *unilateral* military intervention.

On the other hand, would we like the British sovereign bases to remain on the island, even if this would appear to be a possibility? Despite the troubled relations between Britain and Cyprus in the uneasy years of the 1950s, which by now have been overcome (and, if not, they should be), the British presence on the island is, in my opinion, indispensable, particularly in view of reviving Ottoman imperialism. The British have a crucial role to play in the maintenance of security, but they should give explicit assurances (in the form of a legal document, if need be) that they would not allow repetition of the bloody events of 1974. Furthermore, what would be the future of the common Defense doctrine, as it now functions, between Greece and Cyprus? Would that be affected by security arrangements in the context of a future settlement of the Cyprus issue? These matters should be thoroughly examined by all *interested* parties. The Cyprus Government especially should project drafts of military strategy considering these pressing strategic implications.

It remains the case that survival is of utmost importance for a nation. In international affairs, as in the Cyprus case, strategy considerations should be considered in conjunction with international law, the latter providing a basis for international politics and conversely the former conforming to international legality.

NOTES

1. Glafkos Clerides, in his book, *Cyprus: My Deposition* (Nicosia, 1990, vol. III, 343) states the following about the motives of the conspirators: "Bluntly, the real objectives of the conspirators were to oust Makarios and his Government in order to proceed with direct negotiations with Turkey, and use the good offices of the United States, to achieve Enosis of the major part of Cyprus with Greece, conceding a smaller part of Cyprus to Turkish sovereignty. At no time did the Greek junta have in mind to declare Enosis unilaterally and to accept the risk of having a military conflict with Turkey."

2. The meaning of "armed attack" was considered in the *Nicaragua case*, I.C.J. Reports 1986, 14 para.195.

3. S/PV, 1781, 86.

4. For the text of the communiqué see *The Turkish Yaerbook of International Relations*, 14 (1974), 125.

5. Article 181 of the Constitution provided that the treaty guaranteeing the independence, territorial integrity, and constitution of the Republic "shall have constitutional force."

6. *The Turkish Yearnbook of Internaional Realsitons*, *ante*, 130 (italics supplied).

7. *ibid.*, 130

8. Denktash, R. *The Cyprus Triangle* (Nicosia, 1972), 68.

9. *Ibid.*, 68. (It is said therein that "Turkey sent a *peace* force which landed in Northern Cyprus.")

10. *Ibid.*, 69–70. The following is an excerpt from a report sent by Terence Smith from Limassol at the time and published in the *Herald Tribune* on 25 July 1974: "On the sunbaked dirt floor of the Municipal Soccer Stadium here, about 1,750 men from Limassol's Turkish enclave and the surrounding Turkish villages are penned behind

cells of barbed wire. Their days are spent sheltering under the scorching sun that sends temperatures into high 90s. Although the men are dressed in street clothes and claim to be civilians, they are being held as prisoners of war by the Greek Cypriots"; Denktash, *The Cyprus Triangle*, *supra,* 71.

11. Potter notes that many experts on the subject matter readily tends to consider as legal any intervention provided for by treaty. (1930) II *Recueil des Cours*, 657.

12. See Vattel, E. de, *Le Droit des gens ou principes de la loi naturelle appliquee a la conduite et aux affaires des Nations et des Souverains* (Paris: 1863), 22.

13. See Phillimore, R. *Commentaries Upon International Law* (London, 1879), vol. I, 474.

14. See Diena, *Diritto Internationale* (Milano, 1900).

15. See Oppenheim, *International Law, War and Neutrality*, Vol. II (7th ed. H. Lauterpacht, London,1952), 307.

16. See Lawrence, T.J., *The Principles of International Law* (London, 1920), 121–23: "If a state has accepted a guarantee of any of its possessions, or of a special form of government, it suffers no legal wrong when the guaranteeing state intervenes in pursuance of the stipulations entered between them. It is perhaps to this right to intervene in pursuance of a treaty that the course of action adopted towards Greece by the allied powers, Great Britain, France, and Russia, during 1915–1917, must be referred." By the Treaty of London 1863, Greece was put under the guarantee of these powers as a 'monarchical, independent, and constitutional state.' Greece entered the great war on the side of Great Britain and her allies. Most of the nation was enthusiastically in favor of the Entente cause, and of giving effect to a treaty with Serbia (an ally of Great Britain, France, and Russia) under which Greece was bound to assist Serbia in the event of war between Serbia and a third power. On October 2, 1915, the British and French governments landed 150,000 troops at the Greek port of Salonika. They did this, with the hearty approval of Minister Venizelos and of an overwhelming majority of the Greek populace for the purpose of aiding Serbia that was at war with Austria and Germany.

17. See Hodges, *The Doctrine of Intervention* (New York, 1915).

18. See Westlake, J. *International Law* (Cambridge University Press, 1910) Vol. I, 304: "The questions arising from reciprocal rights and obligations of states, it is said, are determined in a notable measure by the body of what are called political treaties, which are nothing else than the temporary expression of transitory relations between the different national forces. These treaties bind the freedom of action of the parties so long as the political coalitions which produced them remain without change."

19. See Seferiades, *Public International Law* (Athens, 1926), Vol. I, 319, and (1930) 34 *Recueil des Cours*, 389.

20. See *Tenekides*, *Vema* (Greek Newspaper, 26.1.1963), 5; to the opposite direction goes the view expressed by the International Law Professor Konstantopoulos by which the UN Charter expressly prohibits intervention. (Konstantopoulos, *Public International Law,* Thessaloniki 1962, Vol. I, 278).

21. Brownlie, Ian, *International Law, and the Use of Force by States* (Oxford: Oxford University Press, 1963), 317.

22. Judgment, Sohn, *Cases and Materials on United Nations Law*, 916–17.

23. This provision, however, did not appear in the later treaty of 29 May 1934: 28 *A.J.I.L.* (1934), Suppl., 97.

24. Art. 1 of a Treaty of Guarantee and Neutrality between Persia and the USSR, signed on 1 Oct. 1927, confirmed the Treaty of 1921. A Soviet statement of Oct. 1958, referred specifically to the Treaty of 1927; *Times,* 3 Nov. 1958.

25. Oppenheim, *International Law, ante*, p.307; Brownlie, *International Law and the Use of Force by States, ante*, 320.

26. Cmd. 9298 (1954), abrogated by Egypt 1 Jan. 1957 (*A.J.I.L.* [1957], 672).

27. *U.N. Charter Article (12):* "To develop friendly relations among nations based on respect for the principles of equal rights and self-determination of peoples."

28. *U.N. Charter Article 2(1):* "The Organization is based on the principle of the sovereign equality of all its members."

29. Brownlie, *International Law and the Use of Force by States, ante*, 321; Oppenheim, *International Law*, *ante*, 307; Jessup, 32 *A.J.I.L.* (1938), 117.

30. On this, Lawrence, *The Principles of International Law*, *supra*, pp. 118–119.

31. See Thomas and Thomas, *Non-Intervention: The Law and its Import in the Americas* (Dallas, 1956), 91–92 (where it is argued that the state is even deprived of its international personality). Indeed, whether a state, under these circumstances, maintains to the utmost its independence and sovereignty, remains controversial.

32. See Lawrence, *The Principles of International Law*, *supra,* 118–19: "Sometimes an independent state finds itself obliged to submit for a while to restraints imposed upon it by superior force, as when Prussia was forbidden by Napoleon in 1808 to keep an army of more than 40,000 men. Such limited and temporary restraints upon the freedom of action of a state are not held to derogate from its independence. The same thing may be said of the authority assumed by the US on the American continent. There can be no doubt that in America a position of primacy has been assumed by the US. But occasional deference to these authorities does not deprive a state of its independent position under the law of nations"; Winfield, *The Grounds of Intervention in International Law* 1924) 4 *B.YB.I.L,* 155–59.

33. *Advisory Opinion*, (1931) 41 *P.C.I.J.* Reports, Series A/B, 59.

34. Instances of the kind are the Soviet intervention in Hungary 1956, the joint intervention of Great Britain, France and Israel in Egypt 1956, and the intervention of the United Kingdom in Jordan 1958.

35. See Thomas and Thomas, *Non-Intervention: The Law and its Import in the Americas, ante*, 96.

36. (1923) 1 *P.C.I.J.* Reports, Series A, 25

37. (1934) 294 US Supreme Court Reports, 330, 353–54. To the same effect, see the Opinion of the Permanent Court of International Justice in the Case of the Greco-Turkish exchange of populations in 1923 (1923, 10 *P.C.I.J.* Reports, Series B, 21).

38. See Harvard University Law School, Research on International Law, (1935) 29 *A.J.I.L.*, Supplement Part III Law of Treaties, 671.

39. Lauterpacht, H. *The Function of Law in the International Community* (Oxford: Oxford University Press, 1933), 109.

40. *Ibid.*, 109. The above considerations, Sir Hersch Lauterpacht observes, will perhaps suggest to the reader a certain criterion for gauging the relative importance of the first two paragraphs of the enumeration of sources of law to be applied by the Permanent Court of International Justice according to Article 38 of its Statute. In particular, he may be inclined to think, not without good reason, that the order in which the first two sources of law have been placed, although technically correct, is not necessarily indicative of the function which they fulfil in the process of bringing about the decision.

41. A. Verdross, *Forbidden Treaties in International Law*, (1937) 31 *A.J.I.L.*, 572.

42. *Corpus Juris Civilis, The Digest of Justinian*, translated by Charles Henry Monro (Cambridge: The University Press, 1904–1909) 26 Pandects, 43,1 and 57 Pandects 17, 2.

43. See Verdross, *Forbidden Treaties in International Law, supra*, 572.

44. *Article 38 (1) (c):* "The Court, whose function is to decide in accordance with international law such disputes as are submitted to it, shall apply: the general principles of law recognized by civilized nations."

45. The Vienna Convention is the outcome of the work of the International Law Commission and two sessions of the United Nations Conference on the Law of Treaties held in 1968 and 1969.

46. Text in *ILM* 8 (1969), 679; *A.J.I.L.*, 875; Brownlie (ed.) *Basic Documents in International Law* (Oxford: Oxford University Press, 1985), 388.

47. Oppenheim, *International Law*, Vol. I (9th ed. Sir Robert Jennings QC and Sir Arthur Watts QC, London: Longman, 1996), 1292: "There is no general agreement as to which rules have this character"; Watts, Sir Arthur, *The International Law Commission* (Oxford: Oxford University Press, 1999, 740–41): " The view that in the last analysis there is no rule of international law from which states cannot at their own free will contract out has become increasingly difficult to sustain, although some jurists deny the existence of any rules of jus cogens in international law, since in their own view even the most general rules still fall short of being universal"; H. Lauterpacht's Report on the Law of Treaties, *Yearbook of the International Law Commission*, hereinafter cited as *YBILC* (1953), ii, 154–55; Waldock's Report, *YBILC* (1963), ii, 52–53; Sinclair, *The Vienna Convention of the Law Treaties* (2nd ed. 1984), 203–41; Rozakis, *The Concept of Jus Cogens in the Law of Treaties* (1976).

48. In the *Barcelona Traction Case* 1970, in an obscure *obiter dictum,* the International Court of Justice referred to 'basic rights of the human person,' including the prohibition of slavery and racial discrimination and *the prohibition of aggression* and genocide, which it considered to be 'the concern of all states,' without, however, expressly recognizing the concept of *jus cogens.* However, in its Advisory Opinion in the *Legality of Nuclear Weapons Case*, the ICJ did not find it a need to address the question whether universally recognized principles of international humanitarian law (applicable in time of armed conflict) are part of *jus cogens* as defined in Article 51. (35 *I.L.M.*, 1996, 828, para. 83).

49. Report of the International Law Commission, 18th Session, [1966] II *YBILC* 172, 248–9, 261.

50. Nicaragua Case (Merits) I.C.J. Rep. 1986, 14.

51. *Ibid.*, 247.
52. *Ibid.*, 199.
53. See American Law Institute, 1 *Restatement of the Law: The Foreign Relations of the United States* 28 (3rd ed., 1986; L. Henkin, Chief Reporter).
54. This peremptory norm may further be said to stem from the principle of state sovereignty.
55. See U.N. Doc. A/5509, Supplement No. 9, 11–12; Watts, *The International Law Commission, ante*, 741: "Some members of the Commission felt that there might be an advantage in specifying some of the most obvious and best settled rules of *jus cogens.* Examples suggested included (a) a treaty contemplating an unlawful use of force contrary to the principles of the U.N. Charter."
56. See G.G. Fitzmaurice, "Third Report on Law of Treaties," [1958] II *YBILC,* 20–40; Dinstein, *War, Aggression and Self-Defence* (Cambridge: Cambridge University Press, 1994), 103.
57. See McNair, *The Law of Treaties* (Oxford: Oxford University Press, 1961), 215: "There are, however, many rules of customary international law which stand in a higher category, and which cannot be set aside or modified by contracting states; it is easier to illustrate these rules than to define them. They are rules, which have been accepted, expressly or tacitly, by custom as being necessary to protect the public interests of the society of states or to maintain the standards of public morality recognized by them. For instance, piracy is stigmatized by customary international law as a crime, in the sense that a pirate is regarded as *hostis humani generis* and can lawfully be punished by any state into whose hands he may fall. Can there be any doubt that a treaty whereby two states agreed to permit piracy in a certain area, or against the merchant ships of a certain state, with impunity, would be null and void? Or a treaty whereby two allies agreed to wage a war by methods which neglected the customary rules of warfare?" Also, authors like Georg Schwarzenberger, representing more or less a traditional view of international law, assert that treaties should not conflict with a peremptory norm of general international law (*jus cogens*), as the principle is expressed in the Vienna Convention on the Law of Treaties, 1969: "Notwithstanding the absence in international customary law of rules of *jus cogens* or of any rule requiring compliance of treaties with *jus cogens,* Article 64 of the Vienna Convention of 1969 on the Law of Treaties provides that if a new peremptory norm of general international law emerges, any existing treaty which is in conflict with it becomes void and terminates" (Georg Schwarzenberger and Brown, E.D., *A Manual of International* Law, 6th edn., London, 1976, 139–40).
58. *U.N. Charter, Article* 103: "In the event of a conflict between the obligations of the Members of the United Nations under the present Charter and their obligations under any other international agreement, their obligations under the present Charter shall prevail." The Vienna Convention on the Law of Treaties 1969 provides that the rules which it sets out regarding the rights and obligations of states parties to successive treaties relating to the same subject matter are subject to this Article; see generally Oppenheim, *International Law* Vol. I, *ante,* 1216; Goodrich and Hambro, and Simons, *Charter of the United Nations* (3rd ed., 1969), 614–17, Kelsen, *The Law of the United Nations*, (New York, 1950), McNair, *The Law of Treaties, ante*, 216–18.

59. This may form a separate argument against the legality of intervention provided for by Treaty right. Given the conventional character of the UN Charter, two treaties conflict: the UN Charter itself on the one hand, and the Cyprus Treaty of Guarantee, on the other. In such a case the Charter, considered as 'higher' law, prevails. The supremacy of the Charter over *any* other international agreement is established by Article 103 (*UN Charter*). Art. 103 refers both to past and future treaties conflicting with the Charter of the UN (on this last point, see MacNair, *The Law of Treaties*, *ante*, 218: "This provision contains no limitation as to time and operates both retrospectively and prospectively"; Oppenheim, *International Law,* Vol. I (9th ed. Jennings and Watts), *ante*, 1216: "Article 103 is widely accepted as establishing the supremacy of the obligations of the Charter over any other contractual agreement of the members whether past or future, and whether between members *inter se* or with non-member states"; Oppenheim-Lauterpacht, *International Law*, Vol. I (7th ed. H.Lauterpacht) *ante*, 807.

60. See Necatigil, *The Turkish Position in International Law, ante*, 118.

61. UN SCOR, 1098th meeting, 5 Aug. 1965, para. 20 (1964).

62. UN SCOR, 1235th meeting, para. 25 (1964).

63. Oppenheim-Lauterpacht, *International Law, ante*, Vol. I, 802–03; Oppenheim, *International Law* Vol. I (9th ed. R. Jennings and A. Watts), *ante*, 1290.

64. See Oppenheim, *International Law*, *supra*. 1290; Lauterpacht, H., *Private Law Sources and Analogies of International Law* (London 1927); Brownlies, *International Law and the Use of by states, ante*, 404–46; Watts, *The International Law Commission, ante*, 737: "There is general agreement that acts of coercion or threats applied to individuals with respect to their own persons in their personal capacity in order to procure the signature, ratification, acceptance or approval of a treaty will unquestionably invalidate the consent so procured."

65. See relevant discussion in Oppenheim-Lauterpacht, *ante,* Vol. 1, 802; Lauterpacht, H., *Private Law Sources and Analogies of International Law*, *supra* 74; McNair, *The Law of Treaties*, *ante*, 209, (1927) 26 *MLR*, 139–51; Brierly, (1936) 58 *Recueil des Cours*, 203–10.

66. Harvard Law School Research on International Law, *ante*, 1148; Grotius maintained that 'the law of nature required that there ought to be freedom of choice by the parties, and that their consent should not be induced by fear' (*De Jure Belli as Pacis, ante*, Book II).

67. Ehrlich, *International Crises and the Role of Law, Cyprus 1958–1967* (Oxford University Press, 1974), 48: "In part, the logical reason may have been concerning that Turkey and the United Kingdom would respond that if the settlement was invalid then Cyprus was still a British colony. But no one seriously urged that position; the Republic of Cyprus had been a member of the United Nations for over three years and its 'sovereign equality' was recognized by the Charter. Much more important, there were strong pressures from at least Turkey and England, and probably Greece as well, against abrogation of all the Accords.

68. Tornaritis, C. *Cyprus and its Constitutional and Other Legal Problems* (Nicosia, 1977), 58–59.

69. *Ibid.*, 42, 60. See also Jacovides, A. J., *Treaties Conflicting with Peremptory Norms of International Law, and the Zurich-London Agreements* (Nicosia, 1966), 15–28.

70. See Crawford, (1976) 48 BYBIL, 93, at 123–24.

71. Ronzitti, N. *Rescuing Nationals Abroad through Military Coercion and Intervention on Grounds of Humanity* (Martinus Nijhoff Publishers, 1985), 128.

72. UN Charter, Article 42: Should the Security Council consider that measures provided for in Article 41 would be inadequate or have proved to be inadequate, it may take such action by air, sea or land forces as may be necessary to maintain international peace and security. Such action may include demonstrations, blockade, and other operations by air, sea, or land forces of Members of the United Nations.

73. Ronzitti, *supra*, 128; Necatigil, *supra*, 131.

74. Tornaritis, *whether any resort to armed intervention in Cyprus would be justified either under the Charter or under customary international law*, (1964) II *Cyprus Today*, 2.

75. The *Textual* or *"plain meaning" approach* to Treaty Interpretation does not seem to be helpful in this case. It should be noted, however, that the International Court of Justice has more than once pronounced that the textual approach is regarded by it as established law (see, for instance, the *Admissions* case, I.C.J. Reports 1948, 57, and the *Competence* case, *I.C.J.* Reports 1950, 4).

76. See *Conference on Cyprus: Documents Signed and Initialled at Lancaster House on February 19, 1959*, Cmnd.679, Miscellaneous No. 4, London, HMSO, 1959, 5, 10.

77. Xydis, S.G., *Cyprus: Reluctant Republic* (London 1973).

78. *Ibid.*, 409–10. On this point see also Bitsios, D., *Cyprus: The Vulnerable Republic* (1975), 102; to the same effect, of interest is a report sent by Averoff, Foreign Minister of Greece, to Prime Minister Karamanlis, briefing him on the points that had arisen during the preparatory London talks: "The most serious point that had arisen concerned paragraph 2 of the Treaty of Guarantee, which provided that each of the guarantors could act unilaterally in order to safeguard the constitutional order, if the other guarantors did not agree as to the manner in which they should act. At the meeting of 12 February, obviously after consulting legal experts, the point was raised by the British that this provision was incompatible with the UN Charter and perhaps would prevent Cyprus from becoming a UN member. Mr. Zorlu, Mr Palamas, Greek expert on UN matters, and Mr Averoff argued that there was no incompatibility. Mr Averoff declared, however, that should any article of the Zurich Agreements create difficulties for the entry of Cyprus to the UN it should be amended in such a way as to remove the difficulty'" (*Story of Lost Opportunities*).

79. More of the international dimensions of the inter-communal strife, see above, Chapter I.

80. 19 UN GAOR 29th Session, 23 Sept. 1974 (A/PV 2793), paras.123–5.

81. 19 UN SCOR, 27 Feb. 1964, S/PV 1098, para.16. On another occasion, he said that the Treaty of Guarantee contains provisions which are contrary to the UN Charter and is consequently void (20 UN SCOR, 5 Aug. 1965, S/PV 1235, para.25).

82. 19 UN SCOR, 1097th meeting, 25 Feb. 1964 (S/PV 1093), para.168. In his view, the Turkish military intervention was aimed at invasion and, in the long run, the partition of the island.

83. S/PV. 1098, February 27, 1964, 48–50. See also Lauterpacht, E. *British Practice in International Law*.

84. *ibid*., 42–46. The representative of the British Government interestingly went on to say that "the legal effect of the provisions of article IV of the Treaty of Guarantee, as in the case of other legal provisions, will depend on the facts and circumstances of the situation in which they are invoked, and there is nothing in article IV to suggest that action taken under it would necessarily be contrary to the United Nations Charter."

85. See Ronzitti, N., *Rescuing Nationals Abroad through Military Coercion, and Intervention on Grounds of Humanity, ante,* 124.

86. Lauterpacht, Eli, Written Opinion, 1964 (the Opinion may be found in Clerides, G., *Cyprus: My Deposition, ante*, Appendix f, 386–87).

87. UNSC S/PV 1781; UN Monthly Chronicle 1974, vol. xi, No.8, 21–3. He proceeded to state that even though it could be assumed that the treaty gave a right to take military action, this right could be resorted to only for the protection of the Constitution.

88. Necatigil, *The Turkish Position in International Law, ante*, 113.

89. U.N. Doc. S/PV.1781, 20 July 1974, 82 (where it is stated: "neither of those prerequisites has been fulfilled . . . exhaustion of consultations did not precede the Turkish attacks nor were Turkey's plans aimed at the status quo ante, but, obviously, at the permanent occupation of large portions of Cypriot territory").

90. See N. Ronzitti *ante*, 121.

91. See, Report from the *Select Committee on Cyprus* together with the *Proceedings of the Committee*, Minutes of Evidence and Appendices, Session 1975–1976, Ordered by the House of Commons to be printed, 8th April 1976, H.M.S.O., London.

92. *Ibid.* However, it must be noted that the UK, according to the Report of the *Parliamentary Debates*, would only intervene to overthrow the Sampson regime and protect the lives of the Turkish Cypriots.

93. It may be inferred that several statements (the present one included) of the United Kingdom, although not without a degree of ambiguity, lead one to believe that, in the eyes of the UK, Article IV permits military intervention on the part of the guarantor states.

94. Report from the *Select Committee on Cyprus* together with the *Proceedings of the Committee*, Minutes of Evidence and Appendices, Session 1975–1976, *supra*, p. x (emphasis added).

95. *Parliamentary Debates (Hansard), House of Lords* (Official Report), vol. 44, No. 80, 20 Apr. 1983, 618.

96. The London Joint Committee, on which the United Kingdom, Greece, Turkey, the Greek-Cypriot and Turkish Cypriot communities were represented, was engaged in drafting the Treaty of Establishment of the Republic of Cyprus.

97. See letter from Sir Gerald Fitzmaurice, Legal Adviser to the Foreign Office, to the Rt. Hon. Sir Reginald Manningham-Buller, Q.C., M.P., Attorney-General. {*Foreign Office* (F.O.) 371/152871, Public Records Office}.

98. F.O. 371/15289, Public Records Office.

99. *Ibid.* "Any question or difficulty as to the interpretation or application of the provisions of the present Treaty on which agreement cannot be reached by negotiation between the military authorities in the cases described above, or by negotiation between the parties concerned through the diplomatic channel, shall be referred for final decision to a tribunal appointed for the purpose, which shall be composed of four representatives, one each to be nominated by the United Kingdom Government, the Greek Government, the Turkish Government, the Government of the Republic of Cyprus, together with an independent chairman nominated by the President of the International Court of Justice."

100. This grave mistake is well spotted by Mr Clerides in his *Cyprus: My Deposition, ante*, p75.

101. *Ibid.*, 75.

102. *Ibid.*, 75; As pointed out by a Greek-Cypriot scholar in international relations, "the particular circumstances of 1974 had made it necessary for Turkey to intervene, and her initial intervention was a legal one" (M. Evriviades, 1975 10 *Texas International Law Journal,* 264).

103. Necatigil, *The Turkish Position in International Law, ante*, 94.

104. U.N. Security Council, 1097thy Meeting, Provisional Verbatim Record, S/PV. 1097.

105. Lauterpacht, *British Practice in International Law, ante,* 8–9.

106. The area of the so-called Attila line comprises the whole of the northern part of Cyprus, covering 37 percent of the territory of the Republic. The most important natural resources, most of the orchards of olive groves, the most important mines, ports including the main ones of Famagusta, Kyrenia, and Karavostassi, the main water resources, the most breathtaking archaeological sites and tourist centers are included within the area occupied by the Turkish forces.

107. On the Geneva Conferences, see generally Clerides: *Cyprus: My Deposition, ante*; Necatigil, *The Turkish Position in International Law*, *ante.*

108. See Necatigil, *The Turkish Position in International Law*, *ante*, 126.

109. See MacDonald, *International Law and the Conflict in Cyprus,* 1981 *Canadian Yearbook of International Law*, 29: "I conclude that the 1974 invasion of Cyprus was in contravention of international law; for an invasion to be legal it must be consistent with the provisions of the United Nations Charter, whether express or implied; compliance with a treaty, on its own, is insufficient to render an invasion consistent with Article 2(4) of the Charter."

110. See page 36 above.

111. Quote from the Turkish Prime Minister, Mr. Ecevit's statement on 14 August 1974 (*Hurriyet* and *Milliyet* newspapers, 15 August 1974); see also Mr. Ecevit's letter to R. Denktash, leader of the Turkish Cypriot community, in R. Denktash, *The Cyprus Triangle, ante*, Appendix 13.

112. *Parliamentary Debates (Hansard), House of Commons*, No.23, 1986–1987, para. 99: "it is our view—evidently shared by most of the international community—that the extension and entrenchment of the Turkish occupation of Northern Cyprus in August 1974 and subsequently, was illegal both in terms of the 1960 Treaties and in terms of the UN Charter and general international law."

113. The U.N. Security Council in Resolution 367/1975 "regrets the unilateral decision of 13 February 1975 declaring a part of the Republic of Cyprus would become Federated Turkish State." The U.N. General Assembly Resolution 37/253 of 20 May 1983 reads: "The General Assembly deploring the fact that part of the territory of the Republic of Cyprus is still occupied by foreign forces . . . demands the immediate withdrawal of all occupation forces from the Republic of Cyprus; considers that the *de facto* situation created by the force of arms should not be allowed to influence or in any way affect the solution of the problem of Cyprus."

114. See MacDonald, *International Law and the Conflict in Cyprus, ante*, 37: "It is concluded that, even if there is jurisdiction in customary international law or in the provisions of the Charter for the intervention in 1974, or for a continued presence in Cyprus, such continued presence over a protracted period of time is rendered legally doubtful by the Security Council resolutions adopted in regard to Cyprus since 1974."

115. See the Resolutions of the Security Council 353 (1974) of the 20th of July 1974, 354 (1974) of the 23rd of July 1974, 355 (1974) of the 1st of August 1974, 358 (1974), 359 (1974) of the 15th of August 1974, 360 (1974) of the 16th August 1974, 361(1974) of the 30th August 1974, 364 (1974) of the 16th December 1974.

The Geneva Conference at its first phase sought to find ways and means for carrying the above resolutions into effect, especially Resolutions 353(1974) and 354(1974) for attaining a cease-fire agreement. It has, however, exceeded its authority in that, though the Security Council demanded *the immediate withdrawal* of the Turkish forces, in the Geneva Conference the three Foreign Ministers of Greece, Turkey and the United Kingdom were content in agreeing that measures should be taken for their *reduction by stages.*

116. UN General Assembly Resolution 3212 (1974): "1. Calls upon all states to respect the sovereignty, independence, territorial integrity, and non-alignment of the Republic of Cyprus and to refrain from all acts and interventions directed against it; 2. Urges the speedy withdrawal of all foreign armed forces and foreign military personnel from the Republic of Cyprus and the cessation of all foreign interference in its affairs;"

117. Goodrich and Hambro, *The Charter of the United Nations, ante*, 545.

118. Ronzitti, clearly adopting a pro-Turkish view, cites Wengler: "a treaty providing for a right to intervene against the will of a future government of the other state is regarded as prohibited by a jus cogens rule of general international law. Nonetheless, an exception may be valid if intervention is permitted to secure the upholding of an arrangement among different peoples each other exercising its right of self-determination, to live together in one state." He then concludes that Wengler's observation "perfectly fits the case of Cyprus." (*Rescuing Nationals Abroad through*

Military Coercion and Intervention on Grounds of Humanity, ante, 134). For the issue of self-determination and its application to the Cypriot Communities, see below Chapters IV and VII of the present thesis.

Chapter 11

United Nations Peacekeeping and Enforcement Action

COLLECTIVE SECURITY AND ENFORCEMENT ACTION

The bitter experience of the League of Nations, ancestor of the United Nations, led the drafters of the UN Charter to create a more effective system of collective security toward implementing peace. Its pillars are Article 2(4) of the UN Charter and a system of complicated political, military and financial measures against violence or aggression based on Chapter VII of the UN Charter.

Chapter VII is entitled "Action with respect to threats to the peace, breaches of the peace, and acts of aggression." The Charter does not purport to interpret these terms, although it is textually plain that 'threats to the peace' and 'breaches of the peace' mean international peace. Article 39, first article of Chapter VII, provides the following: "The Security Council shall determine the existence of any threat to the peace, breach of the peace, or act of aggression and shall make recommendations, or decide what measures shall be taken in accordance with Articles 41 and 42, to maintain or restore international peace and security." The Council, however, may adopt further measures according to Article 40:

> To prevent an aggravation of the situation, the Security Council may, before making the recommendations or deciding upon the measures provided for in Article 39, call upon the Parties concerned to comply with such provisional measures as it deems necessary or desirable. Such provisional measures shall be without prejudice to the rights, claims or position of the Parties concerned. The Security Council shall duly consider of the failure to comply with such provisional measures.

The words "call upon" used in Article 40, have caused certain problem of interpretation. They are often used in Resolutions of the United Nations as synonymous to the verb "suggest," but the Member States of the United Nations Organization seem to agree that the words mean "[to] order." For instance, when on 15 July 1948 the Security Council passed a Resolution calling upon the Arabs and the Israelis to cease fire, this Resolution was taken as obligatory, that is, it was an order or command from which emanated the legal obligation of obedience and compliance.

Strictly speaking, enforcement action, that is, action that tackles threats against peace, violations of peace or acts of aggression, may take two forms: Article 41 provides for non-military action and Article 42 provides for military action.

Article 41 says as follows:

> The Security Council may decide what measures not involving the use of armed force are to be employed to give effect to its decisions and it may call upon the Members of the United Nations to apply such measures. These may include complete or partial interruption of economic relations, and of sea, postal, telegraphic, radio, and other means of communication, and severance of diplomatic relations.

Article 42 provides:

> Should the Security Council consider that measures provided for in Article 41 would be inadequate or have proved to be inadequate, it may take such action by air, sea or land forces as may be necessary to maintain or restore international peace and security. Such action may include demonstrations, blockade, and other operations by air, sea, or land forces of Members of the United Nations.

Article 42 must be studies in conjunction with Article 43, the content of which reads:

> All Members of the United Nations undertake to make available to the Security Council, on its call and in accordance with a special agreement or agreements, armed forces, assistance, and facilities, including rites of passage, necessary for the purpose of maintaining international peace and security. . . . The agreement or agreements shall be negotiated as soon as possible on the initiative of the Security Council. They shall be concluded between the Security Council and the Members of the United Nations.

Collective security has functioned effectively in the cases of Haiti and Rwanda and in other similar cases, but it is very difficult for it to be effective where international political expediencies are at stake.

THE INVASION OF KUWAIT BY IRAQ

When Saddam Hussein invaded Kuwait on 2 August 1990 and declared it to be Iraq's seventeenth province, the Security Council responded immediately by condemning the act as a breach of the peace and of international security, and requiring Iraq's immediate and unconditional withdrawal. Iraq did not abide by this requirement and subsequently the Security Council adopted more than thirty resolutions on the conflict and its consequences. *Inter alia* it imposed an arms and trade embargo upon Iraq and Kuwait on 6 August 1990 and instituted a committee to supervise the implementation of the sanctions. Following a naval blockade authorized on 25 August 1990, on 28 November 1990 the Security Council finally adopted Resolution 678, in which the Council acting under Chapter VII of the Charter authorized Member States co-operating with the Government of Kuwait, unless Iraq on or before 15 January 1991 fully implements, as set forth in paragraph one above, the foregoing resolutions, to use all necessary means to uphold and implement resolution 660 (1990) and all subsequent relevant resolutions and to restore international peace and security in the area.

Under the leadership of the United States the coalition forces launched 'Operation Desert Storm' on 16/17 January 1991 with the airborne attacks against Iraqi targets in Iraq and Kuwait, followed by the main land offensive on 24 February. A suspension of hostilities came into effect on 28 February after the allied forces had occupied Kuwait and a part of southern Iraq.

There is no doubt that the wording in Resolution 678 "to use all necessary means" was an authorization to use armed force. But there are a number of other legal problems concerning the conduct of Operation Desert Storm which have given rise to some concern. One question is whether the Security Council may delegate its responsibility for military action under Article 42 and authorize States to employ force at their own discretion without retaining at least some form of control. It is arguable that the Security Council was not exactly acting according to Chapter VII because Articles 46 and 47 imply that enforcement measures will be under the control of the Security Council and its Military Staff Committee.

However, it must be said that the UN is ill-equipped to effectively handle the complicated command and control functions involved in such complex military operations. Furthermore, it is also clear that the United States would not have been prepared to accept anything other than American control over its forces and their cooperation with the allies. Without the leadership of the United States under these conditions, it is not likely that there would have been any UN- sponsored action room at all, although there would still have been room for Allied support for Kuwait in the sense of collective self-defense under Article 51 of the Charter.

A second issue concerns the point whether the international community should not have waited longer to see whether the economic sanctions would lead to the desired result, before resorting to armed force and its consequences for the Iraqi civilian population. In essence, this is a political question in which also a number of military considerations have played an important role. There is also much doubt as to the general effectiveness of economic sanctions in view of past experience which indicates that they have more political and symbolic importance than real effect. But there is also a legal point, namely whether, in the light of the wording of Article 42 of the Charter and its position after Article 41, the Security Council must first make a formal determination that the economic and other sanctions have been inadequate, before authorizing military measures. It is submitted that such a requirement may be overstretching the matter, if the Security Council decides to adopt measures under Article 42, it implicitly says that other measures have been insufficient in its view and there is no reason to see what would be legally gained form the formal expression of this view except that there may be more debate on the inadequacy of the sanctions because it is then a separate item to be formally decided.

A third problem that should be mentioned is related to Article 50 of the UN Charter which provides that in the case of enforcement measures adopted by the Security Council, any State which finds itself confronted with special economic problems arising from carrying out of those measures shall have the right to consult the Security Council with regard to a solution of those problems.

A number of States tried to obtain compensation under this Article for damage which they incurred by adhering to the UN sanctions imposed upon Iraq. But these efforts remained fruitless. This may be a bad precedent for the future willingness of States to follow sanctions of the United Nations. Therefore, measures to address this problem have been proposed by the UN Secretary- General in his Agenda for Peace.

Harsh conditions were imposed upon Iraq in the ceasefire Resolution 687 of 3 April 1991, which is referred to as the mother of all resolutions because of its length and broad range of application. The resolution requires Iraq, inter alia, to destroy or remove all weapons of mass destruction, including nuclear weapons, as well as missiles with a range of more than 150 kilometers (during the war with the coalition forces Iraq had sought relief and other popular Arab support by attacking Israel with Scud missiles, as it had been attacking Tehran with missiles in the First Gulf War). The respective disarmament of Iraq is supervised and enforced by the United Nations. Other issues addressed by Resolution 687 concern the determination of the border between Iraq and

Kuwait by the Iraq-Kuwait Boundary Commission, the monitoring of the border by the UN Iraq-Kuwait Observation Mission, the coordination of the return of property to Kuwait, and the supervision of the continuing arms and trade embargo, including the prohibition of the export of oil, against Iraq by the Sanctions Committee of the UN Security Council. With the purpose of addressing the serious shortages of food supplies in Iraq, on 4 April 1995 the Security Council adopted Resolution 986 (1995) allowing, under certain conditions and strict control measures, States to import oil and oil products from Iraq amounting to the equivalent of US$1 billion every ninety days. Iraq refused to accept the conditions of this deal because it saw its sovereignty as being impaired, until finally a memorandum of understanding was agreed upon between the UN Secretariat and the Government of Iraq in spring 1996.

Another aspect which needs to be mentioned is the novelty of the reparations regime imposed upon Iraq by the Security Council, also acting under Chapter VII. In October 1990, the Council held that Iraq was liable under International Law for all damage caused to Kuwait, other States and individuals as a consequence of the invasion of Kuwait. After the defeat of Iraq, the Council demanded in a resolution adopted on 2 March 1991 that Iraq accepts its international liability as part of the ceasefire conditions. Paragraph 16 of Resolution 687 confirmed that Iraq, without prejudice to the debts and obligations of Iraq arising prior to 2 August 1990, which will be addressed through the normal mechanisms, is liable under international law for any direct loss, damage, including environmental damage and the depletion of natural resources, or injury to foreign Governments, nationals and corporations, as a result of Iraq's unlawful invasion and occupation of Kuwait.

On the basis of this Resolution the Security Council created a Compensation Fund and the United Nations Compensation Commission (UNCC), seated in Geneva, by a resolution adopted on 20 May 1991. The UNCC is a subsidiary body of the Security Council and its main political organ, the Governing Council, mirrors the composition of the Security Council. Its task is to deal with the unprecedented amount of more than 2.6 million claims filed against Iraq from more than 100 countries, ranging from a mass of claims of persons who had to depart from Iraq or Kuwait or who suffered injury, property and business loss claims, various types of claims by governments and international organizations to the new field of claims for environmental damage caused by Iraq (accusing Iraq of using oil as a weapon polluting the Gulf and burning Kuwait's oil resources during the war) in the estimated total amount of US$160 billion. There are a number of legal questions concerning the establishment and mode of operation of this new body, which is not a form of arbitration or adjudication, but a system of imposed administration of claims, but they are not within the scope of this monograph.

THE UNITED NATIONS OBSERVER GROUP IN LEBANON (UNOGIL) 1958

The clear establishment in the developing countries of nationalism as a genuine force and the degree of understanding which has been achieved in the last few years over limits to Big Power interventions in the Middle East, makes it difficult to recall accurately the political assumptions of 1958.[1] Yet the crisis in Lebanon (and the related events in Jordan and Iraq) which took place in the summer of 1958 occurred at a time when the ability of Arab nationalism to retain an identity distinct from those Communists who supported it was still in doubt; when the United States still believed in the necessity of 'filling the vacuum' in the Middle East; and when a direct Soviet military response in that region was by no means to be ruled out.

UNOGIL covered two phases of that turbulent summer, and its role changed accordingly. It was initially established to observe to what extent the United Arab Republic was giving material support to rebels in Lebanon; later in the year, while continuing with this task, it became a UN body whose very presence would permit the otherwise impossible withdrawal of foreign powers who had become embroiled in the situation. We here seek to provide the background to both these phases.

In February 1958, Egypt and Syria united, forming the United Arab Republic. By way of response, in mid-February Jordan and Iraq decided to form a federation, with the two nations as equal partners, but with King Faisal of Iraq as head of the federation. Cairo indicated in various ways its disapproval of this federation. In the spring, considerable disturbances occurred in the Lebanon, occasioned in large part by the intention of President Chamoun to alter the constitution so as to permit himself an otherwise unconstitutional second term in office. The government of President Chamoun was pro-Western and unacceptable to Cairo for many reasons, including its failure to break relations with Britain and France during the Suez crisis of 1956, and its acceptance of the 'Eisenhower Doctrine' on the Middle East.[2] When widespread revolt broke out in May 1958, President Chamoun declared that he had evidence of 'massive infiltration' from Syria, and that the rebellion was quite small, and its Chief Staff, General Chehab, was evidently reluctant for it to be used for overt confrontation with the rebels, fearing that those soldiers who were Moslem would be sympathetic to pan-Arab Mohammedanism seeking the overthrow of Chamoun's Christian government.

Chamoun appears to have inquired of the United States in early May if help would be forthcoming if requested, and Eisenhower apparently replied sympathetically, though laying down the conditions that there must be the concurrence of another Arab nation and that the United States troops were not to be used to secure Chamoun a second term of office. In fact, at this stage Chamoun made no formal request for aid to the United States; instead, on 22 May, he requested a meeting of the Security Council to consider his complaint that the UAR was instigating a rebellion in Lebanon. The meeting was actually convened on 6 June 1958, after the Arab League, before whom Lebanon had pulled her complaint, had met for six days, without reaching agreement. Dr. Malik, Lebanon's Foreign Minister, flew to New York for the debate. The essence of Dr. Malik's case before the UN was as follows:

> 11. The case which we have brought to the attention of the Security Council consists of three claims. The first is that there has been, and there still is, massive, illegal and unprovoked intervention in the affairs of Lebanon by the United Arab Republic. The second is that this intervention aims at undermining, and does in fact threaten, the independence of Lebanon. The third is that the situation created by this intervention which threatens the independence of Lebanon, is likely, if continued, to endanger the maintenance of international peace and security. I now proceed to the proof of these three claims.
> 12. The actuality of the intervention is proven by adducing six sets of facts concerning:
> (a) The supply of arms on a large scale from the United Arab Republic to subversive elements in Lebanon;
> (b) The training in subversion on the territory of the United Arab Republic of elements from Lebanon and the sending back of these elements to Lebanon to subvert their Government;
> (c) The participation of United Arab Republic civilian nationals residing in or passing into Lebanon in subversive and terrorist activities in Lebanon.
> (d) The participation of United Arab Republic governmental elements in subversive and terrorist activities and in the direction of rebellion in Lebanon;
> (c) The violent and utterly unprecedented press campaign conducted by the United Arab Republic against the Government of Lebanon;
> (f) The violent and utterly unprecedented radio campaign conducted by the United Arab Republic inciting the people of Lebanon to overthrow their Government.[3]

He then offered various items of evidence to support these charges. Of the validity of the charges (e) and (f) there was no doubt. The UAR however, categorically denied the charges listed under (a), (b), (c) and (d) above. Her representative, Mr. Omar Loutfi, noted that virtually all the Lebanese claims were based on reports by the Lebanese police, and these were dismissed as of no probative value. How far the United States actually believed Lebanon's claims—other than the undeniable ones of hostile press and radio propaganda—is not entirely clear; the evidence is conflicting.

The Security Council met again on 10 June, when a further series of accusations and denials took place between Dr. Malik and Mr. Loutfi. The Lebanese case was supported by Iraq, whose representatives spoke of the problems which 'Nasserism' was causing to Iraq, Lebanon and Jordan. The United Kingdom representative indicated 'that my delegation considers that the Foreign Minister of Lebanon has fully made out and substantiated his contention that Lebanon has suffered, and is suffering, interference from the United Arab Republic by infiltrations of armed men, smuggling of arms, attack on frontier posts, incitements to revolt and other subversive methods.'[4] The French representative also felt that 'the very detailed factual information which Dr. Malik cited in support of his complaint constitutes a significant, specific and convincing body of evidence.'[5]

The Soviet Union, on the other hand, categorically supported the position of the UAR. She accused Lebanese leaders of 'speaking for the Western Powers'; of betraying Arab nationalism by supporting the Eisenhower Doctrine in the Middle East; and of causing a threat to the peace by preparing to invite intervention by the United Kingdom and the United States in what was purely an internal quarrel.[6] The smaller nations on the Security Council refrained from supporting either the Lebanon or the UAR, seeking only to find a solution acceptable to all parties. To that end, Sweden introduced a draft resolution (S/4022) authorizing a UN observation group to proceed to the Lebanon to ensure that there was no illegal infiltration across her borders. This resolution was adopted by ten votes to zero, with the USSR abstaining.

Thus UNOGIL was established. Until mid-June the situation was quieter, but on 14 June the rebels—who had been encircled in Basra—broke out from behind their barricades and fighting was renewed. Civil disorder in the Lebanon increased again. Hammarskjold himself arrived in Lebanon on 18 June, and an undeclared forty-eight hour truce began. On 3 July 1958 UNOGIL submitted a report to the Security Council which found that there was no major infiltration occurring from the United Arab Republic. This report was strongly criticized by President Chamoun's government; and it is also fair to say that there was fairly widespread skepticism—among Western countries at least—of the ability of UNOGIL to ascertain the necessary information on which to base its report. It now appears that during June President Chamoun several times endeavored, unsuccessfully, to secure American intervention. Interestingly, it was at this time that President Chamoun announced publicly, for the first time, that he would leave office when his term expired on 23 September, and that he would not seek a second term under a revised constitution. The civil war now quietened down and in early July it appeared that the Lebanon crisis would pass without Western military assistance.

Developments from an unexpected quarter were to prevent this. On 14 July 1958 there was military coup in Iraq. King Faisal and the prime minister, both pro-Western, were murdered and a republic was proclaimed. The coup, led by Brigadier-General Kassim, was violent and brutal. There was a widespread belief at the time that Kassim was pro-Nasser, and Chamoun greatly feared that his success would further encourage the Moslem rebels in the Lebanon. At the same time, King Hussein's throne in Jordan was reported to be in danger. The king declared that the Jordan-Iraq Union still stood, and that, with King Faisal dead, he was now the head of the Union. President Chamoun requested intervention by the United States, and Jordan requested intervention by the United Kingdom. Both requests were this time granted. The United States and the United Kingdom each declared that they were acting under Article 51 of the UN Charter—helping a legitimate government, at its own request, to defend its country against external aggression. The other Arab States and the Soviet Union took the position that the situations existing in Iraq, Jordan, and the Lebanon revealed civil war only; that this view had been upheld, so far as the Lebanon was concerned, by UNOGIL's first report; that no outside State could legitimately intervene; and that collective self-defense under Article 51 was only permitted until the Security Council could act—which it had already done by sending UNOGIL to Lebanon.[7]

On 15 July a meeting of the Security Council was convened. There was some initial confusion over the credentials of the representative of Iraq, due to the fact that King Hussein, declaring himself the new head of the Jordan-Iraq Union, had confirmed the appointment of King Faisal's representative at the UN; while the new foreign secretary in Kassim's government has issued credentials to as new representative. Eventually, however, the Security Council began its debate. Ambassador Lodge of the United States said that although UNOGIL had helped to reduce interference across the border, arms and personnel were being infiltrated into the Lebanon at a greatly increased rate since the revolution in Iraq. He emphasized that the United States regarded her action as complementary to the work of UNOGIL, and would withdraw her forces as soon as the UN could effectively guarantee Lebanon's independence.[8] The Soviet Union, on the other hand, introduced a resolution (S/4047) which would have condemned the United States action as contrary to Article 2 (7) of the Charter, and as a serious threat to international peace, and which would call for the immediate withdrawal of American troops from the Lebanon. While the Security Council was still debating the question, as new Interim Report was cabled from UNOGIL, stating that it had met with success in negotiations for inspection all along the Lebanese border. The report also suggested that UNOGIL's size should be considerably increased.

The United States introduced her own draft resolution (S/4050) which, while commending the work of UNOGIL, would also require

> the Secretary-General immediately to consult the Government of Lebanon and the Member States as appropriate with a view to making such additional arrangements, including the contribution and use of contingents as may necessary to protect the territorial integrity and independence of Lebanon and to ensure that there is no illegal infiltration of personnel or supply of arms or other material across the Lebanese borders.

The Soviet representative opposed this on the grounds that the United States draft resolution, though commending UNOGIL, ignored its findings—namely, that no major infiltration was occurring. France thought that it been able to carry out its tasks. Japan, announcing that she would vote for the American resolutions, did so with "certain misgivings concerning the circumstances which have made the landing of the Marines necessary" and believing that "the first operative paragraph of the United States draft resolution appears somehow not quite consonant with the report of the United Nations Observer Group in Lebanon."[9] These misgivings were stated even more forcefully by the Japanese representative a day later.

So far the debate had proceeded much as expected. There was some surprise, however, when the Swedish representative suggested the activities of UNOGIL be suspended until further notice. The Swedish government rejected the United States argument that her troops were in the Lebanon under the terms of Article 51 of the Charter; and thought that the United States presence made it impossible for UNOGIL to carry out the tasks assigned to it (S/4054).

The next day—17 July 1958—the Security Council had an additional item on its agenda: a complaint by Jordan of interference in her domestic affairs by the UAR (S/4053); and with this came the news that the United Kingdom had sent troops to Jordan at King Hussein's request, to forestall an attempted coup. The arguments now heard ran closely parallel to those concerning the Lebanon; the United Kingdom asserted that she was helping Jordan to face an external threat;[10] while the Soviet Union and the UAR claimed that King Hussein faced no threat save his own discontented people, and that outside Powers had no right to intervene in a domestic quarrel. The Soviet Union now revised her draft resolution to include a demand for the withdrawal of United Kingdom troops form Jordan.

The debate was still in progress, and the draft resolutions still had to be voted upon, when the Second Interim Report of UNOGIL was published (S/4052). Once again the Lebanese delegate felt obliged to point out that the report was based on information which was very limited in certain particular respects.[11]

The voting on the draft resolutions was as follows:

1. *Soviet Draft Resolution* (S/4047/rev.1)
   For: USSR
   Against: Canada, China, Colombia, France, Iraq, Panama, UK, USA
   Abstaining: Japan, Sweden
   Rejected: 1-8-2
2. *US Draft Resolution (S/*4050/rev. 1)
   For: Canada, China, Colombia, France, Iraq, Japan, Panama, UK, USA
   Against: USSR
   Abstaining: Sweden
   Rejected: 9-1-1
3. *Swedish Draft Resolution* (S/4054)
   For: Sweden, USSR
   Against: Canada, China, Colombia, France, Iraq, Japan, Panama, UK, USA
   Rejected: 2-9-0

   No draft having been adopted, a compromise resolution was now introduced by Japan, which, instead of asking the Secretary-General to create a police force in Lebanon, requested him in general terms to make the necessary arrangements which will enable the United Nations to fulfil the general purposes established in the resolution of 11 June 1958. This, too, was rejected by the Soviet veto; and Soviet amendments to the Japanese resolution were also not adopted:
4. *Japanese Draft* Resolutiion (S/4055/rev. 1)
   For: Canada, China, Colombia, France, Iraq, Japan, Sweden, UK, USA
   Against: USSR
   Rejected: 10-1-0
5. *USSR* Amendments (S/4063)
   For: USSR
   Against: Canada, Chona, Colombia, France, Iraq, Panama, UK, USA
   Abstaining: Japan, Sweden
   Rejected: 1-8-2

The Soviet Union and the United States both proposed now that the matter should be transferred to the General Assembly. The Security Council was adjourned, but in fact no action was taken to call the Assembly into session until 7 August: the intervening time was used by the major Powers to engage in negotiations, by letter, between themselves. Khrushchev suggested to Eisenhower, Macmillan, de Gaulle, and Nehru that the recommendations of a summit meeting should be submitted to the Security Council. The secretary-general made it clear that he believed that any such meeting should be held under UN auspices. Eisenhower was not at all enthusiastic about the idea of a summit on the Middle East: he felt that foreign ministers, or even heads of State, could represent their countries on the Security Council, and that any summit should be within the framework of that organ. He obviously also had doubts about the advisability of any summit meeting on the Middle East at which Israel was not represented. He and Macmillan (S/4071) replied in these terms to Khrushchev. Khrushchev indicated that a meeting of heads of government within the framework of the Security Council, would be acceptable to the Soviet Union (S/4064). He emphasized that he thought it essential that India should be invited to attend the Security Council for this purpose. This letter, unlike the previous one, was very moderate in its terminology, and for a brief moment it looked as if an agreement to meet was drawing nearer. Eisenhower, however, now backed away, saying that the suggestion that India should be included was arrogating to the Soviet Union privilege of determining who should participate in a Security Council discussion (S/4074). The prospect of a consensus was further dissipated when de Gaulle rejected the Macmillan-Eisenhower stand on the necessity for any meeting being held within the Security Council, and proposed that a heads of government meeting be held in Europe (S/4075). The Soviet Union thus turned once again to this idea, which tallied with her own original proposal (S/4067). After a further exchange of letter (S/4079) it became apparent that no agreement was going to be reached; and after a brief reconvening of the Security Council on 7 August, all the parties agreed that the matter should be transferred to the General Assembly.

Two events of importance—perhaps sufficient to break the deadlock—had occurred by the time that the Assembly met on 8 August; first, General Chehab, the widely respected and acceptable army leader, had been elected president of the Lebanon by a democratic vote, and thus the question of a second term for Chamoun had been irrevocably removed from the scene; and second, the new Iraq revolutionary government had been at pains to indicate that it regarded itself as bound by the UN Charter, and had now been officially recognized by both the United States and the United Kingdom. There was now a tacit agreement that the best solution to the problem would be an "Arab solution." It was clear that the Americans and British wished to withdraw from the Lebanon and Jordan respectively, and the task was to devise the UN role which would most facilitate this withdrawal. Many delegations thought that some UN presence was required in Jordan, and suggested that this might be achieved by strengthening UNTSO within the framework of the Arab-Israeli Armistice Agreements. Jordan, however, made it quite clear that a force of the UNEF type, or an Observer Group of the UNOGIL type, was not welcome on Jordanian territory. Some other form of UN presence would have to be found. This is what the secretary-general ultimately did. So far as the Lebanon was concerned, the question here was whether the mere enlargement of UNOGIL would facilitate a United States withdrawal, or whether its mandate and functions also needed to be changed. The choices before the Assembly were effectively summarized by a future secretary-general, U-Thant, then speaking as the representative of Burma; and his response to the choices reflected a widely shared view. There was little desire to see a force of the UNEF type established in the Lebanon:

> the only logical step for the United Nations is to find some suitable ways and means, whereby the foreign troops may be speedily withdrawn from Lebanon and Jordan and stability restored to the area.

There also appears to be a general agreement that some kind of United Nations presence in these two countries is necessary to ensure the speedy withdrawal of foreign troops. Only the nature of this 'presence' is in dispute. Some Member States favor the strengthening of the United Nations Observation Group in Lebanon in accordance with the plan presented by the Observation Group inn its second report (S/4069), and to send a fresh United Nations observation group to Jordan to perform similar functions. The advocates of this action insist that the enlargement of the functions of the Observation Group is not warranted by the prevailing circumstances. The other school of thought, however, prefers to enlarge the functions of the United Nations force. It advocates some kind of international constabulary with police, if not strictly military, functions. The functions of this constabulary, recruited from among the small nations, if my interpretation is correct would fall short of the normal functions of a fighting force. It would be authorized to shoot, but would carry only small arms:

> On the basis of all available information in the Middle East, my delegation cannot agree to the substitution of the Observation Group with limited functions by an international police force that would be expected to enforce its authority by force of arms.[12]

These were the essential issues before the Assembly, though inevitably the speeches ranged considerably wider. Eisenhower, for example, addressed the Assembly and made certain specific proposals, including a study on a UN stand-by force, and the establishment of a Middle Eastern regional economic plan involving an internationally-supported development institution.

Further evidence that the UN could play a vital role in facilitating the withdrawal of British and American forces appeared in the following letters which were sent to the President of the Assembly while that body continued its discussions:

LETTER DATED 18 AUGUST 1958 FROM THE SECRETARY OF STATE OF THE UNITED STATES OF AMERICA TO THE PRESIDENT OF THE GENERAL ASSEMBLY

United States forces are now in Lebanon in response to an appeal of the duly constituted Government of Lebanon for assistance in maintaining Lebanon's territorial integrity and political independence against danger from without. United States forces will be withdrawn from Lebanon whenever this is requested by the duly constituted Government of Lebanon or whenever, as a result of further action of the United Nations or otherwise, their presence is no longer required. The United States will in any event abide by a determination of the United Nations General Assembly that action taken or assistance furnished by the United Nations makes the continued presence of United States forces in Lebanon unnecessary for the maintenance of the international peace and security.

(*Signed*) John Foster DULLES [A/3876]

LETTER DATED 18 AUGUST 1958 FROM THE SECRETARY OF FOREIGN AFFAIRS OF THE UNITED KINGDOM OF GREAT BRITAIN AND NORTHERN IRELAND TO THE PRESIDENT OF THE GENERAL ASSEMBLY

United Kingdom forces are now in Jordan in response to an appeal of the duly constituted Government of Jordan for assistance in maintaining Jordan's territorial integrity and political independence against danger from without. United Kingdom forces will be withdrawn from Jordan whenever this is requested by the duly constituted Government of Jordan or whenever, as a result of the further action of the United Nations or otherwise, their presence is no longer required. The United Kingdom will in any event abide by a determination of the United Nations General Assembly that action taken or assistance furnished by the United Nations makes the continued presence of United Kingdom forces in Jordan unnecessary for the maintenance of international peace and security.

I would appreciate it if you would have this letter circulated to the Members of the General Assembly for their information.

(*Signed*) Selwyn LLOYD

UNION OF SOVIET SOCIALIST REPUBLICS: DRAFT RESOLUTION

The General Assembly,

Recognizing the necessity of adopting urgent measures for the relaxation of tension in the area of the Near and Middle East in the interests of preserving universal peace,

1. *Recommends* the Governments of the United States of America and the United Kingdom to withdraw their troops from the territory of Lebanon and Jordan without delay;
2. Instructs then Secretary-General to strengthen the United Nations Observation Group in Lebanon in accordance with the plan presented by the United Nations Observation Group in Lebanon in its second interim report (S/4052) and to send an observation group to Jordan with a view to the supervision of the withdrawal of the United States and United Kingdom troops from Lebanon and Jordan, and of the situation along the frontiers of those countries.[A/3870]

CANADA COLOMBIA, DENMARK, LIBERIA, NORWAY, PANAMA AND PARAGUAY: DRAFT RESOLUTION

The General Assembly,

Having considered the item Questions discussed at the 838th meeting of the Security Council on 7 August 1958,'

Noting the declarations addressed to the President of the General Assembly of 18 August 1958 by the United States regarding United States forces now in Lebanon and their withdrawal by the United Kingdom regarding British forces now in Jordan and their withdrawal,

Noting the Charter aim that States should practice tolerance and live together in peace with one another as good neighbors,

I

1. *Reaffirms* that all Member States should refrain from any threats or acts, direct or indirect, aimed at impairing the freedom, independence or integrity of any State, or at fomenting civil strife and subverting the will of the people of any State;
2. *Calls upon* all Members States strictly to observe these obligations and to ensure that their conduct, by word and deed, in relation to the general area of the Near East, conforms to the above-mentioned policy;

II

Requests the Secretary-General, in accordance with the Charter, forthwith to make such practical arrangements as he, in consultation with the Governments concerned, may find would adequately serve to help in upholding the purposes and principles of the Charter in relation to Lebanon and Jordan in present circumstances, having in mind section I of the present resolution;

III

1. *Notes* that the Secretary-General has studies in preparation, for consideration by the General Assembly at its thirtieth session, of the feasibility of establishing a stand-by United Nations peace force;
2. *Invites* the Secretary –General to continue his studies now under way and in this context to consult as appropriate with the Arab countries of the Near East with a view to possible assistance regarding an Arab development institution designed to further economic growth in these countries;

IV

1. Requests Member States to co-operate fully inn carrying out this resolution;
2. Invites the Secretary-General to report hereunder, as appropriate, the first such report to be made not later than 30 September 1958.

[A/3878]

Neither the Russian nor the Norwegian drafts were put to the vote. With a sense of relief, the Assembly turned toward an 'Arab solution' and adopted unanimously the following resolution sponsored by Iraq, Jordan, Lebanon, Libya, Morocco, Saudi Arabia, Sudan, Tunisia, UAR, and Yemen:

The General Assembly,

Having considered the item entitled Questions considered by the Security Council at its 838th meeting on 7 August 1958;

Noting the Charter aim that States should practice tolerance and live together in peace with one another as good neighbors,

Noting that the Arab States have agreed, in the Pact of the League of Arab States, to strengthen the close relations and numerous ties which link the Arab States, and to support and stabilize these ties upon a basis of respect for the independence and sovereignty of these States, and to direct their efforts toward the common good of all the Arab countries, the improvement of their status, the security of their future and the realization of their aspirations and hopes,

Desiring to relieve international tension

I

1. *Welcomes* the renewed assurances given by the Arab States to observe the provision of article 8 of the Pact of the League of Arab States that each member State shall respect the systems of government established in the other member States and regard them as exclusive concerns of these States, and that each shall pledge to abstain from any action calculated to change established systems of government;
2. *Calls upon* all states Members of the United Nations to act strictly in accordance with the principles of mutual respect for each other's territorial integrity and sovereignty, of non-aggression, of strict non-interference in each other's internal affairs, and of equal and mutual benefit, to ensure that their conduct by word and deed conforms to these principles;

II

Requests the Secretary-General to make forthwith, in consultation with the Governments concerned and in accordance with the Charter, and having in mind section I of this resolution, such practical arrangements as would adequately help in upholding the purposes and principles of the Charter in relation to Lebanon and Jordan in the present circumstances, and thereby facilitate the early withdrawal of the foreign troops from the two countries;

III

Invites the Secretary-General to continue his studies now under way and in this context to consult as appropriate with the Arab countries of the Near East with a view to possible assistance regarding an Arab development institution designed to further economic growth in these countries;

IV

1. *Requests* Member States to co-operate fully carrying out this resolution;

2. *Invites* the Secretary-General to report hereunder, as appropriate, the first such report to be made not later than 30 September 1958.[13]

The resolution placed enormous reliance on the discretion of the secretary-general. All specific suggestions having failed, the secretary-general was authorized to make 'such practical arrangements as would adequately help.' The practice of 'Leave it to Dag' perhaps at this moment reached its height. What Hammarskjold in fact did was to follow UNOGIL's own suggestion, and greatly increase the strength of that group, while continuing to limit its mandate to observer functions. In other words, conditions had so modified, and confidence in the secretary-general was at that time so great, that Hammarskjold pursued a course of action which the Security Council had a month previously failed to agree upon. The secretary-general also secured Jordan's agreement:

> to serve as host country for a United Nations representative, properly staffed, to serve as a Special Representative of the Secretary-General to assist in the implementation of the resolution, specifically with a view to help in upholding the purposes and principles of the Charter in relation to Jordan in the present circumstances. The Governments of Lebanon and the United Arab Republic had both undertaken to grant all the facilities—including liaison offices in Beirut and Damascus—needed in support of the establishment of a United Nations organ in Jordan. Ambassador Spinelli, Under-Secretary in charge of the United Nations Office in Geneva, had proceeded to Amman on 27 September to work out the necessary practical arrangements. He was to serve as Special Representative on a preliminary basis.[14]

By 25 October the United States had withdrawn her troops from Lebanon, and by 2 November the United Kingdom had withdrawn her troops from Jordan. In mid-November the Lebanon requested her complaint against the UAR to be withdrawn from the agenda of the Security Council, and shortly thereafter the Secretary-General put into operation a plan for the termination of UNOGIL. By 9 December UNOGIL had left Lebanon, and normal relations between Lebanon and the UAR were resumed.

UN OPERATION IN THE CONGO 1960–1964

In December 1958, with commendable foresight, UN Secretary-General Dag Hammarskjold told the first session of the UN Economic Commission for Africa that the newly emerging African nations were likely to need substantial assistance from the United Nations. Upon independence most of them were likely to face substantial social and economic problems and they had all too few experts of their own. The United Nations could usefully provide technical assistance.

At the same time Soviet-American relations were at a difficult stage. In April 1959 US Secretary of State Dulles resigned for health reasons. He was succeeded by Mr. Christian Herter. Attempts were made in 1959 to seek a relaxation of tension between East and West, and preparations were put under way for a summit meeting to be convened in May 1960. There was hope that some progress might be made on disarmament. In February 1959 Prime Minister Macmillan had visited Moscow and the Soviet Union accepted the idea of a foreign ministers meeting to be followed later by a heads of government summit. After extensive preparations the foreign ministers began their meeting on 11 May 1959. Important questions relating to the reunification of Germany were on the agenda. They adjourned in June and met again in July, but no agreement could be reached on the key issues. However, President Eisenhower announced on 3 August that Mr. Khrushchev would visit the United States in September. Such news, given the past relations of the Soviet Union and the United States, was momentous. The USSR was by now embroiled in the problems of its rift with China. Eisenhower, with the end of his presidential term drawing near, was eager to achieve some measure of détente with the Russians. Among the many other causes of tension was the increasing readiness of Fidel Castro's Cuba to turn to the Soviet Union.

In London an election was imminent. And in France General de Gaulle was anxious to make clear that the United States was not spokesman of the whole of the West. France did not share the general Western desire to prohibit atmospheric nuclear testing and was increasingly dissatisfied with some aspects of defense integration within NATO. Just before Mr. Khrushchev arrived in America the second Soviet space rocket hit the surface of the moon. The visit of the Russian leader went off well. In October the nuclear test ban conference was resumed in Geneva.

It looked as if the long-promised summit would be held, though prospects for agreement there were not very great. In fact totally unforeseen circumstances led to its abandonment. The leaders did meet in Paris on 16 May 1960 but they were wholly occupied with the shooting down of an American U-2 aircraft over Soviet territory and the alleged earlier violation of Soviet air space by a U-2, announced by Khrushchev on 5 May. The conference proper did not even begin. Many observers criticized the timing of these flights and considered that their outcome provided Khrushchev, who on détente was under pressure from elements in the Soviet hierarchy, with the excuse he needed for calling off the summit.

It was into this background of resumed tension that the new nations of Africa were emerging. Hammarskjold was concerned, above all, to prevent their existing problems being exacerbated by competition on that continent between the United States and the Soviet Union. In May 1960 he arranged for Dr. Ralph Bunche, UN Under-Secretary for Special Political Affairs, to represent him at the independence celebrations of the former Belgian Congo the following month. Hammarskjold realized that the transition to independence was unlikely to be smooth, and Bunche was authorized to explore with the new Congolese authorities ways in which the United Nations, by means of technical assistance, could help. It was therefore natural, when trouble came, that the Congo should turn to the UN.

The seeds of violence had long been sown in this vast country. Under the Belgian administration it was divided into the six provinces of Leopoldville, Equateur, Orientale, Kivu, Katanga, and Kasai. Except for Kasai, this pattern more or less held until the early part of 1962 but by the beginning of 1963 the number had increased to twenty-one. The tribal structure is highly complex. The Ba-Kongo inhabit the strategically important strip of land between Leopoldville and the sea. The Ba-Mongo grouping is found in the northern part of the old province of Leopoldville and in the southern parts of Equateur and Orientale provinces. Of the two main groups of the Ba-Luba, one is in the north of what was the province of Katanga and the other in the south of what was Kasai. It has been said of the Kasai Ba-Luba that 'they took very easily to European ideas and education and were employed all over the Congo as mechanics, drivers, and clerks. Because of their quickness and adaptability, they were always regarded with suspicion by the neighboring tribes. The Ba-Lunda occupy a strong position in the south of the old province Katanga. Other tribal groupings include the Ba-Mbala and the Ba-Pende (in Leopoldville province); the Bena-Lulua, Ba-Tetela, and Ba-Songe (Kasai province); the Ba-Kusu (Kivu province); and the Ba-Tshokwe (Katanga).[15] There also exist ethnological differences that cut across with tribal and linguistic differences. Almost evert tribal group has its own dialect, though four trade languages—Kiswahili in the east, Kikongo in the west, Chiluba in the south, and Lingala in the north—are widely spoken second languages.[16]

European penetration of the Congo, the birth of the Congo Free State under the personal rule of King Leopold II of Belgium in 1885 and the establishment of Belgian sovereignty in 1908 are but later elements in the long and absorbing history of that land. By the mid-1950s a political awareness was sweeping across it. Academic circles in Belgium advanced proposals for a thirty-year plan of decolonization. The Belgian government was prepared to give this serious consideration, but for the emergent politicians in the Congo it was too slow. A decree of 1957 gave the vote to Congolese males aged twenty-five and over in the election of communal councils in towns that had the designated rank of 'city.' The following year Joseph Kasavubu, a member of the Ba-Kongo tribe, became mayor of the African commune of Dendale in Leopoldville and began to build up a power base in the Leopoldville area. Until August 1959 political parties had in fact been prohibited, though they had begun openly to be formed in many cases by the end of 1958. Kasavubu was transforming the Alliance des Ba-Kongo, a tribally based federalist party. Patrice Lumumba founded a national, centrist party that was unique in cutting across tribal and regional lines. His Mouvement National Congolais (MNC) obtained widely based support, though it was particularly strong in the province of Kasai and in Stanleyville in Orientale province. It attracted many Africans of caliber. Cyrille Adoula was its first vice-president and Joseph Ileo was on the committee (both were to break with Lumumba in 1959, when the MNC was split). Joseph Mobutu also joined the party. All four became, in turn, prime minister of the Congo. Although the MNC, and Lumumba in particular, were by early 1960 to be regarded by the Belgians as uncomfortably radical, in late 1958 this grouping had been favored by the Belgians as a counterweight to the secessionist groups.

There were other parties of importance, too. Albert Klonji, President of the Kasai branch of the MNC, supported Ileo when he opposed Lumumba in July 1959 and they formed the party that came to be known as the MNC(K).[17] Antoine Gizenga led the separatist Parti Solidaire Africain (PSA), and Cleophas Kamitatu was President of the province of Leopoldville branch. The Association des Ba-Luba du Katanga was a federalist party organized by Jason Sendwe. And Moise Tshombe led another federalist party, the Confederation des Associations Tribales du Katanga. This party's strength lay in the fact that it belonged to southern Katanga, with its copper mines.

During the first week of 1959 there were serious riots in Leopoldville and many people, both African and European, were killed. Kasavubu and other Abako leaders were arrested. The Commission of Inquiry set up by the Belgian government found that discrimination, overcrowding and unemployment were important factors in the violence. Nor could the Belgian Congo be isolated from the moves for independence in surrounding countries. In a message broadcast on 13 January King Baudouin announced that it was now Belgian policy to prepare the Congo for eventual independence. A Belgian government statement the same day included promises that local government bodies at various levels would be elected and it envisaged steps that would lead to a Chamber of Representatives and a Senate. But there was widespread dissent both in Belgium and among Belgians in the Congo. The Minister for the Congo and Ruanda-Urundi, faced hostility in Belgium and among whites in the Congo for his sympathy for African aspirations. Congolese politicians, suspicious of Belgian intentions, began to build up political support for the future, and the emerging political parties began to grow. In August tribal fighting was reported in Kasai. M. van Hemelrijck resigned in September. M. Auguste de Schrijver was appointed in his place and announced inter alia that, in accordance with the King's message and the government statement of 13 January, elections to the Territorial Councils would be held at the end of the year. In early November 1959 street rioting broke out in Stanleyville and was sternly suppressed by Belgian troops with much loss of life. Lumumba was arrested. Although more than thirty political parties had sprung up, the Abako and PSA decided to boycott the elections, held in December, and the MNC did not participate fully. The poll was small.

King Badouin visited the Congo during December and soon afterward M. de Schrijver issued invitations at a Round Table Conference in Brussels, to open on 20 January 1960, on the future of the country. Among Congolese leaders attending it were Kasavubu (Abako), Gizenga (PSA), Kalonji (MNC(K)), and Lumumba (MNC) who, released from prison on the insistence of the other leaders, arrived in Brussels on 26 January. The Congolese pressed for a date for independence; by the end of the Conference a date had been set a mere six months later—30 June 1960. At this stage the Belgian government still trusted Lumumba (who wanted a unitary state and as yet had shown no hostility to the West) more than Kasavubu, who was regarded as a separatist. The scale of the Congolese success was totally unforeseen; and the Congo had all too little time to prepare for an independent future.

Both Kasavubu and Lumumba had urged that a provisional government should be set up immediately but instead the Conference had agreed on a compromise: an Executive College was to be appointed as the transitional regime. It would consist of six Congolese and the Governor-General, and the Colonial Charter would be amended to give this body executive power. Also, three Congolese were to be attached to the staff of each provincial governor. The College was installed on 14 March with Kasavubu and Lumumba among its members.

Work now began on a constitution, and Tshombe, the President of Conakat, did all he could to achieve a very loose confederal structure so that revenues from the mineral rights of Katanga should remain in that province. The Belgians had governed the Congo as one economic unit, giving extensive concessions to foreign –often Belgian- companies. The Congo state had taken an annual percentage of revenues or shares. In 1906, Union Miniere, then a newly formed Belgian company, was given exclusive rights over Katanga until 1999. Tanganyika Concessions was an important shareholder in Union Miniere. Belgian and British finance was thus closely involved in Katanga mining.

The Loi fondamentale providing the new constitution for the Congo was enacted by the Belgian parliament and on 19 May 1960 signed by King Baudouin. There was to be a unitary State with federal characteristics. There would be two federal chambers, and an assembly for each of the six provinces. The Head of State, to be elected by the chambers, would appoint ministers (but each of the provinces was to be represented), make treaties, and command the armed forces. There was also a prime minister. The Chamber of Representatives and the provincial assemblies were to be elected by universal male suffrage, the Senate by vote of the provincial assemblies. The presidents of provincial assemblies and the members of provincial governments were also to be elected by the provincial assemblies, with the condition that two-thirds of the members in each case be present. In some provinces, for example Leopoldville and Katanga, this produced deadlock and the constitution was hastily amended on 15 June to allow election by a majority of the members present, if, after two meetings, attendance by two-thirds of the members had not been achieved. This amendment provoked serious controversy. An enormous amount remained to be done before independence. But internal order was breaking down, and in some quarters the Belgians were accused of abandoning their responsibilities.

Elections to the Chamber of Representatives and to the provincial assemblies were held between 11 and 25 May. Lumumba's party, the MNC, did very well both in the direct voting for members of the House of Representatives and in the indirect voting to the Senate. In both cases Belgian expectations were confounded. But Lumumba had resigned from the Executive College, and his attacks on Belgium became more and more rancorous. Belgian political and public opinion began to regard him as unstable and inclined to accept support from communist elements.

The Loi fondamentale provided that the Belgian King would now appoint, after taking the election results and consultations with the Congolese political parties into account, a *formateur*. The *formateur* would form a government which would then have to receive the approval of the Chamber and Senate. Although Lumumba's party had gained the greatest number of seats, it had not won an overall majority. The King was advised to wait until a moderate coalition emerged. By 2 June Lumumba was protesting that no appointment had been made. On 13 June he was given until 16 June to report on whether a widely based government could be formed. On 17 June the job of *formateur* was given to Kasavubu, who, although intransigent, was regarded by the Belgians as being more moderate than Lumumba. Now Lumumba declared that he would form a government himself, and when the Chamber met to select its officers it was clear that he commanded a majority. He was then appointed *formateur*. By 23 June Lumumba had formed a full government. He was Prime Minister and Minister of Defense; the MNC(K) was the only main party not represented in his government, but that did not prevent widespread dissatisfaction of various kinds. At a joint session of the two Houses, Kasavubu was elected Head of State.

It seemed clear, however, that law and order were breaking down. There was already tribal fighting in Kasai and a state of emergency had been declared in Equateur, on 23 May, after election riots. In Katanga there was good reason to believe that Tshombe was seeking to declare independence: he tried to appoint a representative (a Belgian) from Katanga to the United Nations, and on 29 June only prompt action by Ganshof van der Meersch and Lumumba prevented Katanga Assembly from proclaiming independence. A state of emergency had been declared in that province on 14 June. Lumumba therefore faced enormous problems, often exacerbated by his own volatile personality. On 29 June the Treaty of Friendship between Belgium and the Congo was signed. On 30 June the Congo became fully independent and at the ceremony King Baudouin's welcome to the new nation was patronizing in tone, evincing a characteristically bitter response from Lumumba. Among those attending the ceremony were Robert Murphy of the United States and Ralph Bunche of the UN.

By 5 July elements of the Force publique, the Congolese army, had mutinied. Soldiers in Leopoldville had been on duty during the extended independence celebrations and were tired and resentful; they saw little prospect of Africanization of the officer ranks; and there was tribal resentment about senior government appointments made by Lumumba. On 5 July, after disorders in Camp Leopold II, General Emile Janssens, commander of the Force publique, placed the reserve garrison at Thysville on alert for a possible move to Leopoldville. The soldiers were mutinied and the Belgian officers lost control. Lumumba's handling of general questions relating to the Force and of particular circumstances in Leopoldville was such as to worsen the situation.

General Janssens wanted to bring to Leopoldville, from their bases in the Congo, Belgian metropolitan troops. Lumumba decided instead to speak to the rioting men of the Force publique next day. On 6 July he offered the soldiers promotion, but they were not satisfied. Realizing that their resentment at Belgian command had to be assuaged, Lumumba now dismissed Janssens. Soldiers from Thysville spread the mutiny to other camps and areas, and drunken soldiers began attacking Europeans. Such raping as did take place inevitably caused rumors of even worse excesses, and soon panic swept through the European community. Exit points to the French Congo became crowded and the Belgian embassy in Leopoldville was overflowing with people seeking repatriation.

On 8 July Victor Lundula, mayor of a commune in Jadotville and earlier a medical assistant in the Force publique, was made the new commander of the Force, and Joseph Mobutu, who had served in it as a clerk, became Chief of Staff. It was announced that the officer ranks were to be wholly Africanized and that the soldiers were to elect their officers (some Belgians staying on as military advisers). Lumumba and others formed delegations which travelled round the country to oversee the implementation of these measures. The tension appeared to have relaxed. However, at the port of Matadi the Congolese soldiers were convinced of rumors that their Belgian officers intended to disarm them as a preliminary to the landing of Belgian metropolitan troops who were to attack the nearby Thysville garrison. The European officers were locked up, European civilians were attacked, and several European women were raped.

In Katanga province there was panic. Tshombe, president of the Katanga provincial government, was still in Leopoldville for the independence celebrations. The senior men were unable to control the non-Katangese soldiers stationed in Katanga, who were violently hostile to the possibility of secession. The situation deteriorated throughout the Congo.

The Belgian government was under considerable pressure from its own public opinion. Two ministers were sent to the Congo to tell Lumumba that he should request intervention by Belgium; but it was made clear that Belgian troops would intervene even if that request were not forthcoming. Only Tshombe supported the idea of Belgian intervention.

On Sunday, 10 July, three hundred Belgian troops landed in Elisabethville airport in Katanga and occupied it and the military camp. Lumumba reacted with anger to what he saw as a clear violation of the Treaty of Friendship between the Congo and Belgium. Belgian troops now landed at Matadi and fighting began. The news spread to Thysville; the earlier violence there had subsided but on receipt of this news brutal fighting, looting and raping broke out. In northern Equateur events followed a similar pattern.

On 11 July, against this background, Tshombe declared Katanga independent. When they learned of this, Prime Minister Lumumba and President Kasavubu took off for Katanga. Tshombe refused permission for their plane to land at Elisabethville airport—an act assumed by Lumumba and Kasavubu to have Belgian backing, as Belgian troops held the airport.[18] Tshombe now placed Belgians in important public posts and sought recognition from the Belgian government of Katanga's statehood.

The Congo government, judging that the Belgians were set to occupy the country, now gave priority to seeking external assistance against Belgium rather than to controlling the mutiny.

On the afternoon of 10 July Ralph Bunche attended a meeting of the Congolese cabinet. He transmitted to Hammarskjold a request made for technical assistance. Bunche had explained to the Congolese authorities that the United Nations might be able to provide technical assistance of a military nature but that there were limitations on any military assistance, as such, that it could give to the Congo. This advice was later to be echoed in the words used in paragraph two of the resolution which established the UN operation in the Congo. Hammarskjold, who was in Geneva, in the meantime scheduled a private meeting of the representatives of the African states at the UN for Tuesday 12 July. At that meeting he asked them about assistance they might provide for a UN operation in the Congo. He then asked the members of the Security Council to meet him, informally over lunch on the 13th, to hear a report from him on the situation in the Congo.

Strangely, on 12 July the United States received a request for assistance from the Congo. Assistant Secretary of State Francis Wilcox notified Hammarskjold; and Secretary of State Herter made it clear that the US would not send troops without UN endorsement.

On the morning of 13 July Belgian paratroops expelled Congolese troops from Leopoldville airport and occupied the European parts of that town. Lumumba now told Bunche that he had asked Ghana for military assistance pending the arrival of UN Force. Joined by Kasavubu, he sent a cable to the UN which made it clear that he wanted military help rather than technical assistance of a military nature.

CONSTITUTIONAL BASIS

ONUC was established by the Security Council on a somewhat unclear basis, Resolution S/4387 of 14 July 1960 spoke of the 'request for military assistance' which had been made by the president and prime minister of the Congo and authorized the secretary-general to provide military assistance until the national security forces could meet their tasks. The precise Charter basis was not specified, but there are very good grounds for suggesting that ONUC was established on the basis of Article 40 in Chapter VII of the Charter, notwithstanding the fact that there was no formal determination under Article 39 of a 'threat to the peace, breach of the peace, or act of aggression.' It is not uncommon for the Security Council, in proposing provisional measures under Article 40, to fail to make any specific reference to Article 39.

In resolution S/4405 of 232 July the Security Council, '*Considering* that the complete restoration of law and order in the Republic of the Congo would effectively contribute to the maintenance of international peace and security' called on the Belgian government to implement S/4387 on the withdrawal of its troops, and authorized the secretary-general 'to take all necessary action to this effect.' It also asked States to refrain from any action which might hinder the restoration of law and order or undermine the territorial integrity and political independence of the Congo.

On 9 August, in resolution S/4426, the Council called on Belgium to withdraw its troops immediately from Katanga under modalities to be determined by the secretary-general. And this time, significantly, it specifically referred, in operative paragraph 5, to Charter Articles 25 and 49 as the basis for calling upon members to 'accept and carry out the decisions of the Security Council and to afford mutual assistance in carrying out measures decided upon by the Council.'

We may recall that the secretary-general initially convened the Security Council on the basis of Article 99 of the Charter—an indication that he regarded, from the outset, the situation as likely to threaten international peace and security. In a statement to the Council on 8 August—just before the adoption of S/4426—the secretary-general said:

> The resolutions of the Security Council of 14 July [S/4405] were not explicitly adopted under Chapter VII, but they were passed on the basis of an initiative under Article 99. For that reason I have felt entitled to quote three articles under Chapter VII, and I repeat what I have already said in this respect: in a perspective which may well be short rather than long, the problem facing Congo is one of peace or war—and not only in the Congo.[19]

Resolution S/4426, with its explicit mention of Charter Articles 25 and 49, may thus be seen as a vindication of the secretary-general's views as to the legal basis of ONUC. That its legal basis may lay in its existence as a subsidiary of the Security Council operating under Chapter VII of the Charter, in spite of the absence of an express finding under Article 39, is a view shared by most commentators.[20] Article 29 provides the basis for the establishment of a subsidiary organ by the Security Council.

Whereas resolution S/4426 confirmed that the Security Council's directives concerning the Congo were binding on member States, it did not specify which article within Chapter VII provided the constitutional basis for action. But, again, most commentators have taken the view—here endorsed—that the language and context of the resolutions of 14 and 22 July and 9 August point to Article 40 of the Charter. Article 40 provides:

> In order to prevent an aggravation of the situation, the Security Council may, before making the recommendations or deciding upon the measures provided for in Article 39, call upon the parties concerned to comply with such provisional measures as it deems necessary or desirable.'

All three resolutions used the terminology 'calls upon.' And the demand for the withdrawal of Belgian troops was seen by most Security Council members as the preventive measure necessary to avoid major international hostilities rather than as enforcement. Significantly, too, the Secretary-General in his third report to the Security Council on 30 August spoke of the UN's temporary authority over Kamina base after the withdrawal of the Belgians as 'a provisional measure in the sense of Article 40 of the Charter, necessary for the mandate given to the Secretary General for the achievement of the withdrawal of Belgian troops "under speedy modalities determined by the Secretary-General.[21]

In so far as ONUC was based on Article 40 (implicitly), with Articles 25 and 49 operational, certain results followed. Members of the UN were bound by these resolutions: and that included not only Belgium and the major powers, but also the Congo itself. Thus there was a delicate balance between, on the one hand, the notion that ONUC was in the Congo with the government's consent, and, on the other, that that government was bound by the Security Council decisions. Moreover, Article 2(7) was still applicable to the situation. Whereas the principle of non-intervention in internal affairs, enshrined in that article, does not apply in the case of enforcement measures under Chapter VII, it continues to be relevant to the application of provisional measures under that same Chapter. The secretary-general put it thus:

> in the light of the domestic jurisdiction limitation of the Charter, it must be assumed that the Council would not authorize the Secretary-General to intervene with armed troops in an internal conflict, when the Council had not specifically adopted enforcement measures under Articles 41 and 42 of Chapter VII of the Charter.[22]

It may also be added that the fact that the early Security Council resolutions were deemed (by the secretary-general, and explicitly by resolution S/4426 of August 1960) to be binding under Article 25 of the Charter in no way implies that their basis had therefore to lie in Articles 41 or 42 (enforcement measures) rather than Article 40. The Security Council is perfectly entitled to deem a call under Article 40 as obligatory.

It seems that Article 25 was seen as being specifically applicable to Belgium and Article 49 as having a wider application, creating an obligation on members to give mutual assistance if so requested through contributions of personnel, transport, and supplies for ONUC sent in to facilitate the withdrawal of Belgian troops.

By the end of 1960 the question was being raised within the UN and without: did the actions of ONUC constitute enforcement measures? On 13 December the secretary-general turned to some of the extravagant claims that were being made about what ONUC could and should do to end the secession of Katanga. He said:

> it is significant that the Council did not invoke Articles 41 and 42 of Chapter VII, which provide for enforcement measures and which would override the domestic jurisdiction limitation of Article 2(7). I mention this as one of the reasons why some far-reaching interpretations of the mandate of the Force, to which we have listened here, are, quite frankly, difficult to understand. Those interpretations would require at least that the Security Council had clearly taken enforcement measures under Articles 41 and 42.[23]

The question was given new impetus by the passing of resolution S/4741 on 21 February 1961, in the wake of the death of Lumumba.

Resolution S/4741 contained two clauses that were to cause suggestions that the basis of UN action in the Congo had now shifted to Article 42. Part A, operative paragraph 1 urged the UN to take appropriate measures

> to prevent the occurrence of civil war in the Congo, including arrangements for cease-fires, the halting of all military operations, the prevention of clashes, and the use of force, if necessary, in the last resort.

Operative paragraph 2 urged measures for

> the immediate withdrawal and evacuation from the Congo of all Belgian and other foreign military and paramilitary personnel and political advisers not under the United Nations Command, and mercenaries.

Thus for the first time ONUC's mandate went beyond the use of force for self-defense, and allowed the use of force—as a last resort—to prevent the occurrence of civil war. It was also the first time that there had been use of the terminology of Article 39 without reference to Article 39 itself: 'the Security Council declared itself deeply concerned at the threat to international peace and security.' Did this make ONUC's basis Article 42—'such any action by air, sea, or land forces as may be necessary to maintain or restore international peace and security?' Some jurists have so argued but there is no evidence that ONUC had embarked upon enforcement action.

Security Council resolution S/5002 of 24 November 1961 extended somewhat further the mandate of ONUC to use force. Whereas S/4741 envisaged force as a last resort to prevent civil war, S/5002 authorized use of requisite measure of force, if necessary, for the immediate apprehension, detention pending legal action and/or deportation of all foreign military and paramilitary personnel and political advisers not under the United Nations Command, and mercenaries. But even though the circumstances in which ONUC was permitted to use force were enlarged, the action was still not a sanction against the Congo. Most important, if the basis of UN action had become Article 42, then the restraint of Article 2(7) would no longer operate. There is ample evidence that the UN still regarded itself as bound by the domestic jurisdiction requirements: it could not convene parliament, it could not impose a constitution, it could not forcibly end the secession of Katanga. Moreover, while it is true that it has been very rare for specific findings under Article 39 to precede action under Chapter VII, this does not warrant the assumption that 'the grave sanctions of Article 42 could be brought into play so casually, and via the 'backdoor' –though the less rigorous terms of Article

40 may well be invoked in this manner.'[24] Finally, the International Court of Justice, when examining in the *Expenses* Case the resolutions relating to the Congo, expressly stated that ONUC was not engaged in enforcement action: 'the operation did not involve preventive or enforcement measures against any State under Chapter VII.'[25]

The initial resolutions on the Congo were taken by the Security Council but in September 1960 an emergency special session of the General Assembly was convened on this subject, and both that and the regular session of the Assembly passed resolutions. Such resolutions were binding only to the extent that they incorporated general principles of International Law. Article 25 could not apply to them, even though both resolution 1474 of 20 September 1960 and 1599 (XV) of 15 April 1961 used mandatory-sounding phrases such as 'calls upon' and 'decides.' It was also the General Assembly which passed the resolutions relating to the financing of ONUC. And these were binding on the membership.

The refusal of the Soviet Union, France, and others to pay their assessed dues rested on the position that all matters relating to military operations, including their financing, lay exclusively with the Security Council:

> we consider that the General Assembly has no right to decide the question of the operations in the Congo and their financing, that it has no right to take any decision on this question, since it is one that lies within the exclusive competence of the Security Council.

Indeed, during the drafting of the Charter, when the decision was taken on the division of functions between the General Assembly and the Security Council, it was prescribed, distinctly and clearly, that all questions involving action should come within the exclusive competence of the Security Council. Indeed, Article 11 of the Charter states the following:

2. The General Assembly may discuss any questions relating to the maintenance of international peace and security . . . and . . . may make recommendations with regard to any such questions—"recommendations," mark you, not decisions—to the State or States concerned or to the Security Council. . . . Any such question on which action is necessary shall be referred to the Security Council by the General Assembly either before or after discussion.'

21. In the present case it is in fact actions with which we are concerned. The resolutions under consideration relate to the question of United Nations operations in the Congo, military operations. These are actions, these are not recommendations, and it is precisely the Security Council which should decide questions relating to actions. The Charter provides

that it is the Security Council which is to determine the extent of operations, their scale, their duration and the facilities to be provided for them. If we examine Article 43 of the Charter, we shall find that it clearly authorizes the Security Council to conclude agreements with Members of the United Nations for the provision of facilities for military operations. It states that the Security Council is to conclude agreements with Members of the United Nations on this subject and that:

2. Such agreement or agreements shall govern the numbers and types of forces, their degree of readiness and general location, and the nature of the facilities and assistance to be provided (including the right of passage). Such agreements are to be concluded, the Charter states, between the Security Council and Members of the United Nations. Thus questions relating to operations, to actions, and, *a fortiori*, to military actions, are of course within the exclusive competence of the Security Council.

22. Are these questions being decided correctly in the United Nations at the present time? No, not at all. They are being decided without the knowledge or approval of the Security Council, in circumvention of the Security Council and, thus, in violation of the Charter. Article 48 provides specifically that the Security Council is to determine which countries are to participate in any action. Article 48 reads:

1. The action required to carry out the decisions of the Security Council for the maintenance of international peace and security shall be taken by all Members of the United Nations or by some of them, as the Security Council may determine.'

23. Is the Security Council determining the questions now being decided in the Congo? Is the Security Council determining what armed forces or whose armed forces are to be sent there? Is this matter being decided by the Security Council? No, it is not. Is this the right way to deal with the question? It is completely incorrect and contrary to the Charter.[26]

The Soviet representative later elaborated on what he saw as the relevance of Article 43, given that the agreements envisaged under that Article had in fact never been concluded. Article 43 provides, inter alia, that the envisaged agreements should cover the assistance to be provided. According to the Soviet argument, this meant the financing of an operation. The proper course to follow was therefore clear: referring to the first part of Article 43, the Soviet representative noted:

> Negotiations for the conclusion of such agreements are to be concluded between the Security Council and the Members of the United Nations. That, as I said, is quite clear and precise. But instead of going with this question to the Security Council and saying: this is how the matter stands, it is necessary to decide how

to finance these operations, since financing is part of the material assistance, they turned to the Advisory Committee with a view to that Committee taking a decision on the appropriation of $40 million.[27]

Most Western and many non-aligned countries, did not accept this reading of Articles 11, 43 and 48. They took the view that the Security Council had a primary, but not exclusive, responsibility for the maintenance of peace; that although generally the Assembly could indeed only make recommendations, in matters relating to finance it had the power to bind; that peacekeeping, though not in terms envisaged in the Charter, was clearly within the UN's major purpose of maintaining international peace and security, and could thus be properly financed by the Assembly, under the terms of Article 17(2); and that peacekeeping by consent was legal, whether authorized by the Security Council or by the General Assembly.

The Soviet Union left no doubt that it thought that the Secretary-General should have sought authorization from the Security Council as to which nations were to provide contingents; and should then have negotiated agreements with them and submitted such agreements to the Council. Comparable authorization for the financing of ONUC should also have been sought from the Security Council. Replying to this, the secretary-general said:

> With regard to the legal basis of the United Nations operations in the Congo, it had to be borne in mind that those operations did not constitute sanctions or enforcement action as contemplated by Articles 42 and 43 of the Charter; they were essentially internal security measures taken by the Security Council at the invitation of the government concerned to counteract the threat to international peace. No one had ever suggested that agreements should be concluded between the Security Council and Member States as contemplated in Article 43 and no member of the Council or of the General Assembly had ever implied that the Security Council had acted on the basis of Article 43. On the contrary, several representatives—and he mentioned those of Ceylon, France and the United States—had made it clear that the Council's resolution had not been adopted under Article 42. He himself had stated on several occasions, without any objection being raised, that those resolutions could be considered as having been implicitly adopted under Article 40, but certainly not under Articles 41 or 42. Consequently, the mere fact that military contingents had been used to maintain law and order and to prevent civil war in the Congo did not mean that it had been intended to apply either the letter or the spirit of Article 43. It was therefore clear that ONUC expenditure was not fully within the meaning of Article 17, paragraph 2.[28]

It was this view which prevailed before the International Court of Justice, when it had to deal with the issues in the context of Article 17(2). However, the Court's Opinion did not resolve the financial crisis.

THE ESTABLISHMENT OF THE STATE OF ISRAEL

Britain held a mandate over Palestine of the 'A' class—that is to say, a mandate which applied to certain communities belonging to the Turkish Empire' which had 'reached a stage of development where their existence as independent nations' could 'be provisionally recognized.'

At the time the mandate was granted the majority of the population was composed of Palestinian Arabs. Nonetheless, the mandate also contained provision for the establishment in Palestine of a national home for the Jews; and the Balfour Declaration also pledged a national home for the Jewish people. The differing interpretations which could stem from these various commitments need no emphasis here. However, the Palestine White Paper of May 1939 had severely limited Jewish immigration to Palestine, at a time when hundreds of thousands of Jews were seeking an escape from Nazi Europe. At the end of World War II the appalling plight of Jewish survivors of the concentration camps was yet another humanitarian reason for pressure for immediate large-scale immigration into Palestine. An active Zionist Movement urged the establishment of a Jewish State in Palestine, and immediately upon the end of the war the Zionists presented the outgoing British government with a series of radical demands.[29] The underground military organization, the Hagenah, became very active in Palestine in smuggling in illegal immigrants and forcibly releasing illegal immigrants who were held by the British. Organized terrorist activities among other Jewish groups now became widespread, and as time went by Hagenah became less and less concerned to dissociate itself from these acts. Violence in Palestine, and intense diplomatic activity abroad, marked the background to an Anglo-American Committee of Enquiry, established at the invitation of the British Labor government's foreign secretary, Ernest Bevin. Although two members of the Committee favored the partition of Palestine, they joined the majority of the Committee which 'having regard to the economic interdependence of the two politically rival communities (and also, no doubt, to the Soviet pressure on the northern edge of the Middle East') clung to the hope, against all the experience of the previous ten years, that somehow the two communities might be induced to live together in peace. The Committed made many detailed proposals, including the rejection of the idea of either a Jewish or an Arab State in favor of a trusteeship, and the recommendation of the immediate issue of one hundred thousand immigration certificates for Jewish refugees.[30] President Truman indicated that he accepted these parts of the report that favored the Zionists, but said of the pro-Arab parts that they required careful study which he would take 'under advisement.' Bevin was widely regarded as unsympathetic to the Jewish cause, and refused to discuss the matter with Richard Crossman, the Labor MP who had been on the Anglo-American Committee. He obtained the support of Attlee for the view that the proposed one hundred thousand immigration certificates should be issued only when the illegal Jewish military organizations in Palestine had been disbanded and their arms handed in. Violence continued, however, and it soon became evident that Britain was not to have the support of the United States in implementing the report of the Committee. And Bevin now indicated that to allow one hundred thousand Jews into Palestine would necessitate the sending of another division of British troops there, which Britain could not afford financially.

British troops already in Palestine became increasingly engaged in fighting with members of various Jewish military organizations, and a period of violence and counter-violence culminated in the blowing up of the King David Hotel in Jerusalem, certain parts of which were the British Palestine government's headquarters. The explosion caused the death of ninety-one persons and wounded forty-five others. Vigorous punitive counter-measures were taken by the British.

The British government soon after announced a new plan—the Provincial Autonomy Plan—but once again could obtain little American support. The plan was also rejected by the Jewish Agency Executive. However, the appointment of a new Colonial Secretary—Creech Jones—allowed a breathing space, for he introduced a series of measures designed to lower the temperature between the Jews and the British and to indicate a measure of goodwill, in spite of the continuing violence.

In January 1947 the Arab States had begun talks with the British government, and separate talks began between the British and the Jewish Agency. A compromise offer was made by Bevin, but was rejected by both sides. The immigration restrictions remained unrelaxed, and terrorism in Palestine continued unabated.

The British government now decided to place the issue before the United Nations. On 2 April 1947 the United Kingdom asked the Acting Secretary-General to place the question of Palestine on the agenda of the next regular session of the General Assembly. It further requested that a special session of the General Assembly be convened as soon as possible, for the purpose of setting up a special committee which would prepare for the consideration of the question at the next regular Assembly session. The letter also indicated that the United Kingdom government would submit an account of its administration of the Palestine mandate to the General Assembly, and would ask the Assembly to make recommendations under Article 10 of the

Charter, for the future government of Palestine. It was at this juncture that Sir Alexander Cadogan made his celebrated statement that Britain 'should not have the sole responsibility for enforcing a solution which is not accepted by both parties and which we cannot reconcile with our conscience.'

Accordingly, the First Committee of the General Assembly devoted some twelve meetings to the question of constituting and instructing a Special Committee on Palestine (UNSCOP). It was readily agreed that the Special Committee should be given broad competence to investigate and report on the facts; discussion on composition took rather longer, and revolved mainly around the inclusion or non-inclusion of the five permanent members of the Security Council. Eventually agreement was reached—in the face of Russian opposition—on an Australian proposal whereby UNSCOP would consist of eleven members, not including the five permanent members of the Security Council. The General Assembly approved the recommendations of its First Committee, and when the first special session of the Assembly came to be held the following resolution was carried by 47 to 7 with 1 abstention:

Whereas the General Assembly of the United Nations has been called into special session for the purpose of constituting and instructing a special committee to prepare for consideration at the next regular session of the Assembly, a report on the question of Palestine,

The General Assembly

Resolves that:

1. A Special Committee be created for the above-mentioned purpose consisting of the representatives of Australia, Canada, Czechoslovakia, Guatemala, India, Iran, Netherlands, Peru, Sweden, Uruguay and Yugoslavia;
2. The Special Committed shall have the widest powers to ascertain and record facts, and to investigate all questions and issues relevant to the problem of Palestine;
3. The Special Committee shall determine its own procedure;
4. The Special Committee shall conduct investigations in Palestine and wherever it may deem useful, receive and examine written or oral testimony, whichever it may consider appropriate in each case, from the mandatory Power, from representatives of the population of Palestine, from Governments and from such organizations and individuals as it may deem necessary;
5. The Special Committee shall give most careful consideration to the religious interests in Palestine of Islam, Judaism and Christianity;

6. The Special Committee shall prepare a report to the General Assembly and shall submit such proposals as it may consider appropriate for the solution of the problem of Palestine;
7. The Special Committee's report shall be communicated to the Secretary-General not later than 1 September 1947, in order that it may be circulated to the Members of the United Nations in time for consideration by the second regular session of the General Assembly;

The General Assembly

8. *Requests* the Secretary-General to enter into suitable arrangements with the proper authorities of any State in whose territory the Special Committee may wish to sit or to travel, to provide necessary facilities, and to assign appropriate staff to the Special Committee;
9. Authorizes the Secretary-General to reimburse travel and subsistence expenses of a representative and an alternate representative from each Government represented on the Special Committee on such basis and in such form as he may determine most appropriate in the circumstances.

The Communist countries, including those represented on UNSCOP, were in favor of the immediate termination of the British mandate and the proclamation of the independence of Palestine. Gromyko appeared to part company from the Arab States, however, in letting it be known that a partition of Palestine between Zionists and Arabs would be acceptable if a single independent State could not be attained. The Guatemalan member of UNSCOP, on the other hand, was a known supporter of Zionism, and the Uruguayan representative was also sympathetic to the Jewish case. By the time UNSCOP arrived in Palestine, the Arab community had decided to boycott it. During the period of the Committee's inquiry the Zionists succeeded in a variety of ways in demonstrating their independence of action and in bringing the British government in difficult position.

UNSCOP considerably divided within itself, retired in August 1947 to Geneva to draw up the recommendations which it was due to present to the General Assembly by 1 September. Although there was general agreement that the mandate had proved unworkable, only the Yugoslav, Iranian, and Indian representatives recommended a bi-national federal State. The other eight members of UNSCOP drew up a plan of partition with economic union. Basically, the country was to be divided longitudinally, with Jerusalem and Bethlehem forming an internationalized enclave. The detailed proposals were submitted to the General Assembly, which referred it to an *ad hoc* committee for consideration. The ad hoc committee approved, with certain minor alterations, the proposals of UNSCOP, and its own recommendations were accepted by the Assembly, when on 29 November 1947 it adopted Resolution A 181

(II) on the Future Government of Palestine. The plan of partition contained in this resolution provided *inter alia* that the British mandate over Palestine should be terminated and British armed forces should leave the country by 1 August 1948; that the Arab State, the Jewish State, and the International Regime for Jerusalem were to come into being two months after the departure of the British armed forces; and that a UN Palestine Commission was to be established in order to implement the resolution. The resolution also called upon the Security Council to assist in the implementation of the plan, to determine whether the situation in Palestine constituted a threat to peace, and to take the necessary measures to preserve the peace. The provisions for the setting up of Palestine Commission were as follows:

B. STEPS PREPARATORY TO INDEPENDENCE

1. A Commission shall be set up consisting of one representative of each of five Member States. The Members represented on the Commission shall be elected by the General Assembly on as broad a basis, geographically and otherwise, as possible.
2. The administration of Palestine shall, as the mandatory Power withdraws its armed forces, be progressively turned over to the Commission, which shall act in conformity with the recommendations of the General Assembly, under the guidance of the Security Council. The mandatory Power shall have to the fullest possible extent co-ordinate its plans for withdrawal with the plans of the Commission to take over and administer areas which have been evacuated.

   In the discharge of this administrative responsibility the Commission shall have the authority to issue necessary regulations and take other measures as required.

   The mandatory Power shall not take any action to prevent, obstruct or delay the implementation by the Commission of the measures recommended by the General Assembly.
3. On its arrival in Palestine the Commission shall proceed to carry out measures for the establishment of the frontiers of the Arab and Jewish States and the City of Jerusalem in accordance with the general lines of the recommendations of the General Assembly on the partition of Palestine. Nevertheless, the boundaries as described in part II of this plan are to be modified in such a way that village areas as a rule will not be divided by state boundaries unless pressing reasons make that necessary.
4. The Commission, after consultation with the democratic parties and other public organizations of the Arab and Jewish States, shall select and establish in each State as rapidly as possible a Provisional Council of Government. The activities of both the Arab and Jewish Provisional

Councils of Government shall be carried out under the general direction of the Commission.

If by 1 April 1948 a Provisional Council of Government cannot be selected for either of the States or, if selected, cannot carry out its functions, the Commission shall communicate that fact to the Security Council for such action with respect to that State as the Security Council may deem proper, and to the Secretary-General for communication to the Member of the United Nations.

5. Subject to the provisions of these recommendations, during the transitional period the Provisional Councils of Government, acting under the Commission, shall have the full authority in the areas under their control, including authority over matters of immigration and land regulation.
6. The Provisional Council of Government of each State, acting under the Commission, shall progressively receive from the Commission full responsibility for the administration of that State in the period between the termination of the Mandate and the establishment of the State's independence.
7. The Commission shall instruct the Provisional Councils of Government of both the Arab and Jewish States, after their formation, to proceed to the establishment of administrative organs of government, central and local.
8. The Provisional Council of Government of each State shall, within the shortest time possible, recruit an armed militia from the residents of that State, sufficient in number to maintain internal order and to prevent frontier clashes.

   This armed militia in each State shall, for operational purposes, be under the command of Jewish or Arab officers resident in that State, but general political and military control, including the choice of the militia's High Command, shall be exercised by the Commission.
9. The Provisional Council of Government of each State shall, not later than two months after the withdrawal of the armed forces of the mandatory Power, hold elections to the Constituent Assembly which shall be conducted on democratic lines.
10. The election regulations in each State shall be drawn up by the Provisional Council of Government and approved by the Commission . . .
11. The Commission shall appoint a preparatory economic commission of three members to make whatever arrangements are possible for economic co-operation, with a view to establishing as soon as practicable, the Economic Union and the Joint Economic Board, as provided in section D below.
12. During the period between the adoption of the recommendations on the question of Palestine by the General Assembly and then termination of the Mandate, the mandatory Power in Palestine shall maintain full responsibility in areas from which it has not withdrawn its armed forces. The Commission shall assist the mandatory Power in the carrying out of

these functions. Similarly the mandatory Power shall co-operate with the Commission in the execution of its functions.

13. With a view to ensuring that there shall be continuity in the functioning of administrative services and that, on the withdrawal of the armed forces of the mandatory Power, the whole administration shall be in the charge of the Provisional Councils of the Joint Economic Board, respectively, acting under the Commission, there shall be a progressive transfer, from the mandatory Power to the Commission, of responsibility for all the functions of government, including that of maintaining law and order in the areas from which the forces of the mandatory Power have been withdrawn.
14. The Commission shall be guided in its activities by the recommendations of the General Assembly and by such instructions as the Security Council may consider necessary to issue.

    The measures taken by the Commission, within the recommendations of the General Assembly, shall become immediately effective unless the Commission has previously received contrary instructions from the Security Council.

    The Commission shall render periodic monthly progress reports, or more frequently if desirable, to the Security Council.
15. The Commission shall make its final report to the next regular session of the General Assembly and to the Security Council simultaneously.[31]

The passing of this resolution by no means represented a common front by the UN. The Muslim countries had continued to press for a unitary state, and there were deep divisions between the United Kingdom and the United States. (Both the United States and the Soviet Union supported the partition proposals, though each had reservations about the precise drawing of the frontiers.) The British government, now firmly committed to a rapid withdrawal from its responsibilities, announced once more that British troops and administration could not be used to uphold any decision on Palestine that was not acceptable to both parties. The United States let it be known that she thought the British attitude un-cooperative. For their part, the Arabs made it clear that their attitude was still one of uncompromising opposition to the Assembly's proposals; while the Jewish Agency declared its willingness to work within the framework of the proposals.

Sporadic fighting had been going on in Palestine during the four months that had passed since the UNSCOP left; the UN resolution now occasioned further outbreaks of violence. Both the Arab and the Jewish communities suffered serious loss of life. In the meantime the UN Palestine Commission was set up, composed of Bolivia, Czechoslovakia, Denmark, Panama and the Philippines. In January 1948, the Palestine Commission invited the United Kingdom, the Jewish Agency, and the Arab Higher Committee to designate representatives to assist it. The first two appointed representatives, but the Arab Higher Committee refused in the strongest terms. Troops from neighboring Arab states began to enter Palestine and open fighting developed. On 16 February 1948 the Commission made a special report (S/676) to the Security Council stating that the conditions prevailing in Palestine made it impossible for it to implement the Assembly's Resolution 181 (II) without the assistance of adequate armed forces. Shortly after this, the Secretariat of the UN, at the request of the Commission, produced a paper on the powers of the Palestine Commission and the Security Council; this paper included a discussion of the conditions under which the Commission or the Security Council could employ an international armed force.

Finally, on April 10, the Palestine Commission submitted a report to the General Assembly in which it stated:

> The Commission therefore has the duty to report to the General Assembly that the armed hostility of both Palestinian and non-Palestinian Arab elements, the lack of co-operation from the mandatory Power, the disintegrating security situation inn Palestine, and the fact that the Security Council did not furnish the Commission with the necessary armed assistance, are the factors which have made it impossible for the Commission to implement the Assembly's Resolution.[32]

The United Kingdom had informed the Commission that she had decided to terminate the mandatory administration of Palestine on 15 May 1948 and that there would be no transfer of any authority to the Commission before that date. The Commission was, therefore, never permitted by the United Kingdom government to enter Palestine.

Meanwhile, on 24 February 1948, the Security Council had begun discussions on Palestine (it will be noted that an interval of three months had elapsed since the Assembly had asked, in Resolution 181 (II), the Council to address itself to the peace and security aspects of the problem). On 1 April 1948 the Security Council called for a truce to the fighting and also for the convening of another special session of the Assembly on Palestine:

The Security Council

In the exercise of its primary responsibility for the maintenance of international peace and security,

Notes the increasing violence and disorder in Palestine and believes it is of the utmost urgency that an immediate truce be affected in Palestine,

Calls upon the Jewish Agency for Palestine and the Arab Higher Committee to make representatives available to the Security Council for the purpose of arranging a truce between the Arab and the Jewish communities of Palestine;

and emphasizes the heavy responsibility which would fall upon any party failing to observe such a truce;

Calls upon the Arab and Jewish armed groups in Palestine to cease acts of violence immediately.

> *The Security Council,*
>
> *Having received,* on 9 December 1947, the resolution of the General Assembly concerning Palestine dated 29 November 1947:
>
> *Having taken note* of the United Nations Palestine Commission's first and second Monthly Progress Reports and the First Special Report on the problems of security,
>
> *Having called,* on 5 March 1948, on the permanent members of the Council to consult;
>
> *Having taken note* of the reports made concerning these consultations;
>
> *Requests* the Secretary-General in accordance with Article 20 of the United Nations Charter, to invoke a special session of the General Assembly to consider further the question of the future Government of Palestine.[33]

Another resolution was adopted just over two weeks later, in mandatory language, calling for specific measures to be taken toward the implementation of a truce.

Considering the Council's resolution of 1 April 1948 and the conversations held by its President with the representatives of the Jewish Agency for Palestine and the Arab Higher Committee with a view to arranging a truce between Arabs and Jews in Palestine;

Considering that, as stated in that resolution, it is of the utmost urgency to bring about the immediate cessation of acts of violence in Palestine, and to establish conditions of peace and order in that country;

Considering that the United Kingdom Government, so long as it remains the Mandatory Power, is responsible for the maintenance of peace and order in Palestine and should continue to take all steps necessary to that end; and that, in so doing, it should receive the co-operation and support of the Security Council inn particular as well as of all the Members of the United Nations;

> *The Security Council:*
>
> 1. Calls upon all persons and organizations in Palestine and especially upon the Arab Higher Committee and the Jewish Agency to take immediately, without prejudice to their rights, claims, or positions, and as a contribution to the well-being and permanent interest of Palestine, the following measures:
>   a. Cease all activities of a military or para-military nature, as well as acts of violence, terrorism and sabotage;

b. Refrain from bringing and from assisting and encouraging the entry into Palestine of armed bands and fighting personnel, groups and individuals, whatever their origin;
c. Refrain from importing or acquiring or assisting or encouraging the importation or acquisition of weapons and war materials;
d. Refrain, pending further consideration of the future government of Palestine by the General Assembly, from any political activity which might prejudice the rights, claims, or positions of either community;
e. Co-operate with the Mandatory authorities for the effective maintenance of law and order and of essential services, particularly those relating to transportation, communications, health, and food and water supplies;
f. Refrain from any action which will endanger the safety of the Holy Places in Palestine and from any action which would interfere with access to all shrines and sanctuaries for the purpose of the worship by those who have an established right to visit and worship at them;

2. *Requests* the United Kingdom Government, for so long as it remains the Mandatory Power, to use its best efforts to bring all those concerned in Palestine to accept the measures set forth under paragraph 1 above and, subject to retaining the freedom of action of its own forces, to supervise the execution of these measures by all those concerned, and to keep the Security Council and the General Assembly currently informed on the situation in Palestine.
3. *Calls upon* all Governments and particularly those of the countries neighbouring Palestine to take all possible steps to assist in the implementation of the measures set out under paragraph 1 above, and particularly those referring to the entry into Palestine of armed bands and fighting personnel, groups and individuals and weapons and war materials.[34]

A few days later a further resolution was passed by the Security Council establishing a Truce Commission, and it is from the concept of truce observance in this resolution that UNTSO eventually sprang.

The Security Council

Referring to its resolution of 17 April 1948 calling upon all parties concerned to comply with specific terms for a truce in Palestine,

Establishes a truce commission for Palestine composed of representatives of those members of the Security Council which have career consular officers in Jerusalem, noting, however, that the representative of Syria has indicated that his Government is not prepared to serve on the Commission. The function of the Commission shall be to assist the Security Council in supervising the implementation by the parties of the resolution of the Security Council of 17 April 1948;

Requests the Commission to report to the President of the Security Council within four days regarding its activities and the development of the situation, and subsequently to keep the Security Council currently informed with respect thereto.

The Commission, its members, their assistants and its personnel shall be entitled to travel, separately or together, wherever the Commission deems necessary to carry out its tasks.

The Secretary-General of the United Nations shall furnish the Commission with such personnel and assistance as it may require, considering the special urgency of the situation with respect to Palestine.[35]

The Members of the Security Council who had career consular offices in Jerusalem were Belgium, France, and the United States. Accordingly, these countries were invited to form the Truce Commission. The urgency of the matter at this stage was acute—not least because of the United Kingdom's insistence that she would lay down her mandate on 15 May, and would not thereafter be responsible for law and order.

The General Assembly, now meeting in its second special session, took parallel action: there being no prospect of implementing the plan form partition, it terminated the existence of the UN Palestine Commission, and decided to appoint a Mediator in Palestine:

The General Assembly,

Taking account of the present situation in regard to Palestine

Strongly affirms its support of the efforts of the Security Council to secure a truce in Palestine and calls upon all Governments, organizations and persons to co-operate in making effective such a truce;

1. *Empowers* a United Nations Mediator in Palestine, to be chosen by a committee of the General Assembly composed of representatives of China, France, the Union of Soviet Socialist Republics, the United Kingdom and the United States of America to exercise, the following functions:
   a. To use his good offices with the local and community authorities in Palestine to:
      i. Arrange for the operation of common services necessary to the safety and well-being of the population of Palestine;
      ii. Assure the protection of the Holy Places, religious buildings and sites in Palestine;
      iii. Promote a peaceful adjustment of the future situation in Palestine;
   b. To co-operate with the Truce Commission for Palestine appointed by the Security Council in its resolution of 23 April 1948;
   c. To invite, as seems to him advisable, with a view to the promotion of the welfare of the inhabitants of Palestine, the assistance and co-operation of appropriate specialized agencies of the United Nations, such as the World Health Organization, of the International

Red Cross, and of other governmental and non-governmental organizations of a humanitarian and non-political character;

2. *Instructs* the United Nations Mediator to render progress reports monthly, or more frequently as he deems necessary, to the Security Council and to the Secretary-General for transmission to the Members of the United Nations;
3. *Directs* the United Nations Mediator to conform in his activities with the provisions of this resolution, and with such instructions as the General Assembly or the Security Council may issue;
4. *Authorizes* the Secretary-General to pay the United Nations Mediator an emolument equal to that paid to the President of the International Court of Justice, and to provide the Mediator with the necessary staff to assist in carrying out the functions assigned to the Mediator by the General Assembly;

Relieves the Palestine Commission from the further exercise of responsibilities under resolution 181 (II) of 29 November 1947.[36]

The ground was thus laid for co-operation between the Mediator and the Truce Commission. Count Bernadotte was appointed Mediator.

On 15 May 1948 the United Kingdom mandate for Palestine came to an end, and the state of Israel was at once proclaimed within the boundaries recommended by the General Assembly partition plan. The armed forces of Egypt, Iraq, Transjordan, Syria, and Lebanon crossed the frontier, and widespread and intense fighting broke out. The Security Council again called for an immediate cease-fire:

The Security Council,

Taking into consideration that previous resolutions of the Security Council in respect to Palestine have not been complied with and that military operations are taking place in Palestine;

Calls upon all Governments and authorities, without prejudice to the rights, claims or position of the parties concerned, to abstain from any hostile military action in Palestine and to that end to issue a cease-fire order to their military and para-military forces to become effective within thirty-six hours after midnight New York Standard Time, 22 May 1948;

Calls upon the Truce Commission and upon all parties concerned to give the highest priority to the negotiation and maintenance of a truce in the City of Jerusalem;

Directs the Truce Commission established by the Security Council by its resolution of 23 April 1948 to report to the Security Council on the compliance with the two preceding paragraphs of this resolution;

Calls upon all parties concerned to facilitate by all means in their power the task of the United Nations Mediator appointed in execution of the resolution of the General Assembly of 14 May 1948.[37]

The Chairman of the Truce Commission informed the President of the Security Council that in order to be able to carry out its allotted tasks the Commission would need military advisers and observers. When the Security Council succeeded, on 29 May 1948, in getting a four-week ceasefire accepted, this request was duly incorporated into the arrangements.

> *The Security Council,*
>
> *Desiring* to bring about a cessation of hostilities in Palestine without prejudice to the rights, claims and position of either Arabs or Jews,
>
> *Calls upon* all Governments and authorities concerned to order a cessation of all acts of armed force for a period of four weeks;
>
> *Calls upon* all Governments and authorities concerned to undertake that they will not introduce fighting personnel into Palestine, Egypt, Iraq, Lebanon, Saudi Arabia, Syria, Transjordan and Yemen during the cease-fire and
>
> *Calls upon* all Governments and authorities, should men of military age be introduced into countries or territories under their control, to undertake not to mobilize or submit them to military training during the cease-fire;
>
> *Calls upon* all Governments and authorities concerned to refrain from importing war material into or to Palestine, Egypt, Iraq, Lebanon, Saudi Arabia, Syria, Transjordan and Yemen during the cease-fire;
>
> *Urges all* Governments and authorities concerned to take every possible precaution for the protection of the Holy Places and of the City of Jerusalem, including access to all shrines and sanctuaries for the purpose of worship by those who have an established right to visit and worship at them;
>
> *Instructs* the United Nations Mediator for Palestine in concert with the Truce Commission to supervise the observance of the above provisions, and decides that they shall be provided with a sufficient number of military observers;
>
> *Instructs* the United Nations Mediator to make contact with all parties as soon as the cease-fire is in force with a view to carrying out his functions as determined by the General Assembly;
>
> *Calls upon* all concerned to give the greatest possible assistance to the United Nations Mediator;
>
> *Instructs* the United Nations Mediator to make weekly report to the Security Council during the cease-fire;
>
> *Invites* the states members of the Arab League and the Jewish and Arab authorities in Palestine to communicate their acceptance of this resolution to the Security Council not later than 6 p.m. New York Standard Time on 1 June 1948;
>
> *Decides* that if the present resolution is rejected by either party or by both, or if, having been accepted, it is subsequently repudiated or violated, the situation in Palestine will be reconsidered with a view to action under Chapter VII of the Charter.
>
> *Calls upon* all Governments to take all possible steps to assist in the implementation of this resolution.[38]

There was thus a clear decision that the Mediator would act in concert with the Truce Commission in supervising the truce. Under a private arrangement between the Mediator and the Truce Commission, the latter's authority was limited to Jerusalem. Count Bernadotte, the UN Mediator, embarked upon a week of intense diplomatic activity, and succeeded in gaining the acceptance of all parties to the conditions of the truce which he had formulated and to its effective date of 11 June.

On 7, 10, and 15 June there were discussions in the Security Council as to how the Mediator should obtain the military observer personnel that he needed; no decision was reached, however, and it was left to the Mediator to proceed as he saw fit.

This point may be said to mark the birth of a body for UN Truce Supervision. The precise functions and responsibilities of UNTSO changed to a considerable degree through time. The role of UNTSO may be seen in four main phases—relating to the truce in 1948–9; to the Armistice Agreements in 1949–1956; to the post-Suez era from 1956 to 1967; and to the period following the six-day war of June 1967. Even within these four phases UNTSO was sometimes given additional duties by Security Council resolutions directed toward particular aspects of Arab-Israeli relations. It remains true, however, that UNTSO has performed, in different circumstances and under a variety of commanders, delicate tasks concerned with supervising a minimum order in the Middle East for some eighteen years.

LEGAL OPINION

Re: The UN General Assembly and Peacekeeping Operations (Use of Force)

1. INTRODUCTION: Action authorized by a Competent International Organ: General statements on instances of lawful resort to force in the modern law and provisos in definitions of aggression frequently refer to action authorized by a competent organ of the United Nations, or taken in pursuance of a decision or recommendation of a competent organ of the United Nations. This category has not been free from difficulties of interpretation and application and it is necessary to notice these difficulties without purporting to give any extended or conclusive treatment of the problems involved. The crucial question concerns the general competence of the General Assembly, in addition to the Security Council, to make recommendations to Members for collective measures, including in the case of a breach of the peace or act of aggression the use of armed force when necessary, to maintain or restore international peace and security. Such powers were conferred

on the General Assembly in the *Uniting for Peace* resolution adopted by the Assembly on 3 November 1950. The validity of this resolution in terms of the Charter has been challenged. Very briefly, the critics of the resolution assert that the primary responsibility for the maintenance of international peace and security lies with the Security Council and refer to the Charter, Articles 5, 24, 39, 50, 53, 99 and 106. From this point of view, Article 39 is particularly significant as indicating an exclusive responsibility of the Security Council:

> The Security Council shall determine the existence of any threat to the peace, breach of the peace, or act of aggression and shall make recommendations, or shall decide what measures shall be taken in accordance with Articles 41 and 42, to maintain or restore international peace and security.

Those who uphold the validity of the resolution argue that even if the Security Council has the primary responsibility, the General Assembly has a residuary or secondary responsibility based on the wide terms of Article 10 and Article 11, paragraph 4 (see Ian Brownlie, *International Law and the Use of Force by States*, Oxford: Oxford University Press, 1963, reprinted 2002, 334).

2. It is noteworthy that Article 11 of the UN Charter provides:

(i) The General Assembly may consider the general principles of cooperation in the maintenance of international peace and security, including the principles governing disarmament and the regulations of armaments, and may make recommendations with regard to such principles to the Members or to the Security Council or both.

(ii) The General Assembly may discuss any questions relating to the maintenance of international peace and security brought before it by any Member of the United Nations, or by the Security Council, or by a State which is not a Member of the United Nations in accordance with Article 35, paragraph 2, and except as provided in Article 12, may make recommendations with regard to any such questions to the State or States concerned or to the Security Council or to both. Any such question on which action is necessary shall be referred the Security Council by the General Assembly either before or after discussion.

(iv) The General Assembly may call the attention of the Security Council to situations which are likely to endanger international peace and security.

It is important to quote the leading authority on the interpretation of the UN Charter, namely, Goodrich and Hambro, *Charter of the United Nations: Commentary and Documents,* 3rd ed., New York: Columbia

University Press, 1969), 114–115: 'Article 11 has been the basis for many of the Assembly's most important actions. By specifically authorizing the Assembly to discuss and make recommendations on questions related to the maintenance of international peace and security, Article 11 provides the basis for the assertion of the Assembly's right to deal with threats to the peace, breaches of the peace, and acts of aggression whenever the Security Council is unable to discharge its primary responsibility for maintaining peace and security.'

3. The inaction of the Security Council during the Cold War led the General Assembly to assume a role greater than originally envisaged. The Charter provides for a division of functions between the two organs. Article 11 (2) says that the General Assembly may discuss questions relating to the maintenance of international peace and security and make recommendations (except as provided in Article 12); but any such question on which action is necessary shall be referred to the Security Council. Article 12 is designed to prevent clashes between the two bodies; it provides that, while the Security Council is exercising its functions with regard to a particular dispute or situation, the General Assembly shall not make any recommendation unless the Security Council so requests. But these two provisions have been flexibly interpreted in such a way that there is no strict division of functions (on the drafting history, see Franck, Recourse to Force, 2002).
4. The General Assembly, concerned at the inaction of the Security Council and its failure to play the role provided in the Charter, passed, as mentioned above, the *Uniting for Peace* Resolution in 1950 (GA Res 377(V)). This allowed it to call emergency meetings in the event of Security Council failure because of lack of unanimity of the permanent members to exercise its primary responsibility for the maintenance of peace and security in any case where there appears to be a threat to the peace, breach of the peace or act of aggression. The General Assembly may then recommend collective measures, including the use of armed force if necessary (see Gray, I*nternational Law and the Use of Force*, Oxford: Oxford University Press, 2018). Using this procedure it recommended the establishment of peacekeeping forces in the Middle East. The legality of this was upheld by the International Court of Justice in the *Certain Expenses Case*; it explained away the provision of Article 11(2) that any such question on which action was necessary shall be referred to the Security Council by the General Assembly on the basis that the Security Council has a primary but not an exclusive responsibility for the maintenance of international peace and security. The Court also relied on the less convincing argument that it is only enforcement

action and not peacekeeping action that must be referred to the Security Council (*Certain Expenses* opinion, ICJ Reports, 1962).

5. Article 12 has also been gradually eroded. The General Assembly has made recommendations even when the Security Council was dealing actively with an issue. If the Security Council was not actually exercising its functions at the moment, or if a resolution was blocked by a veto, the General Assembly has assumed it is free to make recommendations, provided that these did not directly contradict a Security Council resolution. The General Assembly has accordingly passed a series of resolutions condemning certain behaviour when the Security Council could not agree on a resolution or could not take measures against a wrongdoing State. In 1994 the General Assembly regarded itself as free to call on the Security Council to lift the arms embargo on Bosnia-Herzegovina when the Security Council had been divided as to whether to do so. Recently, the General Assembly passed resolutions calling for action with regard to Syria and Ukraine when then Security Council was not able to do so.
6. Further, the role of the General Assembly in the case of Lebanon was an important one and need be cited in this regard. The Soviet Union (as it then was) and the United States both proposed that the matter should be transferred to the General Assembly. The Security Council was adjourned, but in fact no action was taken to call the Assembly into session until 7 August.

Letter dated 18 August 1958 from the Secretary of State of the United States of America to the President of the General Assembly:

> United States forces are now in Lebanon in response to an appeal of the duly constituted Government of Lebanon for assistance in maintaining Lebanon's territorial integrity and political independence against danger from without. United States forces will be withdrawn from Lebanon whenever this is requested by the duly constituted Government of Lebanon or whenever, as a result of the further action of the United Nations or otherwise, their presence is no longer required. The United States will in any event abide by a determination of the United Nations General Assembly that action taken or assistance furnished by the United Nations makes the continued presence of United States forces in Lebanon unnecessary for the maintenance of international peace and security. I would appreciate it if you would have this letter circulated to the Members of the General Assembly for their information.
>
> (Signed) John Foster Dulles
> [A/3876]

Draft Resolution [A/3878]

The General Assembly,

Having considered the item Questions discussed at the 838th meeting of the Security Council on 7 August 1958,

Noting the declarations addressed to the President of the General Assembly of 18 August 1958 by the United States regarding United States forces now in Lebanon and their withdrawal, and by the United Kingdom regarding British forces now in Jordan and their withdrawal,

Noting the Charter aim that States should practice tolerance and live together in peace with one another as good neighbors,

I

Reaffirms that all Members States should refrain from any threats or acts, direct or indirect, aimed at impairing the freedom, independence or integrity of any State, or at fomenting civil strife and subverting the will of the people of any State;

Calls upon all Member States strictly to observe these obligations and to ensure that their conduct, by word and deed, in relation to the general area of the Near East, conforms to the above-mentioned policy;

II

Requests the Secretary-General, in accordance with the Charter, forthwith to make such practical arrangements as he, in consultation with the Governments concerned, may find would adequately serve to help in upholding the purposes and principles of the Charter in relation to Lebanon and Jordan in present circumstances, having in mind section I of the present resolution.

III

Notes that the Secretary-General has studies in preparation for consideration by the General Assembly at its thirteenth session, of the feasibility of establishing a stand-by United Nations peace force

7. It is of crucial importance to note that even before the passing of the *Uniting for Peace* Resolution the explicit provisions of the UN Charter with respect to the initiation of collective measures in case of a threat to the peace, breach of the peace, or act of aggression were

found to be of limited value from the beginning because of the inability of the permanent members of the Security Council to co-operate and, and more particularly, because of their failure to agree on the principles governing the military agreements to be concluded under Article 43. As a result, it was necessary to develop alternative methods within the permissive limits of the Charter.

8. In addition to the express authority that the Council has under Articles 39, 41, and 42 to take binding decisions regarding measures to be applied, it has primary responsibility under Article 24 for maintaining international peace and security and, under Article 39, may make recommendations to maintain or restore international peace and security. At the San Francisco Conference, the view was expressed and accepted by the responsible committee of the Conference that, in so far as the Council was making recommendations under Article 39 its action would be governed by the provisions of Chapter VI of the Charter (see *US Library of Congress, Documents of the United Nations Conference on International Organization*, Vol. 12, 1945). In other words, the authority of the Council to make recommendations had special reference to the exercise of the function of peaceful settlement, while the authority to take binding decisions applied to collective measures taken under Articles 41 and 42 to maintain or restore international peace and security.
9. The competence of the General Assembly with respect to collective measures was considered at some length in the discussions during the autumn of 1950 preceding the adoption of the *Uniting for Peace* resolution. The question had not been directly considered by the Assembly before this time, although certain inferences could have been drawn from earlier practice of the Assembly, especially in the Spanish and Greek cases.
10. In the Spanish case, after the Council had failed to agree on any course of action, either under Chapter VI or Chapter VII of the UN Charter, several Members of the Organization asked the Assembly to consider the relations of Members with Spain. Some delegations questioned the right of the Assembly to recommend measures of the kind that the Council was expressly authorized to take under Chapter VII. But, in reply to those Members, it was pointed out that inasmuch as Members acting individually could adopt the proposed measures, the Assembly could recommend that such measures be taken collectively.
11. The Assembly finally adopted a resolution intended to bring limited pressure to bear on the Franco Government (Res. 39 (I) 12, 1946). There was no assertion in the resolution of the competence of the Assembly to recommend collective measures for maintaining or

restoring international peace and security. But the specific measures recommended—the withdrawal of heads of diplomatic missions and the exclusion the Franco Government from membership in the specialized agencies and participation in conferences held under the United Nations auspices—were of the nature of those measures the Council is authorized to take under Article 41 for that purpose. The responses of Members to these recommendations disclosed no inclination openly to challenge the action of the Assembly (U.N. General Assembly, Second Session, *Official Records*, Supplement No 1, pp. 2–4). Although the Assembly later revoked its recommendations, there is no evidence that this reflected a reversal of the original position of the Assembly with respect to its competence. Rather, it appears to have indicated a change of policy toward the Franco Government on the part of certain Members.

12. In the Greek case, the General Assembly was also requested to take certain action following a deadlock in the Security Council. The situation that the Assembly was called upon to consider was quite different, however, from the Spanish case in that there was, according to the contention of one of the parties and in view of the majority of the members of the Council, an actual threat to the peace. The first resolution of the Assembly, adopted on October 21, 1947, established a Special Committee on the Balkans to perform the functions of investigation, observation and conciliation. When this committee reported its conclusion that aid was being given to the guerillas with the knowledge of the governments of Albania, Bulgaria, and Yugoslavia, and that, so long as the aid continued, a threat to the political independence and territorial integrity of Greece would exist and international peace and security in the area would be endangered, the General Assembly in its third session adopted a resolution of a more forceful nature. This resolution found that continued aid endangered peace in the Balkans, and recommended to all Members of the United Nations and to all other States that their Governments refrain from any action designed to assist directly or through any other Government any armed group fighting against the Greek Government (Res. 193 (III) Nov. 27, 1948).

13. Later, the Special Committee reported in 1949 that Albania and Bulgaria continued to give assistance to the Greek guerillas, but aid from Yugoslavia appeared to be tapering off. At that time, the General Assembly proceeded to take its strongest action and recommended to all Members and to all other States that they refrain from any action designed to assist directly or through any other Government any armed group fighting against Greece; that they refrain from direct or indirect provision of arms or other materials of war to Albania and Bulgaria until the Special Committee or another competent organ of the United

Nations had determined that the unlawful assistance had ceased; and that they take into account, in their relations with Albania and Bulgaria, the extent to which those two countries henceforth abide by the recommendations of the Assembly in their relations with Greece (Res. 288 (IV) Nov. 18, 1949). Thus, the General Assembly, even before the adoption of the *Uniting for Peace* resolution in November 1950, used its powers of recommendation to urge Members and States non-Members of the United Nations to take collective measures—political and economic in character—to induce offending States to cease acts found by the Assembly to endanger international peace and security.

14. The General Assembly in the *Uniting for Peace* resolution categorically asserted its competence to consider any case where there appears to be a threat to the peace, breach of the peace, or act of aggression, with respect to which the Security Council because of lack of unanimity of the permanent members, fails to exercise its primary responsibility (Leland Goodrich and Anne Simons, *The United Nations and the Maintenance of International Peace and Security*, Washington D.C.: The Brookings Institution, 430).
15. The aforementioned opinion is held by the majority of the most eminent Professors of Public International Law (Brownlie, Bowett, Gray, to mention but a handful), whose writings constitute a very important source of International Law. Suffice it to mention in this regard the view of Sir Derek Bowett, late Professor of International Law in the University of Cambridge and Director of the Legal Department of the United Nations, in relation to the role played by the General Assembly in the case of Congo.
16. Let us first see some of the important Resolutions that were passed (and accordingly the part played by the Secretary-General) in the above-mentioned case in related sequence:

On 22 July, having meanwhile received the first report of the Secretary-General, the Security Council adopted a second Resolution unanimously which, in its operative part:

1. Calls upon the Government of Belgium to implement speedily the Security Council Resolution of 14 July 1960, on their withdrawal of their troops and authorizes the Secretary-General to take all necessary action to this effect;
2. Requests all States to refrain from any action which might tend to impede the restoration of law and order and the exercise by the Government of the Congo of its authority, and also to refrain from any action which might

undermine the territorial integrity and the political independence of the Republic of the Congo.

When the General Assembly met on 17 September in emergency session, the debate revealed the same fundamental divergence of views as to what the United Nations force should be doing in the Congo as had already emerged in the Security Council. However, a resolution was adopted without a single dissenting vote on 20 September, the text of which was as follows:

The General Assembly

1. Fully supports the Resolutions of July 14 and 22 and of August 9 of the Security Council;
2. Requests the Secretary-General to continue to take vigorous action in accordance with the terms of the aforesaid Resolutions and to assist the Central Government of Congo in the restoration and maintenance of law and order throughout the territory of the Republic of the Congo and to safeguard its unity, territorial integrity, and political independence in the interests of international peace and security.
3. Appeals to all Congolese within the Republic of the Congo to seek a speedy solution by peaceful means of all their internal conflicts for the unity and integrity of the Congo, with the assistance as appropriate, of Asian and African representatives appointed by the Advisory Committee on the Congo, in consultation with the Secretary-General, for the purpose of conciliation.
4. Appeals to all Member governments for urgent voluntary contributions to a United Nations Fund for the Congo to be used under United Nations control and in consultation with the Central Government for the purpose of rendering the fullest possible assistance to achieve the objective mentioned in the Preamble.
5. Requests:
    a. All States to refrain from any action which might tend to impede the restoration of law and order and the exercise by the Government of the Republic of the Congo of its authority and also to refrain from any action which might undermine the unity, territorial integrity and the political independence of the Republic of the Congo.
    b. All Member States, in accordance with Articles 25 and 49 of the Charter, to accept and to carry out the decisions of the Security Council and to afford mutual assistance in carrying out measures decided upon by the Security Council.

6. Without prejudice to the sovereign rights of the Republic of the Congo, calls upon all States to refrain from the direct and indirect provision of arms or other materials of war and military personnel and other assistance

> for military purposes. in the Congo during the temporary period of military assistance through the United Nations, except upon the request of the United Nations through the Secretary-General for carrying out the purposes of this Resolution and of the Resolutions of July 14 and 22 and of August 9 1960, of the Security Council.

As Bowett very well put it, "the significance of the General Assembly Resolution was twofold: First paragraph 2, in requesting the Secretary-General to continue to take vigorous action in accordance with the Resolutions of the Security Council, virtually amounted to a vote of confidence in the Secretary-General: significantly, the Soviet amendments had been directed to deleting the words 'to continue.' Second, paragraph 5, in addressing a general request to all States, made the demand for non-intervention and the challenging of all aid through the United Nations which the Secretary-General had urged the Security Council but which had there been blocked by the Soviet veto" (see Derek Bowett, United Nations Forces: A Legal Study of United Nations Practice, London: Stevens and Sons, 1964).

NOTES

1. Rosalyn Higgins, *United Nations Peacekeeping 1947–1967: Documents and Commentary* (Oxford: Oxford University Press, 1969), 535.
2. This doctrine, approved by Congress in January 1957, authorized the United States to cooperate with any nation in the Middle East in economic development needed to maintain national independence, and to provide military assistance, when requested, against aggression emanating from any Communist-controlled nation. For the political and diplomatic history of the evolution of this doctrine, see Dwight Eisenhower, *The White House Years; Waging Peace* (1965), 176–83.
3. SCOR, 13th yr, 824th mtg, 3–4.
4. SCOR, 13th yr, 824 mtg, 35–44.
5. Ibid., 45.
6. Ibid., 26 35.
7. Clearly the situation in Lebanon was not only civil war. And, certainly, sending UNOGIL to Lebanon does not amount to an act of collective self-defense.
8. SCOR, 13th yr, 827th mtg, 6–11.
9. SCOR, 13th yr, 829th mtg., p. 14, paras 67 and 68.
10. Harold Macmillan, the prime minister, stated that the request from Jordan had been received a few moments after the House of Commons had concluded its heated debate on the Near Eastern situation. It was thus, he said, not possible to consult parliament on the urgent decision to send troops to Jordan. According to Eisenhower, however, Macmillan told him that he had received a request from Hussein on July 14—some two days earlier (Eisenhower, 273).
11. SCOR, 13th yr, 833rd mtg, 2–8.

12. GAOR, 3rd emerg. Spec. sess., 740th plen. Mtg, 96.

13. GA Res. 1237 (ES-III).

14. A/4132, *Annual Report of the Secretary-General on the Work of the Organization, 16 June 1958–15 June 1959*, GAOR, 14th sess., suppl. I, 21.

15. Rosalyn Higgins, *UN Peacekeeping: Documents and Commentary, Volume 3, Africa* (Oxford: Oxford University Press, 1980), 6.

16. Rosalyn Higgins, *UN Peacekeeping: Documents and Commentary, Volume 3: Africa* (Oxford: Oxford University Press, 1980), 7.

17. Rosalyn Higgins, *UN Peacekeeping: Documents and Commentary, Volume 3: Africa* (Oxford: Oxford University Press, 1980), 7.

18. Rosalyn Higgins, *UN Peacekeeping: Documents and Commentary, Volume 3: Africa* (Oxford: Oxford University Press, 1980), 12.

19. SCOR, 15th yr, 884th mtg, para. 26.

20. See E. M. Miller, 'Legal Aspects of the UN Action in the Congo,' 55 *American Journal of International Law* (1961), 1–28.

21. S/4475, para. 3.

22. SCOR, 15th yr, 887th mtg, para. 44.

23. SCOR, 15th yr, 920th mtg, para. 73.

24. R. Higgins, *The Development of International Law through the Political Organs of the UN*, 236.

25. *ICJ Reports, 1962*, 177.

26. GAOR, 15th ses., 973rd plen. mtg, 3 Apr. 1961, per USSR.

27. Ibid. 995th plen. mtg, para. 112.

28. Ibid. Fifth Cttee, 839th mtg.

29. See Rosalyn Higgins, *United Nations Peacekeeping: The Middle East* (Oxford: Oxford University Press, 1979, published under the auspices of the Royal Institute of International Affairs), 5.

30. US Department of State, Anglo-American Committee of Enquiry, *Report* (1946).

31. G.A. Resolution 181 (II), 29 November 1947.

32. A/532, GAOR, 2nd spec. sess., suppl. I, p.36, para. 5.

33. SC Res. S/714, 1 Apr. 1948.

34. SC Res. S/723, 16 Apr. 1948.

35. SC Res. S/727, 23 Apr, 1948.

36. G.A. Res. 186 (ES-II), 14 May 1948.

37. SC Res. S/773, 22 May 1948.

38. SC Res. S/801, 29 May 1948.

Chapter 12

International Law and Recognition of States Created through the Use of Force

DOCTRINAL CONSIDERATIONS

Jus Gentium and Positivism

In accordance with positivism, the obligation to obey international law derived from the consent of States. Oppenheim's *International Law* provides the most influential expression of positivist theory. International law was seen as the law existing between civilized nations. In 1859 the British Law Officers spoke of International law as it has been hitherto recognized and now subsists by the common consent of Christian nations.[1] Members of the society whose law was international law were the European States between whom it evolved from the fifteenth century onward, and those other States accepted expressly or tacitly by the original members into the society of Nations; for example the United States of America and Turkey.[2] Recognition, express or implied, solely created their membership and bound them to obey international law.[3] States not so accepted were not bound by international law. Only States recognized and accepted as States into International society, were bound by international law and were international persons. States solely and exclusively are the subjects of International Law.[4] Through recognition only and exclusively a State becomes an International Person and a subject of International Law.[5]

The Constitutive Theory

The constitutive view which deduces the legal existence of new states from the will of those already established dates to Hegel, one of the spiritual fathers of the nineteenth-century doctrines of positivism and of the absolute sovereignty of the state in the international sphere.[6] Most of the adherents of the constitutive view of recognition are also positivist in outlook. Sir Hersch Lauterpacht, however, who was not a positivist, was one of the most persuasive exponents of the constitutive position.[7] Lauterpacht formulates the position as follows: The full international personality cannot be automatic. As its ascertainment requires the prior determination of difficult circumstances of fact and law, there must be *someone* to perform that task. In the absence of a preferable solution, such as the setting up of an impartial international organ to perform that function, the latter must be the fulfilled by states already existing.[8]

In modern international law, this argument is not applicable at large. Determination of the legality of the use of force, or the violation or termination of a treaty, may involve difficult circumstances of fact and law, but it could not be contended that the views of States as to such matters are conclusive. If that was the case, every rule of international law would be the subject of an automatic reservation with respect to every state.[9] It is of interest though that Lauterpacht allowed the possibility of an invalid act of recognition.[10] Another objection to the constitutive approach is its relativism. Kelsen says that "it follows from constitutive theory that legal existence of a State has relative character. A State exists legally only in its relations to other States. There is no such thing as absolute existence."[11] Lauterpacht, who accepts the relativity of recognition as inherent in the constitutive view, refers to it as a "glaring anomaly casting grave reflection upon international law."[12]

The Declaratory Theory

According to this theory, a state exists as a subject of international law—i.e., as a subject of international rights and duties—as soon as it exists as a fact, i.e., as soon as it fulfills the conditions of statehood as laid down in international law.[13] If recognition is purely declaratory of an existing fact what is, then, its juridical significance? The answer often given is that recognition is a political rather than a legal act.[14] Others maintain that its sole legal effect is to establish ordinary diplomatic relations between the recognizing and the recognized state.[15] This probably is also the intention of a large number of adherents to the declaratory doctrine for whom recognition signifies the acceptance of the state as a member of the international community.[16] Others still explain the declaratory effect of recognition in the sense that although prior to it the new state possesses all rights which international law grants to states, it is only after recognition that it is assured of enjoying them.[17]

A passage of C.J. Taft's judgment in the *Tinocco Arbitration* is considered as the classical piece of reference: The non-recognition by other nations of a government claiming to be a national personality, is usually appropriate evidence that it has not attained the independence and control entitling it by international law to be classed as such.[18] A German-Polish mixed Tribunal, in reference to the existence of the new state of Poland, stated: "the recognition of a State is not constitutive but merely declaratory. The State exists by itself, and the recognition is nothing else than a declaration of this existence, recognized by the States from which it emanates."[19] Of great importance in this regard is the report of the Commission of Jurists on the Aaland Islands. The passage of the Report dealing with the independence of Finland reads:

> these facts by themselves do not suffice to prove that Finland, from this time onwards, became a sovereign State. . . . The same legal value cannot be attached to recognition of new States in wartime, especially to that accorded by belligerent powers, as in normal times. . . . In addition to these facts which bear upon the external relations of Finland, the very abnormal character of her internal situation must be brought out. This situation was such that, for a considerable time, the conditions required for the formation of a sovereign State did not exist.[20]

The crucial point above is that conditions are required for the formation of a sovereign state apart from recognition.

It is evident that the declaratory doctrine prevails among writers. Brownlie summarizes the position thus: 'Recognition, *as a public act of State*, is an optional and political act and there is no legal duty in this regard. However, in a deeper sense, if an entity bears the marks of statehood, other states put themselves at risk legally, if they ignore the basic obligations of State relations.'[21] Nevertheless, states do not practically regard recognized states as exempt from international law.[22]

States Created as a Result of Illegal Use of Force.

It is established principle that territory may not be acquired by the illegal use of force.[23] The entities created during World Wars by illegal use of force were regarded as puppets and thus not independent. The puppet state situation illustrates the difficulty in any consideration of the relation between statehood and the illegal use of force. Either the entity owes its existence directly and substantially to the illegal intervention—in which case it is unlikely to be independent—or it does not, in which case the normal criteria for statehood would presumably apply.[24]

The term "puppet state" is used to describe nominal sovereigns under effective foreign control, especially in cases where the establishment of the puppet state is intended as a cloak for manifest illegality.[25] It is applicable to two European "states" established in German occupied territories. Slovakia was a nominally independent part of Czechoslovakia under German protection from 1939 to 1945. Croatia was also established on occupied Yugoslavian territory at the same period. A US International Claims Commission held that Yugoslavia was not, either factually or legally, a successor to Croatia:

> At all times during the period of its (Croatia's) existence as a so-called independent State, forces headed by Mihalovic and Tito conducted organized resistance within it. At no time was Croatia's control of its territory and population complete. It was created by German and Italian forces and was maintained by force and the threat of force, and as soon as the threat subsided Croatia ceased to exist. . . . It appears well established that Croatia was during its entire 4-year life subject to the will of Germany or Italy. It was not established through any dereliction on the part of the Government of Yugoslavia. . . . Croatia is defined by contemporary writers as a 'puppet State' or 'puppet government'. . . . A puppet State or local *de facto* government such as Croatia also possesses characteristics of 'unsuccessful revolutionists' and 'belligerent occupants.[26]

In the above-mentioned cases the factors considered include that the entities were established illegally using external military force, and that they did not have the support of most of the population they claimed to govern.[27]

It is also necessary in this context to explore the relation between self-determination and the rules relating to the use of force. Apparently the two legal principles are linked. According to Article 2 (4) of the U.N. Charter prohibits the use of force 'in any other manner inconsistent with the Purposes of the United Nations.' One of these purposes is respect for the principle of equal rights and self-determination of peoples. On the assumption that legal personality derives from the legal right to self-determination of the entity in question, it seems unlikely that the use of force to assert that right should be illegal.[28]It is noteworthy that the Declaration on Principles of International Law approved by Resolution 2625 (XXV) States that "every State has the duty to refrain from any forcible action which deprives peoples referred to in the elaboration of the principle of equal rights and self-determination of their right to self-determination and freedom and independence." The principle of self-determination thus takes priority over the prohibition of the use of force against the territorial integrity of a state.

However, the issue in the present analysis is when an entity is created in violation of an applicable right to self-determination by external illegal force. In such a case, the illegality of the entity's origin is confirmed by the maxim *ex injuria jus non oritur*. Therefore, some situations of military intervention in aid of self-determination must be hereby discussed. The two most relevant cases are Manchukuo and Bangladesh. There are two possibilities. It may be that the effectiveness of the emergent entity is in all situations to be regarded as paramount, so that its illegality of origin- however serious will not impede recognition as a state. It may be that the illegality of origin should be regarded as paramount in accordance with the maxim *ex injuria jus non oritur*.[29] "Manchukuo" came into being after Japan invaded Manchuria, a province of China, in 1934. Next year Japan recognized "Manchukuo" as an independent state. Its territory was that of Manchuria. The League of Nations dispatched the Lytton Commission to "Manchukuo" to find out the facts.[30] The Commission reported the following:

> In the "Government of Manchukuo," Japanese officials are prominent and Japanese advisers are attached to all important Departments. Although the Premier and his Ministers are all Chinese, the heads of the various Boards of General Affairs, which, in the organization of the new State, exercise the greatest measure of actual power, are Japanese. They are doubtless not under the orders of the Tokyo Government, and their policy has not always coincided with the official policy of the Japanese Government. But in the case of all-important problems, these officials and advisers, some of whom were able to act more or less independently in the first days of the new organization, have been constrained more and more to follow the direction of the Japanese official authority.[31]

As Crawford observes, the Lytton Commission's finding was that Manchukuo was not a genuine and spontaneous independence movement.[32] He goes on to say that given its total lack of independence the question whether, had it been effectively independent, it would have been deprived of statehood because of Japanese violations of the Covenant and the Paris Pact, did not really arise.[33] In the light of the Commission's Report, on February 24, 1932, the League of Nations Assembly resolved that "the sovereignty over Manchuria belongs to China."[34]

Interestingly, the puppet state of "Manchukuo" situation prompted the Stimson Doctrine of Non-recognition. On January 7, 1932, Stimson, the United States Secretary of State for Foreign Affairs, sent a note to the Japanese and Chinese Governments, stressing the illegality of the establishment of the "Manchukuo" state.[35] The Assembly of the League of Nations, using identical phraseology with the one employed in the Stimson note, resolved that 'it was incumbent upon the Members of the League of Nations not to recognize any situation, treaty or agreement which may be brought about by means contrary to the Covenant of the League of Nations, or the Pact of Paris.'[36] This resolution was a strong indication that the Stimson Doctrine was a landmark in international law and relations.

Let us now turn to the Bangladesh case. Pakistan, until 1971, consisted of East and West Pakistan, with India between the two parts. In March 1971, East Pakistan declared itself independent under the name of Bangladesh. Evidence suggests that India, which by the time had taken into its territory, about one million refugees from East Pakistan, had militarily assisted the insurgents, and Indian troops came to close quarters with Pakistani ones in the border area. In December Pakistan launched an attack against India. On the declaration of war on both sides fierce conflict commenced. Eventually Pakistan surrendered, and Bangladesh has received recognition including that of Pakistan since December 1971.[37]

Clearly, the Indian intervention was decisive, in the events which occurred, bringing about the creation of Bangladesh. There was a lot of support for independence. As Crawford suggests, 'there can be no doubt that Indian intervention was the dominant factor in the success of the independence movement.'[38] Yet, Bangladesh, despite the Indian intervention, was rapidly and widely recognized as a state. The Indian intervention was criticized by many governments as violating the UN Charter, but that illegality did not affect the recognition process.[39]

Thus, the issue whether East Bengal was a self-determination unit prior to independence is of importance,[40] because, if it were not, or if recognition was granted based on effective control in disregard of the legality of the Indian intervention, then there would be no legal criterion determining the creation of states through external illegal force.

Several writers have supported the view that East Bengal did indeed have a right to self-determination. As noted above, this is not to suggest, however, that the Indian intervention was a legal act.

The case of the "Turkish Republic of Northern Cyprus" is different, though, from the one of Bangladesh examined above. Where a state illegally intervenes and instigates the secession of part of a metropolitan state (as the case with the "TRNC" is), other states are under the same duty of non-recognition as in the case of illegal annexation of territory.[41] An entity created in violation of the rules relating to the use of force *in such circumstances* will not be regarded as a state. On the Cyprus issue, Crawford states:

> The situation in Cyprus after the Turkish intervention in 1974 is illustrative. It is not thought that a Turkish State on Cyprus created as a result of the intervention would have been recognized or accepted: indeed, despite their support of partition, the Turkish government appears to have accepted in practice the formal requirement of a unified Cypriot State.[42]

It is necessary to explore in this context the doctrine of non-recognition. The modern law of non-recognition may be formulated in the following terms. An act in violation of a norm having the character of *jus cogens* is illegal and is therefore null and void.[43] This applies to the creation of states, the acquisition of territory and other situations. States are under a duty not to recognize such acts.[44]

The object of the policy or the obligation of non-recognition is not to render illegal an otherwise lawful and valid act; its object is to prevent the validation of what is a legal nullity.[45] The jurisprudential basis of the principle of non-recognition is the fundamental maxim *ex injuria jus non oritur*, a "general principle of law recognized by civilized nations."[46] An illegality cannot, as a rule, become a source of legal right to the wrongdoer.[47] The principle of *ex injuria jus non oritur* provides a sound basis for the duty of non-recognition, particularly where the illegality has been confirmed by the political organs of the United Nations. In the 1971 *Namibia Opinion* the International Court of Justice stated:

> A binding determination made by a competent organ of the United Nations to the effect that a situation is illegal cannot remain without consequence. Once the Court faced with such a situation, it would be failing in the discharge of its judicial functions if it did not declare that there is an obligation, especially upon members of the United Nations, to bring that situation to an end.[48]

Jus cogens is a central feature of the modern doctrine of non-recognition since violation of a *jus cogens* norm is a prerequisite for the illegality that results in non-recognition. Thus, brief consideration of the doctrine of *jus cogens* is imperative. *Jus cogens* has its roots in the Natural Law doctrine of international law and was revived by the International Law Commission for the purpose of the Convention on the Law of Treaties. In 1953, in his Report to the International Law Commission, Sir Hersch Lauterpacht raised the notion of *jus cogens* when he proposed that the Convention include a provision that a "treaty is void if its performance involves an act which is illegal under international law and if it is declared so to be by the International Court of Justice."[49] Article 53 of the Vienna Convention on the Law of Treaties gives the final form to the deliberations of the Commission on *jus cogens*.[50] Writers have formulated the principle of *jus cogens* in a way that does not confine it to the invalidity of treaties. Verdross, a member of the International Law Commission, wrote:

> In the field of general international law there are rules having the character of *jus cogens*. The criterion for these rules consists in the fact that they do not exist to satisfy the needs of individual States but the higher interest of the whole international community. Hence these rules are absolute.[51]

Dugard regards that the prohibition of the use of force as enshrined in Article 2(4) of the UN Charter provides an example of a *jus cogens* rule. He goes on to argue that the "TRNC" has been created by the illegal use of force, and therefore it bears no legal validity.[52]

NOTES

1. Oppenheim, *International Law* (1st edn.) 17.
2. *Ibid.*, 18. On Turkey's membership see Hall, *International Law* (2nd edn. 1884), 40.
3. Oppenheim, *International law, supra* 17.
4. *Ibid.*, 18. By "States" Oppenheim meant recognized states.
5. Ibid., 108.
6. Lauterpacht, *Recognition in International Law* (Cambridge: Cambridge University Press 1947), 38.
7. Lauterpacht adopts the view that prior to recognition, the community in question possesses neither the rights nor the obligations which international law associates with full statehood.
8. Lauterpacht, *Recognition in International Law, supra* 55.
9. See Crawford, *The Creation of States in Modern International Law* (Oxford: Oxford University Press, 2007), 18.
10. Lauterpacht regarded Italian and German recognition of the Franco regime as 'illegal ab initio': *Recognition in International Law supra* 234 fn. 3.
11. Kelsen, 609.
12. Lauterpacht, *Recognition in International Law, supra* 67.
13. Lauterpacht, *Recognition in International Law, ante*, 41; Crawford, *Recognition in International Law,* 20: according to the declaratory theory, recognition of a new state is a political act which is in principle independent of the existence of the new state as a full subject of international law; Brierly, *The Law of Nations* (5th ed. 1955), 131–32: the better view is that the granting of recognition to a new state is not a constitutive but a declaratory act; it does not bring into legal existence a state which did not exist before. A state may exist without being recognized, and if it does exist in fact, then, whether it has been formally recognized by other states, it has a right to be treated by them as a state.
14. See Brierly, *The Law of Nations* (3rd ed. 1942), 100;also see *Hague Recueil*, vol. LVIII (1936) (iv), 52, where Professor Brierly further says that 'international law prescribes the objective conditions on which States are bound to base their *decision* in the matter.'
15. Lauterpacht, *Recognition in International Law, supra*, 42.
16. *Ibid.*, 42.
17. *Ibid.*, 42.
18. (1924) 18 *American Journal of International Law* 147–74, 154.

19. *Deutsche Continental Gas Gesellschaft v. Polish State* (1929) 5 *Annual Digest of Public International Law Cases* No.5.

20. *League of Nations Official Journal*, Supp. No. 4 (1920), 8.

21. *Principles of Public International Law*, 94 (emphasis original); Writers sharing the declaratory view include: O'Connell, *International Law* I, 123–34; Starke, *Studies in International Law*, 91–100; Fawcett, *The Law of Nations* (2nd ed., 1971), 49, 55; Higgins, *The Development of International Law through the Political Organs of the United Nations* (London, 135–36; Akehurst, *Modern Introduction to Internatonal Law*, 60–63; Waldock (1962), 106 *Recueil des Cours*; Chen, *The International Law of Recognition* (ed. L.C. Green, London, 1951); Brierly, *The Law of Nations, ante*, 139.

22. Brownlie, *Principles of International Law, supra*, 92 fn; Brownlie, *Recognition in Theory and Practice, BYBIL*: the declaratory view militates in favor of a legal and objective method of analyzing situations. Whiteman, 2 *Digest of International Law* (*Washington*, 15 vols. 1903–1973), 604–65; Brownlie, *International Law and the Use of Force by States, ante* 380: non-recognition of North Korea and of Israel was not regarded as precluding the application of international law rules to the Korean and Middle East wars).

23. Whiteman, 5 *Digest*, 874–965.

24. Crawford, *The Creation of States in Modern International Law, ante,* 108. For example, in the Manchurian crisis the question whether Manchukuo could have become an independent state notwithstanding the illegal Japanese intervention was never really in issue, since the puppet nature of the Manchukuo regime was and remained evident (*Ibid.*, 107).

25. *Ibid.*, 62.

26. *Socony Vacuum Oil Claim* (1954) 21 ILR 55, 58–62.

27. It was not regarded as relevant that certain groups in the territory carried out administrative functions if the elements mentioned were present. In such circumstances, any acts of puppet entity must be regarded as void *ab initio,* except to the extent that they can be regarded as acts of the belligerent occupant itself (Crawford, *The Creation of States in Modern International Law, ante*, 65); with regard to the puppet governments in Greece during World War II see Tenekides (1947), 51 *Revue General de Droit International Public*, 113–33.

28. *Ibid.*, 110.

29. Crawford, *The Creation of States in Modern International Law, ante*, 114.

30. For an account of the facts, see Harris, *Cases and Materials in International Law* (London: Sweet and Maxwell, 1996), 109–10.

31. See Harris, *Cases and Materials on International Law, ante*, 109–10. The Commission went on to say expressly that 'this authority, in fact, by reason of the occupation of the country by its troops for the maintenance of its authority both internally and externally . . . possesses in every contingency the means of exercising an irresistible pressure.'

32. Crawford, *The Creation of States in Modern International Law, ante*, 108. The independence movement was only made possible by the presence of Japanese troops and for this reason the present regime cannot be considered to have been called into existence by a genuine and spontaneous independence movement.

33. *Ibid.*, 108.

34. *League of Nations Official Journal,* Special Supp. No. 112, 75 (1933).

35. Extract from the note, formulating what was to become the Stimson Doctrine read as follows: the American Government deems it to be its duty to notify both the Imperial Japanese Government and the Government of the Chinese Republic that it cannot admit the legality of any situation *de facto* . . . and that it does not intend to recognize any situation, treaty, or agreement which may be brought about by means contrary to the covenants and obligations of the Pact of Paris of August 27, 1928, to which treaty both China and Japan, as well as the United States, are parties (Harris, *Cases and Materials on International Law, supra*, 219).

36. *League of Nations Official Journal*, Special Supp. No. 101, 87, 88 (1932).

37. For an extensive account of events surrounding the Bangladesh case, see Harris, *Cases and Materials on International Law, ante*, 892–93.

38. Crawford, *The Creation of States in Modern International Law, ante*, 115.

39. On the illegality of the Indian intervention, see Franck and Rodley (1973), 67 *American J.I.L.* 275–305.

40 This conclusion is reached by Crawford, *ibid.*, 116–17. He also argues that genocide is a clear case of abuse of sovereignty, and this factor, together with the territorial and political coherence of East Bengal in 1971 probably qualified East Bengal as a self-determination unit.

41. See Crawford, *The Creation of States in Modern International Law, ante*, 118.

42. *Ibid.*, 118 fn; also see A.V.W. Thomas and A.J. Thomas (1975), 29 *Southwestern Law Journal* 513–46, 526–27.

43. See Dugard, *Recognition and the United Nations (*Cambridge University Press, Grotius Publications).

44. This formulation substantially accords with that of the 1981 Draft of the American Law Institute's Restatement of Foreign Relations Law of the United States, which provides that "A State is required not to recognize or treat as a State an entity that has attained the qualifications of statehood in violation of international law" (Tenatative Draft No. 2, 3, 8).

45. Lauterpacht, *Recognition in International Law, ante*, 413.

46. Statute of the International Court of Justice, Article 38 (3).

47. Lauterpacht, *Recognition in International Law, supra*, 420; also see *Corpus Juris Civilis, Digest* 50.17.134.i: " Nemo ex suo delicto meliorem suam conditionem facere potest"; but, illegality may, if the rigid conditions of lapse of time and of other requirements have been complied with, crystallize into a legal right as the result of the operation of prescription (acquisitive prescription): H. Lauterpacht, *Recognition in International Law*, *supra*.

48. 1971 I.C.J. Reports 16, 54.

49. Lauterpacht stated: "It would thus appear that the test whether the object of the treaty is illegal and whether the treaty is void for that reason is not inconsistency with customary international law pure and simple, but inconsistency with such overriding principles of international law which may be regarded as constituting principles of international public policy" (1953 *I.L.C. Yearbook* II 154–56); also see Sir Gerald Fitzmaurice, Third Report on the Law of Treaties, 1958 *I.L.C. Yearbook* II 40; Sir

Humphrey Waldock, Second Report on the Law of Treaties 1963 *I.L.C. Yearbook* II 52–53.

50. "For the purposes of the present Convention, a peremptory norm of general international law is a norm accepted and recognized by the international community as a whole as a norm from which no derogation is permitted . . . "; see further Rosenne, *The Law of Treaties: A Guide to the Legislative History of the Vienna Convention of the Vienna Convention* (1970), 290–93.

51. *Jus Dispositivum ans Jus Cogens in International Law* (1966) 60 *American J.I.L.* 55, 58; also see *Conference on International Law, Lagonissi, April 3–8, 1966, Papers and Proceedings: The Concept of Jus Cogens in International Law* (Carnegie Endowment for International Peace); dictum in the *Barcelona Traction, Light and Power Company Case*, 1970 I.C.J. Reports 3, 32.

52. *Recognition and the United Nations, ante*, 110. For the relevant complexities of the Palestinian Question, see Elihu Lauterpacht, *Jerusalem and the Holy Places*, Anglo-Israel Association, Pamphlet No. 19 (1968); Melinda Crane "Middle East: Status of Jerusalem" (1980), 21 *Harvard International Law Journal*, 784; the offer to the Palestinians by Barak at Camp David during July–December 2000, could, I submit, provide a framework for a just and viable settlement of the issue: 96 percent of the West Bank, 100 percent of the Gaza Strip, a sovereign Palestinian State, an end to the occupation, the uprooting of most of the settlements, and sovereignty over Arab East Jerusalem.

Chapter 13

Jus Ad Bellum and *Ius in Bello*

Humanitarian Law of Armed Conflict

This chapter on International Humanitarian Law and International Criminal Law deals firstly with the rules governing the conduct of hostilities once an armed conflict has erupted. The term in Latin for this body of law is "ius in bello" and is distinguished from the rules of the International Law relating to the use of armed force, which is the other category of the Law of War. The rationale behind the existence of this body of law lies in the fact that, if it is not possible to achieve deterrence of war (and international history shows that it is not really possible), at least the armed conflict must be subject to certain humanitarian rules and limitations, in order to protect, for example, prisoners, wounded soldiers and civilian population, and to prohibit the use of certain weapons systems.[1]

Various problems arise in relation to the application of this sub-branch of the law. On the one hand, although the declaration of war is no longer an application criterion, as it has become a rather rare practice, however, is it very difficult occasionally to distinguish between the state of war and non-state of war. On the other hand, International Humanitarian Law requires some sort of synthesis between the Law of War and international Law of Human Rights. But this attitude is not generally accepted, because it is not clear which human rights are applicable in time of war. This does not mean that international conventions of human rights are irrelevant to armed conflict and military occupation.

Secondly, the International Court of Justice's Advisory Opinion on the Threat or Use of nuclear weapons under the Law of Armed Conflict is being considered. International Criminal Law is analyzed in this respect, as violations of the rules of the Law of Armed Conflict constitutes simultaneously war crimes.

LAWFUL AND UNLAWFUL CONDUCT OF WAR—INTERNATIONAL HUMANITARIAN LAW OF ARMED CONFLICT

To many people it seems paradoxical that war should be conducted based on legal rules. Why should a nation fighting for survival allow its struggle to be hindered by legal constraints?[2] The answer lies in the fact that the bipolar system of balance of power of the past century dictated flexibility in political alliances and meant that the present enemy of a state could be his tomorrow's ally. This, of course, has led to a reduction of the degree of intensity in wartime, for precisely the states did not wish to elicit endless bitterness among potential future allies.

A more important reason for these political calculations is that the laws of war, the rules of conduct of armed conflict, are intended to prevent unneeded or unnecessary suffering. Unnecessary suffering means that those tribulations that do not result in any military advantage, or those of which have a military advantage, which is very small compared to the tribulations.

Wars during the eighteenth and nineteenth centuries were wars both among civilians and between armed forces. The great military writer of the nineteenth century, *Clausewitz*, wrote that *"the destruction of the war machine or the military power of the adversary is the cornerstone of all the mercurial action."*[3] According to this logic, it is legitimate for International Law to protect civilians. But this protection cannot always be absolute. For another reason, it is a fact that sometimes an army forces a city to surrender by foreclosing and cutting off supplies for citizens.

During the second half of the nineteenth century, states began issuing manuals of military law. A famous example is the *Lieber Code*. It was prepared by *Francis Lieber* of the University of Columbia and was entitled "*Instructions for the Government of Armies of the United States in the Field.*" The Code was drafted in 1863 under a committee of officers approved by President Lincoln, under the guidance of Lieber himself.[4] The first international conventions of the time were the Geneva Conventions of 1864 and 1906, the three Hague Conventions of 1899 (relating to the conduct of land and sea warships), and the thirteen Hague Conventions of 1907, which concerned all the remaining aspects of humanitarian law.

Since the end of the First World War, human rights treaties were developed from time to time. The London Treaty of 1930 and the London Protocol of 1936 attempted to regulate the use of submarines, but they were already abolished from the start of the Second World War. The Geneva Protocol banned the use of gas, while a Convention and a Protocol were signed in Hague in 1954 to protect the cultural heritage in time of armed conflict.

It is noteworthy to state that the basic provisions of the Convention constituted a landmark in International Humanitarian Law:

Definition of Cultural Property: *Article 1*: For the purposes of the present Convention, the term *"cultural property"* shall cover, irrespective of origin or ownership: (a) movable or immovable property of great importance to the cultural heritage of every people, such as monuments of architecture, art or history, whether religious or secular; archaeological sites; groups of buildings which, as a whole, are of historical or artistic interest; works of art . . . objects of artistic or archaeological interest; as well as collections. . . .

> (b) buildings whose main and effective purpose is to preserve or exhibit the movable cultural property defined in subparagraph (a) such as museums, depositories of archives, and refuges intended to shelter, in the event of armed conflict, the movable cultural property defined in subparagraph (a).

The second, third and fourth Article of the Convention define and explain the protection of cultural property:

> *Article 2:* Protection of Cultural Property: For the purposes of the present Convention, the protection of cultural property shall comprise the safeguarding of and respect for such property.
>
> *Article 3:* The High Contracting Parties undertake to prepare in time of peace for the safeguarding of cultural property situated in their own territory against the foreseeable effects of an armed conflict, by taking such measures as they consider appropriate.
>
> Under the *Article 4.1.*: Respect for Cultural Property: The High Contracting Parties undertake to respect cultural property situated within their own territory as well as within the territory of other High Contracting Parties by refraining from any use of the property and its immediate surroundings or of the appliances in use of its protection for purposes which are likely to expose it to destruction or damage in the event of armed conflict; and by refraining from any act of hostility directed against any such property.
>
> *Article 4.2.:* The obligations mentioned in paragraph 1 of the present Article may be waived only in cases where military necessity imperatively requires such a waiver.
>
> *Article 4.3.:* The High Contracting Parties further undertake to prohibit, prevent, and if necessary to put a stop to any form of theft or misappropriation of, and of any acts of vandalism directed against, cultural property.

> *Article 4.4.:* They shall refrain from any act directed by way of reprisals against cultural property.
>
> *Article 4.5.:* No High Contracting Party may evade the obligations incumbent upon it under the present Article, in respect of another High Contracting Party, by reason of the fact that the latter has not applied the measures of safeguard referred to in Article.

The *Hague Convention*, furthermore, in *Article 5* refers to the significant protection that the Contracting Parties undertake to provide for cultural property in time of military occupation. Under *Article 5.1.*, any High Contracting Party in occupation of the whole or part of the territory of another High Contracting Party shall as far as possible support the competent national authorities of the occupied country in safeguarding and preserving its cultural property. Under *Article 5.2.*, should it prove necessary to take measures to preserve cultural property situated in occupied territory and damaged by military operations, and should the competent national authorities be unable to take such measures, the Occupying Power shall, as far as possible, and in close co-operation with such authorities, take the most necessary measures of preservation.

One convention and three protocols were concluded in 1980 to reduce the use of hard conventional weapons, for example, napalm bombs. The First Review Convention of the Convention on Certain Conventional Weapons of 1980, which was convened in Vienna in 1995, adopted new protocols, which concern blinding laser weapons and landmines. More importantly, however, are the two Geneva Conventions of 1929 for the protection of sick and injured soldiers, sick and injured sailors, and war prisoners, and the four Geneva Conventions of 1949 on the Protection of Wounded Soldiers, Prisoners of War and Civilians, accompanied by two protocols of 1977. It primarily aims to protect only two categories of citizens: those who are in hostile territory at the beginning of war, and those who live in territory ruled and occupied by the enemy during the war. It is noteworthy that in the case of the Geneva Conventions of 1949 ratification is now literally universal. With the accession of the Republic of Cyprus on 18 March to Protocol II of 1977, the number of member states in the Protocol reached 135.

The codification of International Law Humanitarian Law through treaties has not diminished the continuing role of the principles of international customary law. This is expressed by the so-called Martens proposal (*Martens Clause*) in the Preamble of the Hague II Convention:

> Until a more complete code of the laws of war is issued, the high contracting Parties think it right to declare that in cases not included in the Regulations adopted by them, populations and belligerents remain under the protection and empire of the principles of International Law, as they result from the usages

established between civilized nations, from the laws of humanity and the requirements of public conscience.

Nowadays, technological changes occur so rapidly that each war differs dramatically from previous wars. It is astonishing that there is no judicial declaration or judicial precedent on the legality or illegality of bombardment. There are two additional causes which encouraged violations of the laws of war during the twenty and twenty-first centuries. In the first place, the First and Second World Wars caused bitter feelings than previous wars. Secondly, economic, and technological developments have greatly increased the military advantage that one can gain by violating the laws and rules of war.

THE INTERNATIONAL COURT OF JUSTICE'S ADVISORY OPINION ON THE THREAT OR USE OF NUCLEAR WEAPONS

In 1961, the United Nations General Assembly adopted a resolution declaring that the use of nuclear weapons is illegal. Fifty-five states (mainly Communist and Third-Party) have voted in favor of the resolution, twenty (mainly Western countries) voted against, and twenty-six states (mainly Latin American countries) abstained. The diametric difference between the positions of Communist and Western countries is explained by the fact that the Soviet supremacy of conventional (i.e. non-nuclear) weapons in Europe was so great (before the Red Army's withdrawal from Eastern Europe) so that the western states would most probably be forced to use nuclear weapons to defend themselves against an invasion of Western Europe by Soviet forces using conventional weapons. Some rules of International Law can proportionately be applied to nuclear weapons. Nuclear weapons could be compared with massive bombing attacks during the Second World War. However, there was no treaty prohibiting such bombings then. The First Protocol of the Geneva Convention of 1977, nevertheless, set some barriers to this practice of bombardments.

Geneva Convention Article 48 of the 1977 Protocol I provides: *"In order to ensure respect and protection of the civilian population and civilian objects, the Parties to the conflict shall at all times distinguish between the civilian population and combatants and between objects and military objectives, and accordingly shall direct their operation only against military objectives."* However, the United States, when signing the Convention, pointed out in the minutes that the rules established by this Protocol would not apply to and would not determine the use of nuclear weapons. Similar statements were made by the British and French Governments.

The question of the lawful use of nuclear weapons was raised before the International Court of Justice based on a Request from the United Nations General Assembly on 6 January 1996. The General Assembly requested the International Court of Justice to urgently submit its Opinion on the following question: *"Is the threat or use of nuclear weapons under any circumstances permissible under International Law?"* Different majorities arose between the judges during the various phases and steps of the decision. The Court ruled that there is no specific licensing of the threat or use of nuclear weapons (unanimously) in international customary law or in international treaty law, but also that there is no total and universal ban (eleven votes against three). The Court furthermore unanimously adopted the verdict that *"the threat or use of force by form of nuclear weapons, which is contrary to Article 2(4) of the United Nations Charter, and which does not satisfy all the requirements of Article 51, is illegal."* In essence, the Court has advised that the use of nuclear weapons is legal, legitimate, and permissible only for the purposes of self-defense of states under *Article 51* of the UN Charter, a provision which constitutes an exception to the general prohibition on the use of armed force.

In this Opinion, Judge Higgins, a former Professor of International Law at London School of Economic and Political Science in the University of London, disagreed on the issue of the use of nuclear weapons. It is noteworthy that *Article 51* of the UN Charter, as well as *Article 42*, based on which the Security Council is legally entitled to take armed action to restore the legal regional order in accordance with VII of the UN Charter, does not refer to certain weapons. It refers to any use of armed force, regardless of the weapons systems. The UN Charter neither allows nor does it clearly prohibit the use of nuclear weapons. On the other hand, the use of armed force according to Article 51 of the UN Charter (self-defense) is subject to the requirements of necessity and proportionality. In the Case concerning *Military and Paramilitary Activities in and against Nicaragua (Nicaragua v. United States of America, International Court of Justice—I.C.J.—Reports* 1986, p. 94, para. 176): the Court held: *"there is a specific rule whereby self-defense would warrant only measures which are proportional to the armed attack and necessary to respond to it, a rule well established in customary International Law."* The principle of proportionality, however, does not in itself prohibit the use of nuclear weapons in self-defense. At the same time, the use of an armed force which is proportionate to the law or to the doctrine of self-defense must, to be lawful and legal, fulfil the conditions of and rules of Humanitarian Law of Armed Conflict. In this regard, the Court points out that the nature of nuclear weapons and the obvious risks associated with their use must be considered by states which intend to use nuclear weapons in the form of self-defense in accordance with the principle of proportionality. In such case, there will probably be some kind of violation of the *Ius in Bello*, that is the rules of the humanitarian law of the armed conflict. This suggests the general superiority of "*Ius ad Bellum*" over "*Ius in Bello.*" The irrefutable fact remains that the International Court of Justice allows in its Opinion the use of nuclear weapons for the purposes of Self-Defense.

In this context, it is also necessary to underline the fact that the Treaty on Non-Proliferation of nuclear weapons have also emerged in this field. Nevertheless, this Treaty confirms the privilege of the official nuclear nations, the five permanent members of the UN Security Council, to possess nuclear arsenal and excludes the possession of such weapons by other Countries.

INTERNATIONAL CRIMINAL LAW

However, the violation of the Law of the Armed Conflict on part of states generally amounts to commission of war crimes, so International Criminal Law and the need for its implementation is brought into the picture, which virtually penalizes the commission of such crimes. Significant developments have occurred with the adoption of the *Statute of Rome*, which states in *Article 1*: The Court: An International Court is hereby established. It shall be a permanent institution and shall have the power to exercise its jurisdiction over persons for the most serious crimes of international concern, as referred to in this statute. Let us analyze in succession the crimes that the Court may try, and the exact definition of these crimes.[5]

Statute of Rome Article 5: Crimes within the jurisdiction of the Court: The jurisdiction of the Court shall be limited to the most serious crimes of concern to the international community. The Court has jurisdiction in accordance with this Statute with respect to the following crimes:

(a) The crime of genocide
(b) Crimes against humanity
(c) War crimes
(d) The Crime of aggression

> Violence or aggression in International Law, is defined as the use of armed violence by one state against another, which is not justified by self-defense or any other legally recognized exception to the general prohibition of the use of force as enshrined in the UN Charter.

Genocide, for the purposes of the *Statute of Rome* is defined in *Article 6* as follows: Genocide: For the purpose of this Statute, *genocide* means any of the following acts committed with intent to destroy, in whole or in part, a national, ethnic, racial, or religious group, as such:

(a) Killing members of the group
(b) Causing serious bodily harm to members of the group
(c) Deliberately inflicting on the group conditions of life calculated to bring about its physical destruction in whole or in part
(d) Imposing measures intended to prevent births within the group
(e)Forcibly transferring children of the group to another group.

Statute of Rome Article 7.1.: Crimes against humanity: for the purpose of this Statute, *crime against humanity* means any of the following acts when committed as part of a widespread or systematic attack directed against any civilian population, with knowledge of the attack:

(a) Murder
(b) Extermination
(c) Enslavement
(d) Deportation or forcible transfer of population
(e) Imprisonment or other severe deprivation of physical liberty in violation of fundamental rules of International Law
(f) Torture
(g) Rape, sexual slavery, enforced prostitution, forced pregnancy, or any other form of sexual violence of comparable gravity[6]
(h) Persecution against any identifiable group on political, racial, national, ethnic, cultural, religious, gender or other grounds that are universally recognized as impermissible under International Law, in connection with any act referred to in this paragraph or any crime within the jurisdiction of the Court. At this point, an identification of crimes against humanity with the crime of genocide is evident, or otherwise it is possible to commit crimes that constitute both crimes against humanity and genocide.
(i) Enforced disappearance of persons
(j) The crime of apartheid
(k) Other inhumane acts of similar character intentionally causing great suffering, or serious injury to body or to or physical health[7]

Statute of Rome Article 8 paragraph 2: War crimes: For the purpose of this Statute, *war crimes* means: (a) Grave breaches of the Geneva Conventions of 12 August 1949, namely, any of the following acts against persons or property protected under the provisions of the relevant Conventions:

i. Willful killing;
ii. Torture or inhuman treatment, including biological experiments;
iii. Willfully causing great suffering, or serious injury to body or health;
iv. Extensive destruction and appropriation of property, not justified by military necessity and carried out unlawfully;
v. Compelling prisoner of war or other protected person to serve in the forces of a hostile power;
vi. Willfully depriving a prisoner of war or other protected person of the rights of fair and regular trial;
vii. Unlawful deportation transfer or unlawful confinement;
viii. Taking of hostages;

(b) Other serious violations of the laws and practices applicable to armed conflict, within the established framework of International Law, below the name of any of the following:

i. Intentionally directing attacks against the civilian population as such or against individual civilians not taking direct part in hostilities;
ii. Intentionally directing attacks against civilian objects, that is, objects which are not military objectives;
iii. Intentionally directing attacks against personnel, installations, material, units, or vehicles involved in a humanitarian assistance or peacekeeping mission in accordance with the Charter of the United Nations, if they are entitled to the protection given to civilians or civilian objects under the International Law of armed conflict.
iv. Intentionally launching an attack in the knowledge that such attack will cause incidental loss of life or injury to civilians or damage to civilian objects or widespread, long-term, and severe damage to the natural environment which would be clearly excessive in relation to the concrete and direct overall military advantage anticipated;
v. Attacking or bombarding by whatever means, towns, villages, dwellings, or buildings which are undefended, and which are not military objectives;
vi. Killing or wounding a combatant who, having laid down his arms or having no longer means of defense, has surrendered at discretion.

Statute of Rome Article 77.1.: The Court may impose one of the following penalties on a person convicted of a crime referred to in article 5 of this Statute:

a. Imprisonment for a specified number of years, which may not exceed a maximum of 30 years or
b. A term of life imprisonment when justified by the extreme gravity of the crime and the individual circumstances of the convicted person.

Statute of Rome Article 77.2.: In addition to the imprisonment the Court may order:

a. A fine under the criteria provided for in the Rules of Procedure and Evidence;
b. A forfeiture of proceeds, property and assets derived directly or indirectly from that crime.

It is high time for states such as Cyprus and at this very hour Ukraine, which have suffered enormously from the commission of war crimes in the context of expansionist illegal interventions, to appeal to the International Criminal Court and bring to trial those individuals criminally responsible, in order that international justice be properly done, and public catharsis be achieved.

NOTES

1. See generally the leading authority on the subject matter, Roberts, Adam and Guelff, *Documents on the Laws of War* (Oxford: Oxford University Press, 2000).

2. It is my submission that the view expressed by Michael Akehurst that "nations did not regard themselves as fighting for survival in the eighteenth and nineteenth centuries. Wars were seldom fought for ideological reasons and tended not to rouse the same intensity of passion as twentieth century wars" (*Modern Introduction to International Law*, Routledge, 1997, 343). Proof of the opposite is the Greek revolution (the large-scale and perpetual war), which took place both for the national survival of the Greeks as well as for the protection and preservation of the ideology and conscience of Hellenism.

3. On War (1832).

4. In his lecture at the beginning of the seventh annual meeting of the American Society of International Law, which was dedicated to the Lieber Code, the president of Elihu Root stressed the humanitarian content of the Code: *"While the instrument was a practical presentation of what the laws and usages of war were, and not a technical discussion of what the writer thought they ought to be, in all its parts may be discerned an instinctive selection of the best and most humane practice and an assertion of the control of morals to the limit permitted by the dreadful business in which the rules were to be applied"* (Opening Address by Elihu Root at the Seventh Annual Meeting of the American Society of International Law, April 24, 1913, reprinted in 7 *American Journal of International Law* 453 [1913]). Evaluating Lieber's work, Bluntschli, a professor in Heidelberg, said the following: *"His legal injunctions rest upon the foundation of moral precepts. The former are not always sharply distinguished from moral injunctions, but nevertheless, through a union with the same, are ennobled and exalted. Everywhere reigns in this body of law the spirit of humanity, which spirit recognizes as fellow-beings, with lawful rights, our very enemies, and which forbids our visiting upon them unnecessary injury, cruelty, or*

destruction. But at the same time, our legislator remains fully aware that, in time of war, it is absolutely necessary to provide for the safety of armies and for the successful conduct of a campaign; that, to those engaged in it, the harshest measures and most reckless exactions cannot be denied; and that tender-hearted sentimentality is here all the more out of place, because the greater the energy employed in carrying on the war, the sooner will it be brought to an end, and the normal condition of peace restored." (*Introduction: Lieber's Service to Political Science and International Law*, in 2 Francis Lieber: *The Miscellaneous Writings of Francis Lieber: Contributions to Political Science* 12–13 (1881)). In some respects, including the absolute prohibition of rape and the protection of the occupied territories, the Code was more advanced than the Hague Regulations: All wanton violence committed against persons in the invaded country, all destruction of property not commanded by the authorized officer, all robbery, all pillage or sacking, even after taking a place by main force, all rape, wounding, maiming, or killing of such inhabitants, are prohibited under the penalty of death, or such other severe punishment as may seem adequate for the gravity of the offense (Code Lieber, article 44). It is remarkable that the aforementioned crimes are punishable with the death penalty.

5. See the excellent textbook of Cassese, *The Rome Statute of the International Criminal Court* (Oxford University Press, 2002). Respect to the Constitution of the International Criminal Court useful are the reports of Christopher Keith Hall: *The First Two Sessions of the UN Preparatory Committee on the Establishment of an International Criminal Court*, 91 *American Journal of International Law* 177 (1997); *Idem: The Third and Fourth Sessions of the UN Preparatory Committee on the Establishment of an International Criminal Court*, 92 *American Journal of International Law* 124 (1998); *Idem, The Fifth Session of the UN Preparatory Committee on the Establishment of an International Criminal Court*, 92 *American Journal of International Law* 331 (1998).

6. As far as rape is concerned, it is noteworthy that the Statute for the establishment of an international arbitral in the case of the former Yugoslav proposed by the Secretary-General of the United Nations involves rape as a crime against humanity (UN Doc. S/ 25704). This statute was approved by the Security Council resolution 827 (SC Res. 827). In the same climate is notable the letter of Robert Bradtke, executing US Secretary of State for legislative affairs to Senator Arlen Specter, 27th of 1993; violation of the Geneva Conventions is a war crime (FM 27–10, para 499). Article 27 of the Geneva Convention Relative to the Protection of Civilian Persons in Time of War provides that women shall be "especially protected . . . against rape." Article 13 of the Geneva Convention Relative to the Treatment of Prisoners of War provides that prisoners "must at all times be protected, particularly against acts of violence"; article 14 requires that women "be treated with all the regard due to their sex." Both Conventions list grave breaches, including willful killing, torture or inhuman treatment, and (with regard to civilians) willfully causing great suffering or serious injury to body or health. Under the Geneva Conventions and customary international law, all parties to an international conflict (including all parties to the conflict in the former Yugoslavia) are required either to try persons alleged to have committed grave breaches or to extradite them to a party that will. In our reports to the United Nations

on human rights violations in the former Yugoslavia, we have reported sexual assaults as grave breaches. We will continue to do so and will continue to press the international community to respond to the terrible sexual atrocities in the former Yugoslavia.

7. In the case Tadic the International Criminal Court delivered the following important: It is by now a settled rule of customary international law that crimes against humanity do not require a connection to international armed conflict. Indeed, as the Prosecutor points out, customary international law may not require a connection between crimes against humanity and any conflict at all. Thus, by requiring that crimes against humanity be committed in either internal or international armed conflict, the Security Council may have defined the crime in Article 5 more narrowly than necessary under customary international law. There is no question, however, that the definition of crimes against humanity adopted by the Security Council in Article 5 [of the Statute] comports with the principle "*nullum crimen sine lege.*" The statement by the American Government of 23 March 1998 on the criminalisation of acts carried out during non-international conflicts is also on the same wavelength: The United States strongly believes that serious violations of the elementary customary norms reflected in common Article 3 should be the centerpiece of the ICC's subject matter jurisdiction with regard to non-international armed conflicts. Finally, the United States urges that there should be a section . . . covering other rules regarding the conduct of hostilities in non-international armed conflicts. It is good international law, and good policy, to make serious violations of at least some fundamental rules pertaining to the conduct of hostilities in non-international armed conflicts a part of the ICC jurisdiction (Meron, *War Crimes Law comes of Age*, Oxford University Press, 1998). I think, however, that this approach is a bit dangerous, because it allows international criminal law to intervene in cases which may have a purely internal character and an ethnic dimension.

Bibliography

Aeschylus, *Persians. Seven Against Thebes. Suppliants. Prometheus Bound*, Loeb Classical Library 145 (Cambridge Massachusetts: Harvard University Press, 2009).

Akehurst, Michael, 'The Hierarchy of the Sources of International Law,' 47 (1974–1975) *British Yearbook of International Law*, 273.

Akehurst, Michael, *A Modern Introduction to International* Law (London: Routledge, 1997).

Aristotelis, *Politica, Oxford Classical Texts* (Oxford University Press, 1957).

Aristotle, *Nicomachaean Ethics*, Loeb Classical Library 73 (Cambridge Massachusetts: Harvard University Press, 1926).

Aristotle *Ars Rhetorica*, Oxford Classical Texts (Oxford: Oxford University Press, 1959).

Arrian, *Anabasis of Alexander, Books I-IV*, Loeb Classical Library 236 (Cambridge Massachusetts: Harvard University Press, 1976).

Beck, Robert J, 'International Law and the Decision to Invade Grenada: A Ten-Year Retrospective' *Virginia International Law Journal* 765.

Bockh, A., *Corpus Inscriptionum Graecarum* (Officina Academica, 1828).

Bowett, Derek, 'The Use of Force for the Protection of Nationals Abroad.'

Bowett, Derek, *Self-Defence in International Law* (New York: Praeger, 1958).

Brierly, *The Law of Nations* (Oxford: Oxford University Press, 2012).

Brownlie, Ian, *International Law and the Use of Force by States* (Oxford University Press, 1963).

Brownlie, Ian, *Basic Documents in International Law* (Oxford University Press, 1985).

Brownlie, 'Humanitarian Intervention,' in John N Moore (ed.), *Law and Civil War in the Modern World* (Baltimore, Maryland: Johns Hopkins University Press, 1974).

Buckland, *Textbook of Roman Law* (Cambridge: Cambridge University Press, 1921).

Bush, Letter from President Bush to Speaker of the House Thomas Foley, 21 December 1989, in [1989] 2 *Bush Papers* 1734, para 5.

Cassese, ed. *The Current Regulation of the Use of Force* (Dordrecht: Martinus Nijhoff, 1986).

Cassese, *The Rome Statute of the International Criminal Court* (Oxford University Press, 2002).

Chesterman, *Just War or Just Peace: Humanitarian Intervention and International Law* (Oxford: Oxford University Press, 2001).

Chesterman, Simon, 'Rethinking Panama: International Law and the US Invasion of Panama, 1989,' in Guy Goodwin-Gill and Stefan A Talmon (eds), *The Reality of International Law: Essays in Honour of Ian Brownlie* (Oxford: Oxford University Press, 1999), 57.

Christopher Keith Hall: *The First Two Sessions of the UN Preparatory Committee on the Establishment of an International Criminal Court*, 91 *American Journal of International Law* 177 (1997).

Christopher Keith Hall, The Third and Fourth Sessions of the UN Preparatory Committee on the Establishment of an International Criminal Court, 92 *American Journal of International Law* 124 (1998).

Cicero, *On Duties* (*De Officiis*), Loeb Classical Library 30 (Cambridge Massachusetts: Harvard University Press, 1931).

Clarke, Right to Protect Citizens in foreign countries by landing forces, 1912 (US Department of State, revised ed., 1929).

Clark, Memorandum on the Monroe Doctrine (US Department of State Publication No. 37, 1930).

Clerides, Glafkos, *Cyprus: My Deposition* (Nicosia, 1990).

Clowes, *The Royal Navy* (London, 1903).

Conference on Cyprus: Documents Signed and Initialled at Lancaster House on February 19, 1959, Cmnd. 679, Miscellaneous No 4 (London, HMSO, 1959).

Constantopoulos, *Public International Law* (Thessaloniki, 1962).

Cornford, F.C., *Thucydides Mythistoricus* (London: Edward Arnold, 1907).

Couloumbis, Theodore, and Wolfe, James, *An Introduction to International Relations* (Washington: Prentice Hall).

Crawford, James, 'Democracy and International Law' (1993) 44 *British Yearbook of International Law.*

Crawley, *The Question of Greek Independence: A Study of British Policy in the Near East, 1821–1833* (Cambridge: Cambridge University Press, 1930.

D' Amato, Anthony, 'The Invasion of Panama was a Lawful Response to Tyranny' (1990) 84 *American Journal of International* Law, 516.

Darcy, 'Retaliation and Reprisal, *The Oxford Handbook of the Use of Force in International Law* (Oxford: Oxford University Press, 2015).

Dinstein, Yoram, *War, Aggression and Self-Defence* (Cambridge: Cambridge University Press, 2017).

Denktash, R., *The Cyprus Triangle* (Nicosia, 1972).

Diena, *Diritto Internationale* (Milano, 1900).

Dinstein, *War, Aggression and Self-Defence* (Cambridge University Press, 1994).

Dworkin, Ronald, *Law's Empire* (London: Fontana, 1986).

Eisenhower, Dwight, *The White House Years; Waging Peace* (1965).

Farer, Tom, 'Panama: Beyond the Charter Paradigm' (1990) 84 *American Journal of International Law* 503.

Ferrell, Robert, *American Diplomacy: A History* (New York: Norton, 1975).

Fitzmaurice, G., Third Report on the Law of Treaties (1958) II *YBILC.*

Fliess, P.J., *Thucydides and the Politics of Bipolarity* (Baton Rouge, 1966).
Fonteyne, 'The Customary International Law Doctrine of Humanitarian Intervention: Its current Validity Under the UN Charter,' (1974) 4 *California Western ILJ* 203.
Fox, Gregory, 'The Right to Political Participation in International Law' (1992) 17 *Yale International law Journal,* 539.
Fox, Gregory and Brad Roth (eds.) *Democratic Governance and International Law* (Cambridge: Cambridge University Press, 2000).
Frank, Thomas and Nigel Rodley, 'After Bangladesh: The Law of Humanitarian Intervention by Military Force' (1973) 67 *American Journal of International Law,* 275.
Thomas Franck, 'The Emerging Right to Democratic Governance' (1992) 86 *American Journal of International Law* 46.
Gentili, Alberico, *De jure belli* [1612], (Classics of International Law; Oxford: Clarendon Press, 1933).
Gomme, *A Historical Commentary on Thucydides*, volume III (Oxford: Oxford University Press, 1956).
Goodrich and Hambro, *The United Nations: Commentary and Documents* (Boston: World Peace Foundation, 1946).
Greenwood, 'Is there a Right of Humanitarian Intervention?' (1993) 49 (2) *The World Today*, 36.
Greenwood, Christopher QC and Lowe, Vaughan, Memoranda submitted before the House of Commons Select Committee on Foreign Affairs, *http://www.parliament .the-stationery-office.co.uk/pa/ cm199900/cmselect/cmfaff.*
Grotius, *De Jure Belli ac Pacis* (Classics of International Law, Publications of Carnegie Endowment, 1925).
Halberstam, 'The Copenhagen Document: Intervention in Support of Democracy' (1993) 34 *Harvard International Law Journal* 163.
Hampson, 'Belligerent Reprisals and the 1977 Protocols to the Geneva Conventions of 1949,' 37 *International and Comparative Law Quarterly* 818, 837 (1988).
Harris, *Cases and Materials on International Law* (London Sweet & Maxwell, 1998).
Harvard University Law School, Research on International Law (1935) 29 *A.J.I.L.*
Herodotus, *The Persian Wars*, Loeb Classical Library 118 (Cambridge, Massachusetts: Harvard University Press, 1921).
Hertslet, Edward, *The Map of Europe by Treaty*, London: Butterworths, 1875.
Higgins, Rosalyn, *United Nations Peacekeeping: The Middle East* (Oxford: Oxford University Press, 1979).
Higgins, Rosalyn, *UN Peacekeeping: Documents and Commentary, Volume 3, Africa* (Oxford: Oxford University Press, 1980).
Higgins, Rosalyn, *The Development of International Law through the Political Organs of the UN* (Oxford: Oxford University Press, 1963).
Hodges, *The Doctrine of Intervention* (New York, 1915).
Homer, *The Odyssey of Homer* (London: Harper Collins Publishers, 2007).
Hornblower, *A Commentary on Thucydides Volume I: Books i-iii* (Oxford: Oxford University Press, 1997).

Hughes, 'Observations on the Monroe Doctrine,' *American Journal of International Law*, Vol. 17 (1923).

Hoffmann, Stanley, *The Ethics and Politics of Humanitarian Intervention* (University of Notre Dame Press, 1996).

Jacovides, A. J., *Treaties Conflicting with Peremptory Norms of International Law and the Zurich-London Agreements* (Nicosia, 1966).

Jessup, *Modern Law of Nations* (Read Books, 2007).

Kagan, D., *The Outbreak of the Peloponnesian War* (New York: Cornell University Press, 1989).

Kareklas, Iacovos, *International Law and Politics on Salamis* (Nicosia, 2007).

Kareklas, Iacovos, "International Law and Diplomacy on the Turkish Military Intervention of Cyprus," *Policy Paper* (Athens: Hellenic Foundation for Defence and Foreign Policy—ELIAMEP, 2012).

Καρεκλάς, Ιάκωβος, *Διεθνές Δίκαιον και Ελληνικός Πολιτισμός* (Αθήνα: Σιδέρης, 2010).

Kaye, 'Adjudicating Self-Defence: Discretion, Perception, and the Resort to Force in International Law,' 44 *Columbia Journal of Transnational Law* 134, 162 (2006).

Kelsen, *The Law of the United Nations* (New York, 1950).

Kelsen, *Law of the United Nations* (The Lawbook Exchange, 2000).

Kirkpatrick, Jeance J and Allan Gerson, The Reagan Doctrine, Human Rights, and International Law, in Louis Henkin (ed) *Right v Might: International Law and the Use of Force* (New York: Council on Foreign Relations, 1989), 19.

Lauterpacht, Hersch, 'The Grotian Tradition in International Law' 23 [1946] *British Yearbook of International Law*, 27.

Lauterpacht, H., *The Function of Law in the International Community* (Oxford University Press, 1933).

Lauterpacht, H., *International Law and Human Rights* (London: Stevens and Sons, 1950).

Lauterpacht, Elihu, 'Letter to the Editor: Legal Aspects of the Panama Invasion,' *Times*, 23 December 1989.

Lawrence, T.J., *The Principles of International Law* (London, 1920).

Levitin, Michael, The Law of Force and the Force of Law: Grenada, the Falklands, and Humanitarian Intervention (1986) 27 *Harvard International Law Journal* 621.

Lillich, 'Forcible Self-Help by States to Protect Human Rights' (1967) 53 *Iowa Law Review*, 325.

Low, P., *Interstate Relations in Classical Greece. Morality and Power, Cambridge Classical Studies* (Cambridge: Cambridge University Press, 2007).

MacDonald, International Law and the Conflict in Cyprus, 1981 *Canadian Yearbook of International Law*.

McDougal and Gardner, 'The Veto and the Charter: An Interpretation for Survival' Yale L.J., Vol. 60 (1951), 258.

McNair, *The Law of Treaties* (Oxford University Press, 1961).

Meron, *War Crimes Law comes of Age* (Oxford University Press, 1998).

Miller, E.M., 'Legal Aspects of the UN Action in the Congo,' 55 *American Journal of International Law* (1961), 1–28.

Moore, *A Digest of International Law* (Washington, DC: Government Printing Office, 1906).

Mullerson, 'Self-Defence in the Contemporary World' in Lori Fisler Damrosch and David Scheffer (eds), *Law and Force in the New International Order* (Boulder: Westview, 1991), 13.

DeMuth, Christopher, *The Reagan Doctrine and Beyond* (Washington, DC: American Enterprise Institute for Public Policy Research, 1988).

Necatigil, *The Turkish Position in International Law* (Oxford University Press).

Newman, *The Politics of Aristotle* (Oxford: Oxford Clarendon Press, 1887).

Nicholas, Barry, *An Introduction to Roman Law* (Oxford: Clarendon Press, 1962).

Oppenheim, *International Law, War and Neutrality*, Vol. II (7th ed. H. Lauterpacht, London, 1952).

Oppenheim, *International Law*, Vol. I (8th ed., London: Longmans, 1955).

Oppenheim, *International Law*, Vol. I (9th ed. Sir Robert Jennings QC and Sir Arthur Watts QC, London: Longman, 1996).

Pearce-Higgins, 'The Monroe Doctrine,' *British Yearbook of International Law*, Vol. 5 (1924), 114.

Phillimore, R., *Commentaries Upon International Law* (London, 1879).

Plato, *Republic*, Loeb Classical Library 276 (Cambridge Massachusetts: Harvard University Press, 2013).

Plutarch, *Lives* Volume III, Loeb Classical Library 65 (Cambridge Massachusetts: Harvard University Press, 1916).

Plutarch, *Lives Volume IX, Demetrius and Anthony*, Loeb Classical Library 101 (Cambridge Massachusetts: Harvard University Press, 1920).

Rawls, *A Theory of Justice* (Cambridge, Massachusetts: Harvard University Press, 1971).

Reagan, State of Union Address, 6 February 1985, in [1985] *Reagan Papers* 135.

Reisman, Michael, 'Humanitarian Intervention and Fledgling Democracies' (1995) 18 *Fordham International Law Journal,* 794.

Reisman, Michael and Myres McDougal, 'Humanitarian Intervention to Protect the Ibos' in Lillich (ed.) *Humanitarian Intervention and the United Nations* (Charlottesville: University Press of Virginia, 1973.

Reisman, Michael, 'Sovereignty and Human Rights in Contemporary International Law' (1990) 84 *American Journal of International Law* 866.

Roberts, Adam and Guelff, *Documents on the Laws of War* (Oxford: Oxford University Press, 2000).

Rozakis, *The Concept of Jus Cogens in the Law of Treaties* (1976).

Ronzitti, N., *Rescuing Nationals Abroad through Military Coercion and Intervention on Grounds of Humanity* (Martinus Nijhoff Publishers, 1985).

Root, Elihu, 'The Basis of Protection to Citizens Residing Abroad,' Presidential Address to the 10th Meeting of the American Society of International Law; cited in Stowell, *Intervention in International* Law (J. Bryne & Company, 1921), 159.

Brad Roth, *Government Illegitimacy in International Law* (Oxford: Clarendon Press, 1999).

Schwarzenberger, Georg and Brown, E.D., *A Manual of International Law* (London, 1976).

The Cambridge Bible, King James Version (Cambridge: Cambridge University Press, 1611).

The Turkish Yearbook of International Relations.

Seferiades, *Public International Law* (Athens, 1926).

Select Committee on Cyprus together with the *Proceedings of the Committee*, Minutes of Evidence and Appendices, Session 1975–1976, Ordered by the House of Commons to be printed, 8th April 1976, H.M.S.O., London.

Schachter, 'The Rights of States to Use Armed Forces' (1984) 82 *Michigan Law Review*, 1620.

Sofaer, Abraham, 'The Legality of the United States Action in Panama' (1991) 29 *Columbia Journal of Transnational Law* 281.

Ste Croix, G.E.M., *The Origins of the Peloponnesian War* (New York: Cornell University Press, 1972).

Stowell, *Intervention in International Law* (Washington, DC: John Byrne & Co, 1921).

Teson, *Humanitarian Intervention: An Inquiry into Law and Morality* (Brill, 2005).

Thomas and Thomas, Non-Intervention: *The Law and its Import in the Americas* (Dallas, 1956).

Thucydides, *History of the Peloponnesian War* (Cambridge: Harvard University Press, 1972).

Tornaritis, Criton, *Cyprus and its Constitutional and Other Legal Problems* (Nicosia, 1977).

Tornaritis, Criton, *Whether any resort to armed intervention in Cyprus would be justified either under the Charter or under customary international law* (1964) II *Cyprus Today.*

US Department of State, Anglo-American Committee of Enquiry, *Report* (1946).

Vattel, *'The Law of Nations'* (Washington DC, Carnegie Institution, 1916).

Verdross, A., Forbidden Treaties in International Law (1937) 31 *A.J.I.L.*

Waldock. 'The Regulation of the Use of Force by Individual States in International Law,' *Red Cross*, 1952, 505.

Walzer, Michael, *Just and Unjust Wars: A Moral Argument with Historical Illustrations* (New York: Basic Books, 1992.

Walzer, Michael, 'World War II: Why was This War Different?' (1971) 1 *Philosophy and Public Affairs,* 3.

Watts, Sir Arthur, *The International Law Commission* (Oxford University Press, 1999).

Westlake, J., *International Law* (Cambridge University Press, 1910).

William Vernon Harcourt, *Letters by Historicus on Some Questions of International Law: Reprinted from 'The Times' with Considerable Additions* (London: Macmillan, 1863).

Winfield, The Grounds of Intervention in International Law (1924) 4 *B.YB.I.L.*

Woodhouse, *The Battle of Navarino* (London: Hodder & Stoughton, 1965).

Woolsey, 'The Uniting for Peace Resolution of the U.N.,' *American Journal of International Law*, Vol., 45 (1951), 129.
Xenophon, *Anabasis*, Loeb Classical Library 90 (Cambridge Massachusetts: Harvard University Press, 1998).
Xydis, S.G., *Cyprus: Reluctant Republic* (London, 1973).

Index

About the Author

Iacovos Kareklas was born in Nicosia on October 18, 1976. He graduated (with Apolyterion Excellent) first in his class, receiving ten academic awards from the Classics Department of the Kykkos Lyceum.

He got his BA and MA degrees in law from Cambridge University, *Magdalene College*. At the University of Cambridge, where he studied on a Cambridge Commonwealth Trust Scholarship jointly with a British Foreign Office Bursary, he won First Prize in the de Smith Mooting Competition of the Cambridge University Law Society, of which he is a lifetime member. He was particularly keen on constitutional law and theory, which he studied in depth having as tutor Sir Derek Oulton Q.C. (drafter of the Kenya Constitution).

He holds a PhD in International Law from London University (*London School of Economics and Political Science*). He specialized in all aspects of public international law and every aspect of the Cyprus problem. He conducted in-depth research in the Foreign Office Archives with regard to the critical phases of the Cyprus Question. During his doctoral program, he was a teaching assistant in subjects of his specialization.

In the academic year 2003–2004, he was a postdoctoral fellow at the Department of Government, Harvard University. He did postdoctoral studies in international relations theory with special reference to the use of military force and emphasis on classical antiquity under the worldwide distinguished political scientist Professor Stanley Hoffmann. At Harvard, he also taught the course *Classical Theories of International Relations*. In the year 2004–2005, Dr. Kareklas flew to Boston again and was appointed postdoctoral fellow at Harvard's Center for Middle Eastern Studies. Additionally, he is a member of the Harvard Faculty Club. In 2006 and 2007, he was elected fellow of the Faculty of Law (Honour School of Jurisprudence) in the University of Oxford, where he specialized in philosophy of law.

In the academic years 2021–2022, Dr. Kareklas was appointed visiting fellow of Pembroke College in the University of Oxford, Changing Character of War Centre (which is also inseparable part of the Oxford Department of Politics and International Relations). He conducted sustained research in the politics, ethics, and law of war with emphasis on military humanitarian intervention. He gave lectures on international law and the use of force at the Oxford Department of Politics and International Relations and presented his book, entitled *Thucydides on International Law and Political Theory* (Rowman and Littlefield: Lexington Books, 2020), at Pembroke College, Oxford, before Fellows of the College and members of the wider university.

In 2008 Dr. Kareklas was elected lecturer at the European University Cyprus and was appointed coordinator of the law program. As of 2013, he is an associate professor, a rank at which he was unanimously elected. He teaches international law, philosophy of law, constitutional law, and international politics. He further took part in many appointment and promotion committees.

He spent a year as researcher in the Institute of Commonwealth Studies (ICS) of London (2001–2002), the British Institute of International and Comparative Law (2003), and the Oxford Centre for Criminology (2006). He wrote his B.A. dissertation at the Cambridge Institute of Criminology, and he has been a member of the Royal Institute of International Affairs. He has given lectures in English and American universities as well as at various political organizations. Dr. Kareklas is the author of a number of books and articles in the fields of his specialization. In 2014 he launched an original series (of which he is the editor), entitled *Studies in International Law and International Politics* (in Greek) published by the preeminent law publisher SAKKOULAS in Athens.

www.ingramcontent.com/pod-product-compliance
Ingram Content Group UK Ltd.
Pitfield, Milton Keynes, MK11 3LW, UK
UKHW041833031026
15587UKWH00002B/730

9 781666 947335